Drive-in Theaters

DRIVE-IN THEATERS

A History from Their Inception in 1933

by

Kerry Segrave

McFarland & Company, Inc., Publishers

Jefferson, North Carolina, and London

The present work is a reprint of the library bound edition of Drive-in Theaters: A History from Their Inception in 1933, *first published in 1992 by McFarland.*

Photos courtesy of BETTER THEATRES, *Motion Picture Herald,* Quigley Publishing Company, Inc., New York.

LIBRARY OF CONGRESS CATALOGUING-IN-PUBLICATION DATA

Segrave, Kerry, 1944–
Drive-in theaters : a history from their inception in 1933 / by Kerry Segrave.
p. cm.
Includes bibliographical references and index.

ISBN 0-7864-2630-6 (softcover : 50# alkaline paper)

1. Drive-in theaters—United States—History. I. Title.
PN1993.5.U6S37 2006
792'.0973'0904—dc20 92-50319

British Library cataloguing data are available

Manufactured in the United States of America

McFarland & Company, Inc., Publishers
Box 611, Jefferson, North Carolina 28640
www.mcfarlandpub.com

Contents

Introduction

When I began to research drive-ins I had no preset ideas or preconceived notions—with the exception of the drive-in's reputation as a passion pit. Letting my research findings guide me in determining what was important in the history and background of outdoor movie theaters, I have tried to strike a balance in this book between the technical aspects of the drive-in—which didn't fuel its rise but did contribute to its decline—and the sociocultural ones; that is, who the audience was, why they went, the response of the community at large to this new cultural force, what factors led to the outdoor theaters' phenomenal rise and, later, to its steady decline toward its inevitable demise, and so on.

While I have included material from around the world, the drive-in is a uniquely American institution. Only Canada and Australia came close to having the intense love affair with drive-ins that America did. This is understandable, given that before drive-ins could spring up all over, a country had to be wealthy; it had to have a good deal of vacant, accessible, relatively cheap land; and the country's inhabitants had to be financially well placed, have automobiles, and enjoy an emotional relationship with their cars. A country that met all the requirements but whose inhabitants regarded automobiles as simply a mode of conveyance to get from A to B would never develop a drive-in industry of any extent.

Along with the pioneering shopping malls, drive-ins led the post–World War II rush to suburbia. Both catered to families who didn't want to return to the city at night—it was too much of a hassle. But these families were ready to drive to a mall or a drive-in. The latter was ideal, as the family practically didn't have to set foot out of their car once they entered it in their own driveway. Of course, they *did* set foot outside their car. Rare was the family that could avoid the refreshment counter or the kids' playground or sometimes the adult playground or the bingo or the square dance, and so on. For the drive-in was a family outing involving much more than a movie. Parents didn't have to dress up at all, a fact that was more important then than now. Men in the 1940s and into the 1950s were still wearing suits and hats at what we would regard as the oddest times. The informality of dress that would be one of the lasting legacies of the late-1960s youth movement still lay in the future, and its opposite could be a nuisance for those bound up in rules of etiquette. No babysitters were needed—take the kids in their pajamas. There were no parking fees. The kids could play on the mostly free rides. The entire family could eat supper at the drive-in. It was a family outing that satisfied the needs of families to spend time together, to do things together, as a unit. (While teenagers did engage in sexual activity at the outdoor theaters, they formed only a small proportion of the audience.) Drive-in patrons overwhelmingly were families with kids. Solitary adults make up a minority of patrons at indoor theaters; at drive-ins their numbers were much smaller still.

But most of all, drive-ins fueled Americans' love affair with the car. You could drive somewhere, then stay in your car when you got there. The drive-in heyday coincided with the era of the Sunday afternoon drive to nowhere in particular. A trip to a drive-in was something akin to a trip to the beach or a family outing to a low-cost, mini-Disneyland. Real Disneylands and their countless more modest variations would, one day, erode the drive-in base. Had the outdoor theaters paid more attention to technical aspects of screening and to showing a higher-quality product, they might have helped to hold this base. Most of all, a trip to the outdoor theater gave Dad an excuse to drive the car around in semirural areas, which had fewer traffic lights and lighter traffic, and he didn't have to try to find a place to park the car—a place on a city street or in a garage where it could get clipped by another auto or otherwise damaged.

The drive-in thrived for a time. Anyone who opened an outdoor theater in the 1940s or 1950s made money almost in spite of him- or herself. The film on the screen was largely irrelevant, as long as it was wholesome. Some operators recognized this; some didn't; most didn't care. Because patrons didn't seem to care about the film being shown, operators never banded together in a strong way to try to get a better product to screen. If they could fill the lot with a cheap-to-rent fourth-run film, why try to obtain a costlier first-run product? When quality of product became a more important consideration, it was too late: An unstoppable decline was under way.

Today drive-ins usually screen first-run features, but nobody goes. The family-outing mentality is long gone. Automobiles are much smaller and even less comfortable to view a movie from than were 1950s vehicles. Kids' playgrounds at drive-ins went the way of the dinosaur decades ago. One reason was the litigious American nature—too many lawsuits and too much money for insurance. The technical aspects of drive-ins were always poor. But again, since the lot was full, why bother to try and improve? (To this day audio and video remain inadequate.) Operators listened to one wild scheme after another that would produce the daylight screen—touted for more than thirty years—and the daylight-containment screen—touted for more than twenty. The former would allow all-day screenings at drive-ins, while the latter would do that and contain the image precisely within the lot. This latter issue became important in the 1960s as sex on the screen (visible outside the lot) became more of a community issue than sex in the lot. The miracle screen, of course, never arrived. Even if it had, it would have kept critics at bay and increased profits. It was not proposed to enhance the customers' experience.

The rise of the drive-in was most improbable. Climate dictated that it would be functional in much of this country only for part of the year. And during that part of the year the days were long—so long that one show per night was all that was really feasible. They showed a film that had made the rounds and then some by the time it unreeled at the drive-in. Sound quality ranged from abysmal all the way up to poor, with the illusion that the sound came from the actors' lips—always believable in a hardtop house—never even remotely sustainable outdoors. During the height of summer, for the first ten or twenty minutes, the viewer might have trouble seeing anything at all on the screen, as the operator would start the show as early as possible—too early to prevent the sun's illumination from washing out the screen—to try and squeeze in a second show. None of this mattered at all at first. The lot was almost always full.

Total movie attendance was in a steep decline for at least a couple of years before television became a fixture in most homes and thus can't be blamed for the decline. However, once television arrived, it ensured that the decline would never be reversed, that the old high numbers would never be recaptured. During this overall decline, attendance at drive-ins increased by leaps and bounds, in the face of competition from television. It is probably an exaggeration to say that revenues from drive-ins to the studios during this period single-handedly kept the major studios from bankruptcy, but had it not been for one bright spot, the drive-in theaters, the motion picture industry would have been in even more serious trouble.

Drive-ins declined in part because success came too easily at the start. Operators made little effort. When attendance declined, the cavalier way operators treated patrons came back to haunt them. It couldn't be undone.

And so a unique piece of 1950s Americana stumbles its way to extinction. Perhaps it is fitting. This is no longer the 1950s, and it's no longer Eisenhower's America. The family is something different today as well. The drive-in belongs to the era when a working-class family in which only the father had outside-the-home employment could aspire to, and buy, a single-family house on a 50-by-100-foot lot.

As I write these introductory words, Disney World is opening up outside Paris amid cries of American cultural imperialism. Americans have successfully exported most of the cultural icons that have become popular at home, from television series to sports to films to fast food to clothing. In Australia people who have never been to this country can be found wearing 49ers jackets, Dodger caps, or Bulls sweatshirts. But they were never found—with exceptions noted above—at the drive-in. Most European countries had one or two for a time. However, they were mere curiosities, not industries; in a way that makes the drive-in even more quintessentially American. So American that it traveled poorly, the drive-in was a celebration of extravagance, a statement of conspicuous consumption of resources—of cheap gas and a car in every garage. Only a country as wealthy as 1950s America could do it.

Research for this book was conducted at the UCLA libraries. Much of it consisted of reading back files of such magazines as *Variety* and *Motion Picture Herald.* The latter was particularly useful in that its articles contained detail, such as construction costs and so on. Another helpful institution was the Los Angeles Public Library.

Chapter 1

A Backyard Invention

"My invention relates to a new and useful outdoor theater and it relates more particularly to a novel construction in outdoor theaters whereby the transportation facilities to and from the theater are made to constitute an element of the seating facilities of the theater . . . wherein the performance, such as a motion picture show or the like, may be seen and heard from a series of automobiles so arranged in relation to the stage or screen, that the successive cars behind each other will not obstruct the view," wrote Richard Milton Hollingshead, Jr., in his August 6, 1932, application for a patent.

The application provided that aisles be slanted in various ways to allow cars to coast in and out, thus minimizing engine-noise annoyance from late arrivals and early leavers. A special funnel device, with a stream of air pumped through it, was to be placed over the projector lens to keep insects from crossing the path of light too close to the lens and casting large shadows on the screen. The inventor anticipated that seats for walk-in patrons could be added in the space between the screen and projection booth, although he never installed them at his own theater.*

After a favorable patent review, Richard Hollingshead, Jr., was granted patent number 1,909,537 on May 16, 1933 (see pp. 203–214). Like all patents at the time, it would run for seventeen years, during which Hollingshead could collect royalties from anybody who used his invention—or so he thought. After seventeen years the invention's technology became open to use by anyone without compensation to the inventor.

The inventor's grandfather, Richard Spencer Hollingshead, had been born in Ohio around 1843. Later moving to New Jersey, Spencer made his living as a clothing merchant until his death in 1893. Richard Milton Hollingshead, Sr., was born on May 4, 1869, in Millville, New Jersey. In 1887 he started his own business, forming a small company that manufactured harness soap. Initially he made his products at home in the kitchen sink. His successful

**See Notes, beginning on page 239.*

business soon expanded into one that manufactured a full line of products catering to the harness part of the horse-powered transportation system. Along the way the business relocated to Camden, New Jersey. When the age of the automobile arrived, Hollingshead quickly understood the implications for his company. Starting in 1905 he phased out harness products, turning his attention to the manufacture of soaps, polishes, greases, and oils for automobiles. More successful than ever, Richard found himself owner and president of the Whiz Auto Products Company, which produced nearly one hundred products for automobile care. Three children were born to Richard and his wife, Emma Lovett. One was Richard Milton Hollingshead, Jr., on February 25, 1900.

After completing his education Richard junior went to work in his father's company. At the age of thirty he was general sales manager, in a secure but less than challenging position. Wanting not just a job but to create something of his own, he began to do some thinking. Considering credit to be a liability business, he looked for something involving cash. Hollingshead related that he "analyzed the market from the standpoint of what people gave up last. It came out this way: Food. Clothing. Autos. Movies. In order."[2] His idea that people continued to attend movies despite economic hard times was strengthened by his own visits to a neighborhood theater, where the manager pointed out to him that although a majority of his customers were on relief, they remained customers.

Hollingshead's first inspiration was to construct a deluxe gas station, all the better to retail Whiz products. It was to be a Hawaiian Village theme station, complete with thatched-roof buildings and gas pumps made to resemble palm trees. While getting their cars serviced, customers could meet and mingle at an attached restaurant. Or they could watch outdoor movies. These elaborate extras were intended to lure customers in the evening when gas station business tended to drop off. For unrecorded reasons Hollingshead soon dropped the gas station idea. He did, however, pursue the movie aspect of his plan.[3]

Looking at reasons people didn't go to the movies, Hollingshead concluded, "The mother says she's not dressed; the husband doesn't want to put on his shoes; the question is what to do with the kids; then how to find a baby sitter; parking the car is difficult or maybe they have to pay for parking; even the seats in the theatre may not be comfortable to contemplate." However, Richard had the solution to all those woes.[4]

In the driveway of his Riverton, New Jersey, home at 212 Thomas Avenue, Hollingshead experimented. Setting a 1928 Kodak projector on the hood of the family car, he projected the film onto a screen he had nailed to a tree. He tested foul-weather potential by turning on his lawn sprinkler to simulate a rainstorm. With his home radio sitting behind the screen to provide sound, Hollingshead sat in his car watching and listening. With the car windows up or down, with the sprinkler on or off, he liked what he saw and heard.

More research became necessary, however, as many problems emerged.

Richard M. Hollingshead, Jr., the "father" of the drive-in.

Sitting in his vehicle, Hollingshead realized that a car parked in front of his would obscure his view. For many weeks he continued his experiments, placing one car behind another, forty feet apart. Blocks were put under the front wheels of both cars until he got the proper angle to allow the driver in the second vehicle to see over the car ahead. With this vision problem solved for a pair of vehicles, the inventor devised his series of terraced rows with raised ramps providing an unobstructed view for all cars. This concept would be the core of his patent, as well as the source of much litigation, as courts pondered whether such a thing was patentable.

In order to make this new creation pay, Hollingshead felt he would need a 500-foot-long drive-in lot with a screen up to 50 feet wide, much larger than those utilized by indoor theaters. This problem was taken care of when a screen supply company informed him they could give him a screen of that size as well as a projector with a sufficient throw.

Last was the difficulty of providing sound to his potential customers. That stumbling block was turned over to the RCA Victor Company, next-door neighbors in Camden to the Hollingshead company plant. In time for the opening of that first drive-in, RCA came up with what they called controlled directional sound. It meant, they claimed, that everyone in the theater received the same volume of sound—delivered, in this case, from three central speakers (the in-car speaker with individual volume control would not make its appearance until the late 1940s). Patrons may have all been exposed to the same volume; however, cars in the last rows heard the sound later than did cars in the first row. People who lived in the area of the theater, even miles away, could also hear the sound in their homes. They were very unhappy about this.

With his major problems apparently solved, Hollingshead lined up financial backing for his venture. His major partner was Willie Warren Smith of Riverton, New Jersey, a first cousin and an operator of parking lots in Camden; New York; and Philadelphia. The men formed a company, Park-In Theatres, Inc. As soon as Hollingshead received his patent, he assigned it to this company. Other backers include road contractor Edward Ellis, who graded that first drive-in in exchange for company stock; and Oliver Willets, a Campbell's Soup vice president who bought stock.[5]

Construction of the project did not begin until May 16, when the patent was officially granted. Then a group of architects, tradesmen, and laborers descended on the site. Men hired were taken off the Pennsauken Township relief rolls. Pay was forty cents per hour for skilled workers, twenty cents an hour for laborers. Soon representatives of organized labor arrived at the site, demanding that its union men be hired at rates of $1 or more per hour for skilled tradesmen and forty cents an hour for laborers. So heated did the dispute become that a fistfight broke out on the site, with two men injured. One of those was Ernest R. Lewis, president of the Camden County Building Trades Union, who required hospital treatment for his injuries. In some fashion this deadlock was broken, and even with the labor problems, construction was completed in less than three weeks.

The world's first drive-in opened on Tuesday, June 6, 1933. Most sources give the location as Admiral Wilson Boulevard, Camden, New Jersey. Actually the theater was just over the Camden town line, from which point outward the street was called Crescent Boulevard. The location was Pennsauken Township.[6]

The screen tower of the first drive-in at Camden, New Jersey, June 1933.

Looking from a ramp to the screen in June 1933 at the world's first drive-in in Camden, New Jersey.

Ads from Philadelphia's *Public Ledger* for the opening days of the first drive-in in the world, at Camden, New Jersey, June 6, 1933 (*top*) and June 7. The three-show-a-night policy didn't work, and on June 8 it cut back to two shows per night.

The theater was called the Automobile Movie Theatre; the marquee simply read "Drive-In Theatre."

When construction began Hollingshead enthused about the benefits of his creation for the public:

> Inveterate smokers rarely enjoy a movie because of the smoking prohibition. In the Drive-In theatre one may smoke without offending others. People may chat or even partake of refreshments brought in their cars without disturbing those who prefer silence. The Drive-In theatre idea virtually transforms an ordinary motor car into a private theatre box. The younger children are not permitted in movie theatres and are frequently discouraged even when accompanied by parents or guardians. Here the whole family is welcome, regardless of how noisy the children are apt to be and parents are furthermore assured of the children's safety because youngsters remain in the car. The aged and infirm will find the Drive-In a boon because they will not be subjected to inconvenience such as getting up to leave others pass in narrow aisles or the uncertainty of a seat.[7]

Since Camden was separated from Philadelphia by just a few miles, only by the narrow Delaware River, the drive-in had a large potential audience to draw on. One ad in a local newspaper showed a very obese lady trying to fit herself into a narrow indoor theater seat, indicating another group Hollingshead was targeting. Opening night drew a full house, or nearly so. However, many were there for free, Hollingshead and Smith had distributed free passes to as many Philadelphia and Camden media people as they could. The opening attraction was the 1932 release *Wife Beware*, starring Adolphe Menjou. It was then in second-run (or later) status. The partners complained they had been unable to obtain a first-run film from a distributor for fear that the gate at indoor houses would be lessened. This problem of access to first-run films would always bedevil drive-ins. A variety of shorts accompanied the feature. Admission was twenty-five cents for a car and twenty-five cents per person. Three or more in a car were admitted for a flat rate of one dollar.

Initially the plan was to have three shows a night—at 8:30, 10:00, and 11:30 P.M. Allowing for time to empty and refill the house between shows, this left not much more than seventy minutes of actual show time in which to squeeze in shorts and a feature. As this was impossible, early publicity noted the theater would use "abridged features, with all dull or uninteresting parts omitted."[8] It was left unsaid just who would do the abridging.

The partners must have realized the folly of this scheduling idea, for after only two nights, beginning on June 8 and continuing thereafter, only two shows were run per night, at 8:45 and at 10:45 P.M. The program changed twice a week, Wednesdays and Sundays. Camden's scheduling difficulties illustrate another problem faced by drive-ins—the limited number of shows they could program as well as the late starting time, particularly in June and July during the long summer days. People who had to get up early for work couldn't be expected to patronize a late-starting second show, especially during the week.

Business may have been good that first night, but the trade publication *Variety* noted a "marked drop in attendance" during the rest of the week.[9] This publication attributed the decline to particularly hot weather. From June 7 to June 9, the Philadelphia maximum temperature ranged from ninety to ninety-eight degrees, with high humidity. Opening night was only slightly cooler, with a muggy high of eighty-seven degrees.

Besides local newspaper coverage this pioneer drive-in theater drew national coverage in several major periodicals.[10] Most reported on this new creation in a matter-of-fact way, simply rehashing the advantages Hollingshead had previously presented along with a few statistics. No account was enthusiastic. None foresaw the enormous future the drive-in was destined to have within fifteen years. The *Literary Digest* wondered what effect adverse weather would have on this new style theater as well as questioning whether the public would be willing to exchange the intimacy of an indoor theater for the convenience of an outdoor one. Only the *Motion Picture Herald* viewed the newcomer with a degree of open skepticism, asking rhetorically, "Why is it desirable to remain in your automobile when you go to the movies? Only Mr. Average Man in his Chevrolet can answer that one."

That first drive-in was not unlike the thousands that would follow over the coming decades. Cars entered past a ticket booth, then took a spot on ramps laid out in the familiar fan or clamshell pattern. The major difference was the lack of individual speakers. The lot size of the Camden Theater was 500 feet by 500 feet. From ramp to ramp the distance was 50 feet. Of this total, 16 feet were considered to be the length an average car needed for parking. The remaining 34 feet were the width of the driving aisles by which patrons moved to a spot on the ramps. A car leaving had to back off the ramp, since the ramps weren't rounded but featured a short, sharp drop as well as a guardrail at the edge of the drop. When a driver forgot and tried to exit forward, the auto got hung up on the ramp.

Most sources say the Camden drive-in had seven ramps and held four hundred cars. Today both the Camden Public Library and the Camden County Historical Society issue an identical one-page fact sheet on the first drive-in, which states that five hundred cars could be held on nine ramps.[11] All these numbers are incorrect. The projector was housed in a small building in the middle of the first row. With a maximum throw of 150 feet, it was positioned 133 feet from the screen, approximately 180 feet from the lot line. At 50 feet between ramps, nine, or even seven, ramps couldn't be squeezed onto the 500-foot lot. Row number six was about 430 feet from the far lot line. The architect was Howard E. Hull of Camden. His ground plan of the theater shows six rows with space for future pedestrian chairs as well as a free car-parking area behind and around the screen housing for those wishing to use those pedestrian chairs which never materialized at Camden. The number of autos held by rows one through six from front to back were, respectively, 32, 49, 60, 66, 65, and 64, with a total capacity of 336 (see page 215). Twenty percent of these spaces, 67, were—due to their angle of positioning relative to the screen—placed in what was euphemistically termed "an area of distortion." In other words, customers couldn't see very well from these spots.[12]

Some two hundred trees ranging in height from 12 to 20 feet were planted around the perimeter of the lot. A high fence was constructed to prevent people from sneaking in or just standing outside the lot line to view the show for free. The 30-foot-high by 40-foot-wide screen was housed in a wooden screen structure 149 feet wide, 35 feet deep, and 60 feet high. The bottom of the screen was 12 feet from the ground. Most sources cite a screen size of 40 by 50 feet, which Hollingshead seemed initially to have in mind; however, the installed screen apparently was scaled down. Ramps were constructed with concrete retaining walls, paved with gravel and cinders, and then rolled and oiled. (The oiling was done to reduce dust: it was also said to discourage mosquitoes.) The first ramp was inclined five degrees. The highest point, or front edge, of each ramp was five inches above that of the ramp ahead. Ramp number 1 was nine inches above the ground at its highest point, ramp number 2 fourteen inches, and so on. Sound was supplied through three six-feet-square RCA speakers.

The estimated cost of the Camden drive-in has been given generally as $60,000. Considering the small size of this first one, as well as more reliable figures for later 1930s drive-ins, this figure is likely highly exaggerated. A cost of around $30,000 is probably closer to the mark. *Boxoffice* reported it at $25,000.[13] A mainstay for any drive-in, or indoor theater, today, is the concession business. The Camden theater installed one after the first week, when they began to sell beer and lunches. As much as for any other reason, this was done to reinforce the idea that a drive-in was a place to go to watch a movie, have a meal and a beer, things you couldn't do in an indoor theater.

Hollingshead's drive-in didn't prove successful. He sold it in 1935 or 1936 to a man who "moved" it to Union, New Jersey. However, Hollingshead always maintained, "It was a real success in Camden but the high film rental rates continued to plague us. We probably never would have sold it otherwise. The man in Union who bought it had several indoor theaters in north Jersey, so he could easily get films. . . . The first film at the drive-in was three years old and cost us $400 for four days. The last time the film had run was in a little South Camden movie that paid $20 a week for it."[14]

Wife Beware wasn't that old. While Hollingshead justifiably complained that he couldn't obtain first-run product from the major Hollywood studios, or second-run for that matter, there was never a scarcity of *some* product. The many small and independent studios always had something to offer. Nor were their rental rates likely to be extortionate, as they scrambled to find places to show their material. Whether the public wanted to view this type of product was another matter.

The many problems of the Camden drive-in were likely to be off-putting to customers after a first novelty visit. Cars were stuck in "distortion" areas; the sound was terrible; the sound wasn't synchronized with the picture for many patrons; if car windows were shut, it was too hot; if windows were open, people were attacked by insects; the admission charge was not cheap relative to indoor houses which charged an average admission of twenty-three cents in 1933 in the United States; patrons got only one obscure feature film to view in the Camden drive-in, while virtually all indoor theaters showed a double bill, usually from a major studio in either first or second run.

Hollingshead retained his 30 percent interest in the Park-In company—later passed on to his son—but never again was he actively involved in the running of a drive-in. He contented himself with granting licenses under his patent; however, the hoped-for financial windfall did not materialize. By 1934 he had resumed full-time work with his father's company; he became board chairman by 1950.

When Laura Ottinger joined that company as Hollingshead's secretary in 1953 it was doing business in 139 countries. Eventually it was absorbed by Litton Industries. In 1964 he retired from the business to his home in Villanova, Pennsylvania, where he died of cancer on May 13, 1975, at seventy-five years of age. Loyal employee Ottinger was annoyed that Hollingshead had never received any recognition from the film industry for his pioneering efforts. During the 1970s she regularly wrote to the Academy of Motion Picture Arts and Sciences in Beverly Hills, California, urging it to award a posthumous Oscar to her former boss for his contributions to the film industry. Said Laura: "He never even got an acknowledgment and I think it's unfair and unjust. The movie industry would have gone down the drain during the Depression if not for the drive-in theater."[15] There is truth in what she said; however, the period was the 1950s. During the depression era, drive-ins were few and far between, having no real impact on the film industry. During the 1950s, when television hammered indoor houses closing them down regularly and rapidly, the drive-in more than held its own, expanding strongly as it resisted the inroads of television for a much longer period than did its indoor kin. During this time drive-ins truly helped keep the whole film industry afloat.

Not long before his death Hollingshead told an inquiring reporter that he and his wife occasionally attended the Main Line Drive-in near their home. Asked what kind of films he liked to see there, he laughed and said, "I like dirty movies the best."[16] One month after his death the United States Supreme Court ruled that communities couldn't ban the showing of nudity at drive-ins.

Chapter 2

Patent Battles

Two weeks after receiving his patent, on June 1, 1933, Hollingshead assigned it to his newly formed company, Park-In Theatres, Inc. If he, with his 30 percent share of the company, along with cousin Smith and the other minor backers, expected to sit back growing rich as royalty payments flowed in he was to be bitterly disappointed. The drive-in industry turned into a morass of litigation. When *Boxoffice* surveyed the New England scene in the spring of 1938, they wryly commented: "There are already more law suits on drive-in theatres in this territory than there are drive-in localities."[1]

In the spring of 1936 a drive-in was under construction at Weymouth, Massachusetts—the Weymouth Drive-In Theatre. One of those involved was Joseph T. Burchini. A licensing agreement was not obtained from Park-In. The Weymouth opened about May 6, 1936, under the ownership of Thomas DiMaura and James Guarino through their company, Drive-In Theatres Corporation. On July 3 that year Park-In brought an action against the Weymouth in United States District Court in Massachusetts, charging patent infringement. Obtaining a writ of attachment, Park-In placed keepers at the Weymouth the nights of July 3, 4, and 5, 1936, taking possession of the entire gate for those nights. They also attached certain funds of the Weymouth company. The total take was reported to be $5000. According to DiMaura a second such attachment took place in the fall, which caused the Drive-In Theatres Corp. to enter into a licensing agreement with Park-In.[2]

Under the terms of the October 23, 1936, agreement the Weymouth group got exclusive rights for drive-in theaters in a specified New England area. They could build more drive-ins in that area if they wished, provided they signed a licensing agreement for each one. Cost to the Weymouth group was $1000 plus a royalty of 5 percent of gross box office receipts per unit. For its part Park-In agreed to license no other group to build a drive-in in that area. It also agreed to prosecute for patent infringement anyone who built an unlicensed facility in the area. While this was going on Burchini was suing the Weymouth company over an alleged equity claim. Two other individuals had launched separate suits claiming Weymouth hadn't paid them for work done on behalf of the drive-in.

In July 1937 Elias M. Loew and his company opened a drive-in at Lynn, Massachusetts. The Weymouth company considered this a violation of its contract, whether the Lynn theater was licensed in its area or not. After repeatedly bringing this situation to Park-In's attention but getting no action, the Weymouth company initiated legal action in March 1938, in Massachusetts District Court, asking the court to order Park-In to sue the Lynn operation.

Three days after the suit was filed, Park-In countersued Weymouth, claiming that the company had violated the agreement by constructing an unlicensed drive-in at Shrewsbury, Massachusetts. DiMaura denied any ownership of the Shrewsbury outlet but did admit that the construction company he headed had built the theater for a group with which he was not connected. Also admitted was the fact that the company he and Guarino operated would run the house for this other group. The land for the theater had been bought by a man named James Guarino. James Guarino of the DiMaura/Guarino team denied any knowledge of this transaction. This confusing piece of litigation was thrown out of court in June 1938 on the technical ground that service was not performed properly.[3]

Out in California two men, M. A. Rogers and Thomas Burgess, had opened a drive-in without bothering to get a license from Park-In. The company promptly sued for patent infringement. When the case was heard in the District Court for the Southern District of California, the judge dismissed the case on the ground that the subject matter of the patent was not patentable. That is, drive-ins didn't fall into a category of invention for which a patent could be issued. This ruling was appealed by Park-In. On September 14, 1942, the Ninth Circuit Court of Appeals ruled, 2–1, that a drive-in was within a patentable classification, reversing the lower court's decision. The dissenting judge's comment was limited to the brief and inscrutable, "I dissent." If drive-ins as a class were unpatentable then, of course, the Hollingshead patent was invalid on its face. However, if they were a patentable class, then an individual patent in that class, such as Hollingshead's, could be valid or invalid, depending on its own merits. That is what this court ruled. They were not asked nor did they comment on the specific validity of Richard's patent.[4]

At the same time that Elias Loew and his company, Loew's Drive-In Theatres, Inc., opened their Lynn theater, they opened a second one at Providence, Rhode Island, on July 21, 1937. A month earlier they signed a licensing agreement with Park-In containing the same provisions as all the other contracts. Park-In required its licensees to make weekly reports to it on receipts and weekly royalty payments to it based on those receipts. This Loew's did for Rhode Island from July 21 to November 13, 1937, when the theater closed for the season. Gross box office receipts for that period amounted to $29,065.75.

When this drive-in opened for the 1938 season Loew didn't bother sending any more reports or money to Park-In. On June 1, 1938, Park-In terminated the licensing agreement for nonpayment, as it was allowed to do. Park-In sued for royalties owed to June 1 and for patent infringement thereafter. This case dragged on for years. It was not decided until March 1947 in Rhode Island District Court.

Loew's argued that other unlicensed drive-ins had been built and operated in its area and that Park-In has not prosecuted them as the agreement required, despite repeated complaints and requests to do so by Loew's. The judge denied this defense on the ground that Loew's had never submitted such complaints in writing to Park-In. Other lines of defense—that the agreement restrained Loew's from engaging in the business it was organized to carry on and that the agreement violated antitrust laws—were given no consideration by the court. Loew's argument that drive-ins were not patentable was tossed out on the basis of the Rogers decision. This court ruled in Park-In's favor on all counts, setting the stage for an appeal. Evidence indicated that Park-In then had licensing agreements with forty to fifty drive-ins, some not yet built but in the planning stage. Considering that two hundred or so outdoor theaters were in operation, most operators chose to ignore Hollingshead and his patent, at least in terms of paying him any royalties.[5]

Before the appeal was heard, other litigation intervened. Park-In took legal action against Herbert J. Ochs and others in 1947 over patent infringement resulting from two unlicensed drive-ins operated in Dayton, Ohio, by Ochs and associates. In two separate appearances before the Ohio District Court, the complaint was thrown out on technical grounds.[6]

On November 20, 1940, Park-In entered into one of its standard licensing agreements with Elwood R. Clay to operate a number of drive-ins. Clay assigned the agreement to Paramount-Richards Theatres, Inc., of which he was president. Pursuant to the agreement, Paramount-Richards constructed and operated seven drive-ins, as follows: Shreveport, Baton Rouge and New Orleans, Louisiana; Pensacola, Florida; Jackson, Mississippi; Texarkana, Texas; and Mobile, Alabama. Paramount-Richards made only partial and inadequate royalty payments under the contract with respect to five of the theaters, while making no payments at all on the other two. Park-In cancelled the agreements on April 28, 1948, and then sued the seven companies involved, all controlled by Paramount-Richards, for royalties and patent infringement. Arguing that the case be dismissed Paramount-Richards claimed Park-In was using its patent as a monopoly unfairly in restraint of trade. The Delaware District Court judge hearing the case declared, on December 8, 1948, that he couldn't decide, deferring the whole matter.[7]

These two combatants appeared in court at least four more times, as more complaints and amendments were filed. Ultimately Park-In, in May 1950, lost this battle in Delaware District Court. Not satisfied, Park-In went higher, to the Third Circuit Court of Appeals, where the appeal was dismissed, leaving the lower court's decision in force. An appeal to the United States Supreme Court was denied on June 4, 1951.[8]

Hollingshead used these proceedings to vent his spleen against the ill-treatment he felt he had received at the hands of the established film industry. To buttress its claim for damages, Park-In argued that it was the victim of a conspiracy by Paramount Pictures, of which Paramount-Richards was an affiliate. Explaining that the Camden drive-in had been "closed and dismantled in 1936," the Hollingshead company claimed that this had happened "by reason of the fact that affiliates of the defendants, viz., Paramount Pictures, Inc. and Paramount Film Distributors, in combination and conspiracy with owners and operators of conventional theatres in the Camden-Philadelphia area, practiced a film boycott and applied economic duress by refusing to supply new and appropriate film and by charging rental for film substantially in excess of that charged to other theatres in the area." Because of this "economic duress," Park-In was forced to grant Paramount-Richards and the other companies "territorially exclusive licenses at inadequate royalty rates." Being "forced" to enter such agreements brought great expense and disadvantage to the plaintiff, it argued. This lapse in judgment came at a time when Park-In was without benefit of legal counsel, the company claimed.[9] Given that the agreements were the standard ones Park-In used with every licensee, and that this most litigious of companies was never without counsel, these claims were dismissed by the court.

Meanwhile, the appeal by Loew's was making its way through the legal system. The First Circuit Court of Appeals rendered its verdict on April 8, 1949. This was the single most important piece of litigation for Park-In and everybody else who had a similar patent, such as Louis Josserand and others. When this court reversed the lower decision it made such patents worthless.

Focusing on the specific merits of the Hollingshead patent, the judges decided, 3–0, that it lacked invention and was therefore invalid. To their way of thinking, something that was novel, useful, or commercially successful couldn't be subject to a patent on that basis alone, but only from the means for making the system practically useful. In their opinion, the judges wrote: "This arcuate arrangement of parking stalls in a lot is obviously only an adaptation to automobiles of the conventional arrangement of seats in a theatre employed since ancient times to enable patrons to see the performance while looking comfortably ahead in normal sitting position without twisting the body or turning the head. ... There is nothing inventive in adapting the old arcuate arrangement of seats in a theatre to automobiles in a parking lot as the means to achieve horizontal pointing. ... Certainly terracing the parking lot as the means for giving occupants of cars in the rearward rows of stalls a clear field of vision over the tops of cars in front is not inventive. It is again only an adaptation of the familiar sloping floor of the conventional theatre. Nor appropriate vertical angle. . . . Anyone with even ordinary perception would certainly realize that the vertical angles of the automobiles would have to be adjusted with reference to the height of the screen." Finding that the lower court was so impressed by the commercial success of drive-ins that it lost focus on the real issues, the appeal judges termed the lower court decision—that a faculty of invention was required to devise the Hollingshead patent—"clearly erroneous."[10]

Park-In appealed twice to the court of last resort, the United States Supreme Court. A petition for a writ of certiorari to the First Circuit Court of Appeals was denied on October 10, 1949, while a petition for rehearing was denied by the Supreme Court on December 5, 1949. Both petitions were denied without comment.[11]

Hollingshead always had difficulty in enforcing his patent. The majority of people who opened a drive-in did so without bothering to obtain his permission and or sign an agreement. Of the earliest ones perhaps one-fifth were licensed. By the time of the Supreme Court decision Hollingshead estimated that about one hundred out of one thousand or more drive-ins then operating had honored his patent. By that late date, though, many saw the writing on the wall, realizing the patent would fail. Undoubtedly this further lowered the rate of compliance. There was a large resistance to the patent by operators, as many were annoyed with the idea that someone could patent the arrangement and rearrangement of lumps of dirt on the ground. (Essentially that *was* the Hollingshead patent.) The Court finally agreed this was not sufficient for a patent.

Litigation continued apace for a time. A suit brought by Park-In against Newman H. Waters, Jr., of Alabama, for patent infringement bounced in and out of court on technicalities. Out in California, Park-In sued Seth Perkins and others for patent infringement. Even those who paid royalties in the beginning were stopping, before the Supreme Court invalidated the patent. The district court dismissed this complaint, going so far as to award attorney's fees to Perkins. On appeal to the Ninth Circuit Court of Appeals, the best Park-In could do was to get those fees, $3,400, removed from the judgment against itself.[12]

Last was an action by Park-In against four drive-in owners in Denver, Colorado. On July 25, 1946, Park-In licensed two Denver men to build two drive-ins in the area. These rights were later assigned to the Denver Drive-In Theatres Corporation, which erected one, the East Drive-In Theatre. Around the same time the North Drive-In Theatre was being built by Carvue Corporation, without a license. After being threatened with a lawsuit by Park-In, Carvue sold the by-then-completed and operating drive-in to North Drive-In Theatres Corporation, effective September 1, 1948. Subsequently the South Drive-In and the West Drive-In were built. Thus each of the four companies were licensed to operate one patented theater within a certain quarter segment of the territory bounded by a circle within a thirty-mile radius centered on downtown Denver. Even then Hollingshead must have seen the end coming, for the licensing agreements all contained clauses setting out the rights and obligations of the parties in the event the patent was adjudicated as invalid. Each company agreed to pay a $1000 fee on execution of their agreement as well as to pay a royalty of 3.5 percent of the gross box office receipts.

None of the companies paid the $1000. Part payments of royalties were made for what little remained of the 1948 season. Nobody paid anything to Park-In after that. The company sued for royalties owing. It wasn't until 1955 that this case came to trial, well after the Supreme Court decision. Even if the Hollingshead patent had been found valid, it would have expired naturally in May 1950 after the patent's standard seventeen-year lifespan.

Strangely, the Colorado District Court ruled in Park-In's favor, deciding that the license under the Hollingshead patent was not the only consideration for the payment of royalties. As the contract dealt expressly with the rights of each party if the patent was deemed invalid, the judge cited the defendants' failure to exercise their right to terminate the contract in the event. He held this against them. Royalties were awarded to Park-In. On August 22, 1957, the Tenth Circuit Court of Appeals upheld the decision.[13]

A couple of months after the Supreme Court ruled against him, Richard Hollingshead gave the following comments:

> There ought to be an award in the industry for ideas which built it. Like the Oscars. It might stimulate the industry. But as for me, I can assure you I'm not going to think up any more ideas for the motion picture industry. Why should I lie awake nights to think up anything? ... To me, the drive-in stands in the category of the greatest contribution to the industry since sound. Yet since I began the drive-in theatre 15 years ago, I've received very little. Even from this viewpoint, it seems a shame that a person who creates and develops a new idea and goes through the procedure set down by law to obtain a patent cannot obtain remuneration when his patent gives everyone else profits. We're never going to create a better country if we kill initiative, and initiative depends on remuneration.[14]

Hollingshead estimated that the drive-in industry would gross $150 million that year, 1950. At royalty rates of 3.5 to 5 percent, this was $5.25 million to $7.5 million that Park-In would not collect in 1950. With his own share of the company at 30 percent—by then turned over to his son—Richard Hollingshead personally lost out on $1.5 million to $2.25 million in 1950 alone. Whatever amount he collected over the years in royalties has gone unrecorded. However, it must have been very small. Moreover, that much, and perhaps much more, was probably spent in legal fees.

Chapter 3

A Very Slow Start, 1933–1944

Camden's drive-in probably failed for lack of sufficient business. Whatever its cost, it was more-or-less state of the art for the time. It was built to last and expected to last, which was not the case with some of the drive-ins constructed in the 1930s. An illustration of one of these bottom-of-the-line facilities was the world's second drive-in, which enjoyed a very short life in Galveston, Texas.

Louis P. Josserand, an architect in Houston, Texas, came up with a slightly different version of the drive-in theater in 1933. The main difference between his plan and Hollingshead's was that the former allowed for two sets of parking ramps between each aisle. Automobiles could enter or exit a parking space either forward or backward, as the incline was rounded, lacking any rails. Josserand filed his patent application on December 14, 1933. United States patent number 2,102,718 was granted to him on December 21, 1937 (see pp. 216–221).

Along with associate A. H. Emenhiser, Josserand attempted to lease land from T. D. Dunn, Jr., of Houston for the purpose of building a drive-in. Dunn was very skeptical of this proposition, apparently refusing to lease the land for such a risky new endeavor. The cost of constructing a permanent drive-in on Dunn's land was estimated at $30,000 at the time, 1934. Dunn's skepticism may have caused Josserand to worry about the viability of this idea, for he turned to a cheap, "experimental" theater to convince Dunn, and perhaps himself, before establishing a costly and more permanent facility.

Galveston, Texas, was chosen as the spot for the experiment. Emenhiser built the theater to his partner's specifications on a beach, with the cars facing out to sea. Terraces and ramps for the cars were graded out of the sand, then wetted down each night before the show. Soaking the sand made it hard enough so that automobiles could drive over it. Even so, some would occasionally get stuck as they entered or left. Once the sand dried, the wind would blow it around, which necessitated regrading the entire parking area almost daily. At the front of the area were located a number of bench seats for walk-in customers or people who preferred to leave their cars to watch the show. A certain amount of congestion occurred outside the back of the theater, where people parked their cars in an effort to see the show for free. Emenhiser said: "Kids in Galveston had a free show by entering from the ocean side of the theater, which could not be fenced off." (A fence did surround the rest of the area, however.)

The parking area was lit; ushers were used. A sound truck roamed Galveston, publicizing this new marvel, which opened on Thursday, July 5, 1934. That day's edition of the *Galveston Daily News* reported: "The formal opening of the Drive In Short Reel Theater, just off 6th and Boulevard, will be held at 8 o'clock tonight. Programs, featuring news reels, comedies, cartoons, screen novelties, and short subjects of major producing companies will be held nightly between the hours of eight and twelve o'clock, and Saturday's until 2 a.m." Admission for a car and all its occupants was twenty-five cents. For ten cents an adult walk-in could sit in the bench seats, five cents for a child. It operated every night up to and including July 25. On the twenty-sixth this theater was destroyed during a storm. It was not rebuilt. Total cost for construction was just fifteen hundred dollars.[1]

The story of the Galveston drive-in appears in the pages of the *United States Patent Quarterly*, for Josserand's patent was similar to one being sought by a man named Herbert Taylor, Jr.—so similar that the patent office called an "interference," necessitating a lengthy court battle before Josserand's patent would prevail over Taylor's. By then it would not matter, as Hollingshead's patent had been invalidated and the idea regarded as unpatentable. Neither Josserand's patent nor Hollingshead's nor anybody else's then had any value.

Drive-ins didn't exactly mushroom in those early years. Slowly and steadily, however, they did pop up. The second such facility of a permanent nature opened on Sunday, September 9, 1934, in Los Angeles, California at the intersection of Pico Boulevard and Westwood. The opening-night attraction was Will Rogers in *Handy Andy*. Selected shorts rounded out the bill at this five hundred–car capacity theater.[2]

Other early drive-ins included the Merrimack Park Auto Theatre in Methuen, Massachusetts, on the bank of the Merrimack River, which opened in the summer of 1938. Owners Joe Cifre and George Swartz advertised: "A large body of water is Nature's greatest air conditioner." Boston got its first in 1937, as did Cape Cod, Massachusetts. There were owned by the Drive-In Theatre Corp. of America, headed by Philip Smith, Emanuel Kurland, and Sidney Stoneman (see pp. 222–227).

As early as 1938 such theaters were already being referred to as "ozoners," a nickname that would be much used in the future, particularly by *Variety*."[3] Other nicknames showed up in the press once or twice, only to disappear as quickly as they appeared. Some of these were "open-air operators," "fresh-air exhibitors," "outdoorers," "ramp-house," "under-the-stars emporium," "rampitoriums," "auto havens," "underskyer," "mudholes," "cow pastures,"

A photo of California's first drive-in taken in 1934, the year it opened. It was located in Los Angeles at the corner of Pico and Westwood Boulevard.

Cars line up in 1934 to visit the first drive-in in Los Angeles.

Los Angeles's first drive-in, pictured here in 1934 or 1935. Note the large speaker on top of the screen. This was the theater's sole audio system. Its noise generated so many complaints that the city passed an antinoise ordinance aimed specifically at the drive-in.

"autodeons," and "autotorium." "Passion pits" was the only other nickname with any staying power.

When a hurricane from the West Indies lashed the New England area in the fall of 1938, many drive-ins were damaged. Some were put out of business permanently; others reopened in a day or two. Severely damaged was the Merrimack, whose screen housing was flattened into a pile of kindling, seriously injuring three employees. One year passed before the Merrimack reopened for business. Also a victim of the storm was a curious hybrid under construction at Shrewsbury, Massachusetts. In an effort to obtain better-quality films, the owners were building a combination indoor/outdoor house. They hoped that year-round operation would ease film-booking problems. The plan was to use the indoor part after the outdoor season ended. However, after the hurricane reduced the structure to rubble, plans for this hybrid were abandoned.[4]

On February 25, 1938, Miami, Florida got its first one, owned jointly by E. M. Loew and Peter Landatti. It contained ten ramps, representing an investment of $50,000. Initially admission was set at thirty-five cents per person, 50 percent above that charged by an average indoor house. Despite press releases that the drive-in was popular, it quickly found itself in trouble, having to cut admission back to twenty-five cents within two months of opening. Publicly the theater said the move was just for the summer—to bring people in during

Miami's hot and steamy weather. (Mosquitoes would also have been a huge problem there.) When it cut admission prices, the Miami drive-in was also reportedly working on new promotional schemes.[5]

June 1938 saw drive-ins opened in Cleveland, Ohio; Detroit, Michigan; and Shrewsbury, Massachusetts. The first two were owned by the Phil Smith group, while the latter was operated by James Guarino and Thomas DiMaura. Detroit's opened on Thursday, June 2, 1938, to just fair attendance in a slight rain. The first attraction was a double bill consisting of *The Big Broadcast of 1938* followed by *Dead End*. Programs changed twice a week.

The screen was 49 feet by 59 feet, with the projector set 288 feet away. With a capacity of five hundred cars, admission was thirty-five cents per person, also above the level charged by local neighborhood theaters, which featured second-run programs. A staff of thirty people was employed, twenty-two of them in the field, to run the show. The field employees directed all cars, coming and going, with flashlights. They also cleaned car windshields.[6]

During the first month of operation an observer noted a steady buildup of attendance. This observer felt that the Detroit drive-in didn't compete with indoor theaters to any extent, drawing instead from people who would otherwise have gone to some other outdoor attraction. Noting the high admission the writer added: "the Drive-In does not even compete on the same price level, but offers a distinctive seasonal variety in entertainment." Nor did he see much of a future for the idea, writing that the "novelty appeal of the idea appears to be an important factor. First impression is that repeat business is not going to be built up, as is done in a neighborhood house, but that plenty of Detroiters will plan to go once to see what it is like, just as everybody goes to the zoo once a year—but this stream of 'just once' patrons will provide a steady revenue for the summer season."[7]

Maryland's first drive-in opened May 14, 1939. It was the Governor Ritchie Automobile Open-Air Theater, located on the Governor Ritchie Highway near Baltimore. The official opening was held with fanfare and speeches, including one by David Winebrenner, III, a cousin of the late Governer Ritchie. Prior to the opening, local newspapers explained this new marvel to their readers: "Customers drive into the theater in their own automobiles, and are allotted parking places. Special attendants wipe windshields and windows to afford a clear view to the huge screen, which is set up on an opposing hillside, and the amplification is great enough to make the music and speech of the picture audible even in the rearmost tier with car windows closed." In 1984 the Ritchie was torn down to make way for the Chesapeake Square Shopping Center.[8]

On Saturday, July 15, 1939, the Saco Drive In opened in Portland, Maine, featuring Jimmy Durante in *Forbidden Music*. Children under twelve were admitted free while all others paid thirty-five cents. Opening ads proclaimed it as "Maine's first open-air automobile theatre. . . . Avoid Parking Troubles. Sit in your own car and Enjoy the Talkies. Motor in Anytime after 7." Although it was put up for sale in 1987, the Saco was still operating in 1989, able to celebrate its fiftieth anniversary. Featured that night was a double bill of *Say Anything* and *Field of Dreams*. Admission was $8.50 per carload.[9]

New York State got its first ozoner when one opened at Valley Stream, Long Island, on Wednesday, August 10, 1938. A capacity crowd of six hundred cars attended that night despite a torrential downpour. Constructed at a cost of $50,000, the screen was 48 feet high by 60 feet wide. The bottom of the screen was 30 feet above the ground. With a throw of 245 feet, the projection booth was located in the fourth row. Situated on twelve acres, a drive-in of this size occupied a land area about ten times larger than the largest indoor theater (capacity two to three thousand) needed. A *New York Times* reporter who turned out for the opening wrote that although he had to keep his windows closed due to the rain, he could hear everything just fine. Nor, he happily reported, did he notice any distortion of vision.[10]

In Jacksonville, Florida, the Atlantic Drive-In opened on December 6, 1939, one mile past the city line, with a showing of *East Side of Heaven*, starring Bing Crosby, along with shorts and a newsreel. Horace Denning was the man who secured the six-acre plot of land for his company and the 361-car capacity Atlantic. When the entertainment editor of the local paper heard of Denning's plans, he bet him ten dollars that the venture would fail in less than six weeks. While scouting the land he would eventually purchase, the property owner's daughter, Virginia Holden, came by on horseback. The couple soon married, and Virginia became the Atlantic's first cashier. During the early years Denning obtained a daily list of births, both from newspaper listings and local hospitals. To each newborn child in the county he sent a pair of passes along with a letter addressed to the infant, which pointed out the advantage of "movies in the comfort of your car and if you should start to cry, you will not have to leave because you will not disturb anyone." On opening night only one item, Coca-Cola, was available at the concession stand. It was soon joined by popcorn, then candy, and then other foodstuffs. The entertainment editor lost his bet: The Atlantic lasted longer than six weeks, not expiring until the night of September 29, 1973, with a double bill of *Song of the South* and *A[illegible]cats*.[11]

Chicago's first ozoner opened the weekend of May 24, 1941. With space for 1,160 cars on its twenty acres, erected at a cost of $75,000, it was much bigger and costlier than most other theaters of that first drive-in decade. It was a forerunner of many to come. At the intersection of Waukegan and Golf Roads, it lay on Chicago's northwest side, and was owned by N. S. Barger, who also owned the Rialto, a local burlesque house. Admission was forty cents, with children admitted for twenty cents. Usherettes riding bicycles met each car at the ticket booth, from where they escorted it to a parking space. Sandwiches, soft drinks, and ice cream were on tap at the concession stand, along with specially constructed trays that clamped onto car windows to hold those purchases. In addition to washing car windshields, attendants checked autos for oil, gas, water, and air.[12]

Central Arkansas saw its first outdoor theater, known simply as the Drive-In Movies, open on six acres in Rose City on July 27, 1940. It had no competition in the area until a second was built after the war. Newspaper ads placed during the week before opening urged residents to drive out and see the drive-in under construction. Ads touted this "new, different, exciting form of entertainment for all the family," promising "a loudspeaker for each car" and "no more parking worries." On opening night an estimated twelve hundred cars jammed the highway trying to squeeze into the four hundred–car lot. Those that were lucky enough to get in saw Joan Blondell and Melvyn Douglas in *The Amazing Mr. Williams*. News accounts noted that customers bought their thirty-cent tickets from "decorative women," while twenty ushers showed drivers how to park uphill on the "newfangled" ramps. Ushers then cleaned windshields and brought refreshments to the cars. Management promised prices would stay low to "include many persons not now able to attend the movies" in conventional theaters.[13]

The Los Angeles area got its second drive-in on June 10, 1938, when the San-Val opened. Lying just outside Burbank, it took its name from the San Fernando Valley, in which it was situated. Ownership was by the California Drive-In Theatres Corporation, of which Seth D. Perkins was president. This company then also owned the first Los Angeles ozoner, which was then called the Pico. On its ten acres of land the San-Val held 618 cars in nine rows. Excluding land, this drive-in cost $54,563 to build (see pp. 227–228). The screen was 60 feet wide by 40 feet high with a two-foot black border painted around the entire screen, leaving a usable screen 58 by 38 feet.

As with all the early drive-ins, much of the screen tower was built of wood. Made of a metal-lath-and-plastered surface, the screen area itself was then covered with lightweight canvas bedded in white lead and painted a flat white. Ramp-to-ramp distance was forty feet. Sitting in the second row the projector was 186 feet from the screen. Cars in the ninth row, capacity ninety-nine autos, were 550 feet from the screen. Like all projection booths of the time, the San-Val's was set some two to three feet underground to minimize the number of car spaces lost in ramps directly behind it due to obstruted vision.

After the lot was graded into the required terraces and ramps, a light grade of hot penetrating oil was poured over the ground. Then a layer of number 6 decomposed gravel was spread and rolled over this surface; following this a heavy-gravity road oil was laid down. Next came a covering of a layer of crushed rock, thoroughly rolled by a four-ton roller until a hard compressed surface was obtained. Over the lot was laid a huge gridwork of 2 × 6 stringers spaced 3 feet apart, joined by 1 × 6 crosspieces. This grid formed bumpers for parked autos as well as a place to locate the individual speakers. Made of 3/8-inch plywood, these were fixed-position speakers with no volume control.

An aerial view of the San-Val Theatre, Burbank, California, taken in 1938, the year it opened. It was California's second drive-in. Note the rows of rudimentary speakers.

Burbank, California's, San-Val Drive-In in 1938. Note the speakers on a wooden grid. They were an attempt to lessen noise and eliminate complaints from nearby residents.

Regular changes in the types and locations of speakers in early drive-ins were a result of constant and chronic complaints from nearby residents about too-high noise levels. The speakers at the San-Val were connected in such a way that an entire row could be switched off or on. Thus, on a night when the theater wasn't busy one or more rows of speakers could remain off, saving on energy costs. A signal system existed between the ticket booth and projection room, allowing the ticket person to alert the projectionist to increase the sound level if a train or truck passed nearby. The fence enclosing the San-Val was 10 feet high except at the rear, where it stood 7 feet high.

The concession building was very rudimentary and illustrated the small role concessions played in most early drive-ins. Housing a hot-water heater, gas range, and a few appliances, this building was only 10 by 18 feet, with a six-stool counter.

Company president Perkins explained that the Pico charged thirty-five cents for admission while the San-Val charged only twenty-five cents—the difference being that the Pico obtained newer product due to its closer proximity to Los Angeles, necessitating a single-feature program with twice-weekly changes. The San-Val was cheaper and double-billed because that's what indoor houses in that area did. The product was generally older in that locale. There were two shows a night at the San-Val.

Even as early as 1938 drive-ins were engaged in an attempt to win community goodwill. The San-Val offered its facilities free anytime during the day on Sundays to any church that wished to hold its services there. Perkins claimed that this generated much favorable comment, although it is unclear if any church took him up on his offer.

The San-Val employed twenty-eight people in the summer; eighteen of these were ushers. During colder winter months staff was reduced by eight ushers. At the ticket booth were three employees—two of them sellers who took money from customers, took it to the cashier, and then returned tickets and change to the customers. Two other employees at the box office were charged solely with cleaning car windshields. Perkins explained they did this because "the patron appreciates the cleaning of the windshield; with a clean windshield our picture stands out much better. We do not allow these boys to accept tips for this service."

It was claimed that patrons drove as far as twelve to fifteen miles to attend the San-Val. Perkins felt there was very little competition between a drive-in and an indoor house saying:

> Our patronage is really created by what might be termed a "non-theatre-going public." By that I mean people who are in ill health, cripples, old people, especially large people who find that theatre seats are not comfortable, people who have a fear of contagious diseases picked up in any sort of enclosed buildings or auditoriums, people who have little children whom they dislike

> leaving at home or in the care of a neighbor or nurse, as well as a good number of people who do not feel like dressing up after a hard day's work in order to attend a show at the conventional type of theatre. Then, too, there are hundreds of people who bring a lunch and who find their automobile has the desired privacy.[14]

The biggest problem early drive-ins had with their neighbors was complaints from the latter about the noise level. Camden had been hit by such complaints from day one. Some drive-ins utilized a single huge speaker mounted on top of the screen building to pump out the sound. Some used a few speakers on poles, spread around the lot a bit. Complaints led to experiments with individual speakers. Hollingshead tried putting speakers into the ground. Each car parked directly over a grate from which the sound rumbled up through the floorboards. "Sound-in-the-ground" failed miserably. Some ozoners utilized individual speakers that they hung on car bumpers. As always at this time there was no individual volume control. In this case the sound seemed to come out of a customer's hood. The San-Val used fixed speakers stationed beside each car. But whether the sound thundered out of one huge speaker or five hundred small ones, it was far too noisy as far as the neighbors were concerned. It wasn't much good for the customers either. Only a portion got really synchronized sound, while it arrived too early or too late for many. Also it was tinny, often muffled, or garbled. The sound problem would likely have brought drive-in proliferation to a stop had it not been for RCA's development of the individual car speaker hung in each customer's car, with its own volume control in the patron's hands. While RCA announced this invention in 1941, a wartime halt in drive-in construction, among other things, delayed its use until 1946.

So irate did some neighbors become in those early years that drive-in owners were occasionally hauled into court. The first Los Angeles drive-in ran into trouble within a few months of its opening in 1934. Angry citizens brought enough pressure so that the Los Angeles City Council introduced an ordinance on January 31, 1935, passed on February 7, making it a misdemeanor to operate a sound-amplifying system in connection with "any show" in such a manner that the sound was audible at a distance of fifty feet or more from the facility or property line.

In the month after passage of this ordinance, Guy Douthwaite, owner of the drive-in, was arrested, charged, and released on his own recognizance. A warrant had been sworn by a physician and three women neighbors who charged that the noise from the drive-in annoyed them. It could be heard, they said, a mile away. Douthwaite first tested the constitutionality of the new law in superior court. He argued the bill was discriminatory in that it was aimed solely at drive-ins, of which he was the only owner and operator. When he argued that the law didn't apply to amplifying systems broadcasting sporting events or political affairs, he was correct. However, "any show" was broadly defined in the bill to include indoor theaters, stage performances, and so on. The court declined to see things Douthwaite's way, sending him down to municipal court for trial. However, lending support to Douthwaite's idea that the law was specifically designed to get him was the fact that it was enacted just a few months after he opened for business. Also, he was the first person charged under that law, within a few weeks of its passage.

On June 4, 1935, Douthwaite was found guilty of violating the ordinance. The judge fined him $250 or ninety days in the county jail. Sentence was suspended on the condition that Douthwaite not be convicted of a similar offense within one year. Douthwaite died of a heart attack in December 1936, aged fifty. A small obituary in a Los Angeles newspaper called him the "originator of the drive-in theater." Even at that early time Hollingshead was being forgotten and getting little respect.[15]

In Detroit, John H. Flancher filed a petition in court in July 1938 on behalf of residents of three Detroit suburbs. Flancher contended that the Detroit ozoner should be termed a public nuisance because its sound could be heard from two miles away. His petition, which contained five hundred signatures, asked for a restraining order against the theater. A reporter for *Boxoffice* visited the area, reporting that only a slight noise could be heard outside the property line of the show. Hearing the case was Judge Sherman D. Callender, who adjourned it until later in July, intending to visit the theater himself. Before that time, however, the court, with consent of the petitioners, dropped the case. Drive-in management took steps to address the problem, apparently successfully.[16]

A drive-in theater in Bethal Township, near Pittsburgh, Pennsylvania, ran afoul of its neighbors in 1940, when more than one hundred of them testified in court seeking a restraining order against the theater because of its excessive noise. Residents alleged that the sound could be heard "more than a mile away and that nervous systems are being shattered and sleep made impossible until around 1 A.M." Defense attorneys argued their noise was no worse than that emanating from other facilities such as open-air dance floors. When they pleaded that the owners had $30,000 invested in the drive-in, attorneys for the plaintiffs countered that the residents had close to a half million dollars invested in their homes. These neighbors also wanted the drive-in to remove an iron fence which they considered illegal, around the perimeter, as well as financial compensation for alleged injury to the value of their property.[17]

In 1945 another Pittsburgh ozoner, one owned by Norbert Stern, came under fire, when Stern was hauled into court over noise complaints by neighbors. Stern and residents living as far as two miles from the theater had been involved in several legal skirmishes over the preceding summer. Judge William H. McNaughter was slated to attend the season opening of Stern's ozoner the week of May 8, 1945, to determine if it was, as residents contended, a public nuisance.[18] With no other reports in the national media on these two Pittsburgh cases, it is likely that some compromise was reached. There is no record that any drive-in was forced to close due to complaints from neighboring residents about its noise level.

The Riverside Auto Theatre in Columbus, Ohio, was in court in August 1940 over its sound level. This case was dropped when the theater owners brought in a sound expert who reduced the amount of noise from the loudspeakers. Further sound reductions were promised for the future.[19]

As an item of trivia, the first woman manager of a drive-in was Nelle Brock of Cincinnati, Ohio. In March 1940 Nelle was appointed manager of Tucson, Arizona's, only ozoner. Four months later, in July, it was reported that B. A. Reif took over management of the theater from Mrs. C. H. Perry. Presumably Nelle married while in Tucson, then quit work.[20]

There was a tremendous variation in the costs of those early drive-ins. A figure of $30,000 to $35,000 would seem to be a rough average, at least for the better-quality ones. However, the range was from $75,000—as was spent on Nate Barger's Chicago venture, opened in 1941—all the way down to the $1,500 spent on the one in Galveston, Texas. One that opened in Cheektowaga, New York, near Buffalo, in 1941 cost $52,000. Admission was thirty-five cents for adults, with "children and cars free." The drive-in was situated on twenty acres, and its screen was 30 by 40 feet.[21]

Many observers were skeptical of the long-term potential of drive-ins. Elias Loew was offered a share of the Weymouth, Massachusetts, unit but held off from accepting it. Within a year he was enthusiastically constructing his own chain. When the trade publication *Boxoffice* gave a detailed list of new theaters opened in 1939, broken down by quarter and by state, they dismissed ozoners by writing: "Drive-in theatres cropped up in a number of sections during the past year and, in the main, have been eliminated from this survey, since there is no permanency to such open air projects in contrast with regular theatres. In some cases drive-ins have faded from the local scene after one season's operation."[22]

One example of this type was one set up in a flat bean field in North Carolina where a farmer erected two telephone poles with a screen attached. Admission was twenty-five cents a carload, with a "foghorn-blast speaker" at the side of the screen. A film could be rented for twelve dollars a week. The rural audience was described as composed of "old farm boys who would watch anything moving. Anything. They'd come right in the middle of the story and it wouldn't matter a bit. . . . I guess at first it was probably more like a social occasion than anything else."[23]

Some of these hastily and cheaply erected ozoners evolved into permanent theaters. Wilson Shankweiler was a movie buff from Orefield, Pennsylvania, a suburb of Allentown. During a 1933 vacation trip he discovered the Camden drive-in. Pleased by what he saw, he decided he'd like one for himself. Behind the hotel he owned in Orefield was a deserted landing strip, which Shankweiler converted to a makeshift drive-in. The first screen consisted of two poles and a sheet. A 16-mm projector sat on a table in the middle of the landing strip, while audio was provided by one large horn speaker down front. Shankweiler's Auto Park also drew walk-in patrons, who sat on benches near the screen. Wilson never bothered about a patent license. As expected, Park-In sued for infringement. They lost. When the local township instituted an amusement tax, which applied to all types of theaters, Wilson tried to avoid it by advertising "Free Movies. Parking 50c." There was no tax on parking. Shankweiler's opened on April 15, 1934. Fifty years later it was still going, after a great many modifications.[24] If this date is correct, it would make Shankweiler's the second drive-in built. The fiftieth anniversary article, published in 1983, makes the opening in April 1933, which is definitely not correct. Did the author of the article mean that this ozoner was entering its fiftieth year in 1983? Opening dates for Camden, Galveston, and Los Angeles are reliable. They are the first, second, and third ones built. With the Shankweiler opening date unclear, it's hard to say whether it comes before or after Galveston.

While the original Camden ozoner likely closed for financial reasons, other early ones were very successful. Loew's operation in Providence, Rhode Island, grossed $29,065 during its first season, which was less than four months long. The Weymouth drive-in grossed $68,000 in its first year, 1936, and grossed $72,000 in 1937.[25] Each of those years it grossed more than it cost to build. The difference in success may have been due to expertise and or connections in the film industry, which these men had or developed and Hollingshead didn't. However, many of the early operators were men like Hollingshead, who had no connection or experience in the industry. If they rigidly stuck to trying to land first-run, or even second-run, product from the major Hollywood studios, then they were doomed to a lack of product. The film industry was a monopoly at that time, with the major studios making, distributing, and exhibiting the films in theaters they owned. Even independent indoor theaters had problems obtaining product. More experienced men who entered the drive-in business, such as Loew, who owned a chain of New England indoor theaters, knew there was lots of product churned out by independents, and they knew where to get it. If a drive-in owner was willing to take any product—and he had to be—something was always available at a reasonable rental rate. Beginning in 1938 the major Hollywood studios began, one by one, to make their films available, in later runs, to drive-ins. *Time* magazine reported in 1941 that, "despite the fact that producers refuse to sell Drive-Ins anything but old A pictures, punk Bs and westerns, most of them manage to make a respectable profit."[26] By then there was evidence that the majors were starting to become interested in drive-ins. Paramount, through subsidiaries, already owned several. The major Hollywood studios might very well have turned to large-scale ownership of these theaters, as they already had with indoor ones, except for protracted antitrust litigation already under way, which ultimately forced the majors to sell off their theater holdings. Had the majors moved into a position of large drive-in ownership, the ozoners would likely have received easy access to A films. As it evolved, they never did.

Mostly, though, the major studios were hostile to drive-ins because the independent owners of indoor theaters were hostile to drive-ins. This latter group was antagonistic to ozoners because they felt threatened. Since the independent indoor men were the most important customers of the major film studios (excluding the theaters owned by the studios), the studios sided with them. Already at the mercy of the major studios, forced to take product wholly on studio terms, with the emergence of drive-ins, the independents felt themselves squeezed from another direction. Making healthy profits on the monopoly theater system that then existed, the major studios were little inclined to change anything. The system worked very well for them.

Back in the 1930s, some indoor theaters closed for part of the summer, in hot, humid areas. Air-conditioning had not fully arrived, and customers might be permanently lured away. Thus the independent indoor men put pressure on the studios to make sure they got earlier and better bookings than their open-air competitors.

Another point that bound the studios together with the independent indoor owners was the policy—even in those early years—that some drive-ins had of charging no admission for children. Both groups strongly subscribed to the idea that any warm body passing through the gate must pay. A cheaper rate for children might be acceptable, but a charge had to be levied. This free admission policy, thought the indoor people, would also undermine their customer base. It meant a smaller gross for the film distributors at a time when film rental rates were often a percentage of the gross. Neither group considered the possibility that drive-ins might have an overall positive effect on the industry.

During the Great Depression the film industry was nervous as attendance fluctuated wildly. In 1930 weekly attendance at U.S. theaters hit 90 million, a figure that would never be surpassed. In 1932 and 1933 it plunged to 60 million a week. By 1936 and 1937 it had surged back to 88 million per week, only to fall steadily to 80 million in 1940. These figures would climb back to 90 million per week for 1946 and 1947 before the final, and permanent, descent set in.[27] The drive-in was not to blame for any of this, but it was a handy whipping boy. The entire film industry enjoyed nothing but vigorous success from its inception until the depression. Suddenly the industry was not as invincible as it thought.

At the beginning of 1941 the average indoor theater charged 23 cents for admission. Open for business roughly ten hours a day it took in 60 percent to 85 percent of its daily gross in just one hour, usually between 7:30 and 8:30 P.M. Ten percent of its business was done on each of Monday through Thursday while Friday to Sunday business accounted for, respectively, 15 percent, 20 percent, and 25 percent. While 6,972 theaters featured single bills, 10,031 ran double bills.[28]

As early as the summer of 1938 *Variety* articulated the fears of indoor exhibitors, though there were probably no more than 50 to 60 drive-ins in operation, when it wrote they were spreading "alarmingly" and "may eventually represent a serious threat with organized operation in many parts of the country. Up to now confined to the sticks, the drive-ins are beginning to penetrate more important situations ... they are getting more in the way of regularly operated theatres and causing theatre men to raise complaints about which seemingly nothing can be done." The main "danger" of the ozoner lay in its becoming widespread and the difficulty of meeting its competition since it could be constructed more cheaply than an indoor theater. Newly spreading air-conditioning would soon put an end to the need for any house to close for the summer, however, *Variety* worried about even that fearing patrons would prefer the outdoors to an "iced auditorium."[29]

Instead of becoming the natural allies they were and joining together to battle the majors over improved film access the independent indoor owners and drive-in men became bitter enemies. When a drive-in was announced, early in 1940, for construction and opening that May in Cincinnati, Ohio, Wess Huss, Jr., president of the Greater Cincinnati Independent Exhibitors, sent a letter to all the exhibitors in the Ohio territory calling attention to, and protesting, this proposed intruder. The reasons Huss cited in his letter to oppose the drive-in were that it planned to admit children for free and that it operated only part of the year. A group of motion picture theater owners in Massachusetts publicly took a stand against ozoners as early as 1938. Commenting on the New England drive-in situation that same year *Boxoffice* wrote that, "Despite attempts of intimidation ... Boxoffice has exclusively continued to report the various moves as they were made, or premeditated, in the outdoor theatre design. And so will Boxoffice continue."[30]

It was all a vast overraction directed against a small number of drive-ins, many of which were poorly constructed, more likely to turn potential patrons off after one visit. Surfacing of the ramps and drives was usually several inches of crushed stone, slag or cinders. Rolling of this material was often inadequate, leaving a surface constantly in motion under the wheels of a car. It was difficult for people to walk on and needed constant attention from the staff. It was noisy. During periods of dry weather cars coming and going would raise huge clouds of dust. Ramp areas were usually unlit. Most of the concession buildings were tiny, many little more than wooden shacks. Toilets were often just wooden outhouses. Only the few drive-ins in the "better class" had any concrete buildings. Picture quality was at best fair, on a small screen. On a large screen it was poor no matter where your car was parked.

Worst of all was the sound. Drive-ins located normally just outside of a town line where zoning rules were more lenient, taxes less, and the cost of land more inexpensive. However, they had to be close enough to populated areas to attract support. The resultant speaker noise riled up those very neighbors. Underground speakers, "sound-in-the-ground," was once touted as the "real solution." Nate Barger's huge Chicago ozoner utilized this system installing 580 grilled manholes, one for every two cars. The sound was distorted and had a metallic tone after bouncing off the undersides of automobiles. Also, the illusion that the sound was coming from the actors on the screen was ruined as it obviously drifted up from under the cars. During rainstorms these systems were subject to flooding and many grounded out in severe storms.

The overhead horn speaker, either one huge one on top of the screen or several smaller ones on poles spread around was the original system. These horns were aimed downward at the center of the parking area. The same metallic quality was produced as the sound bounced off the tops of autos. Distortion was also obvious. These systems angered neighbors the most. The remaining method tried was some sort of fixed speaker mounted beside the car. It was not taken into the car, nor did it have individual volume control. This system confined sound to the theater better than the other methods, with less distortion for the patrons. Disadvantages included the fact that car windows had to be left open all the time in order to obtain sufficient volume. This was less than satisfactory during rainy weather, windy weather, cold weather or in times of heavy insect activity. A strong wind blowing into the speaker would necessitate the volume control being turned up by the projectionist which would produce distortion. A strong-enough wind could actually lock the diaphragm in the speaker, stopping all sound.[31]

While development of drive-ins was slow during the first eight years it came to a halt for the next four years as building restrictions imposed during World War II stopped all unnecessary construction. It's an old cliché to say that something is ahead of its time but the drive-in was. The economic hardships of the depression worked against any rapid spread of ozoners. As did the structure of the film industry itself. By the 1940s the drive-ins had all the necessary conditions in place to allow them to skyrocket when the war froze that. Technology improved projection to the point where they had a long-enough throw to allow a drive-in to be constructed that could hold well over a thousand autos—Barger's in Chicago. RCA developed the in-car speaker in 1941, although it would not be used until 1946 when every drive-in quickly adopted that method. This ended the major, nagging technical problems, from the owners' perspective.

Most of the early drive-ins had concession stands that were rudimentary and small, added almost as an afterthought it seems. Operators perhaps thought patrons would bring their own food with them. The art of maximizing concession sales would be raised to its highest level after the war. Playgrounds for children were very rare in the first half of the 1940s, but a few were successfully established. Some observers felt that the Hollingshead patent retarded development of the drive-in; that potential owners and builders were turned back because they had to get permission and pay royalties. This is not likely, as most operators who did build ignored Hollingshead anyway. While he had a strong propensity to sue and drag cases to the highest court levels, he usually lost.

The 1930s were not conducive to the large-scale development of drive-ins. The first half of the 1940s may have been, but World War II put an end to that possibility.

The first reliable statistics as to the number of drive-ins in the United States are for January 1, 1942, when *Film Daily* reported a total of ninety-five ozoners spread over twenty-seven states (see pp. 222–227). Ohio led the way with eleven drive-ins. These figures are probably quite accurate. This survey indicated a size range of a 135-car capacity unit up to an 800-car capacity unit with an average-size lot, holding 400 cars. Either this survey underestimated the size of Barger's Chicago facility or other accounts exaggerated it. For a 300-car theater, six to seven acres of land were needed, while twelve acres were needed for 800 cars. The average drive-in employed fifteen to twenty people. Admission charges ranged from twenty-five to thirty-five cents (twenty-five to twenty-seven cents for indoor theaters). The first ones typically had screens 40 by 30 feet, while the later ones in this group were more apt to have a 60-by-50 foot screen. A boom seemed imminent as this survey announced fifty drive-ins planned for 1942—virtually all killed by the war. Yearly totals for drive-ins on January 1, 1943, to 1946 were, respectively, 99, 97, 96, and 102. On January 1, 1947, there were 155. Two years later, 820. Six years after that the total exceeded 3,700.[32]

During those war years totals were virtually unchanged. A few were rushed to completion, it seems, toward the end of 1945. Other problems faced drive-ins during the war years. Automobile tires were hard to come by—rubber was needed for the war. Gas rationing was in effect for some of that period, yet none of the ozoners failed and went out of business. Seasons may have been shortened in some cases, or even terminated totally. Elias Loew's Providence, Rhode Island, drive-in operated every year from its opening in 1937 except during the 1943 season "when it closed down during part of the season because of restrictions imposed by the Office of Price Administration [OPA] in respect to the use of gasoline for pleasure driving and that its operation did not exceed twenty days in 1943." Rationing of gas and tires forced the Ritchie Drive-In near Baltimore to close for two years during the war.[33]

Just before World War II ended, drive-ins offered their patrons obscure B films at prices higher than those indoor houses charged for A films, first or second run. As to the technical quality of presentation the drive-ins offered something ranaging from poor to abysmal. It was not then clear that in-car speakers would solve one problem. Many other "miracle" sound systems had been previously announced only to fall on their faces. Amenities at drive-ins were mainly in place but still small and unappealing. Balanced against this were the facts that patrons could dress as they liked, eat, talk, smoke, and so on. Their kids could cry and scream. There were no parking problems or baby-sitting needs. Patrons could walk from their home to their cars and never leave their vehicles again until arriving back home. No standing in line for tickets. If it could be simplified into a choice between quality versus convenience it was no contest as quality was beaten handily. An analyst looking at the drive-in industry logically in 1944 or thereabouts could be forgiven if he concluded it had little future. Of course he would have been completely wrong. The final factor that drove the drive-in industry to heights even its strongest supporters couldn't have dreamed of in such a short time was the coming immediately after the war, and the full flowering of, America's love of the automobile—American car culture.

Chapter 4

Postwar Surge, 1945–1949

During the 1930s, when drive-ins first appeared, and into the 1940s, they were trying to break into an industry under monopoly control. Hollywood was dominated by eight major companies: Paramount, 20th Century–Fox, Warner Bros., MGM (formerly Loew's), RKO, Columbia, Universal, and United Artists. The first five named companies were the most important for they produced films, distributed them and exhibited them in theaters they owned. Less important but still significant players were the final three companies, sometimes called the "little 3." None of these three owned any theaters. Columbia and Universal produced and distributed, while United Artists only distributed. In addition, three other companies were involved in film distribution, for a total of eleven in all.

Before the monopoly was broken up in 1949 by the courts, these majors produced more than 95 percent of all A features released. After the breakup, in 1957, independent producers made more than 50 percent of all motion pictures, most of them being A's. During the 1943–44 season releases by the five majors accounted for 73.3 percent of the film rentals received by the eleven distributors.

These big five produced enough film product to take up most of the screen times at their own first-run theaters. This left the "little 3" and the other three distributors able to market mostly only B films and westerns. Of the producing, distributing, and exhibiting sectors, it was the last area that was most securely controlled by the five majors prior to the court-ordered breakup. Their control was such that the court held that in cities with populations under one hundred thousand the effect "was largely to eliminate competition," while in cities larger than one hundred thousand the effect was "substantially to limit competition." These five owned 70 percent of the first-run theaters in the ninety-two largest cities. Each of them gave the other four special access to its first-run theaters in exchange for reciprocal rights. Each respected the others' run and clearance policies.

In their licensing agreements these majors set the admission prices that were to be charged by independent exhibitors. A common practice of the majors was to impose block booking on an exhibitor. If an independent theater owner wished to play, for example, a Paramount big-budget film with lots of stars—and all did—Paramount would agree only if the exhibitor agreed to take all Paramount product over a certain period of time. Block booking was much hated by exhibitors, who got stuck playing a lot of films they would never had screened if judgment were passed on a film-by-film basis. However, so great was the power of the majors that they could and did impose block booking.

First-run product from these majors was mostly shown in theaters they owned themselves, although first run sometimes went to independent indoor men in areas where the majors didn't have a heavy concentration of theaters, or if they had a backlog of product. Second and third runs were often referred to as first subsequent run and second subsequent run. After that there were later runs still. These were what neighborhood indoor houses got, and what drive-ins would fight to work themselves up to. One reason the majors disliked the ozoners was that it was difficult to impose block booking on a class of theaters many of which were closed for six months or so over each winter. Whether a neighborhood indoor house got second or third run depended on whether it was a "deluxe" house or not. Such distinctions were arbitrarily imposed by the majors. As the run got later and later the rental rates dropped; however, very likely so did the attendance.

Between each run was a certain amount of dead time, or clearance, as it was called. For example, there might be a clearance of thirty-five/fourteen between first, second, and third runs. In this example thirty-five days had to pass from the time a film ended its run at a first-run house until it could begin a second run. Then fourteen days had to elapse before it could begin a third run. All these numbers were set arbitrarily, running anywhere from seven to ninety days or more. They varied from major to major, from city to city, from year to year.

The United States government had looked at the film industry for possible monopoly control as far back as the 1920s, on several occasions, but never took any action. Finally an antitrust suit was started against all eight majors in 1938 culminating, in 1949, in the breakup of the monopoly. The most important points of the decision, from the drive-in's perspective, were that all five majors had to sell off their theater holdings, block booking was banned, and the companies were not allowed to set admission prices in film rental contracts. Clearances were not banned but allowed to exist as long as they weren't "unreasonable"—language vague enough to continue to favor the distributors.[1]

A major achievement of this court decision probably was to make the industry somewhat more varied and competitive, which may have helped keep it alive (albeit wounded) under the assaults of television. Had the old monopoly been in place, it might have suffered even more seriously.

Drive-ins were the new guys in town. In terms of dealing with the established film industry, life was not easy for them at any time. Before the monopoly breakup, the ozoners found the industry a nearly impossible nut to crack. After the breakup the industry was just a very tough nut to crack. Not that it seemed to matter much. People poured into drive-ins. They couldn't be built fast enough.

The drive-in boom began almost as soon as World War II ended. Hostilities ceased on May 8, 1945, in Europe followed by the surrender of Japan on August 14. On January 1, 1946, there were just 102 ozoners in the country. Three years later there were almost 1,000. Five years after that there were more than 3,000. Driving that boom was the full-blown arrival of the car culture. On its heels came the baby boom. As we have seen, ozoners were an ideal place for a young family with children — no baby-sitter needed, no parking problems, dress as you like, and they offered relatively cheap entertainment for a family group. A love of motion pictures was already well established in the United States. Writer Lloyd Wendt put it as well as anybody when he summed up the mood of the American people at the end of World War II: "What Americans want is to get into their new automobiles and drive someplace."[2]

There was one observer who looked at the outdoor theater situation near the end of 1945 only to find it wanting. Writing in *Boxoffice* Ansel M. Moore declared the drive-in to be sound on certain points but "sorely lacking in patron psychology." Moore found it difficult to accept that people would prefer a "gaseous parking lot" over a comfortable seat in an air-conditioned indoor theater. He explained this anomaly, at least to himself, by claiming that the ozoner's popularity sprang from its concession sales: "It has outmaneuvered and outsold its indoor contemporary. ... Take away its confectionary sales profits and the average drive-in theatre would probably fold in a fortnight."[3] At that time concession sales were still only a minor, rudimentary part of a drive-in's business. What Moore said about concession sales would prove to be true, but it wasn't so in 1945.

For Moore the only future for ozoners was if they were built as adjuncts to modern indoor theaters. Somehow they would then function mainly as parking lots, "feeders" for confectionary items, and as outdoor dining areas. It would have a distinctly secondary role. As for the drive-in as a stand-alone unit, Moore felt: "It is questionable whether the drive-in, as now constituted, will very long survive."[4] His opinions definitely make him odd man out.

The battle to gain better pictures earlier for their screens would occupy the time of a number of owners over the coming years; however, they were a minority. Simply because every new drive-in immediately made money, most owners worried less about whether they showed an A or B film or whether it was six months or three years old. When almost three new drive-ins were opening each and every day of the year — as happened at the end of the 1940s — they still all made money. As a result, drive-in owners never banded together to lobby intensely for changes in the film-booking policies laid down by the distributors. They might have been successful had they tried during the ozoner glory years, but they were all making too much money to try, to care, or to worry.

Annual profits at the most successful ones sometimes hit 30 percent of invested capital—a phenomenal figure in American industry. Many earned net profits of 15 to 20 percent, compared to conventional theaters, which averaged around 10 percent. These profits were achieved in spite of the low-quality films screened at ozoners.[5]

Some owners were more perceptive than Moore in analyzing the new phenomena. One such was Herbert J. Ochs, who was enlarging his drive-in chain at war's end. He opened his first outdoor theater in Warren, Ohio, in 1940. His notion of preferred location was a site not too far from the highway but not too distant from residential areas. In scouting land one had to act surreptitiously, he said, for "farmers are alert to the drive-in possibilities and jack up their prices at the faintest whisper of a prospect."[6]

Admission at the Ochs drive-in was always slightly lower than the prevailing first-run admission price at indoor theaters in the vicinity. However, it was always higher than any of the second- or later-run indoor houses in the area. No complaints on that score were ever received, said Ochs because his patrons didn't go to indoor houses and thus had no standard of comparison. In his view 95 percent of his customers wouldn't go to an indoor theater regardless of price or program. Films were booked to appeal to the family, which meant excluding "heavy sex stuff, the too abnormal and the too gruesome." An Ochs venue mainly booked action dramas, comedies, and musicals.

As a result of this type of operation, Ochs said, his ozoners were "bringing people to motion pictures who haven't even been tapped by the indoor theatre. We have checked out patrons. Not 5 percent of any given night are people who would have gone to an indoor house. Our crowds are made up of couples who can't find anyone to stay with the babies, so they bring them in the car. We get invalids who return as many as four times a week, people who otherwise would never see a picture. Among our regulars are two fat ladies who do not go to indoor theatres because they don't fit into regular seats. No sir, not 5 percent of our crowd is a potential indoor theatre crowd."[7]

Baby-sitters were out there; they just weren't being used. In 1947 six female teenage baby-sitters picketed the Aurora Drive-In near Seattle, Washington. Their placards read: "Down with drive-ins, more work for baby-sitters" and "While you drive in movie theaters, baby-sitters starve." After a brief period of picketing, Aurora management bought off the protesters with an offer of free hot dogs and a free movie.[8]

Ochs regarded the drive-in as an entertainment event, not just a film screening, and he operated that way. When he opened a new ozoner he advertised only the theater, leaving out completely the name of the film believing that the customers simply wanted to enjoy the outdoors along with some form of entertainment. Even when a drive-in had been operating for a while, the Ochs group would sometimes omit the name of the film running from ads as a test. On those occasions Ochs said he got no more phone calls than he got on the days the name of the film was listed in the ads. Ochs's record gross came from "a low-bracket film from one of the smaller distributors." Having asked patrons on his lot why they came to the drive-in that night, Ochs found "in almost every instance, they said they did not know what picture was being shown when they drove into the parking space. They just came to the drive-in for whatever type of entertainment was presented." At an Ochs drive-in the policy was: "we sell the drive-in theatre to the public, not the picture. The program is secondary," he asserted.[9]

The Dayton Ohio Valley drive-in, owned by Ochs, opened in 1941. In 1946 it charged fifty cents for adults, thirty-five cents for high school students, and twenty cents for children. There were two shows a night, starting at dusk. On Saturdays a midnight show was added. On average there were 2.5 adult admissions per car in the Valley. Walk-in business was fairly brisk at this ozoner with enough lawn chairs set up near the front of the screen to accommodate three hundred people.[10] Each of his drive-ins was staffed with from eighteen to twenty-five ushers. "All of our ushers wear uniforms and present a natty appearance. They greet each car, see that the headlights are turned off and, so as not to annoy other patrons, personally guide the driver to a proper location on the lot."[11]

Drive-ins always had that dead space between the screen and the front row of cars. Some used it as Ochs did, by providing seating for walk-ins. From that range and angle the visual aspects of the film must have been of exceptionally poor quality. A better use would be found for this area as more and more ozoners would locate their kiddies' playground there. While the Valley in Dayton still charged for children, this was becoming less common in the drive-in industry. Soon children under twelve would be admitted free at virtually every ozoner. The owners would more than make up for this at the snack bar.

So foreign was the concept of a drive-in theater in the late 1940s that some of them held an open house so patrons could come in to get used to them. Long Beach, California's, Lakewood Drive-In became that city's first outdoor theater in 1948. A week before the opening, the theater held an open house so people could familiarize themselves with the layout, the parking procedure, and the sound equipment. One year before that, the Vermont Drive-In opened in Gardena, California. Frank Diaz was a nineteen-year-old usher at the time. He recalled: "At the time, nobody knew what to expect. . . . So we let people come in and see what it was all about. About 400 cars came through during the open house—we expected about 100—and we showed them how to drive in, pull

The "Rain-A-Way" was designed to keep rain off the windshield (about 1950).

up to a speaker, put it in the car and adjust the sound. Everyone was very excited. We knew we had a winner."[12]

Amenities to be found in a drive-in expanded by leaps and bounds. Many took to wiping motorists' windshields with a glycerine solution if it was raining, or threatening to do so. Supposedly this made it possible to watch a film on a rainy night with the windwhield wipers off. One ozoner's staff wiped the windshield, for reasons known only to itself, with a wet Bull Durham (the tobacco) sack.

Alternatively, patrons could buy a visor made of flexible pastic that could, claimed the manufacturer, be fastened to the car "in a matter of seconds" above the windshield. Dubbed the "Rain-A-Way" visor, it had a gutter along the side that carried the rain away while preventing it from running down the windshield. Anchoring was by means of a fastener extending to the hood ornament. The slogan for the product was supplied by the maker. It went: "No rain—no battery or gas drain—no motor or eye strain."

A newly opened drive-in in Tulsa reported that a party of eight turned up at the gate on horseback. They were placed behind the last ramp, where they watched the show on their horses; all reportedly had an enjoyable time. Many ozoners introduced bottle-warming facilities for their customers. David Flexer, who owned a chain of theaters centered around Memphis, claimed to have been the first to introduce this to outdoor theaters. "The mother just reaches out of her motor car, presses a button and an attendant brings her the bottle warmer," said Flexer. Usually it was located in the concession building.

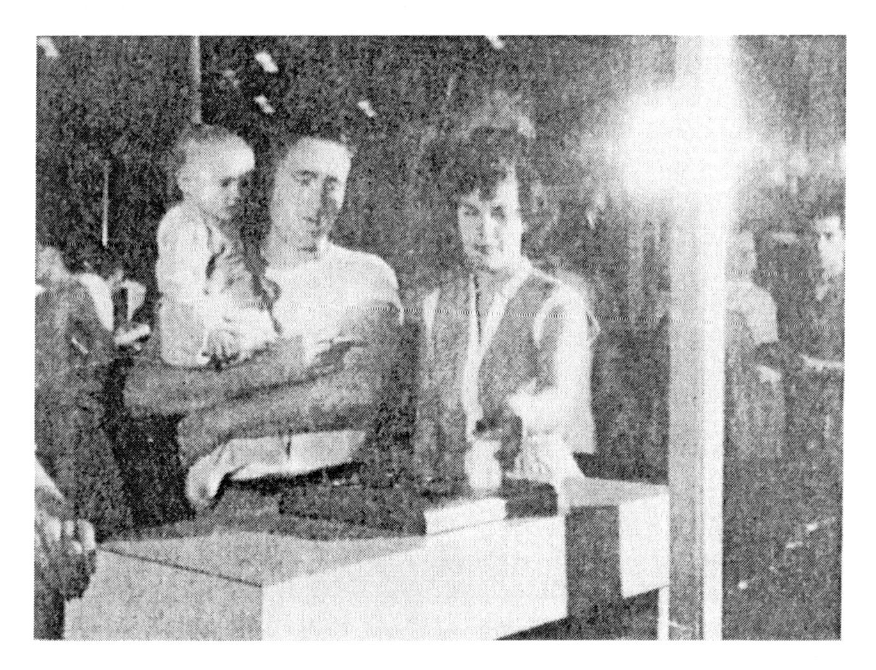

A bottle-warming table provided free by the theater, enabling mothers to attend with their infants (1951). This amenity was widely available.

When the Woodbridge, New Jersey, drive-in opened, it installed a single baby-bottle warmer. Soon it had three in operation, and, said the manager: "It's a slow night when we don't heat three dozen formulas."[13]

At his chain Flexer reported 2.96 paying customers per car. Seventy-two percent of his patrons were family groups, with 10 to 12 percent of patronage coming from convalescents. What little trouble Flexer had came from "spooners": "We have regular police patrons. If a man puts his arm around a girl that's all right. But if she puts her arms around him, too, and they go into a clinch—well, that's out."[14]

Always it was the family group that dominated, sometimes an entire neighborhood group. One night at the Mohawk Drive-In in Albany, New York, manager Leo Rosen watched a man pull in with eleven children in his car. This customer told Leo: "This is my night to take the youngsters from the neighborhood. Others will do the same." Rosen, who had managed indoor houses for twenty years before switching to ozoners, said he'd "never seen so many families coming to a theatre, folks who find it hard to attend indoor houses because they have no one to mind the small children, or have not the time to make a change from their working clothes." In Rosen's mind there was little difference between indoor and outdoor audiences. He said: "If I had complete choice of product I would book a drive-in just like I would a regular

John Wayne stars at the Mohawk Drive-In near Albany, New York (1950). The playground is under the screen.

theatre. Forget this chatter about great differences. Drive-in patrons are like those for indoor houses, except there are more family groups."[15]

Picnic facilities popped up on the lots. Others installed a dance floor directly in front of the screen to entertain early arrivals. In San Antonio, Texas, one drive-in brought in a disk jockey from a local radio station who played records as part of the prefilm warm-up. Singers and other entertainers performed at some of the theaters. Some used vaudeville-type acts. A Kenosha, Wisconsin, facility featured a strong man as well as an aerial act. The strong man had the additional duty of hauling a car through town to publicize his boss's ozoners. Many of these novelties were introduced because of the increasing concentration of drive-ins in some areas. Not that any of them were suffering, but some turned to incidental entertainment just in case. Patrons at a Memphis, Tennessee, outdoor theater could get their laundry done. They turned in their dirty clothes on the way in and picked them up clean as they left. This was not a free service. Another venue, in South Carolina, featured a shopping service. Arriving patrons turned in a grocery list at the ticket booth. An employee of the drive-in did the shopping. Groceries were delivered to the car while the show was still going on.

Indoor seating sheltered from the elements was added by some drive-ins in the 1940s and 1950s, in the hope of promoting year-round use. Reportedly the first to incorporate this feature was one in Oklahoma in 1948.[16]

Fireworks displays were featured here and there. Kennel facilities were available for free at a few ozoners, in case patrons didn't want to keep Fido in the car all night. And—as noted—everywhere sprang up the children's playground. It was the perfect use for the dead space between screen and first row. These playgrounds featured swings, teeter-totters, slides, pony rides, sandboxes,

Pony rides at the Atlantic Drive-In, Atlantic City, New Jersey, 1950.

merry-go-rounds, miniature railroads, miniature golf, and even boat rides. Parents could safely leave their children at these playgrounds, which were always staffed by employees; a few even provided a nurse.

Pacific Drive-In Theatres president C. A. Caballero claimed that Pacific was the first to install a children's playground. In 1947 the Drive-In Theatre in Indianapolis, Indiana, was proclaiming itself as "the only theater in the world with a playground." It then had certain toys and equipment to which were added ponies, a pony track, and trained attendants. Pony rides were given only before the show started. Another contender for first with a playground was Claude Ezell, who operated a chain of ozoners and was credited with installing one in a Texas drive-in in 1944. However, the earliest seems to have been in 1943 at Detroit's West Side Drive-In, where a pull-away merry-go-round was installed that year. So successful was that experiment that the following year the West Side laid out a 100-foot-square area where they placed swings, seesaws, slides, mountain climbers, and other devices. Similar equipment was installed at nine other drive-ins around the country, operated by the same owners.[17]

After a workout on the playground a trip to the concession stand was usually in order. This was facilitated by the development and installation in ozoner lots of bluish or amber lights on tall poles, giving a "moonlit" effect to the lot. This type of light didn't affect the brightness of the film on the screen but did illuminate the lot enough to facilitate the coming and going of patrons to and from the concession building. It also allowed cars to arrive late or leave early without using their headlights. Prior to these moonlights,

Dancing for adults and playgrounds for kids at the Walter Reade chain of drive-ins in the Northeast, 1950. Note the elaborately uniformed attendants.

Shuffleboard, horseshoes, and a baby parade were just some of the amenities and entertainment available at drive-ins before the show started. These took place at the Walter Reade chain of drive-ins in the Northeast, 1950.

Crowds jam the concession area at the 9-W Drive-In at Kingston, New York, during the fifteen-minute intermission, 1949.

the lot was very dark, which tended to make walking around difficult, except during the actual intermission. Cars not coming or going at the film's end had either to use their lights or be guided out by an usher with a strong flashlight. Both methods tended to annoy other patrons.

The concession stand could be operated in one or two ways. Either the owner could lease it to a concessionaire or he could operate it himself. An owner could expect from 25 to 35 percent of the gross concession receipts as his share if he leased out the operation.[18] The major concession problem, not fully ironed out in the 1940s, was how to serve so many people in such a short period of time. Intermissions were normally about fifteen minutes long, and that's when most people wanted to buy their food. A partial solution lay in children's playgrounds, which created an appetite before the show began and perhaps triggered two trips to the concession building. It also brought the whole family out to the ozoner earlier, which increased the chance they would eat their evening meal there. That was also one of the reasons behind installing a dance floor or having prefilm entertainment, such as singers: Get people out early and try to get them hungry.

Some drive-ins adopted a mobile refreshment service, with sellers roaming the lot looking for business. In larger ozoners these employees sometimes used tricycles to cover distance more rapidly. This mobile service didn't always work, for, as one observer noted, "In some theatres attendants wander between the rows of parked cars, offering their wares in a loud voice. This is said to insure a higher sales volume, but at the same time it drives away the better-type patron."[19] Most ozoners stayed with selling just from their buildings. Despite the limited amount of time available to sell refreshments, however, a drive-in could reasonably expect 35 to 40 percent of its total gross receipts to come from concession sales.

Mobile vending carts ready to bring refreshments to the cars at the El Rancho Drive-In near Sacramento, California, 1950.

A mobile refreshment cart, 1950.

Prior to 1945 none of the trade magazines contained ads for equipment or for services directed at the drive-in owner. There were only one hundred or less in the country, too small and insignificant a group to target. All that changed after the war, even before the boom really got going. Manufacturers knew a boom in ozoners was coming, and they wanted in on it. Some fifty or so outdoor theaters had been announced for construction in 1942, but all were aborted after America entered the war. National Theatre Supply Company offered a free booklet, *Planning the Drive-In Theatre*, to prospective owners in a trade ad on September 15, 1945. RCA followed less than five months later with a two-page ad offering prospects a free thirty-page pamphlet, *The Drive-In Theatre*.[20] Soon the trades were full of ads offering various supplies to the expanding industry. In-car speakers sold for around twenty-two dollars a pair at the beginning of 1947. Within a few years they would drop to as little as five or six dollars a pair. Next came the package deal, whereby companies like RCA, and many others, did everything involved from site selection to construction to opening night. All the new owner had to do in these turnkey packages was hand over the money, then show up on opening night to take over the running of the place. Some packages even arranged for film contracts. In 1949 drive-in owners formed an association of their own to look after their interests.[21]

Reported costs for building a drive-in in the late 1940s varied widely. *Business Week* put it as $250 to $450 per car space, compared to $250 to $300 per seat for a five hundred–seat indoor house. Allowing for 2.5 to 3 paying customers per car, *Business Week* noted the investment per admission thus dropped to $100 to $150 per head at the outdoor spots.[22] Using these figures, a five hundred–car ozoner would run from $125,000 to $215,000, with the low end of the indoor range also at $125,000.

Boxoffice claimed drive-ins cost $130,000 to $160,000 to build, compared to $500,000 for a comparable indoor house. In one issue *Motion Picture Herald* said ozoner cost ranged from $150,000 up for a five hundred–car capacity unit. Yet only eight months earlier they pegged the average drive-in cost at $75,000 to $100,000. To this might be added another $20,000 or so if the operator intended to include elaborate recreational facilities.[23] The last figures cited by *Motion Picture Herald* are reasonably accurate, except for the extras. The other figures, for whatever reason, are widely exaggerated.

Illustrating the range was the five hundred–car Magnolia Drive-In in Arlington, California, which opened in 1950. It cost $60,000. At the other end was the Denver Drive-In, which became Colorado's first when it opened in 1947. Holding 750 cars, it cost $125,000.[24] An estimate in another issue of *Boxoffice* was a more reasonable $100,000 average. For indoor theaters not in major metropolitan centers, a six hundred–seat house was estimated as costing $95,500, while a thousand-seat house was $186,000, land excluded in both cases.[25]

One of the more accurate cost estimates was presented by the *Motion Picture Herald*, which gave a detailed cost breakdown based on several ozoners built in 1948 (see pp. 222–232). They found that a seven hundred–car drive-in averaged $96,000, land excluded.[26] That would be $137 per car space or $46–$55 per admission based on 2.5 to 3 admissions per automobile. The average for the indoor examples cited above would be $160 to $186 per seat. This cost advantage per admission was a big reason for the ozoner boom.

During the middle of 1948, the then reported 759 drive-ins had a total car capacity of 314,378 (an average of 414). Most of these were seasonal operations with just 137 (18.4 percent) operating year-round. Sixty-five of these were open six days a week while 678 operated seven days a week. Programs were changed three times a week at 352 venues; four times a week at 309; five times at 42; twice a week at 35; with weekly program changes at 8 outlets. The single feature was much more prevalent than the double bill. Ownership of drive-ins was less dominated by chains than was that of indoor theaters. A chain, called a circuit in those days, was defined as a company owning four or more theaters, not limited to drive-ins. Chains owned 241 (31.9 percent) of the ozoners, with nonchains owning 518 (68.1 percent). Drive-ins owned by chains were bigger. While they owned only 31.9 percent of the drive-ins, the chains had 39.8 percent of the car capacity. The nonchains had 60.2 percent of the capacity against their 68.1 percent of the number of outlets. An average chain drive-in held 518 cars, while an average nonchain venue held 366.[27]

While it was much cheaper to open a drive-in compared to an indoor house, operating costs themselves were not markedly different. In 1948 indoor theaters numbered 17,689, with drive-ins at 820, according to the U. S. Census. Gross box office receipts (less taxes) were $1,312,013,000 for indoor houses, compared to $40,385,000 for outdoor theaters (see pp. 233–236). Payroll expenses for indoor and outdoor houses were, respectively, $293,872,000 and $8,569,000.[28] Drive-in theaters were 4.7 percent of indoor theaters in numbers; receipts were 3 percent of indoor receipts, while payroll expenses were slightly less than 3 percent of those at indoor houses. Each indoor house grossed $74,200 in 1948, versus $49,300 for its outdoor counterpart. Much of this difference is explained by the short season at the drive-ins, whose receipts were squeezed into about a thirty-week season. Each dollar of payroll expense generated receipts of $4.46 indoors. At the drive-in each dollar generated $4.71. This marginal difference would increase somewhat if film rental costs were taken into account, since they were lower for outdoor theaters (earlier runs rented for higher fees).

Seating capacity of indoor houses was 11.7 million. At drive-ins it was roughly 1 million, or 8 percent. Yet drive-ins did only 3 percent of the gross, with 8 percent of the capacity. With total admissions of 3.35 billion at indoor spots, this translated to 65 million admissions per week at indoor theaters. This figure, from the 1948 census, is significantly lower than that given elsewhere for 1948, namely 90 million per week for the years 1946–48 with a drop to 60 million by 1950. While acknowledged to be estimates, these latter figures are widely used in various statistical sources.[29]

According to census figures a huge drop in film attendance had already occurred in 1948—assuming higher figures for earlier years were in fact correct—a drop that couldn't be blamed on television as it barely existed then. Fewer than 200,000 sets were in use in 1948 in the United States. No figures for drive-in admissions are given in the census, but a reasonable assumption would be 3 percent of the indoor number, the same as their percentage of receipts, as average admission prices would have been similar. That would translate into 2 million admissions weekly to the drive-in. This is also too insignificant to explain the huge decline in indoor film attendance. Another indication that the 90 million figure is wrong, at least for 1948, can be found by browsing through issues of *Variety* in 1948 when a large number of articles were published along the lines of: box office down 15 percent in Cleveland, 25 percent in Dallas, and so on. If a large decline in attendance had in fact taken place by 1948 at indoor houses, which seems to be the case, it can't be blamed on television or drive-ins, both of which were then too minor to have any impact. Adding all the drive-in attendees into the indoor figures moves attendance only from 65 to 67 million per week.

This drop in indoor attendance was noted by University of Minnesota professor Rodney Luther, who said it began in the final quarter of 1947. It was, he felt, a postwar phenomenon that had occurred in many established industries. It reflected a relaxation on curbs on other forms of entertainment, which were diverting disposable income. According to Luther the motion picture industry was then taking 75.7 percent of every dollar spent for spectator amusement, down from 79 percent in 1929, 84 percent in 1933, 82.6 percent in 1937, 80.7 percent in 1940, and 83.3 percent in 1945.[30] As well, people were spending money on a variety of big-ticket items such as appliances, cars, and houses, catching up on the missing war years. There was only so much money to go around.

At the end of the 1940s, the attractions of a drive-in over an indoor house to a potential exhibitor were obvious. The drive-in was significantly cheaper to build on a per-admission basis. It was cheaper to operate as well. There was greater profit at the concession stand. Rental of product was likely less costly. While the country was saturated with indoor houses, drive-ins were still relatively scarce. Neil Hellman, a partner in the Fabian chain, which owned several ozoners, was one of the very few who worried about overbuilding. "Too many drive-ins are being built throughout the country and they are being piled up too near supposedly choice spots," he said. "The result is sure to be harmful to this business. Some operators are going to lose money if this overbuilding and saturation continue." Hellman subscribed to the theory that most of the drive-in patronage never went to indoor theaters. The reverse was also true, he felt: "Despite the advantages and attractions of drive-ins, there are a great many persons who will not attend any but the standard type of theatre. The chances of converting them into drive-in customers are slim."[31] Hellman's fears would become reality, but not for a long time. The drive-in boom would surge into the 1950s.

Chapter 5

Drive-ins Battle the Industry

It was the end of the 1940s before the battle by drive-ins for better access to major Hollywood studio product heated up. However, there were skirmishes before that time. When Eddie Joseph opened an ozoner in Austin, Texas, in 1940, the major studios refused to let him have product on any basis, not first run, second run, or any other run. It was their policy, they told him, to protect their old customers, which meant the indoor houses. Not satisfied with this treatment, Joseph filed an arbitration suit—settled out of court a few hours before the hearing was slated to start—against Fox, Warner Bros., and MGM. Joseph argued that the majors should be forced to establish clearances and rent product to him. The majors agreed to submit various matters to arbitration at that time in an ultimately unsuccessful attempt to forestall the breakup of their monopoly.

Seven years later Joseph was back in court. What he had won the first time was access to product on a six-months-after-downtown-release basis, later reduced to ninety days. Now Joseph wanted it down to thirty. Carrying his campaign to the public, he gave out printed matter on his battle to his drive-in patrons, took out newspaper ads, and even discussed it on the trailers shown at his drive-in. Joseph urged patrons to write to the head offices of the major film studios.[1]

The San-Val followed the arbitration route in California against Warner Bros., MGM, Paramount, and RKO when it tried, in 1942, to force them to lower clearances from sixty-three days down to seven following Burbank first run.[2]

An example of how independent indoor theater owners sometimes responded to drive-ins could be seen in Minneapolis, Minnesota, in 1947. Before that year the Twin City independents had successfully blocked permits that had been applied for by various groups who wanted to erect a drive-in in the area. David Flexer and Al Avery of Memphis managed to obtain a drive-in permit for the Minneapolis suburb of Bloomington. The permit was put through without any publicity, leaving the independent exhibitors no time to respond. Opening in August 1947, this drive-in did a roaring business its first week, with thousands of cars turned away.

In response the independent owners held a couple of "secret" meetings. Putting on more pressure, they complained that the state highway department had to spend more taxpayers' money by stationing extra police at the drive-in to handle the massive, miles-long traffic tie-ups that ensued, forcing police to ban lefthand turns and preventing many cars from entering the drive-in. One solution proposed by the independents was to have each of their number contribute money to a new company that would build its own drive-ins in the Minneapolis–St. Paul area. At least this would keep out outsiders.

David Flexer said the independents were trying to throttle competition. He claimed that when these owners failed to keep him from obtaining his permit and license to build the drive-in, they contacted film distributors, urging them not to furnish him with any product. Other complaints voiced by Flexer were that the independents tried to get state officials to kill the project as well as "siccing" health and other officials on him to increase his difficulties."[3]

Three years later the independents owned four drive-ins in the area—a fact that displeased film distributors. The distributors found that the money they made from an independently owned drive-in (although its season was only four months) was usually greater than from a late-clearance neighborhood indoor house. The later the run and or the longer the clearance, the less the amount of money a theater had to pay in rental fees. Distributors found that independent drive-ins, having no indoor houses to protect, utilized a picture as early as possible, which increased rental fees. Newer films drew more of an audience, which also increased rental fees, which were often on a percentage-of-the-gross as opposed to a flat-rate basis. Those four drive-ins owned by the indoor exhibitor group used the very last runs for films, which drew the smallest crowd, to protect their indoor houses. This resulted in a much lower return to the distributors for these drive-ins.[4]

Jack Farr owned the Skyway Drive-In, open year-round, in Bryan, Texas. In 1949 RKO granted Skyway the opportunity to enter first-run bids for its product for the Bryan and College, Texas, area. Farr thought his drive-in was the first in Texas to be granted the right to make first-run bids by a major studio. Even so the victory was a hollow one. No way could RKO or any of the other majors be forced to accept the best bid, if they preferred to freeze out drive-ins.[5]

Publicly, however, the majors insisted that they displayed "scrupulous fairness" to all their customers. Considering their court difficulties over their monopoly position, this public stance was not unexpected. In 1949 spokesmen for the majors were unanimous in declaring that "the drive-in theatres are being treated just like any other theatre, just like any other customer. If they ask for a certain run, and if they can prove they can pay for it, we consider the request."[6]

As the 1940s ended and the 1950s began, pressure from the drive-ins for better product increased. Spurring the drive-ins on in their fight was their sheer number. Owners worried that the novelty effect had worn off. Ozoners had to compete with ozoners. Patrons were no longer content with just anything thrown up on the screen, operators feared. Commenting on the situation in 1949, *Boxoffice* wrote: "Now the drive-ins find the novelty wearing off and they want to move up to third- and second-run status, and, in some cases, into the first-run classification."[7] (If they wanted to move "up" to third-run status one can imagine what they had been screening!) What little change did take place came about because of financial return to the distributors. So old were most of the films the ozoners played that rental was usually on a flat-rate basis. When an ozoner occasionally ran a third-run film or better, it paid a percentage of the gross. Distributors found that this amounted to a much greater return for them.

Open hostility still remained the normal reaction to the drive-in pressure. Andy W. Smith, Jr., 20th Century–Fox vice president, reiterated that his company would protect indoor houses from "unfair competition" by ozoners. Smith acknowledged that many drive-in owners sought first-run product from his company. However, Fox would not permit this, he said. His company considered drive-ins to be in the same classification as first-run subsequent, with product being sold to them on that basis.[8]

Pressure from the Interboro circuit, which owned indoor theaters, and an alliance of theater owners was strong enough in New York State that Assemblyman Samuel Roman introduced a bill, sponsored by those groups, to prohibit the building of drive-ins throughout the state. The bill failed to pass.[9]

In the summer of 1949, William F. Rodgers, an MGM distribution chief, announced the results of a survey his company had taken. Results disclosed that drive-ins were creating new customers rather than competing for the old ones. This set off a flurry of angry letters to the studio from drive-in owners who argued that if they were not competing they should get first runs. It caused no change in policy. *Variety* noted that "the rule against granting first-runs to drive-ins is fairly uniform among the majors."[10] Working against any acceptance of the outdoor theaters was the suddenly decreasing film attendance. Immediately after the war weekly film attendance hit 90 million for the years 1946 and 1947, matching the all-time high from 1930. But it was the end of the great years. Over the next six years, from 1948 to 1953, weekly attendance went into a tailspin, down to 45.9 million in 1953.[11] This was the very period of dynamic drive-in growth. The older and established film industry was in no mood to be benevolent to a newcomer it feared was stripping its business away. Even when it was shown that box-office grosses of indoor theaters in towns having no ozoner competition dropped by the same proportion as they did in towns with drive-ins it made little or no difference.

In Ohio the Greater Cincinnati Independent Exhibitor Organization took a firm stand, opposing the giving to drive-ins of films less than thirty-five days after the end of their first suburban run, which was actually second run. Clearances in other cities ranged from twenty-one to ninety days.[12]

The Skyhigh Theatre, located near Urbana, Ohio, tried to buy advertising space in the *Urbana Daily Citizen* in 1952. When its copy was refused it sued but lost. Judge David S. Porter of Common Pleas Court ruled that the publisher of the *Citizen* could turn down any ad he wanted to. The drive-in advertisement wasn't rejected because of its content, said the judge, but because it would injure the business of the Urbana area indoor theaters, which also advertised in the paper.[13]

So important were drive-ins becoming that 20th Century–Fox planned to create an executive head-office position to deal exclusively with the ozoners. Fox did alter its way of dealing with drive-ins by selling them more and more film on a percentage instead of on a flat-rate basis. This studio found that by changing over to this method they reaped two to five times the earnings they achieved from a flat-rate rental. As with indoor theaters, Fridays and Saturdays were the busiest nights for drive-ins. Sundays and Mondays were next best; Tuesday through Thursday came third.[14]

Some owners claimed that they did more business than their indoor competition. Phil Smith operated a chain of outdoor theaters in New England and fought with the majors for earlier availability of product for his ozoner at Natick, Massachusetts, which he said had outgrossed two indoor houses at Framingham, Massachusetts. What Smith wanted was the right from film distributors to bid against these Framingham houses on behalf of his Natick drive-in. None of the majors would let him bid against the indoor spots, except MGM, which did comply with his request. Even had Smith been allowed to bid and win, it would not have amounted to much. Warner Bros. once let him play the film *The Flame and the Arrow* at his Natick drive-in at the same time it played at a Natick indoor spot. They both played it one week after it ended at Framingham. Framingham played it twenty-one days after it finished its run in Boston.[15]

Failing to get much satisfaction for their demands, many drive-in owners began to mutter about suing. Responding to this threat in arrogant fashion, executives of the major studios said again that they had no intention of backing down. Several of the distribution arms of these studios claimed they had gone so far as themselves to notify the Department of Justice of their refusal to license drive-ins for first-run exhibition of their product, and their reasons for doing so. Failure of the antitrust division of the Justice Department to protest this action meant, said the distributors, agreement with this policy.

Reasons cited by the distributors for not altering their stance included the fact that ozoners were seasonal; while drive-ins might return higher revenues in some situations, the overall loss might be greater; suburban locations of drive-ins broke up geographical servicing of theaters; drive-ins could play successfully after regular theaters while the reverse might not be true; and, drive-ins were limited to automobile owners and exclude nonowners. Business at independent indoor houses would be "murdered" if they gave first runs to drive-ins. One unnamed distribution company executive said his company, "will not discriminate against people without cars. Films are a form of mass entertainment and should be available first-run to the public whether they have a car or not."[16]

A distributor could rent a film on a first-run exclusive or first-run nonexclusive basis. In the former case no one in the area of the exhibitor playing a film could show it at the same time. In the latter case other venues were allowed to play it simultaneously. Whenever they did try to get first-run rights to a film, the drive-in operators always sought nonexclusive rights. Thus a film having a first run at a drive-in could also be playing a downtown indoor house to service people without cars. On very rare occasions drive-ins did get a first-run film from a major studio. So unusual an event was this that it would be expected to merit a small item in one of the trades, such as *Variety*.

Threats to sue turned into action as many lawsuits were launched and under way by drive-in owners by the end of the 1940s. In the Chicago area Robert C. Nelson sued 20th Century–Fox, Universal, Warner's, RKO, and United Artists. Also in Illinois, John Reckos sued all the majors except Universal. During the course of a similar suit in South Bend, Indiana, owners of several indoor houses in the area sent six of their employees to the South Bend Auto Drive-In to copy down information from license plates of patrons entering the ozoner. The idea being to show that the patrons came from the town itself to substantiate the claim of competition. The drive-in argued unsuccessfully before the judge than an injunction be granted to prohibit such activity as it was "injurious to business" and an "invasion of private rights." Generally the ozoners were suing for injunctive relief to obtain access to first run films on a nonexclusive basis.[17]

By far the most important legal case over access to first-run films was that started by David E. Milgram, who owned, with four others, the Boulevard Drive-In Theatre near Allentown, Pennsylvania. When the Boulevard opened on October 19, 1949, Allentown had six first-run indoor theaters, all of which were independently owned. That is, none was owned by a major studio. Also in the city were five neighborhood indoor subsequent (second) run houses. Very soon after opening his theater Milgram wrote to the eight biggest studios, MGM, Paramount, RKO, 20th Century–Fox, Universal-International, Columbia, United Artists, and Warner Bros., and their distribution arms, requesting that he be allowed to compete for their first-run films on an equal basis with the indoor Allentown houses. Six of these companies refused to allow Milgram access to any run—no run. Only RKO and Fox were prepared to deal with Milgram at all. The best they offered was product on a twenty-eight-day, second-run basis. Milgram sued all eight companies alleging restraint of trade. No money damages were sought, only access to product.

After this suit was filed four more of the companies offered Milgram twenty-eight-day second-run status. Columbia offered only last-run licensing. United Artists continued to refuse to hold any negotiations with Milgram. During the trial in United States District Court the majors contended that they acted independently in dealing with Milgram with each having no knowledge of what the other seven were doing. Understandably Judge William Kirkpatrick found this contention to be "incredible." On November 28, 1950, he found all eight guilty of acting in concert in violation of the antitrust laws. The companies were ordered to give the Boulevard Drive-In the same treatment as was given to the indoor houses. Drive-ins had to be given the same opportunities, said the judge, as were indoor theaters.

In their appeal to the Third Circuit Court of Appeals the majors argued that the trial record was "bare of evidence to support the court's crucial finding of an industry-wide policy." As well, they said, the trial judge erred in holding, "that evidence of consciously parallel business practices is sufficient proof by itself of antitrust conspiracy." Milgram also won this round.

Continuing on, the majors appealed to the Supreme Court. Asking those judges for a rehearing, the majors claimed they were still living under a dark cloud based upon the "proclivity to unlawful conduct" that the Supreme Court found against the majors back in 1949 in the big antitrust case in which their monopoly was ended. They majors wondered how long they would have to live under such a cloud before they got "fair consideration" in new matters from the courts. Because of the Milgram ruling, the majors said they were at his "mercy." On April 21, 1952, the U.S. Supreme Court refused to hear the majors' appeal, letting the Milgram ruling stand. It meant that distributors legally had to treat drive-ins the same as indoor houses. Favoritism couldn't be shown to the latter group. At least, that's what it said in theory.[18]

From the time the lower court ruling was handed down in this Allentown case, a flood of first-run bids from drive-ins poured into distribution offices. Sales executives confidently predicted that these bids would quickly trickle away to nothing, for they believed ozoners would be unable to gross high enough to outbid an indoor first-run house.[19] This was an indirect way of saying that drive-ins were unlikely to win any such bidding contests if the majors didn't want them to. The courts could force the majors to receive first-run bids from drive-ins but could not force them to accept those bids. So many factors were involved—location, length of run, advertising, capacity, and so on—that it was nearly impossible to state objectively that one bid was financially better for a distributor than was another. The drive-ins had scored a hollow victory in court. Other suits launched by ozoners during this period did go after monetary damage awards from the majors.[20]

Overwhelmingly the drive-in owners wanted better runs for their operation.

In a survey conducted by *Motion Picture Herald*, 88 percent of the owners polled were in favor of aggressive competition for better and earlier runs. Only 12 percent were satisfied with the current booking conditions ozoners were subjected to.[21]

With theater attendance then in the early stages of what would be a long and sharp decline, distributors put the squeeze on ozoners. More and more of the product, regardless of run, was available only on a percentage basis—which was more favorable to distributors—as the percentage itself moved up higher and higher from 25 percent of the gross to 35 percent, for example.

The Independent Theatre Owners of Arkansas (ITO) asked the Theatre Owners of America (TOA) to take drastic action to halt free child admission as well as the admission of car- and truckloads of people at fifty cents to a dollar a load at drive-ins. These practices were "abnormal and unbusinesslike" methods of attracting attention, said the Arkansas group. Further, these techniques had a damaging and detrimental effect on indoor houses. The ITO wanted the TOA to survey these "extraordinary and destructive methods" and draft a plan to put a stop to them.

Unless this was done, the Arkansas group predicted, these methods would "bring about a dangerous cheapening of the operating standards of the industry among the American public," destroying normal and fair competition. According to this group, some ozoner operations in the Memphis area went so far as to admit bus- and truckloads of as many as forty people at a single per-car price. Free admission for kids under twelve should be stopped, complained the ITO, as this practice, "serves only one purpose, namely, to create the impression that motion pictures are free and convenient rather than important entertainment that should be appreciated and bought."[22]

The vice president of MGM, William Rodgers, took an equally hard line when he addressed a TOA convention. Carefully saying that he felt MGM had no alternative but to treat drive-ins as it did the indoor houses, he added that this held only if the ozoners operated the same as conventional theaters. Rodgers believed that practices at some drive-ins could clearly be classed under the heading of unfair competition:

> I refer here to those types of operations who have free admissions; those who advertise and invite busloads of patrons to attend the drive-in theatres at a specified price for the entire busload, and others who subordinate the attractions and level their sights on the development of their business on concessions. All of these we consider to be a deterrent to the development of our business. We do not believe that these offenders are entitled to the same availability on our product as those drive-in theatres that operate on a legitimate basis.[23]

If drive-ins were engaging in those practices, and they were, it was partly because of the difficulty in obtaining acceptable product. With ozoners springing up everywhere competition was fierce; drive-in against indoor and drive-in against drive-in. They turned to putting emphasis on concessions to ensure their survival.

As the attendance at indoor houses dropped, that at the ozoners increased, as did the number of such theaters. Rather than being viewed in the early 1950s as holding the film industry together in the face of the television onslaught, the drive-ins were seen as even a greater threat than in the old days. The reasoning was that in the early years drive-ins drew a different audience than did conventional theaters. However, as they succeeded they demanded better and better access to films. If granted this access they would then compete for the very same audience that attended the indoor houses. Said one distributor: "This movement can do us serious damage and is in many cases unnecessary. The primary attraction of a drive-in is not the early availability of the pictures it plays, but its convenience and novelty. It's unfair for the drive-ins to take early runs that don't materially help their business, but can seriously hurt competing four-wall houses."[24] More than a little snobbishness was involved in at least one piece of conventional wisdom, which had it that second-run indoor houses in large cities would refuse to play a film that had its first run at an ozoner.[25]

Despite the Milgram court decision, drive-ins had little luck obtaining first-run product. Several more lawsuits were initiated in the mid–1950s by drive-ins against the majors for the same reasons that had motivated the earlier spate—lack of access to product.[26] Generally such suits slowed down, finally stopping. Drive-ins by then had been around in a big way for close to a decade. They had learned to adapt to their film-access problem in a variety of ways. What had initially perhaps been viewed as temporary measures until equal access was a fact soon became a way of life for drive-ins. After so many years of fighting—winning in theory but not in reality—they carried on as they had been doing. The times that a drive-in would play a first-run film from a major Hollywood studio would always remain rare. Ozoners would always feature distinctively different programming from that shown at indoor houses.

In 1978 *Variety* commented on the fact that several major films opening in Chicago that summer played drive-ins and indoor theaters at the same time. The article went on to discuss theories that audiences for the two types of theaters were different. However, the article noted: "There have not been enough first-run pictures at outdoor screens to make a definitive statement."[27] This underscores how infrequently drive-ins aired such films, even twenty-five years after they had "won" equal access in the highest court in the land. Those court battles did little tangibly to improve access to first-run Hollywood product, but they may have aided drive-ins in moving up to second- and third-run status—as did their success in attracting customers and expanding in number. Initially in dealing with the majors the drive-ins had little more to choose from than third run, last run, or no run.

Chapter 6

Communities Battle Drive-ins

The upsurge in the number of drive-ins after the war was upsetting to highway officials around the country who feared a nightmarish scenario of blood and death on the roads. In Ontario the provincial Department of Highways worried about the potential of accidents resulting from heavy traffic conditions, particularly when the last show let out from the drive-ins. This caused the local Motion Picture Board, in 1947, to notify film distributors that they must not supply outdoor theaters with film.[1] Apparently this ban was very short lived.

At a meeting of the Institute of Traffic Engineers in Washington, delegate J. E. Johnston of Nebraska's Department of Roads and Irrigation stated that the outdoor theaters added to countryside traffic problems. It was a sentiment echoed by C. M. Wilhelm, head of Pennsylvania's Highway Department, who ordered a statewide survey of these "highway hazards."[2]

A comprehensive report on drive-ins was prepared by the American Association of State Highway Officials and issued as a booklet in 1950. It was prepared by the association's Committee on Roadside Control after surveying 282 ozoners during 1948 and 1949. Soon after its release, officials of forty-four of the forty-eight states approved its contents. Acknowledging that the outdoor theater was accepted by the public and here to stay, the report outlined ways of controlling them to minimize their effect on increasing traffic congestion and accidents.

The first and easiest way to tackle them was through zoning regulations, by prohibiting them entirely. Said the report:

> Lack of location control has resulted in 90% of the drive-in theatres being located on major highways. Theatres are being located in the main on highways already overloaded and are dumping short-time peak loads onto high speed highway facilities not well suited for absorbing such loads. About 32% of the theatres reported are located on curves and 28% on hill crests

> where limited sight exists. The location of 58% of drive-ins cause loss of speed by cars in the adjacent vicinity and create potential traffic accident areas.

This group wanted no drive-ins located on major highways, only on secondary roads.

If control couldn't be accomplished through zoning, the association recommended control over access, design, traffic control, and other aspects, be achieved by requiring exhibitors to obtain state permits to build. These permits would then prescribe the various specifics. When that failed and no legal authority existed, the association recommended that state officials approach the exhibitor to talk him into cooperating with their demands.

Other problems mentioned included inadequate holding areas between the parking ramps, ticket booths, and highway, which often caused waiting patrons to back up onto the highway. The screen should not face the highway, thought the association, but if it did a fence or tree should be used to obscure the view. It was considered too distracting for passing motorists to be able to see the film on the screen as they drove past the theater.[3]

That same organization was still worried several years later. Charles Curtis, U.S. commissioner of public roads, made a tour of outdoor theaters as "just another motorist." Reporting to the executive committee of the American Association of Highway Officials, Curtis said he noticed with marked concern that an increasing number of ozoners had the screen sited in such a way as to "tempt night drivers to take their eyes off the road." Curtis suggested the exhibitors be given a final chance to police themselves "in advance of drastic action to curb the safety hazard."[4]

Any anticipated carnage on the roads didn't materialize, which is one of the reasons these worries soon were forgotten. There were plenty of traffic jams, of course, but they were of brief duration and orderly. They took place in areas where the normal pre–drive-in traffic had been light to almost nonexistent, lessening any impact. Some drive-in owners went out of their way too ease the situation by building, for example, their own cloverleafs so patrons entering or leaving their theater never had to make a left turn across traffic. When kiddylands became popular, drive-ins opened their gates much earlier than if they had no such facility. This ameliorated the traffic problem of any inadequate holding area they may have had by spreading out the arrival period. Of all the worries expressed by the American Association of State Highway Officials, the only one that would return to haunt the drive-ins was that of screens being visible from the highway.

Many cities and towns continued to try to prevent the erection of drive-ins in their areas through proscriptive legislation. In Milwaukee, Wisconsin, the county park commission recommended that both the town and county boards ban ozoners in all parts of Milwaukee County. Parks Commissioner Robert Moses of New York City took a firm stand opposed to outdoor theaters in his bailiwick to avert serious traffic congestion and to "protect the health" of the people. Moses added: "We do not attack this application from moral grounds."[5]

Middletown Township, New Jersey, voted to adopt a zoning ordinance against ozoners while at South Huntington, Long Island, the town board rejected an application to build an outdoor theater citing the proximity of a high school and an already heavily traveled road. Just a week before leaving office, having been defeated in his bid for reelection late in 1949, Boston's mayor James Curley granted permits to build two drive-ins in that city in January 1950. These permits were granted without a public hearing, which, while not a legal necessity, was a custom. Opposition to the proposed ozoners came from religious, school, civic, and hospital groups. New mayor John B. Hynes tried to quash the permits but after study of the situation had to admit that they could not legally be revoked.[6]

The city ordinance Chicago passed in 1949 banning drive-ins from its jurisdiction was thrown out of court the following January when Judge Harry M. Fisher ruled the city had no legal right to ban a legitimate business from all parts of the city. Fisher did leave Chicago a loophole when he pointed out that the city had a right to ban certain businesses from certain areas of the city. The city council took quick advantage of this by passing an ordinance prohibiting an outdoor theater from being closer than two thousand feet to a residential area. They also banned any whose screen would be visible to passing motorists on nearby streets. Together these restrictions effectively banned ozoners from Chicago.[7]

In Skokie, Illinois, the city had denied a drive-in permit to an applicant in the summer of 1949. The applicant filed suit claiming Skokie had no zoning provisions against ozoners on its books when he had been denied his permit. After filing of the suit the Skokie leaders hastily passed an ordinance banning outdoor theaters from the area where the applicant proposed to build. Skokie lost the suit but appealed to a higher court, basing its claim on safety factors. According to Skokie the planned outdoor theater "would create a health menace to the community, since Skokie is a heavy industrial, heavily trafficked area." City officials also claimed it would be a traffic menace as well as acting "as an harassment to the safety of the villagers and theatre patrons."[8]

Woodbridge, New Jersey, was unable to stop contruction of ozoners, so it tried another method by imposing a 12:30 A.M. curfew on all drive-ins within its judisdiction. During court action to overturn this ordinance, Woodbridge police officers testified that the ordinance had been motivated by a desire to keep down teenage petting and to eliminate ozoners as a potential place for teens to hang out during the early morning hours. This curfew law was thrown out by the judge, who called it arbitrary and discriminatory because indoor theaters as well as other places of amusement didn't come under the curfew restrictions.

Mayor Richard Daley of Chicago had a unique way of dealing with the problem. When it seemed likely that one would be built near the city's O'Hare Airport, Daley ordered city officials to proceed with a plan to purchase 850 acres near the airport, including the proposed drive-in site. Mayor Daley opposed the drive-in because he thought its screen and signs would endanger planes landing and taking off at O'Hare.[9]

Getting approval from local authorities to construct a drive-in could be very difficult. In 1950 longtime outdoor theater manager Wilfred P. Smith offered some ideas on easing the way in his weekly trade-paper column. A prospective owner, he wrote, should be a resident of the area in which he planned to operate. If that wasn't possible, then he should at least establish contact with the area, perhaps selecting a manager or "partner" from the area, "especially if the person were given the appearance of at least partial proprietorship." (Local people had smoother going for their projects than did outsiders.) When the prospective owner was an outsider who didn't want a partner, Smith advised starting preliminaries with a local manager hired from the area's regular theater field. This manager should be well liked in his community, and, said Smith, "He probably will be a member of a fraternal organization, perhaps also of the Kiwanis Club or similar society. If he is a regular attendant at some church, so much the better. These associations can move a lot of stones."[10] Police and city officials would wage more frequent and intense campaigns against drive-ins when these theaters were targeted for allowing sex both in the drive-in and on the drive-in.

Chapter 7

The Golden Years, 1950s

By the very early 1950s the drive-in had fully arrived. *America's Baby Book*, one of a number of manuals of the period devoted to child rearing, contained the following sentence: "If you have a car, baby can sleep in the back seat while both parents enjoy the movie at a drive-in theater." Comedian Bob Hope joked: "There will soon be so many drive-ins in California that you'll be able to get married, have a honeymoon, and get a divorce without getting out of your car."[1]

Journalist John Durant related the story of how an ozoner prevented a family from breaking up. It seems there was a working-class couple with a young son. She liked going to the movies on Saturday nights. He wanted to stay home drinking beer. There was a battle every weekend over this issue, with the wife going off to the show alone while the husband stayed home with the child. Tension remained high. One Saturday he reluctantly agreed to accompany his wife to the drive-in, provided he could take his beer. After that all was happy in this family, with no more talk of a split-up. Durant wrote: "They now go every Saturday night. She sits in the front seat with Junior and watches the flickers. He sits in the back alone, with his beer in a bucket of ice, and pays little attention to the movie as he sips the brew and smokes cigars comfortably with his legs crossed."[2]

The cost of erecting outdoor theaters continued to climb, but it remained much cheaper than building an indoor house. Typical of the period was the Del-Sago near Oneonta, New York. Built for $75,000 by twenty-nine-year-old veteran William Warnken and his partner, Bert Mitchell, this facility included a miniature golf course. Neither man had any previous experience in show business. By their second year of operations, however, the pair grossed between $3,000 and $4,000 per week. Patrons regularly traveled up to thirty miles to attend the Del-Sago, or any ozoner, compared with a limit of around ten miles for indoor houses. Operations like the Del-Sago often got their entire investment back in three years. In some cases financial institutions took to loaning money for new ozoners just on the strength of the theater's own value, with no collateral.[3]

During 1952 sixty-five indoor theaters were built, containing 35,000 seats for a total cost of $8.5 million. Some 690 drive-ins were built, holding 263,879 cars, at a cost of $52,125,800. Each indoor seat cost $243, while each outdoor seat (on the basis of 2.7 admissions per car) cost just $73.[4]

Estimated income and expenses for a seven hundred–car operation in 1953 were presented by George Petersen in his drive-in manual (see pp. 231–232). Over the course of a twenty-six-week season, he estimated an operating cost of $42,333. Gross receipts from the box office were estimated at $87,294 (after taxes). To this net of $44,961 from admissions, Petersen added $15,000 net from the concession business. Thus Petersen's drive-in, an average of twelve ozoners then in operation, netted a total of $59,961 in twenty-six weeks. He estimated that a five hundred–car theater cost $81,050 to build.[5]

What helped ventures like Warnken's was the public's willingness and eagerness to attend drive-ins as an entertainment event. Quality and or age of the film being shown just weren't important considerations. Indoor theaters were closing at a much faster rate than they were being built, better than five to one. From 1946 to 1953, 851 new indoor theaters were built, while 4,696 were closed permanently. During that same period, 2,976 ozoners were built, with just 342 shut down.[6] The newly built indoor houses were much smaller than the ones built during the prewar period. The opposite was true for the new drive-ins, which kept getting bigger and bigger. Somewhere in the neighborhood of 1,300 cars was the maximum size for outdoor theaters in the 1950s. Larger than that and the screen became postage-stamp size for those in the back rows. Moreover, beyond that limit, the picture—if you could see it—tended to be fuzzy and distorted. Technology dictated the maximum size. Nevertheless many operators exceeded these limits in an effort to make more money, perhaps reasoning that if customers flocked in when a third- or fourth-run, two-year-old Hollywood film was screened, they might not mind if they couldn't see it very well. They were right.

Stanford Kohlberg owned the Starlite Drive-In near the Chicago suburb of Oak Lawn. It was big originally, holding 1,200 automobiles, but it got even bigger in the mid–1950s, when Kohlberg expanded it to accommodate 1,875 cars plus an enclosed auditorium to seat 1,000 walk-in patrons. For the 1956 season, admission to the Starlite was $1.25 per adult, with children under twelve getting in free. Admission included a free door prize for each child, dancing under the stars to a name band, free milk and diapers for babies if needed, the standard kids' playground, and a miniature golf course and driving range. Three separate concession buildings dispensed the regular fare; chicken dinners went for a dollar.

The Starlite kicked off the summer season in May with a weekend of live entertainment—such as singers, dancers, acrobats—that cost Kohlberg $2,000. Also on sale at this ozoner was the "Starlite Happiness Book," which was good for from five to fifteen dollars worth of admissions and or refreshments. Purchasers could charge it. "Parents know their youngsters won't wind up in a beer hall," explained Kohlberg. "With a Happiness Book a youth brings his girl to the Starlite, where we don't sell any alcoholic drinks. We even have attendants in the rest rooms to see that nobody spikes the soft drinks. The drive-in is the answer to the problem of wholesome amusement for teenagers."[7]

In fact, so important was the family trade and image to the drive-in that one consultant recommended that prospective operators shouldn't consider nightclubs and drinking spots an asset when selecting a site, no matter how close they were, because "patrons of those types of entertainment are not the family type of people who are the backbone of the drive-in theatre patronage, so no consideration should be given to their possible business."[8]

One of the biggest ozoners was the All-Weather Drive-In near Copiague, New York. Sprawled over twenty-eight acres, it held 2,500 cars; a 1,200-seat air-conditioned indoor house; a playground, a cafeteria, a restaurant offering full dinners, and a trackless train that ferried customers at no cost from one part of the complex to another.[9] Film quality was bad from the back ramps of such huge venues; however, it was even worse from the front rows, where patrons were overwhelmed by immense images.

The trend to huge outdoor theaters reached its peak in the mid–1950s, when the country was dotted with some true giants. Besides the All-Weather, there was the 110 Drive-In in Melville, New York (2,500 cars); the Newark Drive-In, in Newark, New Jersey (2,400); the Belair Drive-In, in Cicero, Illinois (2,300); the Timonium Drive-In, in Timonium, Maryland (2,479); and the Los Altos Drive-In in Long Beach, California (2,150). The biggest-ozoner award was a tie between the Panther Drive-In in Lufkin, Texas, and the Troy Drive-In in Detroit, Michigan. Each reportedly held 3,000 cars. On the other hand, a few tiny outdoor theaters could also be found. At Norwood, Colorado, the Norwood held a maximum of 64 cars; the Ponce DeLeon Drive-In in Ponce DeLeon, Florida held 60; and the Twilite Drive-In at Nakina, North Carolina, held 60. The competition for the smallest was also a draw. The Harmony Drive-In, Mt. Harmony, Pennsylvania; the Highway Drive-In at Bamberg, South Carolina; one at Sulphur Springs, Arkansas; and one at Yemasee, South Carolina, held 50 autos each.[10]

While Manhattan never had a drive-in, New York City did have perhaps the most urban drive-in in the country. Located in the Bronx, at the intersection of Bruckner Boulevard and the Hutchinson River Parkway, the Whitestone held 900 cars. So urban was it that the platform of a nearby elevated subway stop afforded a view of the ozoner's interior. Broadway was just thirty-five minutes away, and within literal walking distance were a cluster of high-rise apartment buildings housing tens of thousands of families. Despite this

The closest Manhattan ever got to a drive-in was the Whitestone in the Bronx. Here it is, seen from the Hutchinson River Parkway in 1949. Note the concentration of apartment buildings at the right. Despite this, no provision was made here for walk-in patrons.

enormous potential walk-in trade, the Whitestone, which opened in the summer of 1949, decided to install no seats for walk-in trade. It was management patrolled, with a seven-foot-high, or taller, fence to keep out gate-crashing youngsters. The Whitestone closed in 1983.[11]

Kohlberg kept his Starlite open all year, as many owners did, or tried to, even in cold areas of the country. Enough turned out to make it worth his while, he claimed. Patrons didn't complain about idling their car engines all night to keep their heaters going, or about the sleet that reduced visibility, or about the "borealis" around the screen images projected through icy rain and snowflakes. Only fog caused him to close. Said Kohlberg: "When the airports close down, we're closed down too." In Ledgewood, New Jersey, Wilfred Smith touted his winter openings by appealing to his customers' macho instincts. He believed that people loved to brag to their friends that they attended an outdoor theater when there was frost on the screen and ice on the roadside. Before the start of each show in the cold weather, Smith flashed a pep talk on the screen, which went, in part: "You hardy folks may be interested to know that the temperature is now twenty-five degrees. We have always been of the opinion that real drive-in patrons would attend during the winter, just as they bundle up to go to a football game or ice-skating. . . . Pass along the good news that we will be here all winter, bringing you top entertainment."[12]

Operators put more effort into the architectural design and gardening of their properties than in the early years. One in Miami called itself a "theater in a garden." It contained exotic palm trees, flowering shrubs, and a hanging garden with vines and tropical flowers. Several, like the one in Rome, Georgia, disguised themselves as Southern mansions or full-scale plantations. The one

A colonial residence design at the Riverview, near Carrollton, Kentucky.

in Rome had twin landscaped lakes near the entrance. The screen tower was concealed behind a colonial facade, which included Greek columns, pavilions, and loggias.

Near Cincinnati, Ohio, stood the 760-car Dixie Summer Gardens ozoner. Situated beside Kentucky's Route 42, known as the Gateway to the South, the Dixie styled itself as a country amusement park. Against the back of the screen tower stood an administration building in Southern Colonial–style, designed to resemble a Southern mansion. Patrons entered along a winding drive, passing an artificial pond that was used for ice-skating in the winter. Constructed to match the "house" architecturally, the ticket booth even had a dovecote on its roof. The attractions signboard stood over a goldfish pond. Gates and fences matched those found on Kentucky horse farms. The lobby of the projection/concession building had walls of glazed tile and a floor of colorfully rich terrazzo.[13]

Though it was unusual for a drive-in to get this carried away in its architecture, most spent some time and effort in landscaping in an effort to soften the drive-in's rather ugly, barren, daytime appearance. Not all this was altruistic. Owners believed it was the housewife who decided whether or not the family went to the movies that night, and to which one. A well-landscaped ozoner might catch her eye as she passed on her way to or from the store during the day.

So heady did success become, and so easy was it, that in 1957 some drive-in owners predicted that there would be ten thousand ozoners in the United

Ornate living quarters attached to the screen tower exterior at the Cedar Valley Drive-In, Rome, Georgia.

States within two years. Building restrictions on theaters were imposed during 1951–52 due to the Korean War. Not as severe as those of World War II, these restrictions barely slowed the construction of new drive-ins.

Cocky owners criticized Detroit, complaining that automobiles were not yet designed for maximum movie-viewing convenience. Sixteen million miles were logged every day, said the owners, by people going back and forth to the drive-ins. Operators wanted Detroit to kill the tinted windshields that were then just making an appearance as a new innovation. They were supposed to be a boon to drivers; however, it was more difficult to watch a film through them as they blurred and distorted the image.

So worried were drive-in owners that they undertook a campaign to eliminate the tinted windshield. Texan Claude Ezell, founder and organizer of the International Drive-In Theatre Owners Association, commissioned Paul Short, a National Screen Service executive, to conduct a survey about the issue in 1953. Not surprisingly Short concluded that these new windshields were bad news. Drive-in patrons who already had tinted windshelds were questioned. All expressed a variety of negative reactions. Sixty-three percent complained of distortion of the picture. Around 85 percent claimed that color films appeared unnatural when viewed through tinted windshields. Many spoke of diffused and blurred images. Managers of ozoners stated that black-and-white films appeared badly out of focus while color movies were "altogether devastating" when watched through tinted glass. These windshields were also said to neutralize 3-D films. At the time 3-D movies were expected to revolutionize the film exhibition business, both indoors and out.

None of this was likely to have much impact on the auto industry, so the Short survey concentrated on the supposed safety defects of tinted windows. The report claimed that a substantial portion of car accidents in Texas happened at night as a result of these windows. Tests proved, said the report, that the eyes of a person driving 50 mph in daylight began to tire after only two hours behind tinted glass, while this fatigue set in even quicker at night, after just thirty-six minutes. Ezell's group calculated that during the peak summer ozoner season, patrons drove 17,631,720 miles each and every day going to and from drive-ins. Therefore the auto industry, and allied businesses such as tire manufacturers, owed the drive-ins a great deal. Short concluded: "These industries are compatible with the motion picture industry, since the public wears out a voluminous number of cars to use the facilities of drive-in theatres, and that the automobile industry will be cooperative to the intelligent and constructive program" devised by Ezell's organization. It was a simple plan: Discontinue tinted windshields.[14]

Detroit was also urged to invent a horn that was inoperable with the ignition off as well as windshield wipers that operated from the battery and didn't require the engine to be running.[15]

Sneaking into the drive-in was almost a rite of passage back in the 1950s and 1960s. Here is journalist John Durant again with another story. This time the place is Toledo, Ohio, where police got a frantic call from a Mrs. McManus saying she has just seen a kidnapping. Two men pushed a woman into the trunk of a car, then raced off at high speed. Mr. McManus gave chase while his wife phoned the police. Soon Mr. McManus was back home telling the police to forget the whole thing. The kidnappers pulled into a drive-in, bought two tickets, and drove inside. Then the woman got out of the trunk to join her companions and watch the movie for free. Not a very likely story, but it could have happened.[16]

Certainly people sneaked into the drive-in on a regular basis. When admission was on a per-car basis it didn't matter. During the 1950s, though, most ozoners charged on a per-adult basis. An ozoner circuit in Florida issued the following written instructions to its ticket sellers: "Cashiers must train themselves to be ever watchful for unusual behavior on the part of the occupants of any car. They must call the manager's attention to any car which seems to be extraordinarily heavy or weighted down upon its springs. This can indicate patrons hiding in luggage compartments, etc."[17]

Many people successfully sneaked into outdoor theaters, but they usually did so as a result of management's not bothering about the practice. Even when charging admission on a per-head basis, most ozoners chose to ignore sneaking in as opposed to the Florida chain's attempt to control it. Another, even cruder, method to get in for nothing involved crouching down beside the car on the side away from the ticket booth and walking in at the speed of the auto. Virtually everyone who sneaked in by hiding in the trunk had his or her presence detected by staff, who after a short period of time became skillful in knowing just how low a car's back end should ride under normal conditions. Since outdoor theaters were doing so well, the owners just looked the other way.

Early in the 1950s a poll of drive-in owners found that 88 percent charged admission on a per-person basis and favored that method. Only 12 percent favored a per-car charge. With regard to children, the survey found 81 percent in favor of free admission for kids, while 19 percent thought a charge should be made. Those opposed to per-car admission felt that the practice cheapened the industry, ultimately causing it to lose its appeal. Free child admission was necessary, it was argued, to bring out the entire family. Any loss at the gate was more than made up for at the concession stand.[18] At one ozoner a man drove up in a truck containing himself and twenty-two children. He paid his adult single admission and entered the lot. Over the course of the evening, the children consumed forty hot dogs, eight packages of popcorn, and more than fifty soft drinks. The owner figured he came out ahead of the deal.[19]

That same poll also queried exhibitors on the type of films best suited for outdoor theaters. The results (some voting for more than one category) were: Western, 36 percent; action, 35 percent; comedy, 30 percent; musical, 22 percent; family, 19 percent; others, 9 percent. They were best summed up by Ed Marian of the El Rancho at Bridgeville, Pennsylvania, who said, "Anything with a theme or message is murder at the B.O."[20]

When writer Marguerite Cullman looked at the ozoner phenomenon, she found that most patrons admitted that the movies screened were older and less desirable than those to be found at more conveniently located indoor houses. As well, she found the admission price, for adults, to be as much or more than that charged for comparable films at indoor locations. Cullman concluded that people went for the by-then-standard reasons: cheaper and convenient for families and easier for people with any kind of disability. She also wrote that people went "who are extremely health-conscious. Despite the fact that sitting in a car provides no more fresh air than sitting at home next to an open window, a surprising number of people look upon drive-ins as healthful, out-of-doors recreation. Others, who fear to expose their children or themselves to local epidemics of flu, measles, or whooping cough feel safe in the privacy of their own cars."[21]

When asked, in 1951, if they thought drive-ins were less affected by television than were indoor theaters, owners of outdoor theaters responded yes by a vote of 86 to 14 percent. Many thought that the decline of television programs in the summer, along with people's desire to go out more in the warm weather, worked to the ozoners' advantage. Said Edwin Teltzell, who owned a drive-in in Utah, "We do not believe television hurts the theatre. We have television in our town and when we play good pictures we have a good turnout." F. G. Prat, Jr., who owned the Colonial in Thibodaux, Louisiana, commented, "Families with small children still want to get out of the house to be entertained. TV will not keep them home every night, especially in the summer." The rather bumptious, not-without-reason, attitude of the outdoor operators was best expressed by Jack Farr of Houston, Texas, who stated, "We are not scared of TV or other theatre competition." One exhibitor did complain about what he felt to be overdramatization of weather reports on TV. "Just let there be a small cloud in the sky and right away the T.V. boys warn people to be careful not to drive, to stay home if possible," he said.[22]

A couple of years later Gus Valentine reported that his ozoner at Georgetown, Texas, suffered a 20 percent drop in business after a television station went on the air in nearby Austin. Though others had experienced similar declines, all expected business to return to old levels once the novelty wore off.[23] The outdoor men were starting to worry just a bit about competition from the tube.

If patrons loved the ozoners no matter what, parts of the film industry still didn't. As drive-ins increased in popularity from the 1940s to the 1950s, film distributors switched over from charging rentals at a flat rate to a percentage of the gross take. Films screened were still the same second, third, or later runs, but the different method of renting invariably yielded more money to the distributors. No sooner had they congratulated themselves on achieving this than drive-ins overwhelmingly moved to free admissions for kids and, to a much lesser degree, flat per-car rates for adults. Distributors felt they were losing money, not considering that free admission for children might increase the take because the kids brought along adults. These companies checked with their legal departments to see if they could do anything to stop this "injustice." However, the legal proceedings—which ended in the 1940s by breaking up the industry monopoly—had, among other things, expressly forbidden any admission-price-fixing in distributors' film-rental contracts, something they had done with impunity in the past. Drive-in pricing policies could not be altered by the distributors. One frustrated film executive suggested to a drive-in owner that his company should get a percentage of the refreshment sales as it was the movie that brought customers in. Setting him straight, the owner replied, "The worse the pictures are the more stuff we sell."[24]

Indoor houses continued to blame ozoners for much of the decline in their attendance figures. Charlotte, North Carolina, saw three of its five first-run theaters close down in the early 1950s. Film distribution men in New York blamed these closures not on television but on the growth of drive-ins in that state. Other industry executives, when surveying the situation across the country, agreed adding, "the tremendous impact of drive-ins on conventional houses, as a prime cause for the shutterings both past and future, has been underplayed." M. E. Shively of Mid-State Theatres blamed a number of indoor theater closings in Pennsylvania on drive-in competition. Shively had complained to executives of distribution companies about the ozoner practices of free admission for kids and of flat rate per car admissions.[25]

So upset was the industry lobby group, the Theatre Owners of America (TOA), that it delegated a group of members to lobby senators and representatives in order to try to obtain what it felt would be a more equitable admission tax from drive-ins. The tax was levied as a percentage on each admission. The TOA objected to the fact that outdoor houses paid less of this tax if they charged a per-car admission (no matter how many people were in the vehicle.[26]

The TOA Arkansas unit did have some success, in that it got Rep. Wilbur Mills (D., Ark) to take its proposal, for a per-person admission tax, to the House Ways and Means Committee to amend the Treasury code. The committee rejected the proposal on the grounds that it would be a major administrative problem for the Bureau of Internal Revenue. Furthermore, some members argued that it was the intention of Congress to levy the tax on admissions on whatever basis a private company chose to establish. If ozoners wanted to work on a per-car basis that was acceptable.[27] This whole affair added to the ill feeling and antagonism existing between indoor and outdoor exhibitors.

That indoor theaters attacked them on an issue like flat-rate admission, which was practiced by only one in five drive-ins at most, indicated the desperate state of the indoor exhibitors as they tried to come to terms with their declining attendance.

Owners of drive-ins continued to believe they drew mostly from a population that didn't generally attend conventional theaters. One survey indicated that ozoners drew just 15 percent of the customers of indoor houses.[28]

When operators across the country were polled and asked what percentage of the average drive-in attendance did they estimate was made up of people who didn't normally attend indoor houses the results were: under 20 percent don't normally attend indoor theaters, thought 9 percent of respondents; 20 to 30 percent, said 18 percent of owners; 30 to 40 percent, 15 percent; 40 to 50 percent, 25 percent; 50 to 70 percent, 19 percent; over 70 percent of our audience don't attend indoor theaters, said 13 percent, of operators. René L. Carneau, of the Midway Drive-In Theatre, Ascutney, Vermont, claimed, "Many who had given up attending indoor theaters now attend them outdoors. We do not think they attend indoor theaters in the winter when we are closed, however. Some say they don't care for indoor movies since attending outdoors. Ardent fans, however, never try outdoors, as they see everything first run." By a margin of 98 percent to 2 percent respondents in the poll thought drive-ins were helping the movie-going habit in general. David Ginsburg, manager of a Beltsville, Maryland, outdoor house, said, "Former patrons who have been going to movies spasmodically because of television, like the informality and many conveniences of a drive-in. Many get back into the movie-going habit and carry their business indoors when cool weather comes."[29]

Weekly attendance at films continued to spiral downward through the 1950s—from 60 million a week in 1950 down to a low that decade of 39.6 in 1958 before stabilizing in the low 40s range for the next while. These figures were low compared to the high marks of 90 million per week hit both in 1930 and right after the end of World War II.[30] Considering the population was greatly increased, these numbers become even worse on a per-capita basis. During the 1950s the total included those who attended outdoor theaters, which helped hold up the overall total. Indoor attendance alone, then, was even lower than the numbers indicated. From the end of the war until 1957 the population grew by 35 percent, while disposable income rose even faster, moving from $159 billion to $287 billion.[31]

A company by the name of Jack H. Levin Associations surveyed the ozoner industry to determine which influences acted on it. Levin stated that the average drive-in was open 8.05 months of the year with the two warmest regions, the south-central and west-south-central states, having the longest seasons at 10.35 and 10.30 months, respectively. Shortest seasons occurred in the coldest regions with New England and the west north central states averaging 6.75 and 6.46 months. A close relationship was found between car registration and number of drive-ins. In the first seven years after World War II registered automobiles increased from twenty-eight to forty-three million. At the time of his survey Levin found that the five states with the most drive-ins—Texas, North Carolina, Ohio, California and Pennsylvania—had 32.54 percent of the country's drive-ins and 29.74 percent of the nation's private automobiles. Illinois ranked sixth in both categories, while Kansas came twentieth in each group. The area of a particular state didn't influence the number of outdoor theaters but the density of roads did. The more miles of roads per square mile the greater the density of drive-ins per square mile. Precipitation had no effect on length of an outdoor theater's season. Arizona had the driest climate and the longest season. Nevada had the next driest climate but one of the shortest seasons. Louisiana had one of the longest seasons but the wettest climate. Three-quarters of all the drive-ins Levin surveyed operated seven days a week.[32]

A high-water mark was reached by the ozoners sometime in August 1952. For that month, average weekly attendance at indoor theaters was 39.6 million, while 40.9 million attended outside venues.[33] For at least one week during that month the outdoor theaters drew more people than did the indoor houses—the first time this had ever happened.

The cost of building a drive-in continued to increase. The *Motion Picture Herald*'s detailed cost breakdown gave a total cost of $254,000 for a one thousand car-capacity venue, land excluded, in 1956 (see pp. 228–229). To operate in the winter meant adding $22,000 more.[34] This example was a by-no-means-average installation. First of all it was almost twice the capacity of the average drive-in. It also included estimates for fairly elaborate amenities such as a playground and landscaping. Some items, such as in-car speakers, actually cost less in 1956 than they had in 1948. Nor by any means is this example the most costly. Drive-ins built during the 1950s could and did run from $20,000 up to close to $1 million. The former were simply open lots; the latter were ornate shrines to the automobile. At the lower end of the scale the ozoners might rent a film for thirty-five to forty-five dollars for a two- or three-day run, or perhaps $125 for a week. At the top end of the rental scale were giant drive-ins, which might pay out $2,500 or more in weekly film rentals. The odd one ran its tab as high as $5,000 per week.[35]

Ozoners remained in the hands of independent exhibitors to a greater extent than did the indoor houses. In early 1952 chains owned 46.8 percent of indoor houses but 61.8 percent of the seating capacity. For indoor houses seating more than one thousand people the chains owned over four times as many venues as did non-chain operators. Just 28 percent of drive-ins were owned by chains. However, of those with a capacity of more than five hundred automobiles, the chains owned 54.9 percent.[36]

Estimates as to the proportion of drive-ins that remained open during the winter generally ranged from about a third to a half. The Levin survey suggested a fairly lengthy season. However, the only data in the literature would seem to indicate that that percentage is an exaggeration, or that the ones open were losing money. Attendance during the outdoor theaters' best month, August, was at least one hundred times greater than in the worst month, January or December, from 1952 to 1954. In that period the average weekly attendance in August ranged from 33.8 million to 40.9 million, while in January it was .3 or .4 million per week. Indoor theaters were much more consistent. Of those 36 months the range was 31.2 million per week, up to 42.1 million, with the exception of December 1953, at 24.0 million. In 1954 49.2 million admissions were paid each week to film theaters with about one quarter (12.47 million) being visits to outdoor theaters. Attendance at indoor theaters was actually higher during the summer months, when drive-in visits were at their peak, than in the winter even though ozoner attendance in those months was close to non-existent. For the months of June, July, August, and September 1954, average weekly attendance at drive-ins was 29.2 million, 40.2 million per week at indoor houses; for April, May, October, and November ozoner attendance averaged 7.5 million per week, 35.1 at indoor venues; for January, February, March, and December, drive-in attendance was a negligible .5 million per week, 34.2 million at indoor locations.[37] This reinforces the idea that outdoor theaters didn't steal customers from the indoor houses as indoor attendance not only did not rise but declined slightly when ozoners were shut. These figures also support the idea that drive-in patrons didn't transfer their movie-going habits to indoor locations in bad weather. The groups were by and large two different populations.

While the cost of building drive-ins during the 1950s increased, it was still cheaper than that of constructing comparable indoor venues. They thus remained more profitable. Using figures from the 1954 census, each dollar of payroll expense generated $4.72 of gross receipts (including taxes) for an indoor theater, while that same dollar generated $5.34 at the drive-in. Outdoor theaters took in 16.2 percent of gross revenue for the two types of exhibitors combined. For each dollar spent on admissions at indoor theaters, 9.6 cents was spent at the concession stand, 20.3 cents at drive-ins. Admission averaged 60.2 cents at indoor theaters, 74.7 cents outdoors. There were 3,611 drive-ins with a payroll that year, 3,775 in total.[38]

Four years later the 1958 census revealed a similar edge for ozoners. Each dollar of payroll generated $4.13 in gross receipts (tax included) indoors, $4.96 outdoors. Drive-ins took 20.1 percent of combined gross sales. This increased percentage over the prior census was due more to the continued decline of indoor attendance than at outdoor increase. Every dollar spent on admission generated 11.6 cents spent at the indoor concession stands, 22.5 cents outdoors. Admission indoors averaged 73.4 cents, 76.5 cents at drive-ins. There were 3,805 drive-ins with a payroll in 1958, 4,063 in total.[39]

While concession revenue at outdoor theaters was twice that at indoor spots it was considerably less than the 30 to 50 percent of ticket sales often reported in the literature. The 22.5 cents per dollar for 1958 is based on gross admission sales including tax. When tax is excluded, the figure goes to 29.5 cents, still low. The census figures are understated to the extent that income from a refreshment stand leased to a concessionaire is not included. However, since less than 10 percent of ozoners did this, it would only add a couple of cents to the total. Drive-ins had an even greater edge in profits over their indoor kin than these numbers indicate as they usually paid less for film rentals, the only other major business expense, than did the indoor houses.

Growth was stagnant for ozoners during the latter part of the 1950s. Their numbers increased faster than did their revenue. In 1954 the average drive-in drew 93,100 admissions, enough to fill the lot to capacity (based on 2.7 paid per car) 72 times. Four years later the draw was 82,900, enough to fill the lot 58 times. Problems were starting to surface. The drive-in was growing both in number and size faster than the public cared to visit it. While the numbers indicated this by 1958 nobody in the industry seemed to notice. There was no spate of articles warning of overbuilding or of stagnant or lagging attendance. Drive-in exhibitors were still enjoying the golden decade. However, the golden years were coming to an end.

Chapter 8

The Golden Years, Showmanship

More and more drive-ins turned to selling an evening of fun in which the film being screened was only a part—and not necessarily the most important one. Some of this was due to competition between ozoners, but most of it was aimed at getting families out as well as being due to the limitations imposed on outdoor theaters by long summer days, which meant later starts, exacerbated by the much-hated daylight saving time. With films unable to be screened until 8:30 to 9:30 P.M. operators could open their gates several hours earlier, increasing concession business, if they could entertain the patrons during that time.

The National Association of Drive-In Theatres encouraged its members to book live talent. Many did so. A few of the ozoners had an area of the screen tower that, while not built for that purpose, could serve as a stage. Others constructed special platforms for the acts or had them perform on top of the concession building. One popular group that played at a number of ozoners was a hillbilly singing group called the Sleepy Hollow Gang. Up in the Northeast, the Walter Reade chain was partial to booking circus acts. Acts booked for the 1952 outdoor theater season included Penney Millette, swaypole artist; the Great Wilno, a human cannonball; the Stardusters, also a swaypole act; and Will Hills' Circus, which consisted of a dog, a pony, and an elephant. Reade often has these acts perform an afternoon free "teaser" show in the playgound area. During one of these shows Millette climbed a 125-foot pole in front of a group of kids. "She waved to the kids and urged them to come back at night."[1]

The Reade chain was typical in promoting drive-ins as something more than just a place screening films outdoors. In 1950 each of their six ozoners offered playground equipment, fireworks, pony rides, dancing, baby parades, midnight spook shows, gift nights, cartoon carnivals, old-fashioned game parties, and picnic and play areas open free of charge during the day for use by the community. To the Reade circuit the drive-in represented a combination

Participants at a "Home Talent Show" strut their stuff at a Walter Reade drive-in on a stage built in front of the screen tower, 1953.

of motion pictures and a carnival. When patrons arrived on a summer evening at 6:00 P.M. knowing the show couldn't start until 9:00 P.M., they were looking forward, argued Reade,to more than "a few hours at the movies." It was a family outing, a sort of holiday. Older patrons were said to enjoy horseshoe pitching and shuffleboard tournaments. Popular old-fashioned game nights included three-legged races, musical chairs, and potato races.[2]

One of Reade's more popular attractions was its "Beautiful Child" contest. Over a period of four weeks two boys and two girls were selected each night. Finals were held in the fifth week. These winners then went on to compete against winners from other Reade drive-ins. Local newspapers provided free publicity, with photos of the winners along with free ads, in return for screen credit at the ozoner. Merchants donated prizes while area women's clubs donated judges. Reade executive Paul Petersen explained his company's drive-in philosophy by saying: "Unlike the conventional theatre, which primarily sells its screen attraction, drive-in theatre advertising must concentrate on the full evening's inexpensive entertainment it offers to the entire family, of which movies are only a part."[3]

Some ozoners began to cultivate potential future patrons almost from the moment they arrived. Reade sent congratulatory cards to newborn babies with free passes for the parents. Don McNally, manager of the Derby-Port Drive-In

An animal circus entertains at one of the Walter Reade chain of drive-ins in the Northeast, 1953.

in Derby, Vermont, mailed a complimentary pass to each newborn in his area granting free admission to the baby until is reached the age of 12. A letter to the parents reminded them that no baby-sitter was required. They received a pass good for one admission.[4]

Rules for staff selection and attire tended to formality and rigidity. The Reade chain dressed attendants in uniforms that looked like a cross between those worn by the military and a marching band. Some used police-style outfits for those attendants involved in traffic movement. At the Lakeland drive-in in Lakeland, Florida, male attendants had to wear a coat and tie on Sundays and holidays, long-sleeved shirts on other nights. Snack bar staff wore white cotton jackets.[5]

Manager Wilfred P. Smith felt that a manager must always wear a shirt and tie if not a jacket. Colors were to be conservative; the shirt must be white. All staff had to be uniformed, with dark neckties. To get hired by Smith an applicant had to be between thirty-five and forty-five for traffic-control positions, having the authority of deputy police, and between twenty-one and thirty-five for all other posts. Smith leaned toward married men with at least one child—he believed that they were more responsible. In any case no one got hired unless they could produce three character references. For unstated reasons Wilfred preferred to hire fully employed people who were looking to moonlight. Employee motivation at a Smith theater consisted of giving one $25 savings bond at the end of the season to the employee who made the best suggestion to improve operations.[6]

In Long Island, New York, the Hempstead Turnpike Drive-In joined with the few ozoners that did the grocery shopping for its patrons. A dozen ushers were employed to provide this service. A few others even provided laundry

An usher directs traffic at the Gilmore in Los Angeles, 1950.

service: "We wash your dirty shirts while you watch the show," advertised one. Flat tires were fixed at the drive-in, cars jump-started, and gas and oil were available, while in some you could get the car washed. Everything from talent shows to baby contests to boxing matches to car stunts was featured at some venues. A cage of monkeys could be rented cheaply for the season, or a litter of rabbits. These animal displays were reported to be very popular.[7]

Some extra attractions were a natural part of the drive-in. In 1951 James Beach was manager of a newly opened ozoner near Winter Haven, Florida. Struck by the natural beauty of the place, located on the shore of Lake Hartridge,

A family watching a movie at a drive-in in the early 1950s.

Beach was sure it would attract plenty of customers. It did, but the film was only a secondary attraction. After the drive-in had been open just a short time, patrons took to arriving with their fishing gear. Being well stocked with perch and bass, the attraction of Lake Hartridge soon took precedence over the attractions on the screen. Patrons entered the lot, parked, and started to fish—most could do so right from their cars. Beach started to advertise this as one of his features. The fish were billed ahead of the Hollywood stars on the marquee. A few fans came by boat from across the lake. They anchored near the drive-in, fishing while viewing the movie for free. Not minding these freeloaders, Beach installed a couple of loudspeakers near the water so those in the boats could hear as well as see the film.[8]

Meands Drive-In near Albany, New York, reportedly was the first drive-in to sell beer (though Hollingshead's outlet in Camden apparently did in 1933, at least for a short time) which it did in 1950 as part of an experiment to assess exhibitors' attitudes about the selling of beer in their outlets. A total of 2,500 cases were sold that summer at Meands, at twenty-five cents a can. No beer was allowed to be taken from the concession area. Attendants opened and poured all cans.[9] Breweries were anxious to get in on what they saw as a potentially lucrative market. Exhibitors had mixed feelings at best about the idea, and this attitude—coupled with the fact that liquor laws were different in each state—ensured that beer and the drive-in would never mix to any great extent. Moreover, the family image of drive-ins worked against any widespread or easy access to alcohol at these theaters.

Prior to the 1950s ozoners had sometimes allowed churches to use their facilities at no cost to hold services. Usually these were limited to Easter Sunday services and the odd religious pageant. In the 1950s, however, more and more drive-ins gave their facilities up to churches, which used them every Sunday during the summer to conduct their regular services. The Whitestone Drive-In in the Bronx, New York, made its facilities available Sunday mornings and afternoon to all faiths. Services were conducted by the Protestant Council of the City of New York.[10] Churches favored the drive-in because it afforded an opportunity for the physically handicapped to attend. They also eliminated any baby-sitter problem. By granting free use of their premises to churches the drive-ins hoped to build up general goodwill in the community. From their point of view, communities would all too often attack any plans to locate an outdoor theater in their area. There was always the chance that some of these people making their first visit to an ozoner for religious reasons might like what they saw and return one night for a film.

The Central Christian Church of Orlando, Florida, held regular services at the Winter Park Drive-In. Three drive-ins in Jacksonville, Florida, had their facilities used by three different churches in that city. Printed programs of the services were provided to patrons. Each theater had a choir, soloists, and an electric organ. Services were conducted from the top of the projection booths. Patrons listened through the regular in-car speakers. Local firms donated coffee and doughnuts, which were dispensed free from the concession booth before and after the service. Services went ahead rain or shine.[11]

In Lakeland, Florida, the Lakeland Drive-In's playground was used for a church kindergarten after the services were conducted. A portable organ was placed on the roof of the utility building to provide music for the services. When the Neponset outdoor theater in Massachusetts, on the road from Boston to Cape Cod, was converted to a church on Sundays, many of the 350 families who arrived showed up in bathing suits and other sportswear. The Parkman Street Methodist Church set up at the Neponset to combat summer religious backsliding. After services the families headed for the seaside.[12]

As attendance at indoor theaters sagged, those exhibitors tried to fight back with gimmicks of their own—usually technical ones such as 3-D projection, CinemaScope, and so on. Ultimately they would be unsuccessful. The hype surrounding them lasted for several years. Ozoners were only marginally involved in trying to adopt these "advances." The few that attempted to do so suffered immediate failure. Technical aspects of the ozoner, with regard to regular projection and audio, were already poor compared to those found at indoor houses. For example, far more light was required than drive-in projectors could muster. Nor could the ozoner produce stereo sound, a feature of CinemaScope.[13] If the few who tried failed, the ozoner industry as a whole didn't worry. The drive-ins were thriving; attendance was booming. They needed no help at all. It was the indoor houses that were suffering.

The playground at the Bay Shore–Sunrise Drive-In on Long Island was busy at 6:30 P.M. when the gates opened although the film would not start for hours.

Everywhere, of course, was the kiddies' playground. Rare was the drive-in of any size and scope that didn't have something in this line, however modest. Most were very elaborate, and as time passed, they tended to grow more and more so. As drive-ins competed against each other, each theater's playground would add more free rides to its collection. They took to opening these playgrounds many hours before show time. Competition in this regard became so intense in the Hartford, Connecticut, area that one of that city's indoor houses, the Lyric, instituted the unheard-of, allowing kids under twelve, accompanied by parents, in for free after 6:00 P.M. seven nights a week. (It was, as it still is, an article of faith that nobody gets into an indoor theater for free. Something, even a small amount, must be paid.)[14]

In 1956 an estimated 90 percent of drive-ins had a playground or were planning on installing one. While the area in front of the screen remained a favored location for the playground, it was soon rivaled or exceeded in popularity by an area directly behind the snack bar/projection building. Due to lack of sight lines, about eighty feet back of this structure couldn't be used to park cars. Having a central location, this area was more convenient for parents and children. And, as one writer noted at the time: "The advantages of such proximity to the snack bar are obvious."

An example of a small playground installation was the one found at the

The playground at Loew's 35 near Keyport, New Jersey, 1956.

Hilltop Drive-In near Escanaba, Michigan, which held six hundred cars. Called a "basic layout," the Hilltop playground had a primary castle walk; a 12-foot, all-steel slide, a merry-go-round, a seesaw set, and two swing sets. Such basic layouts could be bought for no more than $600 in 1956. Bigger drive-ins had bigger playgrounds. Norfolk, Virginia's, Visulite Theatres set aside a triangular area 300 by 215 by 185 feet at one of their ozoners, which they divided into a jungle and senior playground. The senior division contained a combination unit on a frame 10 feet above ground, consisting of two seesaws, four swings, two trapeze bars, and two sets of flying rings; a castle tower, 7 feet 9 inches high, capable of holding thirty-six children; an all-steel slide with a 16-foot-long chute; a horizontal ladder 6 feet high and 12 feet long; and a wave stride, which children could whirl around by gripping the handrail and pushing against the ground with their feet. The junior division had a six-swing set with chair-type nursery seats; a merry-go-round with a seat board 10 feet in diameter and an enclosed safety platform, which one child could easily propel when it carried the capacity load of twenty-five; a castle walk whose walk was 6 feet long and 5 feet 3 inches high and whose towers were 7 feet high; a six-swing set on 8-foot-high frames; and a steel slide with a 12-foot chute.[15]

At the Lake Park Outdoor Theatre in Fond du Lac, Wisconsin, a total of 150,000 free rides were enjoyed by children in 1953 on the merry-go-round and miniature train. The playground opened one hour before show time and was staffed by two attendants. The Lake Park was one of the few ozoners in the country, and the only one in its area, to charge an admission for children aged five to twelve. Paying nine cents a head, the 20,000 child admissions in 1953 grossed the theater $1,800. Operators of the Lake Park found their child patrons continually in and out of the concession building to make purchases on

Kids arriving at the Westport, Massachusetts, ozoner in 1954.

breaks from the playground. After the playground was installed, the concession gross showed a "definite increase."[16]

That, of course, was the reason for the playground in the first place, and for the policy of free child admission. Preshow play stimulated the kids' appetites, which led to more refreshment sales. As a 1950s writer stated in his manual for ozoner operation, commenting on the playground: "Attendance may be substantially increased if the younger members of the family can be made eager patrons. . . . If the youngsters' visit to the drive-in can be made happy and pleasant, they become excellent advertising agents whose parents are prone to indulge a request which costs so little. . . . It has been proved that it is during this period of a child's life that he exerts the greatest influence on family spending. . . . There can be no question but that playgrounds provide a sound reason for the average youngster to want to come to the show and to ask daddy to 'Take me to the drive-in!'" The playground was also touted as something that would wear the children out so they would rest quietly while the adults watched the show. Or, if not worn out, the kids could be sent back to the playground during the film to give the adults some peace and quiet.[17]

The logical extension to these playgrounds was the super kiddyland, which was spun off of many a drive-in. This became a separate entity, though still part of the ozoner complex. It kept its own hours. It charged admission and or a per-ride fee. An example was the Oxford Drive-In at Oxford, Massachusetts, which had Kiddyland in addition to the free children's playground on the lot. The former was open all day, charging fifteen to twenty cents per ride on attractions more elaborate than those in the free sections. At dusk Kiddyland closed while the drive-in opened its gates. Kids could then go and play on the free playground.[18]

Hollywood's major studios generally issued press books to accompany each of their releases. These books contained promotion ideas local exhibitors could implement to hype the picture. Columbia became the first of the majors, in the mid–1950s, to insert a special page into its press books with promotional ideas specifically geared to the ozoners. The other major studios soon followed suit.[19]

Not that drive-in owners needed much help in the promotion department. At Garden Auto-Torium in Ledgewood, New Jersey, operator Wilfred P. Smith kept things buzzing. From Friday to Sunday Smith directed his approach to family groups with costume shows, pet shows, and so on. Children winning these contests would get a prize consisting of a basket of items from the refreshment stand. Even the winning pet got a can of dog or cat food. Parents' involvement was sought by encouraging them to tell a story about their child and his pet — broadcast over the lot. During the Monday–Thursday period, Smith directed his promotional activities more to adults, who were a proportionally larger share of the audience of those days. Games and giveaways were favorites. Prizes for games, such as "lucky license number," were refreshment-stand items as Smith felt these were more appreciated than passes. A disc jockey was usually featured, who spun records and talked up the crowd. By having him announce as many names and different hometowns of patrons as possible and by dedicating records to various patrons, the disc jockey was supposed to generate goodwill. Discreetly he was also expected to point out the number of different and "delicious" items for sale at the snack bar. Smith cultivated the friendship of nearby high school and elementary school principals. In return he was often asked to address school assemblies to discuss the "attractiveness of the drive-in and the part it plays in community family life." When speaking to these groups Smith made it a point to invite the students, and their parents, to his drive-in. Each year he sent congratulatory cards to every member of nearby graduating classes, with an invitation to the Garden Auto-Torium.[20]

Some suggested promotional stunts that a drive-in might use in the course of a season included anniversary celebrations, good for seven days of activity, including a giant cake displayed downtown with special contests and so on; disc jockey shows two or three times a week to originate from the refreshment stand; dancing for teens as part of the disc jockey program, with other forms, such as square dancing, to appeal to adults; a fashion show by a local merchant to fill several hours in a long midsummer preshow period with the merchant to pick up most of the expense; air shows with stunt pilots and with prizes dropped by plane; and fireworks displays. Other ideas included a hot-rod display by local youths; motorcycle exhibition by a local club; a horse show put on by area saddle clubs; the giveaway of a used car on "Bucket of Bolts" night; a treasure hunt with clues hidden on the lot; and displays by local groups, such as the Boy Scouts, the National Guard, and the Air Force. The tie-in of many of these ideas to the concession stand was their major selling point. Mystery music could be played, with prizes awarded. A photo could be taken of each car entering the ozoner on a given night with one randomly picked for a prize. The airplane could drop not prizes but numbers. In all cases the patron had to go to the refreshment booth to check song titles, or photos, or numbers, to see if he won. If many people could be induced to go there, perhaps they would buy some food on impulse.

The Joy Lan Drive-In in Florence, Alabama, ran a coop deal with a local television store in 1952, offering a free set to the car that brought in the most people. The contest night must have been viewed with horror by area highway officials, as a parade of packed cars groaned its way into the ozoner. For a while manager Dan Davis thought he had a winner after one car arrived bearing thirty-five people. However, later, a 1941 Ford entered with fifty-eight people crammed in, on, and over the vehicle. When told of his winning number, driver Ray Gene Bevis joked, "Only 58? I must have dropped somebody on the way."[21]

Many slogans were used to publicize the outdoor theaters. Some of them were; "Smoke When You Please," "Leave Your Girdle at Home," "Save While You Spend," "Eat While You Look," and "Knit While You Sit."[22]

Boat shows, auto shows, and swap nights were encouraged since something like a boat show brought vending receipts all day long for the entire weekend. One grueling idea was to hold a movie marathon, wherein each patron punched a time clock on driving into the ozoner. The winner was the person who stayed the longest, "weeks if necessary," without leaving the lot. Contestants, of course, produced all-day vending income. These last few suggestions were, as the suggester noted, all "great for vending traffic."[23]

Some operators wanted even more elaborate gimmicks added on. Industry consultant George Petersen desired early evening attractions, such as wrestling and boxing matches, dancing contests, and popular concerts. A small extra fee could be charged for such events which would soon pay off the cost of stadium seating in front of the stage. Petersen felt current showmanship ventures were too petty, that a higher financial return could be achieved. "It is my personal opinion," he said, "that the financially successful drive-in theatre of tomorrow, when erected in the vicinity of the larger metropolitan areas will be built in connection with dance floors, swimming pools, ice skating rinks, cocktail lounges, restaurants and other popular types of entertainment." The trade paper *Motion Picture Herald* tended to agree, editorializing: "There is every reason to consider the feasibility of other adult amusements than motion pictures. . . . How many city people get a chance to play good, old-fashioned croquet? They might like badminton. Tennis courts would be practicable. Where will be the first drive-in to have a bowling pavilion?"[24]

Chapter 9

The Golden Years, Selling Food

The drive-ins were noted for their uninhibited emphasis on refreshment sales. While the concession business certainly was an important part of the ozoner industry in the 1940s, it was in the 1950s that it was studied, researched, and refined into the efficient moneyspinner it became for the outdoor theaters. It was reported in 1952 that for every dollar taken by drive-ins at the ticket booth another 45.0 cents were taken at the concession stand. By contrast, for every dollar in ticket sales at an indoor theater, an additional 26.0 cents was added from refreshment sales. Concession sales per ticket at drive-ins were 15.6 cents and 31 percent of the combined ticket and concession gross. At indoor houses sales were an average 8.6 cents per ticket and 21 percent of the combined gross.[1] While numbers were often exaggerated, drive-in owners definitely did well at the snack bar, much better than the indoor exhibitors.

An early, and apparently unsuccessful, attempt at modernizing the snack bar came in 1950 with the introduction of the talk-back system at the Park Drive-In in Greensboro, North Carolina. On arriving at the ticket booth patrons were given a menu that listed such items as Southern fried chicken, hamburgers, barbecued sandwiches, and soft drinks. If a patron got hungry during the film, or just didn't want to leave the auto, he or she merely had to depress a switch located in the side of the speaker. This allowed him or her to give an order to a switchboard operator. When ready the order was delivered to the the car. One drawback to this system was the fact that an extra employee was required, the operator. A second disadvantage was that an entirely extra set of wiring had to be installed. If the ozoner used 10,000 feet of wiring for the in-car speakers, then an additional 10,000 feet of wiring was needed for the talk-back system.[2]

At most ozoners in the 1940s the concession area setup was a single-station type, or two or even more stations at large facilities. Whatever food or beverage the patron wanted to buy, he or she had to ask for it. The employee collected it, handed it over, received money, and gave out change. It was a slow system

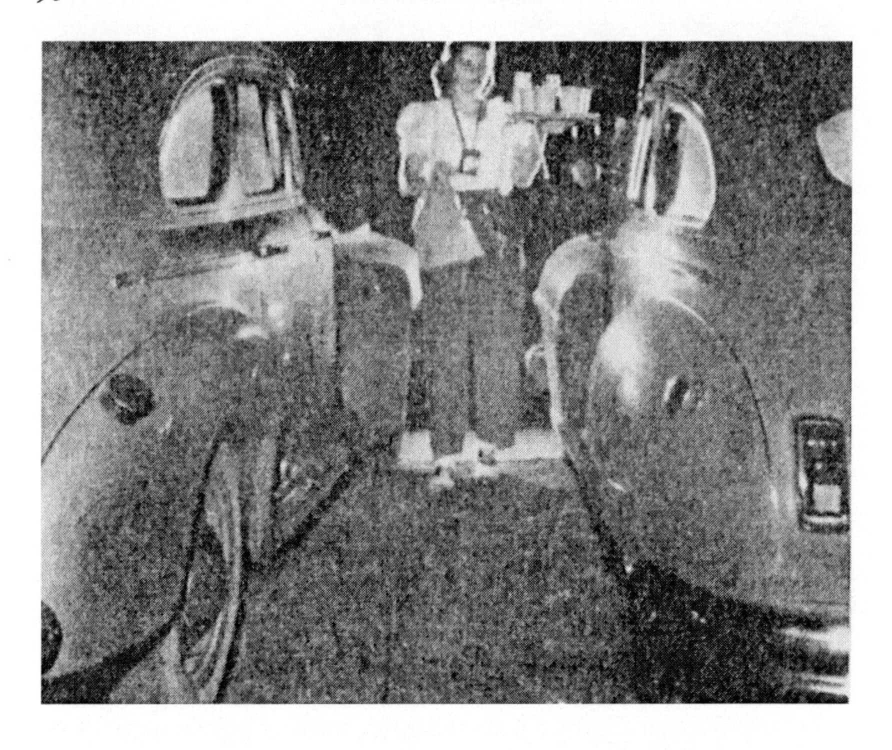

A carhop serves refreshments to the audience in 1951.

for drive-ins since they did so much of their business in a short period of time—the length of the intermission.

By 1950 many drive-ins were in the process of changing over to the more efficient cafeteria style layout. Using this method, patrons passed by the food helping themselves, as much of it was laid out self-service style. At the end of the counter was the cashier who did nothing but handle money. Al Gordon, president of Morris Gordon & Son (hotel and restaurant equipment business), urged the owners of outdoor theaters to convert their snack-bar layout. Gordon felt the concession department should take in a minimum of 50 percent of the net revenue of the admission price while at the same time doing 75 percent of its business during the ten-minute break. "In our experience, we have discovered that the cafeteria style counter is vastly superior to the older type of front counter service," said Gordon. "In theaters holding from 600 to 1,000 cars, the four-lane cafeteria should be installed. The four lanes should be identical, each serving the same wares, preferably with turnstiles at the beginning of each lane for protection against pilfering."[3] For drive-ins holding fewer than six hundred cars two lanes were sufficient. Gordon claimed that his company had designed the restaurant turnstile in 1951 so a patron couldn't enter the line, grab a couple of items, and then exit without passing the waiting cashier.

As far as Gordon was concerned the ozoner was a magnet for families who got in their cars on a fine evening not necessarily to actually go to the movies. "The lights and signs on the marquees sometimes prove a magnet to draw them inside and the concessions can be an irresistible lure," he thought. "It has been proved that the title of the motion picture attraction on the marquee is sometimes of lesser importance than the offerings sold in the concession building." When his company remodeled one drive-in from the old station style to the cafeteria method, concession sales increased 14 percent per patron. E. M. Loew, who used the Gordon cafeteria-style concession building in his new ozoners, reported a 27 percent per-admission concession sales increase over the old-fashioned-style counter.[4]

Given the money generated by concession sales, it is little wonder that operator Wilfred P. Smith advised his peers not to neglect their "profiteria." Another operator felt that neatness and cleanliness were essential at the snack bar. To this end he suggested that the ideal vending manager would be a "responsible middle-aged housewife." Others suggested that females were preferable for counter sales, with male employees used for car-to-car sales. Smith considered that a properly operated concession should do at least 43 percent of the box office gross on a clear night, 25 percent on a wet night, and an additional 15 percent from car-to-car vending.

Some exhibitors reminded their patrons about the snack bar every chance they got. Edward E. Vaughn, manager of Sacramento's El Rancho, used refreshment-menu reminders distributed to entering autos, a public-address-system announcement two or three times a night, and film trailers and special newspaper ads stressing the refreshment stand. Striving for greater efficiency and faster turnover in the necessarily rushed intermission period, Smith noted that speakers near the concession building allowed patrons to hear and see the film, thus tending to hold them in line longer if the film started while they still hadn't been served. Space should also be available for patrons to eat at the snack bar itself on the theory that having finished one item there they might buy more. Smith noted: "An attendant behind the refreshment counter can hold two cups of normal size in one hand while turning the faucet to allow the flow of a soft drink with the other hand. If this same attendant had a pedal attached to the dispensing unit, he could then hold two cups in each hand and double his sales." Pedals could also be used to speed up hot dog and popcorn sales and delivery, thought Smith.[5]

When the *Motion Picture Herald* polled drive-in theater owners in 1951 to find out what percentage of total gross receipts came from concession sales they reported that 6.3 percent of respondents received 10–20 percent of the gross from refreshment sales; 33.0 percent received 20–30 percent; 40.8 percent received 30–40 percent; 17.8 percent received 40–50 percent; 1.9 percent received 50–70 percent; and .2 percent received 70–90 percent. In the 30–40 percent range, a heavy majority of respondents hovered around the 35 percent mark.[6] Most were doing very well, although about 40 percent were grossing less than 30 percent from refreshment sales. Usually, it was felt, these owners were operating in an inefficient manner. Some were slow in converting to the cafeteria style. In 1955 53 percent of the outdoor theaters were still using the single station system; 11 percent using two or more stations and 36 percent featuring the cafeteria method. Just one year later the numbers reversed, with 56 percent using the cafeteria method; 34 percent the single station and 10 percent utilizing two or more stations.[7]

The practice of admitting children, usually defined as under twelve, to the drive-in for free was widespread in the 1950s. It was strongly supported by the industry since it promoted family business, the industry mainstay, and a heavy selling point was the fact that baby-sitters weren't needed. Much of this edge would be lost if child admission were charged. Perhaps more important, children were the "salesmen" who got their parents down to the refreshment counter.

While they were important to the concession business, children could be a bit of a nuisance by slowing down lines plus the fact that they normally had much less to spend than adults. Dean Fitzgerald of the Badger Outdoor theater in Madison, Wisconsin, thought that a potential solution lay in the increased use of coin-operated vending machines as "auxiliary salesmen" since machines naturally appealed to kids. "While children are continuously favored customers at theatre concession areas," Fitzgerald explained, "there is little doubt that they are the toughest shoppers and the most time-consuming patrons. The appeal of the machines for them is unquestioned, and many times the child—with his lesser amount to spend—will head for the machines, leaving the stand open for a man or woman buying either for themselves, their friends and/or their families, with more money to spend and a greater buying potential."[8]

One way of getting patrons out of their cars and into the snack bar was to run food trailers just before the break for intermission. These trailers existed for virtually every product on sale. Supplied to the drive-in by the manufacturer at no charge, provided the theater offered the product for sale, they were a cost-free bonanza for the operators. The only problem was to decide the maximum number that could be shown together before the patrons became irritated.

An example of one of these was the one produced by Hygrade Food Products Corporation to tout its frankfurters. Actually Hygrade produced six different trailers, each of which was one minute in length with full orchestral accompaniment. Virtually no brand identification was used in these ads, which, said the company, would also boost the sales of other snack bar items. A drive-in that sold Hygrade Hot Dogs got these ads free. Irving Goldberg used them at his Detroit ozoner. Pleased with the result he said: "This film is exactly what we need. Commercial identity is minimized, with emphasis on

Patrons watch an Armour Company intermission trailer for hot dogs, 1953. Such trailers were commonplace, free to the drive-ins, and successfully boosted refreshment sales.

whetting the patron's appetite for refreshment items. We believe the Hygrade trailers have been responsible for an estimated 20% increase in sales per customer during the 30 days we've been using them. It has helped sell all refreshment items and it certainly hasn't hurt the sales of Hygrade Frankfurters."[9]

Armour and Company of Chicago also produced trailers to tout their franks. After announcing the intermission and reminding patrons it was time to "stretch their legs and perk up with a cooling drink, a box of popcorn and a delicious Armour Star Frank on a bun," these one-minute commercials then showed scenes of family groups and teenagers enjoying all these refreshments. Words and music for the accompanying jingles were written by employees of Armour's merchandising department. A typical verse went: "So step up—buy your Armour franks / And give the kids permission / To eat the finest hot dogs made— / Enjoy this intermission!" The Armour trailers were reportedly highly successful in generating sales; some drive-ins had sales of one frank for every six patrons before running the Armour trailers and one for every three patrons after airing them. Wade H. Renick, manager of the Hays Drive-In at Hays, Kansas, was enthused about these Armour trailers saying, "During the first four months of our season we sold franks at the ratio of one per every 16 adult admissions. After using the trailers for the duration of the season, we found the ratio to be one to every ten."[10]

Fully 83 percent of all drive-ins used these trailers to promote their refreshment business. Some that didn't use trailers made personal announcements preceding intermissions. Indoor theaters lagged very far behind in this regard, as only 30 percent used trailers to boost their food sales.[11] All that selling had to be squeezed into a short period of time. In the mid–1950s 53 percent of the ozoners had a ten-minute intermission, while 23 percent had one of fifteen minutes. Other periods ranged from three to twenty-five minutes.[12]

Henry Tollette, Wisconsin division manager for a theater chain, had a few tips on how to expand the intermission period. He reported that snack bar sales at his theaters increased when a new trailer was used just before the newsreel. This trailer simply announced that the newsreel would be next, followed by the intermission. "Letting the patrons know ahead of time just when to expect the intermission helps to prevent jam ups at the concession counter," Tollette explained. "Some came during the news, others waited until after." Another method he suggested was to run a cartoon or coming attraction trailer right after the intermission — instead of in their usual spot of after the main feature. "People will buy more if they know they have plenty of time before the main attraction begins," he said.[13]

A Boston drive-in owner named Philip Lowe chastised any of his peers who played double features with no intermission, claiming they "really are as big darned fools as their competitors and brother exhibitors think they are! ... Wake up, boys, you can have an intermission without being labeled a money-grabber." To Lowe's way of thinking, an ozoner with a single-feature policy would always rate low, while one that ran a double feature with an intermission would rate high. "If you run first feature, intermission, second feature, intermission, first feature, you are as high in this category as you can go," he concluded.[14]

One way of trying to increase concession sales was to take food to the people; that is, provide car service. However, most didn't adopt this method. Ozoners owned by chains offered car service in 44 percent of their drive-ins, while the nonchain outlets offered it in just 23 percent of the cases. In both cases it was more likely to be offered in smaller venues than in larger, more than five hundred–car outlets. Car service was given by employees who used either carts they pushed or shoulder equipment. Carts contained much more food but were noisier and harder to maneuver on what was often a gravel surface. Of the drive-ins providing car service 28 percent of the chains and 14 percent of the nonchains used carts exclusively. Owners who didn't provide car service usually claimed it was because they didn't want to disturb patrons with hawkers and carts wandering all over the lot. They may have been more concerned with the idea that it was better to forego car-service gain in order to get the patron to the concession building where he or she would be exposed to the full line of food items and perhaps buy more than he or she intended. According to those who offered automobile refreshment service, 28 percent of their concession dollar volume was done through this portable service.[15]

Cart service direct to cars was established by the summer of 1949 at the latest. One story had it that a Midwestern owner was wandering through his lot one night during the intermission. Although he was aware of the crush of people at his refreshment stand, he wanted to find out how many cars had not sent out supply missions. From his observations he determined that 40 percent of cars on the lot didn't use the break to visit the snack bar. What crystallized this owner's decision to find a better way came when he spotted a large, well-dressed family, in a new car, who had brought their own food and beverages in a picnic cooler. Talking to the family, the owner came away satisfied it wasn't cost but convenience that had lost him this family's refreshment business. Wondering how much snack-bar patronage he lost because patrons were reluctant to make the long walk to the stand, were limited by the amount of food they could carry in two hands, didn't like the crush of people jammed into the snack bar, and couldn't get served in time, the owner added cart service to provide "constant availability" of refreshments to all patrons throughout the show.[16]

In some drive-ins the carts cruised among the cars, while in others a system was used to summon these vendors. When a car entered the lot the driver received a card, which he placed in a designated spot to summon a mobile vendor. Operators claimed to take as much as fifty dollars per night from the vending cart. They were particularly useful on inclement evenings, when patrons were reluctant to leave their cars.[17]

Among the companies who developed these carts were several Coca-Cola bottlers. Weighing seventy-four pounds empty, they held one hundred pounds of merchandise. While their range of food was necessarily limited, they could hold 125 soft drinks, 365 hot dogs, 280 bags of popcorn, 288 ice cream bars, 150 boxes of Cracker Jack and 150 bags of peanuts. The payload of a full cart was $150, with a profit of $95.

Philip Lowe came up with some interesting facts about his concession patrons. Women ate less than men between meals, with children having no limit except for money. People from West Virginia and Pennsylvania were much heavier eaters than those from Maine, Vermont, or New Hampshire. Not surprisingly he found that factory workers ate more than office workers, which led him to conclude that an ozoner would be better located in an industrial area than in a "class location" such as Grosse Point, Michigan, at least from the point of view of concession business. After surveying one of his venues, Lowe found concession sales to be twenty cents per person in April, twenty-seven cents in May, and thirty cents in June. This verified the obvious for Lowe: Rain and cold weather kept people in their cars.[18]

Favorite foods sold in the drive-in were the traditional and familiar—popcorn, soft drinks, hot dogs, candy, and ice cream. Many, many other items were available, right up to full dinners in some outlets. Mostly these were in locations that operated year-round, which helped to justify the purchase of special cooking equipment needed to prepare some of these items. At a typical drive-in concession stand in 1953, products sold, in relation to total refreshment sales, were as follows: plain popcorn, 12.7 percent; buttered popcorn, 12.06 percent; candy, 4.61 percent; hamburgers, 8.91 percent; frankfurters,

12.23 percent; tamales, .68 percent; coffee, 4.3 percent; hot chocolate, .56 percent; small cold drinks, 9.61 percent; large cold drinks, 13.26 percent; ice cream sundaes, 5.59 percent; ice cream cups, 2.45 percent; ice cream bars and Popsicles, 3.94 percent; ice cream bon bons, 3.1 percent; small potato chips, .04 percent; large potato chips, 1.16 percent; peanuts, .77 percent; taffy apples, .55 percent; cigarettes, 4.66 percent; and aspirin, .05 percent.[19]

Other items that could be found in some locations included Kleenex, comic books, tops, apples, and milk. The number of candy bars sold ranged from three to sixty-five, with the average theater offering fourteen different kinds. A half a chicken with an order of french fries could be had for ninety-five cents, in 1951, as well as doughnuts at forty cents per dozen or a six-and-one-half inch pizza at twenty-five cents. Not strictly for patron convenience, picnic tables were often found around the concession stand. It was felt these tables, with people sitting at them, prompted other patrons to get out of their cars and head for the snack bar.[20]

At least one of the items on sale at drive-ins, candy, tended to be more expensive than at indoor houses. For all types of theaters, in 1952, 12.7 percent sold some candy at a minimum price of 1 cent, only 4.8 percent of ozoners did so. Just 2.1 percent of all theaters sold candy at the top end minimum price of 7 or 10 cents, while 14.3 percent of drive-ins did so. At the other end of the price scale, 1.1 percent of all theaters sold candy at a maximum price of 50 cents or more, while 9.6 percent of drive-ins sold in that price range.[21]

Other items were just as profitable. For a box of plain popcorn selling at 10 cents, costs were as follows: corn, .917 cents; seasoning, .363 cents; box, .755 cents; for a total of 2.03 cents. The same size buttered popcorn sold for 20 cents: corn, .917 cents; seasoning, .363 cents; butter, 2.533 cents; box, 1.584 cents; total, 5.39 cents. Costs for a 10-cent small soft drink were: syrup, 1.744 cents; cup, .669 cents; total, 2.41 cents. A 10-cent coffee broke down thus: coffee, 1.6 cents; cream, 1.536 cents; sugar, .313 cents; cup, 1.140 cents; stirrer, .075 cents; for a total of 4.66 cents.[22]

At the beginning of the 1950s about 13 percent of drive-ins leased out their refreshment business to concessionaires, content to take a percentage of the gross. Even this small percentage shrank, dropping well below 10 percent, as more and more ozoners took over the operations themselves. Presumably they made more money that way. Not counting the cost of the refreshment building itself, the cost of concession installation ranged from about $3,000 to $6,500 depending on the size of the ozoner. Full soda fountains were operated at seven percent of the outdoor theaters while three percent ran full restaurants. The concession building would cost in the neighborhood of $20,000 for a five hundred– to six hundred–car facility.[23]

By the very early 1950s such then exotic items as Chinese egg rolls and pizza were well entrenched at drive-in snack bars. Egg rolls cost 11 cents and were sold for 30 cents. Pizza cost 20 cents and sold for 60 cents. A pizza oven set

An outdoor seating patio, which was a feature at Claude Ezell's Texas circuit (1953).

the ozoner operator back $350 to $400. Food was such a draw at outdoor theaters said Walt Thayer of Washington state's United Drive-Ins that, "People would come to get pizza and not stay for the movie. There were no pizza parlors then, and drive-ins were one of the first places you could buy a cooked pizza."[24]

At Jack Farr's 960-car Trail Drive-In located in Houston, Texas, the concession department employed eighteen people, five of them cooks, in turning out high volumes of chicken, tamale, shrimp, chili, and steakburger dinners. Arriving at 5:45 P.M., the cooks began to prepare the dinners, which had to start appearing on the cafeteria counters half an hour later when the theater opened. Priced at 65 cents, the chicken dinner, served on a glazed paper plate, consisted of three pieces of fried chicken, two pieces of toast, a lettuce leaf, and a cup of ketchup. For one dollar a patron could buy a shrimp dinner—six pieces of french-fried shrimp, french-fried potatoes, a lettuce leaf, a package of NBC crackers, and ketchup. Patrons could eat outside on the patio on in their cars. According to Farr, 60 percent of the Trail's food was sold before the show started. "We use trailers to stimulate snack business. The Armour Co. trailers are particularly good," he explained. "Our 15-minute intermission follows a period of approximately 15 minutes devoted to trailers. This gives us a 30-minute shot at snack business. In going after a family-type business all our newspaper advertisements stress a come-out-for-dinner, bring the family theme."[25]

At the Loew chain in New England seven attendants staffed an average-size drive-in refreshment stand with fourteen employed at his largest outlet, which held sixteen hundred autos. Sixty cents an hour was the going rate of pay for these workers. Everything at the drive-in from kiddy playgrounds to entertainment for adults—such as dance floors or live acts—was designed with the snack bar in mind.

Playgrounds offered free rides because if a fee were charged families often

Loew's Miami Drive-In had a special area for children in its concession building — the Little Drivers Club (about 1953).

didn't arrive until the show was due to start. This hurt concession sales. Jeff Jefferis held regular Friday night square dances at his Pine Hill Drive-In, near Piedmont, Maryland. Box-office receipts didn't increase much as a result of this added attraction but, said Jeff, "the concession business is outta this world."[26]

Other lures included horseshoe pits, Ping-Pong tables, checkerboards, barbecue pits, raffles, draws, and giveaways of such items as free gas and oil were all used, as one writer noted, to "get people to come early and stay late (they eat more!)."[27]

Chapter 10

Strange Drive-ins

Even though the typical drive-in theater was almost a guaranteed money-maker, a few people felt compelled to dream about or actually to construct an ozoner that was a little off beat. One of these opened near Asbury Park, New Jersey, on June 3, 1948. Billed as the world's first fly-in, drive-in, it was operated by Edward Brown, Jr., a former navy pilot. His ozoner had room for five hundred cars and twenty-five airplanes. Planes landed at an airfield adjoining the ozoner, then taxied over to the theater's last ramp, where they were equipped with speakers for the pilot and passengers. When the film was over Brown provided a jeep service to tow the planes back to the airfield for take-off.[1]

Within a few years there were several fly-ins in the country. The Roxy Fly-In and Drive-In was Iowa's first, opening near St. Ansgar in 1953. It had eight ramps for autos and one ramp to park about eight airplanes. By that time other fiy-in drive-ins were reported to be in operation at Belmar, New Jersey; Mobile, Alabama; and Spearman, Texas. At Belmar the charge to admit a plane was sixty-five cents.[2]

Almost always the trend in drive-ins was to bigger and bigger, but not quite always. Tom Smith was a theater owner in Urbana, Missouri, during the early 1950s. An advocate of the even then not new technique of rear-projection, Smith spent two years tinkering until 1953, when he displayed his Multiscope Drive-In working model. This system had small screens placed around the perimeter of a circle with one car in front of each screen. In the center of the circle sat the projection booth, which back-projected the film onto each screen. How one projector put the identical image on any number of screens was a secret that Smith would not reveal. According to the inventor a full circle would be 600 feet in diameter, which would allow space for one hundred fifty to two hundred cars. Tom's working model used 270 feet of the circle, accommodating forty-two cars. Each 30-by-40-inch plastic screen, with a wide black masking border, was recessed slightly into a wooden frame. With those measurements the diagonal of the screen was around fifty inches, smaller than many of today's big-screen home television sets.

The Fly-In Drive-In, Belmar, New Jersey, 1951. Planes were allowed to taxi over from a nearby landing field.

Smith was unsure of the cost of his invention to a prospective purchaser as he had built the entire model by hand out of wood. However, he felt the savings with his Multiscope system would be great, as ramping costs and screen-tower costs were eliminated. As well, the projector used much less power to produce a picture Smith claimed was better than that found at a standard-size ozoner. The relatively small number of cars it held would be just right for small towns and remote rural areas, thought the inventor. "You could say it's rather crude, but there is no denying that the result is comparable with the best of front-projection, indoors and out," said Tom. "I don't think we'll make a million dollars out of this brain-child, but I do think we've got something here."[3]

This rather bizarre attempt to miniaturize the drive-in didn't end there, although Tom Smith's name would not resurface. Ten years after Smith unveiled his model the Autoscope Drive-In appeared in Albuquerque, New Mexico. In this incarnation 260 screens for individual cars were provided in a series of rows. One central projector conveyed the image to all screens at once by means of a series of mirrors. Each screen was 3 by 5 feet, a diagonal of about seventy inches. Albuquerque reportedly had two of these Autoscopes operating in 1963.[4] The idea didn't catch on, and they quickly died out.

The Autoscope in Albuquerque, New Mexico, 1963. It featured a screen for every car.

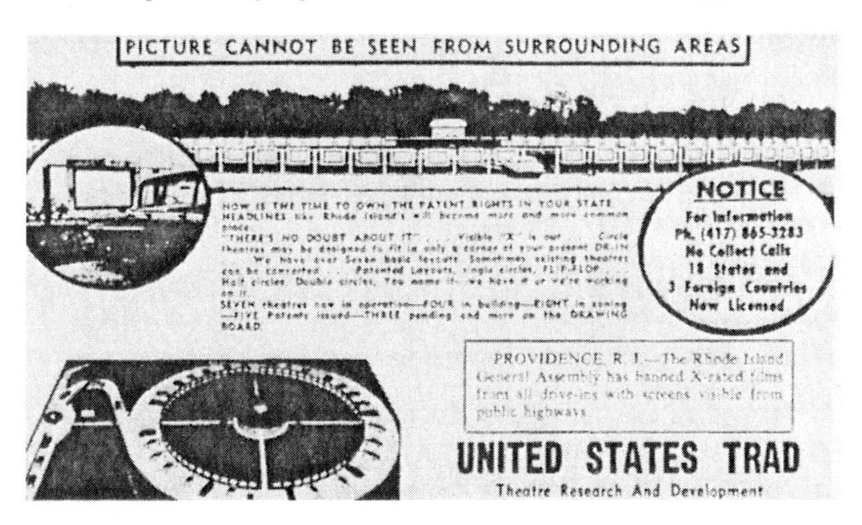

A 1975 ad for a circular, screen-for-every-car drive-in. It was an idea that never caught on. It was advertised as a way of screening X films without them being visible to passing motorists from the highway.

Ten years after Autoscope, we were back to a very Smith-like ozoner, in Richland, Washington. The Smith patent, if he had one, would by then have expired, putting the technology behind it into the public domain. Lloyd Honey of that city already owned a couple of standard-size drive-ins in the area when he opened a miniature one on May 30, 1973. It was circular in shape, with 120 individual screens each of which was 3 by 4 feet, a sixty-inch diagonal. The projection booth was located in the center of the circle, 165 feet from the viewing area. Using 120 lenses and reflecting mirrors, the image was back-projected to all the screens. Sound was picked up on the car radios. Honey said that this theater—built at a cost of $70,000—needed just two people to operate it. While not designed specifically for X-rated films, this new theater "could very well show them," Honey conceded. He claimed that it was the "first of its kind on the West Coast."[5] It was also the last.

Then there was the drive-in in Brattleboro, Vermont, where the Theatre Motel faced a one hundred–foot screen. Owner Norman Bonneau had equipped his motel rooms with speakers. For seventy-five cents a patron could attend Bonneau's drive-in in the normal fashion or for sixteen dollars and up per couple, patrons could view the film from their motel room, which also came with air-conditioning and television.[6] As strange as this idea may seem, it got another incarnation at the end of the 1980s in conjunction with Toronto, Canada's, much-heralded new sports facility, the SkyDome. A luxury hotel overlooked the field from the outfield, allowing hotel guests to watch the baseball game. However, it was the sexual activities of the guests in one room during a game that captured all the attention. Whether automobile patrons at Bonneau's facility were similarly entertained has gone unrecorded.

As the size of the drive-in screen enlarged, so did the supporting screen-tower structure. One South Carolina operator went so far as to try to create apartments inside his eight-story tower. From time to time other elaborate projects were announced, such as an indoor drive-in with space for one thousand cars as well as one thousand regular theater seats. In addition, other amenities, such as an ice rink, would be included.

Fanciful ideas of the future of drive-ins have often been expressed. In 1950 theater executive A. J. Balaban predicted the imminent coming of the "super" ozoner. This would be like the current drive-ins but would also offer television shows, dancing, and eating facilities, with as many as four different types of entertainment screened. One screen would play first-run films, another would be a newsreel theater, while the remaining two would be a foreign-film screen and a combination film-vaudeville theater. A few years later a writer speculated that future ozoners would be integrated with large entertainment or shopping facilities. California distributors were talking about drive-ins being connected to full-size restaurants or built next to bars so patrons could watch a film while sipping drinks, or serving as the main attraction in a diversified entertainment area. One idea was that drive-ins could be integrated with shopping centers so that the drive-in could be a parking lot during the day and a theater at night. Stores would be kept open right up until showtime so patrons could go straight to their cars from shopping and stay to watch a film. This idea was appealing in the mid–1950s, based on a premature hope that car-radio sound would soon arrive, thus eliminating speaker posts, making the shopping-center/drive-in-theater combination lot feasible.[7]

By the mid–1970s the system of delivering soundtracks to patrons over

One of the earliest multiplex drive-ins was this four-plex in Chicago in 1951. Three of the screens are visible in this photo. Unlike more recent multiplexes, this one showed the same film on all four screens. On two of the screens the show began twenty minutes after the first two, to stagger the traffic.

their car radios had been perfected and was starting to come into considerable use. Some operators, such as Steven J. Eisner, who operated nine ozoners in Arizona, thought this might usher in a new golden age for drive-ins. Many of these car-radio systems eliminated the speaker posts entirely. Eisner felt that because of this development virtually any large parking lot was a potential ozoner site. All that was needed was a building with a blank wall large enough to function as a screen, after being properly coated, and a sloping parking lot.[8] However, this revival in drive-in construction failed to come to pass.

Perhaps the prize for grandiose ideas should go to William R. Forman, president of Pacific Theatres, who revealed the drive-in future in 1970. At that time the ozoner industry was in a state of irreversible decline. Forman announced that Pacific would soon build a pair of five thousand car capacity drive-ins in Southern California. These giants were to have car spaces specially designed to vary with car size, from minis to Cadillacs. A moving, electric, center-aisle pedestrian conveyor walkway would lead to super snack bars with computerized ordering systems. Other features would include the daylight screen, an aesthetic, parklike atmosphere and "self-maintaining" restrooms. "The time has come to strike out daringly with fresh ideas and concepts," said Forman.[9] Strike out he did. These giants were never built.

Chapter 11

Foreign Drive-ins

The drive-in is a uniquely American invention. With its need for a great deal of land, a culture dominated by the automobile, and an affluent population, the United States is one of the few countries able to support a large, thriving ozoner industry. It is because of these specific needs that almost no other country adopted the drive-in, even though most things American are widely imitated in other lands. At best, most countries have had only a token drive-in or two, ranging up to a handful, at any one time.

André Fortin was associated with the French Gaumont company, which owned forty indoor theaters in France. This company had no plans, in 1951, to build any drive-ins in France because, as executives of the company explained, they "are not suited to the French temperament. People won't sit in cars to view a film." However, Fortin announced, his company would soon build a drive-in in Morocco. To Fortin this country was a natural for outdoor theaters possibly to become "the greatest drive-in territory in the world." The reasoning behind this was that religious custom forbade women from going to public places but didn't forbid them from traveling in a car. Thus they could watch a film without getting out of their car yet still obey their religious proscriptions. Apparently Fortin forgot that both affluence and widespread automobile ownership were prerequisites to the emergence of drive-ins.[1]

The first drive-in in Europe apparently was in Italy. It opened on August 19, 1957, just outside Rome on the highway linking Rome with its beach at Ostia. With no Italian word for ozoner, the theater was called Drive-In Cine. The snack bar was called just that, in English. So much use of English brought forth many complaints from Italians who lamented the Americanization of their country. On tap at the refreshment stand were such American staples as Coca-Cola, popcorn, ice cream, and hot dogs side by side with Italian favorites such as espresso. Jointly financed by MGM and an Italian company, this drive-in had a 121-by-69-foot screen, accommodated 750 cars and 250 scooters, and was built for an estimated cost of $1.5 million. Indoor theaters in Rome charged about one dollar admission. At the Drive-In Cine admission was about fifty cents (then three hundred lire) for each car plus about eighty cents (five hundred

The Drive-In Cine near Rome, Italy, in 1957. It held 750 cars and 250 motor scooters.

Denmark's first drive-in, near Copenhagen, when it opened in 1961. With no speaker poles, each patron received a tiny transistor radio to pick up the sound track. The radios were collected after the show.

lire) for each person in the vehicle. Motorcyclists and scooter drivers paid fifty cents per head, nothing for their vehicles. Opening night attraction was an Italian film, *Nonna Sabella*. When a foreign film was screened, patrons could listen to the dubbed Italian soundtrack or, by flipping a switch on their speaker, hear the film in its original language.[2]

After that first one opened in Rome, the growth of ozoners in Europe was very slow. Eleven years later there were reportedly just four drive-ins in all of Europe—Rome, Stockholm, Madrid, and Toulon in France. This number may underestimate to some degree; however, they were clearly not in abundance on the European mainland. When a second one was planned for France, near Cointrin, promoters were planning to hype the fact that patrons could smoke in their autos as a major selling point. The practice was then banned at indoor houses in France. In order to placate those who opposed the desecration of the French language by the use of English phrases, *franglais*, the promoters called the ozoner not "le drive-in" but *le ciné-auto*.[3]

Denmark's first opened near Copenhagen in 1961. Built in an old gravel pit, holding 550 cars, beer was sold at the snack bar, in addition to the usual fare. Minus the standard in-car speakers and posts, this theater provided each car with a tiny transister radio to receive the film's soundtrack.[4]

In other areas of the world, Mexico got its first outdoor theater when the Auto Cinema Lomas opened in Mexico City in May 1950. Owned by Raul Castellanos, it held 650 cars. Opening attraction was MGM's *Till the Clouds Roll By*. Mexican president Miguel Aleman turned out to cut the ribbon at the opening ceremonies. Israel's first ozoner, with a nine hundred–car capacity, opened in February 1973 near Tel Aviv.[5]

The 350-car-capacity Auto Cine Juarez at Ciudad Juarez, Chihuahua, Mexico, 1950.

Japan's first drive-in held just 150 automobiles. Located near the city of Iwata, it was part of a recreation center that included a bowling alley, gas station, and restaurants. The extremely high cost of land in that country assured that American-style ozoners would never be possible. By the mid–1980s there seem to have been none in that country at all, with the exception of those resulting from a short-lived experiment by one company. Shochiku-Fuji was a company that produced, distributed, and exhibited films in Japan. In 1983 they utilized the parking lots of shopping malls in Tokyo suburbs as temporary drive-ins. The malls were closed in the evening anyway, enabling the company to rent the parking lots relatively cheaply, 10 percent of the gross box office. Portable 37-by-13-foot screens were trucked in along with portable projection equipment with its own power generator. Sound was delivered to patrons through their car radios. Ken Umebara, company manager, acknowledged that his company "could never justify the cost of constructing drive-ins." During the first year of the experiment, Umebara said, three locations did very well while the remaining two were "so-so." In any event, the experiment quickly failed.[6]

West Germany's first outdoor theater was the Gravenbruch at Frankfurt, which opened around 1967–68. Ten years later the country had eighteen to twenty ozoners, the highest number it would ever have. At that time there were some three thousand indoor theaters in the country. Ironically, eight of the twelve theaters in West Germany that sold the most tickets were drive-ins, while the remaining ozoners were reportedly on the verge of bankruptcy, still existing only because they were part of a large film chain.[7]

Building an ozoner in West Germany was much more costly than in the United States. In 1976 an eight hundred–car capacity facility ran as high as $1.2 million, excluding land, which was normally leased for an average fee of $70,000 per year. Four or five years were often necessary to obtain the appropriate government clearances. Replacement parts were difficult to obtain, since few companies manufactured items catering to such a small segment of the film exhibition industry. As in the United States, German drive-ins customarily never got to screen first-run films, having to wait two or three months after their release. Business at German drive-ins suffered losses in the 1980s, when the country adopted daylight saving time. Rainy weather was also often blamed for keeping customers away. To generate extra income in the 1980s, German ozoners took to opening their gates on Saturdays and Sundays in the daytime to people who wanted to sell or buy used cars. By charging each seller ten dollars, a drive-in could gross $7,000 to $10,000 on a busy weekend.[8]

It appears that the United Kindom has never had even one commercially viable drive-in theater. As in most of Europe, the cost of land makes such a venture unlikely. Furthermore, the British climate works against such a project. American ozoners brag that nothing can shut them down except fog—a noted feature, along with rain, of the British climate. In addition, in the far northern parts of the country, daylight can linger until 9:30 P.M. or later at the height of summer, making early starts impossible.

The few British drive-in ventures have been very primitive affairs, harking back almost to the sheet-between-two-poles types sometimes found in the United States in the 1930s. During the summer of 1983 the Alford Film Society (located near Lincoln, England) operated a drive-in for three nights. Using the side of a building near their indoor venue, this group hung a 12-by-8-foot screen on the wall only to find it far too tiny. Searching for something bigger, they settled on a 20-by-20-foot truck tarpaulin, which they painted white. Projection was with a 16-mm projector placed on the back of a Land Rover. Sound was amplified through two ten-inch speakers. Waitresses were available to serve refreshments. Anyone wanting service simply had to turn on their interior car lights. A capacity crowd turned out on each night; however, capacity was only thirty cars. Some freeloaders watched from outside the fence. These people were sent on their way by turning on the Land Rover's headlights, which shone in their faces, preventing them from seeing. A similar event was staged a couple of years later in the Midlands by the Weston Coyney and Caverswall

Great Britain never had a "regular" drive-in, however, a few makeshift ozoners did appear for a few days at a time, such as this one in the Midlands in 1985. Here a crew is seen erecting a screen for a two-day event to mark British Film Year. Generators were used to supply power for the projection and sound systems. To summon refreshments a patron merely had to turn on his interior lights.

Film Society. This group had a larger area to work with, drawing 270 cars on the first of two nights.[9]

Around that same time Bob Martin began a similar operation in Maidstone, Kent, forty miles southeast of London. A garden-center parking lot by day was transformed into a drive-in at night, with a 25-by-18-foot screen. Martin planned to open other such ventures if this one was successful. It wasn't. London got its first ozoner in 1989; however, it was only for one night. Greenwich Film Festival organizers converted a south London parking lot into a temporary outdoor theater, with a 40-by-15-foot screen. *American Grafitti* was the film screened that June night.[10]

New Zealand has no drive-ins at all due to the fact that government approval for such a venture was withheld for some twenty years. By the time the government was prepared to allow such facilities to be built, it was probably too late. During the mid–1960s a company called Skyline Drive-Ins was formed, with the intent of building at least two drive-ins. Sites were selected but despite its lobbying efforts, this company could never get the needed government approval. Eventually it gave up.

Next was Barry Everard, an Auckland film distributor, who began his efforts around 1973. Everard immediately found the indoor theaters, both chain and independent, to be firmly opposed to his plans to build an outdoor theater. A poll commissioned by Everard found that 41 percent of those questioned said they didn't go to films because of baby-sitting problems. Everard used these facts to push his case with the government. He felt the climate in his country to be ideal for drive-ins, not too cold or too wet. Standing in his way, besides indoor theater owners who wanted no more competition, were a vocal minority of "bluenoses" who opposed the ozoners because of their passion-pit image. Last, all the equipment for the ozoner would have to be imported into New Zealand. Economically difficult times made it unlikely that Everard would be able to obtain permission for the foreign currency necessary to import. After a few years of lobbying Barry Everard gave up.[11]

Finally the government gave in on the issue. In December 1986 Internal Affairs Minister Peter Tapsell announced that restrictions on drive-ins had been lifted. The film industry was to be allowed to run or not run drive-ins based on commercial considerations. The two major theater chains, Amalgamated Theaters and Kerridge-Odeon, both said they had no plans to build. These two companies had jointly formed Skyline Drive-Ins back in the 1960s. Said Joe Moodabe, Amalgamated managing director: "What may have been in demand in the 60s may no longer be in demand in the 80s." The following spring another company announced it was planning to build an ozoner near Auckland, but nothing seems to come of this announcement.[12]

Australia was one country where the outdoor theater did catch on, although it attained nowhere near the penetration that was achieved in the United States. The first drive-in in that country opened in 1954. Within two years every major city, except Sydney, had several. Melbourne, the country's second largest city at more than 2 million then, had close to ten ozoners in operation, with six more to open in 1956. Perth opened its first on October 24, 1955, Australia's third. Within a year or so Western Australia had a dozen in operation. During the year ending July 1957, twenty-one new drive-ins opened in Australia, pushing the total number up near fifty. On April 20 that year an ozoner with a 120-foot screen and capable of holding one thousand autos opened in Perth. In size it was exceeded only by a newly opened drive-in at Sydney, which could accommodate fourteen hundred cars.[13] This particular boom came late, by U. S. standards, but still took place mostly before television's arrival—1956 in Australia. During the middle 1950s the ozoners reportedly all grossed well and didn't adversely affect attendance at indoor theaters.[14]

Despite an ideal climate almost everywhere in Australia for the ozoners, the outdoor theaters quickly went downhill as patronage waned, for the same reasons as in the United States. First television, then videocassettes, cut into patronage. Also cited as a reason for the decline were the police random breath tests on drivers, which caused motorists who liked to drink at drive-ins to stay away.

The Metro Drive-in near Sydney, Australia, 1957. The screen is 120-by-50-feet asbestos board mounted on steel towers.

In the early 1980s a company that owned several drive-ins in Western Australia converted some to indoor-outdoor combinations, the idea being that parents would leave their kids in the car to watch the drive-in film while the parents strolled over to the indoor venue to see a film they wanted to watch.[15] A desperate measure to reverse the decline of the ozoner, it didn't work.

The year 1984 saw many drive-ins finally being closed down permanently. Most were owned by one of the three theater chains in the country. While executives of those companies wouldn't comment on how much attendance had dropped at outdoor theaters, all conceded that most of them operated at a loss. Admission was approximately $5.50 (Australian) per person at the drive-in that year. Melbourne saw the number of its drive-in screens reduced from twenty-two to ten over the period 1982–84. Just as in the United States these drive-ins, built originally near open fields, were then surrounded by development, making the land worth a great deal. Terry Jackman, managing directing of the Hoyts chain, said, "We are seeing the slow stangulation of the drive-in. There will always be a place for some drive-ins but as a large part of the market they have had it. They have been going backwards for the last five years."[16]

Only Canada took the drive-in to heart with as much passion as the United States. At its peak Canada had slightly more than three hundred ozoners in operation, equivalent to over three thousand in the United States since Canada's population is only one-tenth the size of its southern neighbor's. Considering that Canada's climate is nowhere conducive to year-round operation of outdoor theaters, and that Quebec—with one-third of Canada's population—barred them totally until 1967, when the peak had passed, the numbers are even more impressive. Outside the United States, Canada is the only other country to have had operating drive-ins in the 1940s. In all other countries of the world they came in the 1950s or later.

An almost full house at the Delta Drive-In in the Vancouver suburb of Richmond, B.C., Canada, in the early 1950s.

Canada's first ozoner, the Skyway, opened July 10, 1946, near Hamilton, Ontario, in the suburb of Stoney Creek. That same summer one opened on the West Coast in Burnaby, B.C., a suburb of Vancouver. Initially the Skyway used a central speaker to deliver the sound, but as with most such systems this led to a flood of complaints from neighbors about the excessive noise. Less than one year after opening, the Skyway converted to individual in-car speakers.[17]

Quickly the outdoor theater spread to other provinces, except Quebec. That province enacted a law in 1947 prohibiting them. The generally accepted reason was that the Roman Catholic Church—a much stronger and more significant force in Quebec than in any other province—pressured the government to press this legislation as the church was convinced the outdoor theaters were indeed passion pits, not conducive to good moral development. Those more cynically inclined felt that the church exerted pressure simply because they wanted no more head-to-head competition with their own revenue-generating activities, such as evening bingo games. Other laws on the books also worked against the ozoners. Back in 1928 a fire broke out in a Montreal indoor theater. It was only a minor blaze, but it touched off a panic stampede resulting in seventy-eight children being suffocated to death. Immediately thereafter the Quebec legislature passed a law prohibiting children under sixteen from attending films, anywhere, anytime. It was 1961 before this changed and only to the extent that it was amended to allow children ten and over to attend special children's film shows, but only if they were presented between the hours of 9:00 A.M. and 6:00 P.M.[18]

With easing clerical pressure, changing societal attitudes, and different political leaders Quebec finally succumbed to the siren call of the drive-in by passing a law in June 1967 that allowed outdoor theaters to operate in the province. During debate on this bill, opposition members tried unsuccessfully to tack an amendment to the bill that would have allowed only Canadians to own any drive-ins. Even though the drive-in boom was past, the ozoner soon sprouted throughout the province. Twenty years later, in 1988, one million patrons watched films on forty-eight screens at twenty-seven drive-ins, which generated revenue of $4.4 (Canadian) million that year.[19]

With the exception of a somewhat later start, the growth of drive-ins in Canada paralleled that in the United States. Canadian ozoners never played first-run films. Estimates were that up to 75 percent of the audience, at least in the first decade, were family groups. In 1949 admission averaged fifty cents per adult. Each of these adults then spent twelve to fifteen cents at the refreshment counter. Over its normal six-month season in those days, each drive-in averaged around one thousand admissions per day. To build an indoor theater in the downtown area of a Canadian city in 1949 would cost three hundred to three hundred fifty dollars per seat. Drive-ins averaged two hundred to two hundred fifty dollars per car space, however; since each car averaged 3.25 paying customers, the original investment was reduced to sixty-two to eighty-two dollars per space.[20]

Canada even had its own inventor who was going to produce the miracle daylight screen that was so often announced but never surfaced in the United States. Ottawa resident Gordon F. White announced in 1953 that he had invented a screen to allow drive-ins to show films in the daylight. His idea involved a one-piece transparent screen, "energized by a coating of icipolarized material," partly covered by a protective canopy to keep out extraneous light. The projector was enclosed in a "shadow box" behind the screen. White was asking $50,000 for this unit. There were no takers.[21]

Throughout the 1950s the Canadian drive-in season was extended, to seven months in most places except for British Columbia, which squeezed the season to ten months. Many, with the aid of in-car heaters, took to year-round opening, even in Alberta, one of the coldest regions in the country. In size the Canadian ozoner ranged from the one thousand–cars-plus variety all the way down to a twenty-car-capacity unit at Loon Lake, Saskatchewan—perhaps the smallest drive-in in the world.[22]

Norm McDonald opened Edmonton's first drive-in in 1949. When he first approached film distributors for product they all told him he was crazy—that no one would go to an outdoor theater in Edmonton as the sun didn't set until after 10 P.M. from June to September. Yet Edmonton moved on to have more drive-ins than any other city in the country, even though some were triple its size.

McDonald remained involved with Edmonton drive-ins for thirty years. The biggest response he got to a film was in 1959 when he screened Disney's *The Shaggy Dog*. "It ran three weeks and the cars were lined up for 30 blocks almost every night," he said. As in the United States, however, the audience began to change. One survey in 1962 showed that 36 percent of patrons were between twenty-four and thirty-four years of age, 24 percent were between fifteen and twenty-four, while 21 percent were between thirty-five and forty-four. By the 1970s McDonald was alternating his screen fare between soft-core, low-budget porn films, such as *Nazi Love Nest* and *The Erotic Schoolgirls*, and Hollywood big-name action pictures. Sex films drew mostly men by themselves who were either in their early twenties or mid-forties. While these sex films were profitable McDonald said, "Give me a Clint Eastwood or Charlie Bronson movie any day. Everybody comes out. Fathers, mothers, teenagers—everybody. The media makes a big thing about the lack of family films, but do you know something? A Disney film doesn't draw flies compared to an action picture."[23]

On a typical summer night McDonald started his double bill at 10:20 P.M.—the late-setting sun wouldn't permit an earlier start. He found cars lining up at 8:30 P.M. When asked why ozoners were so popular in Edmonton, Norm said, "I can't tell you why Edmonton is the hottest drive-in town in the country. Nobody else can either. Some say it's because there are more unsophisticated people here than anywhere else. Others say it's because Edmonton has one of the highest cars-per-capita ratios on the continent. One theory's as good as the other."[24]

Slowly and relentlessly Canadian drive-ins disappeared. In Alberta they dropped from thirty-five to seventeen from 1973 to 1987. The number of ozoners in Canada reached 242 in 1955, then barely moved at all until 1966, when there were 245. An apparent boom set in, with the total passing 300 during 1974–76 (315 in 1975), but this was illusory, the result of Quebec's suddenly adding a bunch after the lifting of the provincial ban. In 1986–87 the number of Canadian ozoners was 183. The most recent year for which figures are available, 1988–89, has the number of drive-ins in Canada down to 132.[25] Just as in the United States, they are being gobbled up by encroaching cities. Ever-increasing land values make them too valuable to remain outdoor theaters.

Chapter 12

Drive-ins Battle the Elements

Being as open as they are to the elements, drive-ins have had much greater difficulty in dealing with the weather than do their indoor counterparts. All their attempts to ameliorate the climate to their patrons' greater comfort have been singularly unsuccessful.

One of the attempts to air-condition the great outdoors was seen in 1953 at Phoenix, Arizona's, Cinema Park Drive-In. A number of fourteen-foot poles were installed on the lot. Each was topped by vertically mounted propeller blades behind water pipes containing tiny holes. With the blades whirring around, water was forced up the pipes, out the holes, and then blown across the lot in the form of a fine mist. It caused the temperature to drop, said the marketers, several degrees. A few years later a similar invention was announced. Again it was a tall pole with blades mounted on top, horizontally this time. The idea was just to circulate the air, thus lowering the humidity. Models were said to be available especially to control fog and frost as well as humidity. These units, called "Fogmaster" and "Weathermaster," could operate satisfactorily over seven acres or more. Another feature touted was that they helped overcome the mosquito nuisance. Presumably they blew them away.[1]

Winter seemed to be an ideal time to operate a drive-in. With shorter hours of daylight there was no problem in running two complete shows and having the last one end at a reasonable hour. All that had to be done was to find a way to keep patrons comfortable in their automobiles during the cold weather. This was no problem for the ozoners located in the southern parts of the country, but most drive-ins had to close for a portion of the year. A typical shutdown period lasted from early November until the middle of April or the first of May. During the first and last couple of weeks of that period, the theaters might operate only on the weekends.

Some ozoners did nothing to address the problem except to stay open as long as enough patrons kept driving up to make it financially worth their while. These hardy patrons presumably utilized their car heaters to ward off some of the cold. Other operators gave away a gallon of gas, or a coupon for one, to induce patrons to come, idle their engine, and run the car heater at

The "Weathermaster," a 1956 unit featured water pumped through the pipe then sprayed over the lot as a mist by the rotating blade. The idea was to air-condition the lot.

This "Auto-Voice" was supposed to be an in-car speaker and heater, delivering both sound and warm air to the auto through the one tube, 1949.

the ozoner's expense. Not constructed for such an effort, the car heater delivered less-than-adequate heat. It soon was abandoned as a feasible solution to warding off the chill of winter.

When the Chalk Hill Drive-In in Dallas, Texas, gave away a coupon good for one gallon of gas it didn't cost them very much. A nearby gas station agreed to sell the drive-in half a gallon at cost and donate the other half free. The gas station felt it would be a good deal for them, as they didn't expect anybody

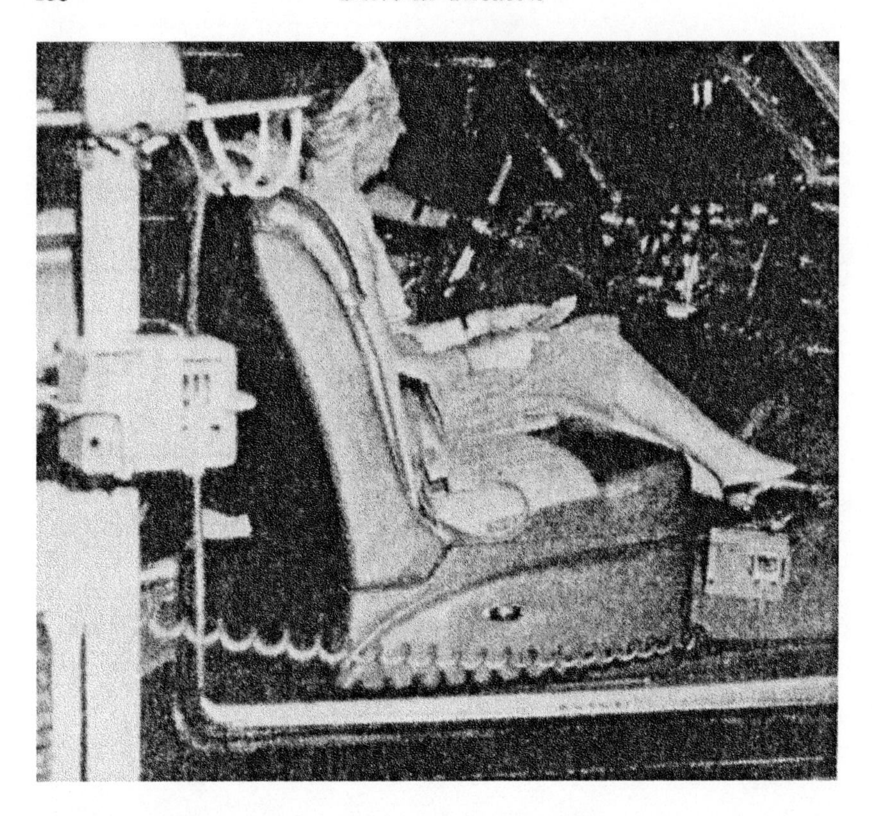

A photo of an in-car heater used by the Walter Reade drive-ins in New Jersey, 1950. This shot was to instruct patrons that the best place for the heater was on the floor of the car.

to show up and just order one gallon, but to buy at least four more. The cost to Chalk Hill for this free gallon of gas they gave away on chilly nights thus was just eight to ten cents.[2]

As early as 1949 more elaborate systems were devised to deliver in-car heat in the winter, and sometimes air-conditioning in the summer. An elaborate piping system was installed underground, connected to each speaker post. In addition to speakers the posts then held large, flexible tubing, which was hooked to the car window, like the speaker, to deliver warm or cold air. These methods were claimed to be well worth the cost, quickly paying back the investment by extending the season.[3]

One of the earliest users of an in-car heating system was Rube Shor, who owned the Twin Drive-In Theatre in Cincinnati, Ohio. With his electric system in place, Shor claimed he had stayed open all but three weeks of the 1950–51 winter. In 1950 an in-car electric heating system cost eight dollars per speaker post (one for every two car spaces) for the wiring of an existing ozoner—one-third less for new construction. Shor estimated an electricity cost of five cents per person when the system was in use. For an electric system the underground installation consisted of wiring instead of piping.

Shor used five hundred–watt heaters. It was said that for every one hundred watts of power provided by the heater, the temperature of an average car was raised by seven degrees. Thus Shor's system elevated the temperature in a car by thirty-five degrees, plus one degree for the body heat of each person in the auto. This kept the car temperature from 57 degrees to 62 degrees when the outside temperature was in the range of 20 to 25 degrees, if two people were in the vehicle. A major problem was that people stole the heaters. To stem this loss Shor handed out a heater at the ticket booth to patrons as they entered, or a brass check to those who didn't want a heater. On leaving, the patron turned in either the heater or the check. Still, theft was so prevalent that manufacturers of these heaters began to produce them in 220-volt models instead of the more normal 110 volts, to try to assist the owners. A drive-in using this type advertised extensively on its screen how to use them, also pointing out that since they operated at 220 volts they were completely useless at a patron's residence on household current.[4]

A system patented in 1949 was called the "Auto-Voice." It consisted of a thinner flexible hose, something of the size found on a vacuum cleaner, the end of which was attached to the car window from a large box on the speaker post. What was unique about the Auto-Voice was that its inventors claimed that both hot air and the film's sound track passed through the one hose without interfering with each other.[5] It didn't sell.

With five hundred–watt heaters the Auto-Voice at least didn't skimp in this area, using the same wattage Shor utilized. Others, like Wilfred P. Smith, economized. Smith just had two hundred–watt heaters at his Ledgewood, New Jersey, outlet, said to be efficient for temperatures down to forty degrees. Smith admitted that below that they weren't "worth a hoot."[6]

Exaggeration seemed to play a part in some of the stories on how much business drive-ins did in winter. Bill Waring, Jr., of Carbondale, Illinois, operated Waring's Auto Theatre where he had 250 heaters in the 530-car lot. Waring claimed that on average he only lost three nights per winter season (December 1 to April 1) due to poor road conditions, excluding Mondays when he was normally closed in the winter. Twenty-two percent of his business came from winter trade, he said, and he said that he operated when the temperature dropped as low as zero degrees.[7]

One inventor came up with an electric in-car heater, which was hung in the car by an employee. To operate it the patron had to feed it coins. This was not a successful idea.[8]

One advantage of an electrically operated system was the lack of the huge and cumbersome flexible ducting, which covered the lot like so many octopus tenacles at ozoners that used forced-air systems. Outweighing this was the high rate of heater theft, 10 percent or more per season, and the cost of electricity. Utility companies sometimes imposed higher rates during certain peak-demand hours—which were precisely the hours the ozoners drew from the system.

Propane heaters were tried in some drive-ins, but with little success. They tended to concentrate their heat all in one spot leaving one patron overly hot while the others in the same car stayed cold. Some states banned them as a fire hazard. To guard against theft of these heaters, one operator required a patron to leave his or her driver's license at the ticket booth when picking up the heater, retrieving it on the way out upon surrender of the heater. This caused a long and tedious traffic tie-up for exiting customers.[9]

Of the few drive-ins that tried an in-car heating technique, most went with an oil-fired system that used ducts six to eight inches in diameter. Nobody stole those things, but even patrons who always carefully hooked the speaker back on the post usually just pushed these giant hot-air hoses out the window onto the ground. Being some three to six or more feet in length, they fell every which way. Cars regularly ran over them.[10]

In the end none of these systems worked. Even if installation costs were reasonable, the cost of upkeep escalated rapidly beyond that level in the eyes of most owners. For the most part drive-in owners understood this, as most never bothered to try them, resisting the lure of articles extolling their virtues. In-car heating systems at the drive-in didn't work because they didn't keep patrons warm and comfortable.

The one element of environmental control at which drive-ins were successful—at least for a time—was insect control, particularly mosquitoes. From the beginning outdoor theaters were plagued by insects. Being in rural or semirural areas, the drive-in was often located near breeding grounds for insects. Being lit up at night, they were a natural magnet for insects of all kinds.

A company in New Jersey came out with a cloth net that was designed to fit over car windows to keep out bugs. Called "Car-Net," they came two to a package, one for the driver's side window and one for the passenger side. This net took only seconds to install, fitted snugly on all types of car doors, and didn't interfere with in-car speakers. When the manufacturer pretested his product he found half his sales were made to patrons who had children asleep in the car. Drive-in owners were urged to sell Car-Net directly to patrons, who could reuse them throughout the season, storing them in the glove compartment between visits.[11]

Far and away the most popular method of dealing with insects at outdoor theaters was by pesticide spraying, using DDT. The most-used method was by foggers with an oil-based DDT insecticide. Some considered this method objectionable due to the kerosene-like smell of the fog and the oily deposit or residue that was sometimes left on cars. Shrubbery could also be damaged by the residue. The problem was thought to be the oil base, not the DDT. Other

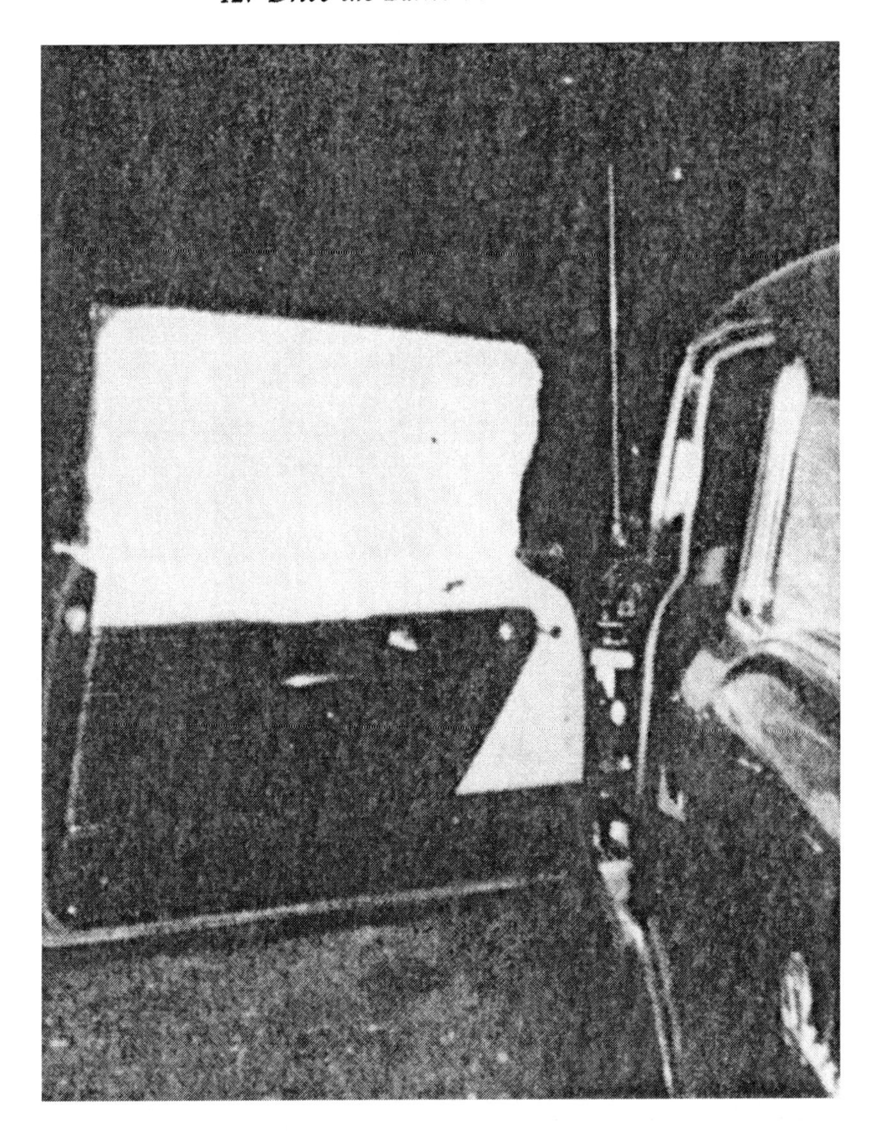

The "Car-Net" was to keep insects out while allowing the car window to remain open (about 1956).

methods used were water-based insecticides and dusts. DDT was the mainstay in all. Miami's Boulevard Drive-In used a water-based solution of 2.5 percent DDT. Emulsified, it clung to leaves, branches, and grass. Spraying was done at the Boulevard during daylight hours, daily during months of high insect activity.[12]

In Woodbridge, New Jersey, the Walter Reade circuit's ozoner used a

A 1949 ad for drive-in owners, touting the advantages of "death-dealing" DDT fog to get rid of mosquitoes and keep them out.

A DDT fog is sprayed at a New Jersey drive-in to control insects, 1949.

Pesky Pests Pilfer Profit

"SWINGFOGGING" Gets it Back

Protect your Drive-In and Concession area against mosquitos, gnats, eye-midges and pests that cause patron discomfort and reduced receipts.

Insure patron relaxation and profit protection— "SWINGFOG" YOUR DRIVE-IN.

Know More About "SWINGFOG" Portable Pest Control Units

SWINGFOG DISTRIBUTORS—c o The FOG-AIR Company

415 LEXINGTON AVENUE, NEW YORK 17, N. Y. • MUrray Hill 7-1488

A 1956 ad for a hand-held fogging machine to control insects at drive-ins.

10 percent DDT solution with a fuel oil base around the outside of the property. Inside the lot a lighter solution, 5 percent DDT and 10 percent chlordane, with a kerosene base, was used. Even inside the concession building was sprayed with what was described as a "non-toxic" solution. Finally, soluble capsules containing DDT concentrate were placed in the drainage ditches, catch basins, and other areas where water could lie for a lengthy period. This treatment was carried out every three weeks in May and early June, then every two weeks after that.[13]

Fogging could be done by a person wearing equipment on his back or larger equipment could be used, mounted on a truck or Jeep. Sometimes an outdoor theater owner bought his own fogging equipment or cooperated with a few other nearby owners to purchase a set between them. Usually, though, outside companies were hired to do the fogging. Alexander Cochran was one such contractor who ran a fogging service. He operated out of Montclair, New Jersey. In the summer of 1948 he treated nine ozoners in that state. Cochran used 10 percent DDT with Sovacide F, a special fog oil. According to him, this fog left no objectionable residue. It didn't stain or smear windshields, nor was it harmful to humans. Ideally Cochran liked to make his first spraying early in June, fogging inside and outside the drive-in. No more than three applications a week were needed after that. If he started early enough, Alexander found that by August the insecticide had built up such a residue that fogging was then needed only once every ten days or so. By Labor Day his services were no longer needed. However, if he got a late season start on the problem, fogging was needed right through September. During periods of heavy insect infestations it was necessary to do an extra fogging at night right after the last show let out. Cochran sprayed everything—inside the projection booth, inside the ticket booth, and inside the snack bar.[14]

Moran McDaniel operated the first drive-in in Galveston County, Texas. He was also one of the few people in the area to own his own fogger. Recalled Moran, "That was before the county did any fogging. On occasion, I'd get asked to fog football fields. People would even want me to spray for their outdoor parties." During the early years McDaniel's theater advertised, "We have large, powerful spraying machines, covering the entire area daily, building a concentration of DDT over the entire surface of the drive-in. However, should any individual become annoyed with insects, we will be glad to spray their auto anytime."[15]

At the Trail Drive-In in Houston, Texas, insect fogging became a spectator sport. Operator Jack Farr promoted his insecticide spraying with top billing in his advertisements, inviting the public to come out to see it in action. After those ads ran they did, in large numbers. Farr said the Trail became so packed and plugged up that people parked outside then walked in on foot to virtually jam the theater.[16] A deadly, carcinogenic poison, DDT was banned almost totally by the United States government in 1972.

Once again outdoor theaters were plagued by insects. There just weren't nearly as many customers to be annoyed anymore. Drive-ins that did have an insect problem dealt with it like the remaining ozoners in Arkansas in the middle 1980s. They sold their customers aerosol insect repellents and mosquito coils.[17]

Chapter 13

Drive-ins Pray for a Miracle

Some drive-in owners might indeed have prayed for their miracle. All fervently hoped for it. Certainly much money was spent trying to produce it. That desired miracle was the daylight-containment screen, which would solve so many problems. Its arrival was heralded as imminent in the 1950s, the 1960s, the 1970s, and the 1980s. It never arrived.

Like Dracula, drive-ins fear the daylight—one of the greatest banes to drive-in owners—for they can't operate during those hours. The days with the most daylight come in the heart of summer, right at a peak time for the drive-in season. Starting as late as they have to makes it difficult to get a second show started and over at a reasonable hour. This is a particular problem on weekdays, when people have to get up early for work the next day. As might be expected, the ozoners have always been vociferous opponents of daylight saving time. Their lobbying against this measure failed, for it arrived permanently right across the United States in 1967. Before that time the change to daylight time came and went randomly in various cities, regions, and states.

One of the earliest documented fights against daylight saving time came in California in 1949. The measure was being voted on in that fall's election. Sero Drive-In Theatres, operators of four ozoners in Southern California, screened special trailers in their theaters urging patrons to vote against putting their clocks ahead one hour. This issue came to the floor of the national TOA convention. Pacific Drive-In executive Charles Caballero insisted that delegates be polled and that TOA take an official stand against daylight saving time. A delegate named Leonard Goldenson said the matter was purely a local one. He was shouted down by drive-in owner Sidney Lust of Washington, D.C., who stated it had done harm to attendance in his area. TOA convention chairman Roy Cooper handled the fight by turning the question over to a committee.

California did institute daylight saving time, and ozoners' fears proved unfounded. It was reported in 1951 that with regard to admissions, the majority of theaters were equal or up over their figures under standard time. More important: "At the concessions, daylight savings has been a bonanza for some ozoners." It seems that the family came earlier, with the result they stocked

A colonial mansion design at Sidney Lust's Drive-In, about 1953.

up at the refreshment stand. The preshow concession business was greater than the take at intermission — normally by far the high spot. Pacific Drive-In, with sixteen ozoners, saw concession sales increase 50 percent after daylight saving time was introduced.[1]

In spite of these results, drive-in owners would continue to fight the time change. Some would always consider it a major reason for their decline. Longtime Texas operator Moran McDaniel looked back from the mid–1980s to recall: "Twilight time began for drive-ins when daylight savings time rolled in. Movies couldn't start till it got dark around 9 P.M. or after. All the big newspapers wanted daylight savings time. And they all owned television stations with one exception — the *San Antonio Light* — and they were on our side, but that wasn't enough." Texas reporter Orlando Blackburn commented at that time: "It is easy to understand how this would effect movies. Either you have less sleep or less movies."[2]

Also in the mid–1980s Jerry Dean, an Arkansas reporter, writing on the decline of the drive-in, cited daylight time as one of the factors affecting business negatively. More unequivocal was Jack Absher of Kentucky, who closed the last of three drive-ins he once owned in 1986. When asked why business fell off, Absher replied: "I blame it solely on daylight savings time."[3] There is nothing to suggest that daylight saving time had any impact on drive-in attendance. Figures for the 1963 and 1967 censuses show virtually no change in number of outdoor theaters or receipts. Almost every state instituted daylight time in 1967, so any effect should show in the census figures.

In the early drive-ins the screen tower was usually made of wood, which tended to rot over the years. By the 1970s and 1980s, the majority of towers were constructed from steel—more costly but much longer lasting. The screen itself was made of weatherproof panels of a variety of materials such as plywood, asbestos, aluminum, galvanized iron, transite, among others, to which white paint was applied. In some cases the surface was finally plastered before it was painted to ensure a smooth surface. However, the panel joints or seams were never mentioned in the literature as causing a problem for the viewers. One of the more commonly used screens consisted of 4-by-8-foot waterproof plywood panels joined together. Several undercoats of paint were sprayed on followed by a final coat of flat white paint.

Whenever new material was introduced as a drive-in screen, it was always heralded as being a great improvement over plywood or asbestos. Always it failed to deliver. An all-aluminum screen was hyped in 1955, with the claim that it offered three times more brightness than a normal screen. It would permit ozoners to double the size of their lot since the image could be seen from farther away. A more exotic screen, of enameled porcelain, was introduced in 1964, with the claim that it offered a 25 percent gain over other screens.[4] If these newer screens couldn't deliver on their promises, they could certainly be depended on to cost more than a wood screen.

Even when newly painted, however, the outdoor theater screen offered only one-fifth the brightness of an indoor screen. This was because the drive-in screen was much larger. To illuminate it as much as an indoor house required an energy system so intense that the film would immediately burn. For example, an ozoner with a 50-foot-high screen needed 22,500 watts for full brightness. Typically used was a 4,000-watt xenon system. Larger systems were available but even a 6,000- or 7,000-watt system was considered too risky—likely to incinerate the film.[5]

These screens were subject to considerable weather damage. Ideally a screen should be painted once every year or two. After six or so coats, there was little point in adding yet another layer; a resurfacing was then necessary. In 1977 it cost an estimated $400 to $1,500 to clean and paint a screen, depending on size and condition. Refacing cost $2,000 to $3,000.[6] To save money some owners didn't paint or reface as often as they should have. Special, more reflective paints existed, but some owners used cheaper paints, the same ones that might be applied to the walls inside a house or apartment. Those who saved money that way made the poor visibility of the ozoner image that much worse. But not to worry, the miracle screen would solve everything.

"Daylight Drive-Ins Are Next," trumpeted the *Hollywood Reporter* in early 1953. This new development was said to be then on the market. It promised to permit daylight operation of the outdoor theater, with a "vastly improved picture quality." Its effect on the box office was going to be "stimulating."[7] That this attempt at achieving the miracle aborted didn't bother the industry too much. Ozoners were still in their period of heady ascent. Even with the late starts—nine-thirty or later in some northerly locales at the height of the season—drive-ins were very profitable. Each succeeding shot at the miracle would become more frantic and desperate, as by then the industry was in rapid decline.

The next major attempt came in the mid-1960s. A committee of TOA members investigated a pilot project in 1965. This daylight screen was more modest, in that it would enable ozoners to start their shows an hour or two earlier, as opposed to all-day operation. Some sources estimated that an hour or two's earlier start would increase box-office gross by 25 percent. The major problem with any of these proposed screens was how to diminish the reflection of natural light while at the same time amplifying the reflection of the projected picture.

The National Association of Theatre Owners (NATO) established a formal committee, the Drive-In Technical Committee, to shepherd the project along. Under consideration was a screen composed of tiny mirrors. Robert Selig, an executive with Pacific Drive-In Theatres, was chairman of this committee. His company was ready to kick in $25,000 if the project looked feasible. "The potential of an effective, efficient daytime screen," he said, "is so great in terms of dollars and other benefits that it needs no elaboration." So great was the problem of twilight operation that ozoners always tried to run color features, as color registered much better at twilight than did black and white. If they had to run a monochrome feature, they would often start off with a number of color cartoons.

That the ozoner industry was worried about its status at that time can be seen in Selig's search for other innovations. The daylight screen was number one priority, but Selig also was to investigate the daytime use of drive-ins; to try to generate some revenue during the many "dead" hours in an ozoner's day. Perhaps, they thought, ozoners could be used as park-and-ride lots in conjunction with public transit. Selig was also badgering the distributors "to furnish prints which would improve the quality of light on drive-in screens." That is, if the drive-ins couldn't innovate an improvement, they wanted somebody else to do it for them. Given the less-than-cooperative relations between ozoner and film distributor, it was no surprise when the latter failed to respond.

Some sort of test of this pilot screen took place early in 1967 in Los Angeles. The company trying to sell the screen called the test a success. Drive-in owners could do no better than to try to save face by rendering a noncommittal verdict of "encouraging." Aborted miracle number two was history.[8]

During the second try no mention was made of containment of the picture for while the first complaints about porn playing on ozoner screens had started, they hadn't yet reached major proportions. They would have though, at the time of attempt number three. It seemed that the companies and individuals promoting their miracles offered the drive-ins exactly what the theaters needed. As the problems of ozoners multipled, so did the number of solutions offered by the miracle screen.

So great was the need for the miracle that in 1972 no fewer than five techniques were under consideration. That was just after a Supreme Court decision in which Chief Justice Warren Burger implied that cities and states would be on safe constitutional grounds if they enacted specific legislation prohibiting ozoners from showing sexually explicit films if those films could be seen from outside the grounds by motorists, nearby residents, and so on. As many as twenty-six different jurisdictions had then passed, or had pending, such bills.

So it was in the spring of 1972 that the *Hollywood Reporter* trumpeted: "Revolutionary new process to permit daylight operation of drive-in theatres . . . the greatest innovation in motion picture screens since CinemaScope and Panavision." First up was Agis I. Mihalakis, whose demonstration evoked the above quote. Mihalakis had a screen, he claimed, that would allow those earlier starts of an hour or two, that would "contain" the picture within the property of the ozoner. That is, patrons just inside the back fence would see perfectly while anybody just outside the fence would see only a blank screen. The containment idea was then more important to owners than the daylight aspect. Mihalakis's screen would also allow up to three separate films to be projected simultaneously on the same screen. Each patron would only see one film. Thus a person on the left third of the lot would see one film, while a patron in the middle third could see a different film, and so on. This was a handy development for the huge drive-ins, which were becoming white elephants in the same manner as the huge indoor houses had done previously. This would allow the twinning or tripling of a big ozoner into more economical units of a smaller size without making any alterations to the property, except buying the screen.

Mihalakis had an embossed stainless steel screen composed of quarter-inch lenticules (small, curved mirror surfaces)—essentially a dimpled steel screen. When he gave a demonstration indoors on a tiny prototype, he simultaneously projected two stills and one motion picture. Those present reported that this innovation seemingly did what its promoter said it would. No one wondered why an innovation intended for the outdoors would be given a demonstration indoors under "simulated" daylight, but then these were desperate men. Mihalakis enthused that his newly formed company could produce forty screens a week within the next six months. As to the price, the best he could do was to peg it at "a very small fraction of $100,000." He could be no more specific. As if he weren't offering enough, he promised sharply enhanced color fidelity and brightness as well as assurances that grain would not be seen beyond seventy-five feet. (The first row at a drive-in was normally farther from the screen than seventy-five feet.) While the Mihalakis proposal would remain technically under consideration by NATO for some time, no more would be heard of it.[9]

Later in 1972, during its convention, NATO considered five different proposals for a screen. One was that of Mihalakis's while three others were somewhat similar. The fifth was a project initiated by NATO itself when it approached the Motion Picture & Television Research Center with its problem. Chief scientist Peter Vlahos undertook to find a solution. NATO was not involved as an organization in funding the project. A group of three dozen drive-in owners got together to fund the Vlahos project by raising $100,000 among them. One selling point of this plan was that it involved only patents issued between 1914 and 1925. This meant that the technology was in the public domain and could be used without cost. All four other methods involved active patents, which required payment to use the underlying technology.

With the funding to develop a full-size prototype screen, Vlahos went to work. His system, like the others, consisted of a series of lenticules on sheets 1.5 by 2.5 feet, electroformed of pure nickel, with the surface coated by rhodium or chromium. Various technical problems cropped up immediately, with the lenticule needing to be redesigned. The timetable for a demonstration was set back, and set back, and set back again. Vlahos did announce, as he ironed out bugs, that because of the redesigned lenticule, the new screen would increase screen brightness, making for an even earlier starting time than he had been hoping for.[10]

As the project dragged on, costs increased, both to the funding group as well as the projected cost of the screen to potential purchasers. At first the estimated price of one of these screens was to be two to four dollars per square foot, comparable to a conventional drive-in screen. An average screen was on the order of 50 by 100 feet, or 5,000 square feet. By mid–1974 the estimated cost of one of these new screens was up to $30,000. The most commonly used screens then were either plywood sheets painted white or white asbestos, either of which were priced at approximately $15,000. Selig still insisted that the new screen would be well worth the price with its brighter picture and its ability to allow earlier starting times. Even this early start was then reduced to perhaps twenty to thirty minutes in southern locales, ranging up to one hour in extreme northern areas of the United States. The dream of a true daylight screen that would allow operation at any time of the day was pronounced dead—for a time—as the sun was just too strong.[11]

Time continued to pass with no results. As the cost rose the innovators tried to soften this impact by pointing out to owners how to save money with it in other ways. The new screen was to increase screen brightness fivefold, making it equal to the brightness of a screen at an indoor house. Previously this had been heralded as a great bonus for the patrons. Now Vlahos suggested operators negate that totally, or at least by half, to save money. He said: "For one quarter the energy he uses today, he can have the same picture he has now. For one half the size lamp bulb, he can still have a picture that's 2½ times brighter than now."[12] While once touted to have a fifty-year lifespan, the innovation would be good for just twenty years, it was now admitted.

Finally, a demonstration was held in spring 1975, not with a full-size prototype but only a tiny one. The full-size screen would be about two thousand times larger than the tiny sample piece. A company by the name of Pichel Industries was then in charge of marketing the screen. Results of the demonstration ranged, said observers, from "excellent" to the much gloomier "some engineering" has to be done. The pilot project would cost a "few thousand" dollars more than the $128,000 already paid by the group of funding drive-in owners. Originally Vlahos had developed his lenticules on the assumption that all drive-ins had a similar shape, layout, and so on. When he discovered that they didn't — that many were very irregular — he realized his lenticules couldn't be fine-tuned enough to cover all possible situations. He began to envision "a family of five or six screens" to cope with installation problems. The one most suited to the configuration of an individual ozoner would be installed and then fine-tuned. Estimates of $30,000 for the screen were too low. The cost of the containment screen would run "considerably higher."[13]

Things got desperate as the whole project started slipping away. NATO announced in September 1975 that the containment screen was a reality. In an enthusiastic letter sent out to drive-in owners, NATO said that Pichel Industries was ready to take orders for the screen. If enough letters of intent were received, Pichel would then proceed to build a prototype full-size screen. None had then been built. Robert Selig enthused: "The unbelievable, unpredictable problems have been solved. Inside and outside containment are now a reality. Vastly improved light is a fact. Earlier starting times are genuinely possible." Wilton Holm, Vlahos's boss, asserted the new screen "may well revolutionize the drive-in industry." Six months after that, Pacific Theatres, owners of a chain of drive-ins in the Southwest, announced they would build the prototype at their own expense to hasten the availability of the containment screen to the drive-in market.[14] And that's where it died, never to be heard from again.

The concept, however, was one that would never die. In 1983 an industry analyst, Harris Plotkin, looked at the potential impact of an earlier starting time on the drive-in industry. Plotkin concluded that by starting three hours earlier or so, weekday grosses could increase by 25 to 60 percent. Ozoners could introduce weekday "early bird discounts," which had been so successful at indoor theaters. Weekend grosses could be increased by a similar amount. Concession revenue would rise because people who came to the drive-in earlier would be more likely to eat their dinner there. With a containment screen, state and local authorities would get off the backs of the ozoners, allowing those so inclined to show as much X and R fare as they liked. This, said Plotkin, could increase profits by 10 to 30 percent. It could all add up to as much as $20,000 in extra profit per year per drive-in. All this analysis was undertaken by Plotkin at the request of Protolite Corp., which had developed a new containment screen. It was made of stainless steel composed of small, curved mirror surfaces. Brightness was four times better with Protolite's innovation than with a regular drive-in screen. As well, it offered better contrast, color, and sharpness while containing the picture within the drive-in's property. Oh, yes, it was a true daylight screen. Operators could begin their shows at any time during the day. Protolite would very shortly, reported Plotkin, give a demonstration.[15] Needless to say, they were never heard from again.

With the passage of time and the continued decline in the number of existing drive-ins, the likelihood that this concept of a miracle screen will stay dead increases. There soon won't be enough drive-ins to make the development of such a screen economically feasible, even if technology advances to the point where it becomes a real possibility. The remaining ozoners operate on a season-to-season basis. Few would be willing to invest a lot of capital for a new screen that may not reverse a decline. There is no point in innovating for something that will soon be extinct. Drive-ins have passed the point where such an innovation could radically alter the course of their future.

One thing that did emerge from all those efforts to produce a miracle screen was how poor the picture quality was on a normal drive-in screen, in terms of brightness. The American National Standards Institute had a standard of sixteen foot-lamberts for indoor screens. Most drive-ins measured between two and four foot-lamberts.

This standard was never applied to ozoners because, said the institute: "Outdoor theatres have been excluded from this Standard because of their inability to meet it. It is recommended that outdoor theatres approach the indoor standards as closely as possible in view of the fact that the same release prints are generally used for both types of theatres." Having only three foot-lamberts was bad enough, but some of the largest ozoners had only one foot-lambert, one-sixteenth as bright as that required of indoor houses. Musing over this number, one observer wrote that it "gives food for thought and shows how very adaptable the human eye, and perhaps how very amenable the human being, can be."[16]

Vlahos stated that screen light intensity in ozoners was less than 20 percent of that found in an indoor house. When once touting the advantages of the never-to-arrive miracle screen Selig said: "For the first time in drive-in history the light will be improved to a minimum of five times—equal to or better than the indoor theatre. Drive-ins have never had adequate light, because so much was diffused or spread out." Motion Picture & Television Research

Center director Wilton Holm noted that the proposed containment screen would "increase the well-known marginal-to-poor screen brightness of drive-ins by approximately five times."[17]

What it all meant was that when you went to the drive-in you had a hard time seeing the picture—much, much harder than at an indoor theater. It was something the industry never mentioned except when it occasionally slipped out in conjunction with other matters. It was a problem the drive-in industry never solved. Oh, yes—a 1987 newspaper report said that research was then under way in Japan on a new drive-in screen that would contain the images within the lot.[18]

Chapter 14
Drive-in Sound

RCA's development, in 1941, of the in-car speaker with individual volume control revolutionized the drive-in industry. The speaker's use was delayed until 1946 as resources were diverted to the war effort. It was reasonably sturdy, compact, and weatherproof. The coiled cord it came with made it easier for people to handle and move around, as compared with the earlier long, straight cord of the 1941 model. Prior to this innovation a whole line of speakers would often go dead if there was a short circuit in just one. This was not a problem with RCA's development. For the first time a drive-in patron could close the car window almost all the way and still hear the film's sound track. In a small way this expanded the operating season for an ozoner in the colder areas of the country.[1]

Other companies besides RCA soon began to manufacture these speakers. Every new drive-in installed them. All the older ones quickly converted to this system. For about thirty years this remained the only system in use in the industry. It was a method with many disadvantages, however: There was a high initial cost of buying hundreds of speakers, poles, and wiring and of trenching the lot to lay the necessary wiring. Yearly costs for upkeep and maintenance were high reflecting worn speakers, damaged posts, vandalism, speakers accidentally ripped from the posts by patrons who forgot to put them back as they left the lot, and theft of speakers. Daily checks had to be carried out on the lot to look for defective speakers.

Speaker theft got so bad that some theaters implemented a policy of offering rewards, fifty or one hundred dollars for example, for reporting speaker theft. Those who initiated such policies claimed that they worked. A common way for the owner to publicize this was to run trailers at the theater explaining the rewards. Other owners said this method didn't work—that it merely drew attention to the problem, thereby making it worse. Some ran trailers to remind customers to replace the speakers at the end of the show so patrons would prevent any chance of a broken window. (There was no real chance of that happening as the cord always gave first.) Still other owners adopted their own methods of attempting to control the problem. One had employees patrol troublesome areas taking down license numbers, trying to prevent theft before it happened. A disproportionately high percentage of speaker thefts reportedly took place in areas teenagers liked to park. One writer said speaker theft ran as high as sixty units a month at some venues.[2]

Bill Poglitsch was employed as a salesman for a Chicago chain company in 1953, when he attended the Double Drive-In in Cincinnati. After he pulled into a parking space, Bill discovered that the speaker was missing. Later he asked theater manager Raymond Marks if this was a problem. Marks replied: "A problem! In the spring when attendance is low, we lose about 20 speakers weekly at each theatre. In the summer, when attendance is high, the number jumps to about 35." Each speaker cost as much as ten dollars. Poglitsch considered the problem, then suggested securing the speakers to their posts with a straight-link chain. At first Marks was skeptical, fearing it might damage car finishes and break car windows if an auto pulled out with the speaker still attached. Nevertheless, he agreed to try it. When all the speakers had been attached to the posts with the one dollar chain, it was reported that no more speakers were stolen—although there was some evidence of attempted theft. A happy Marks said, "I'll spend a dollar anytime to save $10."[3]

At some theaters a steel cable was used to attach the speaker to the post. In fact, the use of such material to secure speakers was short lived because automobiles did suffer damage when they inadvertently pulled away with the speaker still attached. Windows were broken. Doors were damaged. In one instance a car door was torn off.[4] The Sky-Vue Drive-In tried to end the problem by using special speakers that had to be plugged into the junction box on the posts. Patrons entering the ozoner were issued a speaker or a small tag that read, "No speaker issued." Attendants patrolled the exit ramps collecting speakers from departing patrons.[5]

Hope that a way could be found to carry the sound over the car's radio was expressed as early as the start of the 1950s. One writer envisioned that this development would make drive-ins even cheaper to construct, as it would eliminate posts and wiring. With no posts to hinder parking, this writer thought, the number of cars per acre could be increased from sixty-five to one hundred.[6] One of the earliest, and unsuccessful, methods of transmitting drive-in sound over the car radio was that devised and patented in 1951 by R. J. Singleton, assistant manager of the Eagle Drive-In Theatre, in Hobbs, New Mexico. Singleton's method involved the installation of a small black box inside the car, connected to the radio. Holes had to be drilled in the dashboard, if none were already there. Rigging a car to accommodate this device took an average of thirty minutes, ranging from five to fifteen minutes for a Ford to one hour for a Packard. If a theater wanted to convert to this system, several weeks' notice had to be given to allow patrons to have their cars outfitted. Those who chose not to have this device installed could still attend the

Eagle. They were handed a plug-in speaker as they entered the lot. Eagle's management tried to discourage theft of these speakers by taking down the name, address, and license number of the customer.[7] Singleton's system didn't catch on.

Worst of all for drive-in patrons everywhere was the quality of the sound. If the drive-in failed the customers in the video portion of its presentation it failed them again with the audio portion. Sound fidelity produced by the speakers was barely adequate for dialogue. It was useless for music. Volume, even when turned up high, was insufficient for some. When patrons compared drive-in sound quality with that from an indoor theater or a home stereo system or even a television set, it clearly finished last.

More serious work on producing car radio sound started in 1966. Fred J. Schwartz owned a chain of theaters in New York State. Having already enjoyed the film *Zorba the Greek* at an indoor theater, he went again to see it that summer at a local drive-in. Shocked by the experience, he said: "It was not the same picture. The sound quality was so bad that the film lost much of its impact. I decided to explore ways and means of achieving better sound."[8]

Thinking of using the car radio in some fashion to deliver the sound, Schwartz approached the automobile industry but found no one willing to do any research in that area. An acquaintance then steered him to William Halstead, who was a leader in the electronic low-power broadcast field. After ten years of work Halstead had perfected a cable to meet low-power broadcast needs. What was needed was a radio signal strong enough to overcome interference in the field while restricting reception of the signal to a very limited area. Halstead's company had just installed such a system, using the car radio, on an approach road to Los Angeles International Airport. When motorists got to within a certain distance, they could tune their car radios to a specific AM frequency to receive flight information and road reports. Many other places such as hospitals, college stations, shopping malls, and army camps used this method. The two men got together to adapt the system for a drive-in.

Schwartz sold his theaters, and in the 1970s he formed a company, Cinema Radio, to market the system. Transmitting a radio signal normally requires a license from the FCC, but if certain specific low-power conditions are met, which Cinema Radio did, then no license is required. With this system special co-axial cable was laid underground, throughout the drive-in lot. A car sitting over the cable picked up the signal from this "leaking" cable on an AM frequency. Sound was not transmitted outside the drive-in. Speakers and posts were eliminated entirely.

With an estimated 97 percent of cars equipped with an AM radio, the time seemed right. For those who came to the drive-in with no car radio, it was suggested that they be loaned a small transistor set by the exhibitor. It was advised that a deposit be required for the transistor radio, "which, even if the movie fan forgets to return it, can also spell a small profit."[9]

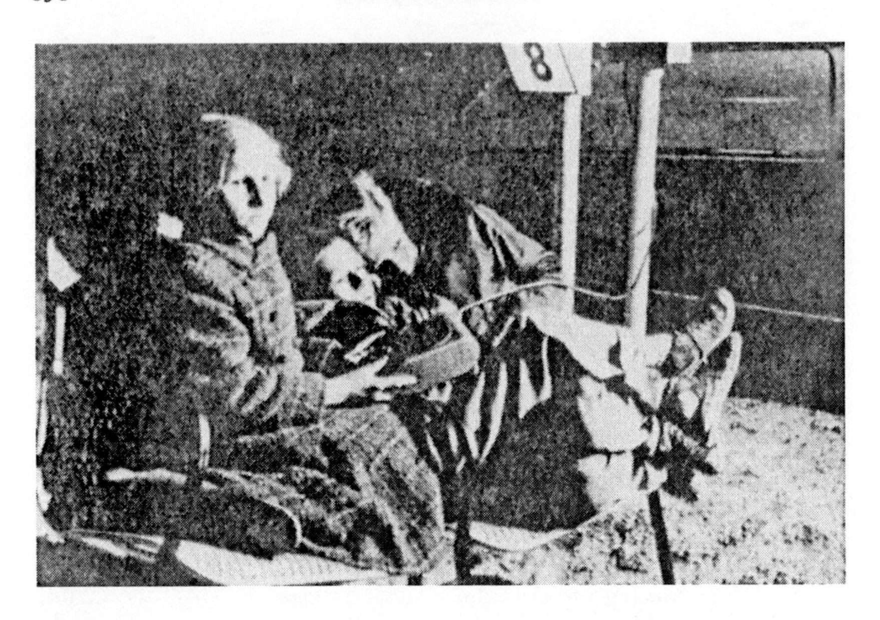

Kids enjoy the show from outside the car in 1955 at Long Island's Bay Shore–Sunrise Drive-In.

Some worry was expressed that the new system would be resisted by those afraid that playing the radio with the motor off would drain the battery. With old tube radios this would have happened, however, Cinema Radio claimed that all automobile radios were then solid state, which meant an ozoner customer could run the car radio as long as ten hours and still use less energy than it took to start the vehicle just once. Besides a much-improved sound quality, Schwartz claimed a big cost advantage for this method. For a thousand-car drive-in, Cinema Radio estimated a cost of $7,000 for installation, compared to a conventional speaker installation of $24,000 just for wiring (12,000 feet at $2 a foot). In addition Cinema Radio charged a license fee for transmitter and cable of $1.25 per car space per year. Since no posts or speakers were used, yearly maintenance would drop to near zero. Schwartz estimated that a drive-in with conventional in-car speakers then spent $5.00 to $7.00 per speaker annually on upkeep. An added bonus was said to be a possible enlargement of an ozoner's capacity, with the elimination of all posts.[10]

Just a few years after Schwartz started his research, a second innovator began work on a new drive-in audio system. This was Kiichi Sekiguchi in the unlikely country of Japan, which (as we have seen) was not noted for its drive-in population. In 1970 a major department store called Sekiguchi in to consult on problems they were having in attracting people to a large suburban shopping mall just outside Tokyo. The solution Sekiguchi came up with was to build a drive-in, the Nissan Sky Theatre, on the roof of the complex. The idea was that people would park their cars on the roof, shop until it got dark, then watch a film.

It was a novel idea, which was financially backed by the Japanese government. At first Sekiguchi wanted to build a standard American drive-in, but the idea was vetoed as the owners didn't want speaker poles installed on their mall roof. Coaxial cable was used instead, with the car radio. Word of this unique drive-in system made its way to the United States. Soon Sekiguchi was in this country doing research. Feeling that coaxial cable would be too costly to use in the conversion of existing ozoners, he spend months researching until he finally found a way to convert his system, Cine-Fi, to the needs of American drive-ins, using the wiring already in place, or field wiring as it was called. With this system the Cine-Fi transmitter picked up the film sound track, sent it from the booth out over the existing field wiring to the speaker post. In place of the removed speaker was a small antenna fastener cable, which was clipped to a patron's car aerial or attached by suction cups to the windshield of autos with hidden aerials. The patrons then tuned the car radio to the appropriate AM frequency.[11]

Cine-Fi was a joint venture between Sekiguchi and Pacific Theatres. The latter quickly installed this system in the ozoners in its chain. The Winnetka Drive-In in the San Fernando Valley achieved a breakthrough when 20th Century–Fox allowed it to screen *Star Wars* when it was still in first-run status because of this sound innovation. Said Pacific executive Ted Minsky: "Fox, when first approached, refused the very thought of drive-in exposure. But, when one of the picture's producing executives tried out the AM radio system, he enthusiastically recommended that the test go ahead."[12] Cine-Fi had another advantage in that it could simultaneously broadcast a film in more than one language. A year later on July 21, 1978, Pacific's Fiesta Drive-In in Los Angeles became the first ozoner to do so when it broadcast *Star Wars* in English and Spanish.[13]

A few other systems were marketed to compete with Cinema Radio and Cine-Fi. All either sent sound waves through special wiring, such as coaxial cable, from which they went direct to the car's radio with no physical connection, or the system sent sound over the existing field wiring to the post, where a small cable was attached to the car's antenna. Rumors that battery drain would follow the extended use of a car's radio continued to plague those trying to market radio sound systems.

When there was no physical connection between car and cable, there could be a problem with signal containment. Exhibitors considering these systems worried that if the signal spilled over outside the property line, freeloaders parked outside would be able to pick up the sound track on their radios. This didn't happen. It was a problem that couldn't happen with a system in which a cable was attached to the aerial, but this meant a certain amount of maintenance as the cable had to be attached and removed. However, touting the system that eliminated posts as perhaps allowing an increase in a drive-in's car capacity immediately backfired. Owners found patrons parking every which way, some even sideways. If anything, capacity was decreased. The old posts—in addition to being a place to hang the speaker—had functioned as parking controllers and directors. Those systems that promised a cost savings by using existing wiring failed to deliver in many cases, as the existing wiring had to be up to a minimum standard to carry the sound. In some ozoners it was so old and in such poor condition it proved unequal to the task. A complete rewiring job then had to be undertaken.[14]

Static was occasionally troublesome with AM reception at the drive-ins. FM would have been a better choice, since it was immune to interference from lightning, neon lights, and other sources that sometimes produced static on AM. A second advantage with FM was that it offered stereo. However, even in the late 1970s most cars didn't come with FM radios. More important, the FCC rules made such systems illegal. The physical laws of radio propagation on the AM band made low-power AM inherently short range. This meant it was unlikely to interfere with licensed commercial AM stations. In the FM band, conditions were different, with long-range transmission being possible even with very low power. Nonetheless, a few companies manufactured radio sound systems that utilized FM. Some drive-in owners bought them. Invariably, the FCC paid them a visit followed by an order to shut the system down.[15]

All the radio sound systems ended up costing more to install than if the exhibitor chose conventional in-car speakers. Whatever advantages there were lay in maintenance savings over time—and, of course, in greater customer satisfaction from improved audio quality. In 1982 *Boxoffice* estimated that 20 to 30 percent of drive-ins were using some form of AM radio broadcasting. Three years later the same source claimed that approximately 70 percent of all drive-ins were so equipped.[16]

An abortive attempt to bring stereo sound to the drive-in patrons was made in 1984 at the Union City Drive-In in Union City, California. All the speaker poles were fitted with plugs. For $19.97 a patron could buy a gizmo that was said to pipe stereo drive-in sound into his car. A patron plugged the gizmo into the speaker post, then into the car's tape deck, which sent out the sound. The catch was the car had to have a tape deck. Theater management said that the gizmo would also work on certain types of Walkmans and ghetto-blasters. Once purchased, the gizmo was the buyer's for life, and the drive-in often threw in a free pass in addition. Needless to say, few were sold. The writer reporting on this invention summed up forty years of ozoner sound when he wrote: "The gizmo allows the drive-in patron to forego those tinny, scratchy dinosaur speakers you hang in your window. Those things sound like 1940s Trans-Atlantic telephone calls in most drive-ins, and you only get sound on one side of the car."[17]

During the summer of 1989 the FCC put into effect a ban on low-power AM broadcasting for unlicensed applications. The agency had decided to assign low-power AM wavelengths to new radio stations. It was a decision that angered the drive-ins as well as numerous other establishments that used such systems. Walt Disney World and EPCOT in Florida had only just completed installation of a car audio system to enable motorists to turn to programmed events on three miles of approach roads.

Most of the battling and lobbying in the effort to rescind this ban on behalf of the drive-ins was done not by the ozoners themselves but by the manufacturers who supplied the theaters with hardware. NATO sent a letter to all its members, noting the upcoming FCC action and stating that the proposed rule "kills the use for broadcasting [of] the audio portion of a movie" on AM radio. The California NATO group acknowledged that the FCC action would make sound systems hooked into car radios "obsolete." When it checked out the scene CAL/NATO said that its "survey would seem to indicate few drive-ins today use low-power AM broadcasting to bring the sound to their patrons." CAL/NATO president Robert Selig, thought the consequences for drive-in owners would be very minor, since many of those who had installed cinema radio sound had returned to the old speaker-on-a-post because "a lot of people did not want to run down their car batteries." There were many complaints, he said, that car batteries went dead on double bills. Selig's attitude as CAL/NATO president may explain why the company he was an executive with, Pacific Theatres, refused to join efforts by hardware manufacturers to petition the FCC to remove the ban. Dick Burden of Burden Associates was a major organizer in the fight against the FCC regulation. Burden's engineering firm designed and installed low-power AM broadcast systems for drive-ins and other venues. Burden vigorously disagreed with the idea that car batteries could go dead using such a system.[18]

Industry apathy in the face of the proposal was curious. Burden and other manufacturing company representatives understood that if the ban stood it could put out of business any ozoner relying on one of those systems. Yet the year was 1989, the industry had long realized it was dying. Whatever fight it might have had in it was gone. None of the "miracle" systems of the past had ever worked out. Either they didn't come to pass at all, or they weren't what they were touted to be. By 1989 the drive-in exhibitors had given up and were lying down. They were ready to die.

Chapter 15

The Audience

The idea that outdoor theaters attract a different type of audience from indoor theaters, that the former don't simply steal business from the latter, has existed since the very first ozoner opened. Partly this idea was advanced because it was believed. Partly it was advanced, and maintained, to try to lessen the hostility displayed toward drive-ins by indoor exhibitors and film distributors. If they could all be convinced that they weren't losing business to ozoners, they might come to see them as actually helping to create more business for films—which might spill over to the indoor houses. Seen less as competitors, perhaps the drive-in exhibitors would gain access to better quality films, they hoped. However, if both types of theaters drew from the same audience group, merely splitting it up, the worse fears of indoor exhibitors—that drive-ins were costing them business—would be realized. Drive-ins could then expect to receive even worse treatment at the hands of indoor operators and film distributors.

Even before the first one opened in Camden, inventor Richard Hollingshead was inclined to think the people who would attend would not be regular filmgoers. He spoke, in his patent application, of his invention serving "an audience, particularly in rural sections."[1] As to the characteristics of drive-in attendees, Hollingshead envisioned a very strong component of family groups coming with their children, due to the convenience a drive-in offered such a group over an indoor house. Another group he felt would obviously be drawn to his invention was one comprising people who had trouble with seats in a conventional theater, such as the obese, the elderly, those with disabilities, and so on.

Fifteen years later this was still the conventional wisdom as to the makeup of a drive-in audience. It made a great deal of sense since the drive-in did afford a family the chance to go out together with a minimum of fuss and formality. People who didn't want to leave their pet dog at home could also take Rover along.

Another piece of conventional wisdom had it that a drive-in should be constructed near working-class communities rather than white-collar areas since the majority of the audience was thought to be blue collar. Veteran Albany, New York, exhibitor Harry Lamont apparently subscribed to this idea. In the middle 1950s he felt the quality of the audience was changing, that drive-ins were attracting a "better patronage." Lamont knew this because he was finding more Cadillacs on his lot.[2]

By 1949 and 1950 a number of individuals were beginning to take surveys of the ozoner attendees to see just how much truth there was in the conventional wisdom. By then indoor attendance was dropping significantly; television was ascending. Rather than blame television for the decline in filmgoing, however, some thought drive-ins were the major culprit.

Support for the idea that ozoners drew a different crowd came from one unlikely source in the person of William F. Rodgers, MGM vice president, whose company surveyed the situation in 1949. Before the survey was concluded Rodgers said: "I believe that drive-ins are creating new patrons for motion pictures, that a new motion picture clientele is being formed attracting folks who are not regular attendants in theatres." According to this executive indoor houses were doing as well as before even after an ozoner opened nearby. "In these places, there are drive-ins, which did not exist last year, doing $5,000–$10,000 weekly without regular theatres taking in one iota less.... Drive-ins do not affect regular theatres nearly as much as some people believe." Rodgers felt if this were true then his company should give them better treatment. "If they are catering to people who seldom go to theatres," he added, "and if they are giving service to young parents with small children, or folks who heretofore have had difficulties because of infirmities to attend theatres regularly, certainly we should give them every encouragement as another department of motion picture service."[3] It was a view held by few in the established part of the film industry.

W. R. Wilkerson, a journalist for the *Hollywood Reporter*, went to a local drive-in that same year, where he conducted his own informal survey. Questioning the 1,286 people he found there in attendance he found that approximately 700 of them would not have gone out that evening at all if there had been no drive-in to attend. Another 400 would not have gone to an indoor theater at any time. When this group went to the movies it was only to an ozoner.

Besides the obvious reasons for going to a drive-in, such as being able to take kids who could be as noisy as they pleased, plus the availability of food, drink, and even full meals, Wilkerson thought people went because "There is great relaxation. If the occupants of the car do not like the picture, or certain parts of the picture they can talk about anything that hits them without disturbing anyone else. They can discuss, and cuss, the picture; they can sing the songs with the singers on the screen and relieve themselves of a lot of desires that would be pent up if they had to go to a closed-in house."[4]

Somewhat more detailed was a survey conducted by Rodney Luther,

University of Minnesota marketing researcher, who interviewed 1,624 drive-in patrons in the summer of 1949 in the Minneapolis–St. Paul area. This survey was repeated the following year. Luther found that 55 percent (54 percent in 1950) of the cars contained family groups with children. Each car contained an average of 3.28 persons (3.45) made up of 2.34 adults (2.48) and .94 children (.97) under age twelve. The cars containing children had an average of 1.6 children (1.8). Ten percent (19) of the adults were in the twelve-to-twenty age range; 48 percent (45) were twenty-one to thirty, and 42 percent (36) were over thirty years of age. Adults attended in pairs, with 74 percent (67) of the cars containing two adults with another 10 percent (14) containing four adults. The average patron made a round-trip of 15 miles (17.6) to and from the drive-in where interviewed. In both years one-third of the patrons said they attended no other type of theater during the summer, with one-half reporting they attended drive-ins a majority of the time. Eighteen percent had a television set at home.

Average attendance per month at all types of theaters was 5.2 times during the summer, 3.9 times in winter. At ozoners average attendance was 2.5 times a month during summer 1949, 3.25 in the summer of 1950. In the 1949 survey Luther found that patrons at drive-ins during weekday first performances attended drive-ins almost exclusively; that patrons found at drive-ins during weekend first performances attended drive-ins 60 percent of the time; and that patrons at the drive-in second show attended drive-ins 54 percent of the time.

Picture preference of those questioned in 1949 and 1950 were; comedies 25 percent (33 percent in 1950), 23 percent drama (23), 21 percent musicals (18), 18 percent Westerns (14), 5 percent romance (8), and 15 percent expressed no preference (4). The ratio of city dwellers to suburban or rural inhabitants was 73 percent to 27 percent in favor of cities. Even though they attended the drive-ins regularly, 60 percent of those polled said they thought films screened at drive-ins were less desirable than those at an indoor house. Many complained that the pictures shown were too old.

Luther concluded that almost 40 percent of total movie attendance by drive-in patrons was at indoor theaters; that the typical drive-in patron was different from the typical indoor patron in terms of age, family status, and other characteristics:

> The drive-in theaters surveyed do not draw a major part of their patronage from what might be termed regular theater fans.... There is probably no better illustration of the strong drawing power that drive-in theaters exert than the evidence that patrons, many of whom own television sets, will drive a total of nearly 18 miles, undoubtedly right past one or several conventional theaters, in order to attend a drive-in theater, even though a majority of the patrons believe that the pictures shown are either not as desirable as, or older than, those showing at conventional theaters.

Enthusiastic about the ozoner industry, Luther felt it had attained its position with late-run product and could advance farther if allowed access to first- and second-run product. Attendance at drive-ins was restimulating the entire industry, he thought, benefitting indoor exhibitors. Luther concluded by calling drive-ins the most dynamic force in the entire film industry at the time.[5]

More than five thousand patrons who attended Chicago's SkyHi Drive-In were surveyed during the summer of 1950 by a public relations man, at the request of owner Louis F. Jelinek, who wanted to access the effects of television on his theater. Fifty-two percent of those questioned owned TV sets, however, 82 percent preferred ozoners to home television programs while 68 percent preferred indoor theaters over television. According to this survey, 85 percent of the respondents attended indoor theaters when drive-ins weren't available. However, in the summer ozoner season 47 percent didn't attend indoor theaters. Refreshment stands were kept busy with 85 percent of the patrons making a purchase there. Ninety-nine percent checked the newspaper to see what film was playing. Film genres preferred at this drive-in were, in order, comedies, Westerns, dramas, romances, historical epics, and mysteries. Cartoons topped the list of favorite short subjects followed by travelogues, sports, news, musicals, and educational films.[6]

Pollster George Gallup entered the scene to report that people who attended films infrequently (less than once a week) went to a drive-in once out of every six trips to see a film. Frequent filmgoers selected a drive-in once in every twelve of their trips. More women than men attended drive-ins, as compared to an even split at indoor houses, with attendance heaviest among the eighteen-to-thirty age group. In July 1950 Gallup reported that drive-ins captured one-eighth of all film patrons in communities of ten thousand-plus. In cities of ten thousand to one hundred thousand the percentage was 19. For cities over five hundred thousand, six percent of all film patrons went to a drive-in.[7]

As late as 1953 the Sindlinger Company reported that their data indicated one-third of all patrons who attended a drive-in for the first time—for its novelty properties—didn't return. They preferred an indoor house. One year later Sindlinger stated: "On a national basis, the drive-in theatre does not appear to be in direct competition with the 4-wall theatre, for, as the attendance and gross of the drive-in commences to climb in June to a peak in August, so does the attendance and gross of the 4-wall theatre."[8]

Contradicting this was the conclusion drawn by the Morton Research Corporation, which said, after reviewing longitudinal economic data: "Over the long run drive-ins made substantial inroads into indoor theaters, however since 1967 the outdoor theatre has been losing ground." Morton added that ozoners did a larger share of business in less urbanized areas of the country.[9]

Another early researcher was Leo Handel, who concluded in 1950 that outdoor theaters "create new business.... A large portion of the drive-in theater audience is composed of regular movie-goers who would not have attended a conventional theater on the day of the drive-in theater attendance." Handel found an attendance unit of four persons more frequently at drive-ins. A two-person unit was, and is, the most common unit found at indoor theaters. This was corroborated by a 1957 study undertaken by the Opinion Research Corporation (ORC). ORC found that 32 percent of indoor admissions were accounted for by groups of three or more people. At drive-ins it was 57 percent. Of those polled by ORC, 72 percent had been to a drive-in, with 35 percent reporting that the last visit they made to the movies was to a drive-in.[10]

Sindlinger found that 54 percent of his respondents preferred indoor houses; 30 percent favored ozoners; and 16 percent had no preference. Females consistently preferred conventional theaters. Luther reported that 67 percent of his respondents had no preference for a particular type of theater. When the ORC did its study, it found that 32 percent preferred indoor shows, 30 percent favored outdoor theaters, and 10 percent opted for the no-preference category.[11]

Some ten years after Luther another marketing professor, Dr. Steuwart Henderson Britt of Northwestern University, put drive-in patrons under the microscope. Sixty percent of twenty to thirty-four year olds attended an ozoner at least once during the summer in question. Of families that attended, 19 percent had one child nineteen years or under, compared to 18 percent of the total population. Twenty-nine percent of drive-in families had two children (18 percent in the total population), while 21 percent had three children (10 percent in the total population).

Britt concluded that "the drive-in audience was noticeably different from the general population." However, he felt that they were different in ways going against the conventional wisdom because his respondents "generally had better jobs, higher income, more education, more children, more home ownership, more cars, more major appliances, and more conveniences" than the national averages.[12] Almost two decades after that the Leo Burnett advertising agency reported the results of its survey—results that contradicted Britt's findings. Burnett reported that "while the heavy filmgoer is socially active, confident, future-oriented, financially stable, and career-minded, the drive-in patron tends to be a dissatisfied lonely blue-collar worker with financial worries.[13]

During 1981 and 1982 Bruce Austin, an associate professor at Rochester Institute of Technology, interviewed a total of 607 patrons at one Rochester, New York, drive-in. Asked if a film they wanted to see were playing at both an indoor and outdoor theater, which they would choose, all things being equal, 76.5 percent opted for a drive-in. Austins's respondents averaged one visit a month to drive-ins. Males made up 57.9 percent of the patrons, whose average age was twenty-four. Family groups made up only 16.7 percent of the audience. The respondents' most common companion was an opposite-sex friend (41 percent), followed by family (16.7 percent), then spouse (16.5 percent), and then mixed-sex group (12.5 percent). Size of the average attendance unit was 2.66 (mean) and 2.23 (median), down considerably from earlier surveys. Over one-third of the respondents held blue- or pink-collar jobs. Those who attended drive-ins the most frequently tended to have less prestigious jobs and were more likely to be unemployed than those who attended outdoor theaters less frequently. The most frequently cited reasons for drive-in attendance were: less expensive than indoor houses (18.1 percent), more comfortable than indoor houses (17 percent), privacy (15.6 percent), can have fun—party, drink, smoke (15.6 percent), to be outdoors (7.9 percent), and to see the movie (7.5 percent). Even though "to see the movie" ranked only sixth in general reasons for ozoner attendance, on the particular night people were interviewed the most frequently cited reasons for attendance were: for the movie playing (58.1 pecent), closest drive-in (15.7 percent), and nothing else to do (4.9 percent). Fifty-nine percent of the patrons said they didn't expect to buy food at the snack bar and 12 percent weren't sure, while the rest already had purchased, or were going to purchase, something. Seventy-eight percent brought refreshments with them. These patrons visited indoor theaters as often as outdoor ones, once a month.[14]

One observer wrote in 1953: "The general feeling seems to be that drive-in patrons are not greatly concerned with the age of pictures; they seem to be content with second and third run pictures." Around the same time another writer noted: "It doesn't seem to make much of a difference what kind of pictures are shown, because drive-in fans are far less choosey than the indoor variety." Austin reached a similar conclusion stating, "At least for some individuals, drive-in attendance occurs regardless of interest in what film is being shown."[15]

Chapter 16

Sex in the Drive-in

Sex on the drive-in was a monumental headache for the exhibitors. Sex in the drive-in caused them no end of trouble as well. That the drive-in afforded an excellent opportunity for sexual activity was obvious to observers from the very beginning. Just a few weeks after the first one opened in Camden, New Jersey, in 1933, a writer noted, "Perhaps it will occur readily enough to the reader what fun Young America could have in a coupe under the added stimulation of a sophisticated romance!"[1]

Another who noticed the possibilities immediately was the editorial writer of *Motion Picture Daily* who commented: "The Romeos who lost out in the back seats of picture houses when West Point ushers and super-service came into the deluxe houses are waking up in a new world." The inventor of the drive-in, and the owner of the one at Camden, Richard Hollingshead, found himself having to deal with angry parents. Many felt that every time he licensed somebody to build an ozoner he was issuing a license for immoral conduct. Said Hollingshead: "We always had a lot of criticism about kids necking, but I've always said that I'd rather see my daughter in a drive-in than parked in a dark alley somewhere."[2]

Pacific Drive-Ins hired uniformed policemen to combat amorous adolescents in the very early years. Toward the end of the 1930s, when *Variety* discussed the advantages of ozoners over indoor theaters, the publication wrote: "Another box-office element in favor of the drive-ins is the fact that patrons may spoon in their cars as they watch a picture. Or spoon without watching it." *Time* reported that prewar drive-ins were spots "for young bloods looking for a place to make two-bit love."[3]

Some owners have steadfastly denied that any sexual activity took place on their lot, or that it was a minor element, or it took place only in the past. One such was the West Side Drive-In in Detroit, the city's first. Open only a few months, this theater felt compelled to state publicly that most of its customers were regulars, family trade, "the reputed petting party trade being a very minor part of the total patronage."[4]

During an unusually late snowstorm at Rochester, New York, in May

1945, manager Grandon Hodges of the Driven-In went out to the theater expecting only to make a quick check of the premises, then go home. Surprised to find cars waiting in line, he went ahead with the planned screening. By the time the show started he had fifty cars on the lot. Reporting on this event, a writer wondered: "Could it be necking has something to do with it?"[5]

By then the idea that drive-ins were passion pits was well entrenched. So entrenched that residents of a Toronto, Canada, suburb complained to the authorities about new ones being planned. These citizens were worried about "petting parties." Seeking to reassure them, Canadian Drive-In Theatres, Ltd., general manager James Brandon told them that when his latest ozoner opened there would be two police officers and thirty ushers to break up any necking. Reassurances also came from pioneer drive-in operator Herbert Ochs, who owned several in the Dayton, Ohio, area and who was a crusader to keep outdoor theaters out of the "park-and-pet" class. Ochs said: "We have promoted our place as a family theatre and if you watch the cars as they come out you will see that it is the family trade we are getting. We keep plenty of attendants on the lot and the cars are parked from the front in the order they enter. There is no such thing as parking in isolated spots."[6]

Not long after the Whitestone Drive-In opened in New York, manager Harvey Elliott was boasting how well the new theater was doing. "The only thing that can slow us down is an ugly rumor going around that drive-ins are perfect for neckers," he worried. "No such thing—not real necking. I had a police officer check the cars one night, and he reported that no one was paying the least bit of attention to anyone else. Of course, we were showing an exceptionally good movie that night."[7]

When writer John Durant questioned dozens of outdoor exhibitors as to what sort of sexual behavior took place on their lots, he wrote that all firmly replied that nothing took place in the cars that didn't happen in the rear seats of indoor theaters. All the exhibitors were reportedly touchy on the issue with only one admitting to ever having received a patron complaint on that issue. Typical of those who spoke to Durant was Leon Rosen a manager for the Fabian Theatres chain, which had seven ozoners in the Middle Atlantic states. Rosen said he's never had a single complaint. "Sure, a fellow slips his arm around his girl in the drive-in," he said. "The same as in the regular theaters or on a park bench. No more than that. And there's one thing you don't get in the drive-in that you get inside. That's the guy on the prowl, the seat changer who molests lone women. There's none of that in drive-ins."[8]

One ozoner chain included the following in their manual of instructions for managers:

> One of the most important managerial tasks falling under the general heading of proper supervision is that of preventing breaches of good conduct. In this regard a special officer or night watchman should be assigned to patrol

> the lot after 10 P.M., looking casually into every car without disturbing the occupants. He should go from the front ramp to the back ramp and back again, never stopping, so as to prevent any sort of misconduct.

Another manual advised: "There is also the rare undesirable patron who insists upon parking on the last ramp. There can be only one reason for this attitude and it is advisable to refund the admission price and request such a patron to leave the theatre."[9]

Some critics of the passion pits couldn't even bring themselves to mention the "sin" by name. During a hearing in Cook County Circuit Court over an ordinance to bar outdoor theaters from Chicago, Assistant City Counsel Morton Nathanson said to the judge, trying to point out that such theaters were an invitation to immoral practices on the part of youth: "Now there are features of an outdoor theatre that are different from an ordinary theatre. They are out in the country with the moon shining, in automobiles. Why, some of the things that happen there, Judge—it's terrible." Appearing before a Senate subcommittee investigating juvenile delinquency William Mooring, film critic for *The Tidings*, official newspaper for the Roman Catholic Diocese of Los Angeles, asserted that some drive-ins "condone and encourage among their young customers behavior that called for some police action."[10]

Citizens and communities reacted more angrily to the outdoor theaters as their numbers increased rapidly. When Sidney Lust obtained a license to build one near Rockville, Maryland, the county board put through an ordinance setting an annual license fee of $1,000 while imposing an 11:00 P.M. curfew on outdoor theaters. This action was taken after various prominent citizens described drive-ins as "licensed petting places." Representing several area ministers, the Rev. J. Virgil Lilly told the board that ozoners were "a demoralizing influence leading to promiscuous relationships." Speaking for the County League of Women Voters, Mrs. Thomas M. Bartram insisted that the "invasion of such amusements into the county will increase juvenile delinquency." Juvenile Court judge Alfred D. Noyes backed up Bartram by claiming that a drive-in in nearby Prince George county was a contributing factor leading to juvenile delinquency in his jurisdiction.[11]

At a hearing at Fall River, Massachusetts, to determine if a permit should be granted to construct an outdoor theater within the city limits, an attorney for the opposition attacked them as "noisy, not clean from a physical or moral point of view, regardless of the claims of the proponents that drive-ins are family institutions" arguing they should be "forced to remain out in the country where they belonged."[12]

During the early- to mid-1950s many drive-ins in the Midwest and then in the Southwest adopted a policy of all-night dusk-to-dawn movie marathons. It was a result of intense competition among the drive-ins. Five of the twelve ozoners in San Antonio, Texas, had adopted the all-night policy. Those who did not opposed it, fearing that it would arouse church and municipal authorities bringing their harassment down on all outdoor theater operators—which is what did happen in San Antonio. Local clergymen combined to condemn the dusk-to-dawn policy, complaining that young people who attended these shows stayed out so late that they couldn't attend Sunday morning church services. One minister pointed out that some of these theaters were showing the film twice during the same night, "and teenagers are not interested in seeing the same picture twice just for the sake of seeing a movie." This pressure was effective, for all five San Antonio drive-ins stopped screening all-night films.

All-night activity made other drive-in owners uneasy. Later that year at a convention, Jack Braunagel, chairman of the Theatre Owners of America drive-in committee, told delegates that exhibitors screening all night movies were courting a stigma for the entire industry by reviving the image of ozoners as "passion pits with pix." From this would come more harassment, raids, complaints and bad publicity he warned. "One of the dangers we are confronted with is the advent of policies that will earn a 'quick buck' tonight and cost many times that much to drive-in operators in weeks to come," Braunagel added, citing the all night policy.[13]

In later years Woodbridge, New Jersey, tried to impose a 12:30 A.M. closing time on drive-ins. A court challenge led to a Jersey City judge's quashing the ordinance ruling that "the fact a drive-in can be the scene of an immoral act is not sufficient ground for such severe regulation." Trying to circumvent such difficulties, the New Jersey State Assembly passed a bill in 1972, effective from October 1 to April 30 each year, which fined an ozoner operator one hundred dollars if any autos remained on his premises one hour after the end of the show. The purpose of the act, they said, was to prevent carbon-monoxide deaths.[14]

The Whitestone in New York was still protesting the purity of its lot in 1970, when manager Larry Barrett said, "If we find cars with no heads sticking up, then we make them either sit up or get out. Nine times out of ten the reason for the no heads is that the family is at the concession stand." Robert Selig of the Pacific chain commented, "Parents would rather have their daughters here than up on Mulholland Drive. We patrol but we don't rap on windows." There was less need for patrolling anyway, as sex seemed to be more confined to vans and campers. Agreeing with that was Bob Hernandez, projectionist at Marin County, California's, last ozoner. Hernandez said: "The lovemaking isn't like it used to be. Everyone has a camper or a friend with an apartment. They don't need the drive-in for that any more."[15]

Some continued to deny, like manager Dick Stemen of the Corral Drive-In near Flatwoods, Kentucky, who claimed that the "back seat" myths vanished a long time ago. Others were more forthright, like owner Max, in Georgia, who said, when asked about sex on his lot, that it had not fundamentally changed.

> Back in the Forties and Fifties it was all rassling and steaming up the windows. Now they come out here with pillows and plug in eight-track stereos.... I can look out some nights on my back row and I won't see a single head. Not one. Everybody's going at it. I could be running black leader. But I'll tell you something, we don't have any trouble out here. I mean none. Kids are more sophisticated.[16]

By the 1980s many felt the era of the passion pit was past. Vicki Slate recalled the pre-1960s ozoner, saying, "We certainly couldn't go to his house or my house. Our parents would have killed us." Families traditionally parked in the front rows; teens who were just dating parked in the middle rows; while those with serious sex on their minds took up the back rows. Ronn Teitelbaum recalled: "At that time nobody would even consider living together. There was no way you could get into a motel, so the drive-in was really the only place to go." Near Chicago, SkyHi's projectionist Jack Cerrone commented: "They used to be the cheapest motel in town, but that's no longer the case. Today's kids can do it anywhere. Things have changed." The owner of Shankweiler's Drive-In in Allentown, Pennsylvania, Bob Maklames, said: "Now—and I'm not putting a moral judgment on this—girls have their own apartments. Guys have their own places. Everybody is on The Pill. The fear of premarital sex is gone.... Motels advertise singles' weekends. It's a different world. And so, the drive-in doesn't have the same function it had years ago."[17]

According to others, however, the old image remained alive. A source at the Addison, Illinois, police department stated: "They are still passion pits for some kids." In the Washington, D.C., area the back rows were often devoid of speakers. Yet on weekends especially these rows tended to fill up. Whoever was there watched the entire movie without hearing it. A manager at a Texas ozoner said: "They're out there drinking beer and smoking that marijuana. Some of them come through the ticket booth with their clothes half off, just ready for love. Drive-in's a cheap motel, I guess. Somehow the fights will start. It got so crazy last summer we had to call out the SWAT team."[18]

Texas film critic John Bloom, better known under his redneck drive-in movie critic persona of Joe Bob Briggs, explained, "Drive-in owners try to duck their reputation as proprietors of sleaze on the screen and sex in the seats. They've been denying it since 1948. You thumb through the old exhibitors' journals, and once a year you'll find an article which reads, 'Drive-ins Used to Be Passion Pits, but Now They're Family Entertainment Centers.' To this day you'll find articles like that, and it's always last year they were passion pits."[19]

Chapter 17

Sex on the Drive-in

Drive-ins have been plagued by sex—sex in the drive-in and sex on the drive-in. Both have brought many problems to owners and operators of outdoor theaters, with the on-screen sex perhaps the most troublesome. The bulk of attacks directed against drive-ins for the content of the films they screened came beginning in the mid- to late-1960s although a few incidents took place prior to that.

In the fall of 1951 letters to the editors of Detroit newspapers complained about the nature of films at area drive-ins. H. F. Reves, a writer for *Boxoffice*, investigated the situation, finding such ads in the *Detroit Times* as the following: "Fort Drive-In—Three adult hits. . .*The Burning Question, Guilty Parents,* and *How to Take a Bath*. Grand River and Gratiot drive-ins — 'Revealing all the facts of life! Children must be accompanied by parents. Now it can be shown! It will amaze you! Exposing the stark naked facts of life!'"

Reves reasoned that as it was nearing the end of the drive-in season, some operators were tempted to change their booking policy for a few weeks to try to generate more profit. Noting that some of these films had already played conservatively operated indoor houses, securing respectable approval and receiving no complaints, Reves wondered if the "reaction of the public indicates that people are quicker to suspect trouble on film content at a drive-in because of the reputation flamboyantly given to the outdoor houses by some newspapers and magazines." Sound operating policy might require drive-ins, he thought, to be more conservative than indoor houses in selecting films.

A showing of *Hurly Burly* brought sheriff's representatives to the Division Drive-In in Grand Rapids, Michigan, for the opening-night screening. No complaints were received that night, with no action taken by the sheriff's men. *Hurly Burly* had been approved by the censors for showing in Detroit, Chicago, and elsewhere. A couple of days after this film opened, the situation was inflamed by a Michigan Catholic archdiocesan newspaper that headlined: "Two Drive-Ins Push Sex Films." On the night *Hurly Burly* was to finish its run area lawmen confiscated the film. What Reves noted then would hold true many decades later. He wrote: "The combination of drive-in plus exploitation films apparently has set up a very sizable adverse public reaction."[1]

Later that decade the police in one unnamed city were able to compel an ozoner operator to remove a film they considered to be objectionable by threatening to charge the patrons with fornication.[2]

During the evening of August 28, 1968, a police officer stood outside the fence that surrounded the Park Y drive-in at Richland, Washington. Playing at the ozoner was *Carmen, Baby*. It definitely was not the average X-rated film, for it was reviewed in the *New York Times* by Vincent Canby. On August 29 the police officer was back in the same place. He brought the city attorney with him. According to the police, the film was visible to people standing outside the fence. *Carmen, Baby* had many objectionable scenes in it, said the state, so the manager was arrested and the film confiscated. In court the manager, William Rabe, was convicted of violating the state obscenity law and causing to be exhibited an "obscene, indecent and immoral show." The Washington State Supreme Court upheld the conviction and six hundred dollar fine against Rabe.

The U.S. Supreme Court reversed the decision holding that a state could not criminally punish the exhibition of a film at a drive-in when the statute didn't give fair notice "that the location of the exhibition was a vital element of the offense." It was agreed that this film could have been shown at an indoor theater with impunity.[3]

The state argued that even if a film wasn't lewd enough to be banned at an indoor theater, it should be a crime for an outdoor theater to show a film that "illuminates the nighttime sky of a residential area with a vivid portrayal of erotic sexual scenes."[4] The Supreme Court reversal in this case didn't sit well with some members of the Court. Chief Justice Warren Burger, joined by Justice William Rehnquist, noted that *Carmen, Baby* was clearly visible outside the fence and that young teens were watching. Burger said that if a state enacted a law banning films like *Carmen, Baby* from exhibition in places where they could be viewed by the general public, such as at drive-ins, he would support such a law. "That this record shows an offensive nuisance that could properly be prohibited, I have no doubt," Burger wrote, "but the state statute and charge did not give the notice constitutionally required."[5]

Some operators who tried to ensure a film couldn't be seen outside the drive-in's property line found a catch-22. In North Carolina a drive-in operator was charged under an ordinance forbidding any "nude or semi-nude picture" to be visible to the general public outside the theater. This operator volunteered to erect a nine foot fence around the theater to solve the problem. Local authorities refused to allow this citing local zoning regulations that limited fences to a height of three feet.[6]

In October 1967 police seized copies of the film *I, a Woman* at two drive-ins in Indiana, one in Indianapolis, the other in Marion County. Four people involved in the film's distribution were arrested. All of this activity was carried out without judicial warrants. The authorities barred the film from being distributed in the state even though the state of Maryland censors had licensed it as had a Chicago board of censors, with the latter ordering four deletions to the film. The version shown in Indiana was the one with the deletions. The court threw all the charges out and ordered the police not to interfere with further exhibitions of *I, a Woman* in Indiana on the ground that proper procedure—the issuance of warrants—had not been followed.[7]

Activity against drive-ins for the showing of so-called sexual material intensified from the mid-1960s onward. By then the drive-in industry was into its decline. In order to survive, the ozoners experimented with different types of films. More and more turned to the screening of X-rated hard-core porn or soft-core R-rated material. Standards applied to such "public" exhibitions at drive-ins were often more restrictive than the standards for obscenity that applied to indoor theaters. An ordinance in Texas forbade the showing of any film visible from any public street in which "the bare buttocks or the bare female breasts of the human body are shown or in which striptease, burlesque or nudist-type scenes constitute the main or primary material."[8]

Some actions taken can be viewed as nothing more than harassment by local authorities. Pennsylvania's Lancaster County had three drive-ins, all of which had been operating seven days a week for twelve, seven, and six years respectively. Suddenly the county attorney invoked a state blue law enacted in 1794 to bring a halt to Sunday screenings at all three ozoners. Numerous complaints had been received about films playing at two of the three theaters, claimed the attorney. In Grand Rapids, Michigan, the license of one drive-in owner was revoked on account of the purported obscene films it screened. Undaunted, the man continued to operate. Police raided this drive-in, seizing the family-type film then playing along with the day's box-office take.[9]

Some actions were little more than a macho show of force. When a drive-in in Pittston, Pennsylvania, was raided eight state troopers along with six city police officers entered the theater in unmarked cars. They arrested the manager and seized the film. They also checked the cars of patrons one by one as they left the lot making a count of the "juveniles" and taking down their names and addresses.[10]

A large, coordinated raid took place on the night of July 9, 1969, in the state of Alabama. Acting under the orders of Gov. Albert P. Brewer, the state police raided six drive-ins, seizing six different films: *Inga, Starlet, Thar She Blows, Barbette, The Shanty Tramp,* and *The Secret Lives of Romeo and Juliet.* All the managers were charged with violating a 1907 antiobscenity law that prohibited any display of nudity except in art galleries. Charges of contributing to the delinquency of minors were laid against some of the managers. According to Brewer the "trash and filth being shown on some Alabama picture screens is almost unbelievable." City police in Montgomery were upset by the action:

when the raid took place a detail of the Montgomery vice squad was at the drive-in playing *Inga*—attempting to gather evidence to seek a court injunction against the film, they said. The raid surprised them. Said police chief D. H. Lackey, "It's an insult to us." Also upset was Montgomery District Attorney Dave Crosland, who complained that the state police "sort of muscled in on our show."[11]

During the period 1965 to 1966 the Ohio state legislature proposed that no ozoner be allowed to operate after 1:30 A.M. Given the late summer starting times, this proposed law would have made many drive-ins unprofitable during the summer. More restrictive was an Indiana proposal that would have required outdoor theaters to hire a security guard for each carload of customers. In Nebraska a bill to bar anyone under eighteen from attending a theater that let out after 10:00 P.M. was defeated. The city of Parma, Ohio, enacted an ordinance requiring all drive-ins to be closed no later than 12:01 A.M. At times the authorities proceeded against ozoner patrons under morality laws.[12]

As complaints against the outdoor theaters mounted, states and cities became more involved as they passed or tried to pass legislation restricting the types of films drive-ins could screen. Governor Nelson Rockefeller of New York State vetoed such a piece of legislation in 1970. The proposal would have made it a felony to exhibit a film that "depicts nudity, sexual conduct or sadomasochistic abuse which would be harmful to minors" at sites near the public highways that could be viewed by people not inside the theater. Rockefeller said the bill was too broad in scope. Yet two years later he changed his mind by signing into law a bill that added theater screens to a list of display areas where it is illegal to present "offensive sexual material" if it was visible from public thoroughfares. Other areas where such material couldn't be displayed included windows, billboards, newsstands, and so on.[13]

Action took place in Arizona without benefit of a specific statute. Several complaints were reportedly registered by citizens against *The Last Picture Show* when it played a Phoenix drive-in because it could be seen "upon the public way." The city attorney wrote to the theater manager stating that in his opinion the film violated both the "explicit terms" and the "spirit" of a state criminal obscenity law. The manager ceased to show this film under the threat of prosecution if he didn't desist. When the city attorney later demanded a four-second cut in the film before it could be reshown, the film's producer and distributor filed in court claiming their civil rights were being violated. The court held that it was the prosecutor's threats that had caused the film to be pulled—that it didn't violate state law and therefore could not lawfully be suppressed. Down the road in Tucson the city attorney brought suit to have the film *Lysistrata* banned from further exhibition after it played a local drive-in. It was an obscene film, said the attorney, which could be seen outside the theater. It was a public nuisance. The Arizona Court of Appeals upheld the injunction, granted by a lower court, finding that "a drive-in theater that exhibited films in such a way that they were visible to the public outside the theater invaded the rights of that public by imposing its pictures upon persons without their consent."[14]

Pennsylvania came close to passing legislation that would have banned the showing of X-rated films in drive-ins "to protect the public on highways and streets from accidents caused by distractions." Massachusetts also considered such legislation, in which the class of material barred from screening at a drive-in would have included "a visual representation of actual or simulated human sexual intercourse, masturbation, bestiality, oral intercourse, anal intercourse, direct physical stimulation of unclothed genitals, flagellation or torture in the context of a sexual relationship."[15]

Sex on the drive-in screen even made itself an issue in the 1970 reelection campaign of sixty-six-year-old United States Senator Roman Hruska (R., Neb). The senator, a noted opponent of violence and pornography, was part owner of a chain of drive-ins located in the Nebraska cities of Omaha and Lincoln as well as one in Carter Lake, Iowa. Running against Hruska was Frank B. Morrison, who labeled Hruska a smut peddler and glorifier of brutality because of the type of films played at his drive-ins. Films cited by Morrison included: *The Blood Drinker, Catch-22, The Shanty Tramp,* and *Easy Rider.* As far as sixty-five-year-old Morrison was concerned, the senator showed some of the "most filthy pornographic films made." Hruska defended himself by saying his theaters showed lots of Walt Disney pictures and no X-rated films. Besides, said Hruska, he was just an investor, who didn't actively participate in the management of the chain. Morrison continued to imply that the senator voted against pornography on the Senate floor but "peddled smut" in his drive-ins. As election day neared Morrison fulminated: "Can Roman Hruska deal effectively with drugs and violence among youth while he glorifies them in his drive-in movies? Can Roman Hruska sermonize against loose sex and low morals while displaying filthy situations upon the public screen for money?"[16] The answer must have been yes, for Hruska was reelected.

One drive-in located on the border between two communities found itself in a bind when it came time to expand. The Orange Drive-In operated wholly in Orange, California, in 1970, when it decided to expand by adding a second screen behind its existing one. This would extend into Anaheim, California. This ozoner had no trouble from Orange officials over the types of films it played; however, when Anaheim officials approved the expansion they stipulated that the exhibiting of any X-rated material would have to be confined solely to the screen located in Orange. Anaheim wanted to retain its reputation as a family recreation area, which came, it thought, with the arrival of Disneyland. The Orange Drive-In got a measure of revenge because one-third of the expansion area would still be located in Orange. It was an important part as it contained the ticket booth, projection booth, and concession stand. With this revenue end in Orange tax revenue would stay there, not passing over to Anaheim.[17]

The not-so-subtle comments Justice Burger made in the 1972 case against Rabe (see p. 154) as to the type of law he would like to see drawn against drive-ins didn't pass unnoticed. Cities and states throughout the country began to draft this type of legislation, hoping it would be upheld if and when it reached the high court. Hopes got a little higher again in 1973 when the U.S. Supreme Court issued a ruling that made possible the application of "local community standards" in determining obscenity. Drive-ins were not involved in that particular case, but its implication seemed to be that it would be easier in the future to convict the ozoners on obscenity charges.

Immediately after the Rabe decision, Councilman Joe Carlucci in Jacksonville, Florida, introduced legislation banning nudity films from drive-in screens visible from public places. The owner, operator, and all employees of a drive-in were subject to public-nuisance charges if a film showed "human male or female bare buttocks, human female bare breasts or human bare pubic areas." In due course a drive-in breached this law, resulting in an arrest. The Jacksonville ordinance was upheld at three levels of Florida courts before it landed in the Supreme Court. There, on June 23, 1975, the ordinance was struck down as an unconstitutional interference with free speech, by a vote of 6 to 3. Burger and Rehnquist had been unable to switch votes to their side, which was to favor the Florida legislation. While the majority justices agreed that such films could possibly be offensive to inadvertent viewers, the solution was simple. "The offended viewer readily can avert his eyes," wrote Justice Lewis F. Powell, Jr., for the majority. Joe Carlucci was disappointed when news of the decision reached him in Jacksonville. Promising to pray for the justices who held his law unconstitutional, Carlucci commented: "Filth seems to prevail ... the ordinance was not designed to legislate morality but to rid neighborhoods of a public nuisance."[18]

People were disappointed in many other areas such as Salt Lake County, Utah; Dallas, Texas; Fort Worth, Texas; Toledo, Ohio; Middletown Township, Pennsylvania; Delaware; and New Jersey. All these places had legislation similar to the Jacksonville ordinance. Most agreed that the Supreme Court decision appeared to declare these laws void. Captain Norbert DeClerq of the Toledo police wasn't worried, though. He did receive occasional complaints about drive-ins but said that in each case "the issue was resolved after the theatre management agreed to eliminate offensive scenes." Some New Jersey communities were angry with the decision. In Palmyra, John R. Makin, township manager, said, "It's unfortunate that the Supreme Court struck down the nudity ban. The town should have the right to protect its residents' privacy."[19]

Over in Gloucester City, New Jersey, the manager of the Starlight Drive-In was arrested on public-nuisance charges just days before the high court ruling. Mayor William Gartland said, "We'll continue to fight against obscenity.... The kids park their cars along the road to watch the movies and many of the area's residents are afraid to sit on their front porches with their company for fear of seeing some bare parts."[20]

None of these court decisions stopped or even slowed the attack on ozoners. In October, 1975 state police in Palatine Bridge, New York, arrested Elmer Rossi, Jr., operator of the El Rancho Drive-In. He was charged with the public display of offensive sexual material after motorists and nearby residents were reported to have complained to the police they could see *Coming of Age* and *Night After Night* emanating from his screen. When complaints that X-rated *The Story of O* was playing at an Oakland, California, drive-in police investigated. Before they could make their arrest they said they had to make their way through a traffic jam of free moviegoers, many of whom were juveniles. All were parked within a few blocks of the theater, around the perimeter. The operator of the Airport II was charged. Some drive-ins gave up the battle, such as the one in Greenport, New York, that showed X-rated films until 1975, when it was bought by St. Peter's Lutheran Church. The church switched it to family films, specializing in Walt Disney. St. Peter's hoped to raise money from the drive-in to help in the construction of a retirement village. The town of Greenport was happy with the drive-in's change of direction.[21]

Some areas persisted in trying to find ways around the 1975 Supreme Court ruling. The Baltimore, Maryland, County Council first passed legislation prohibiting drive-ins from showing X-rated films that could be seen by the nonpaying public in 1974. Councilman Harry F. Bartenfelder sponsored the bill which initially applied to both X- and R-rated material but was amended to just X-rated material. Support for the bill came from Rev. Robert T. Woodworth, who was chairman of the county's long-inactive Decency Committee. That committee had been established in 1963 by Spiro Agnew. Woodworth told a hearing on the bill that children gathering at night in a schoolyard and teenagers parked on the grounds of a trailer park so they could watch X and R films at nearby drive-ins. Worried about traffic hazards, the reverend said: "Looking up into a dark sky and seeing a twelve-foot bosom is more distracting than [seeing] a cowboy picture."[22]

Howard Waggonheim, owner of the Valley Drive-In, was the first person charged under this Baltimore ordinance after a citizen complained he could see scenes from Russ Meyer's *Supervixens* from the road. By then the Supreme Court had declared the Jacksonville legislation invalid. District Court Judge William T. Evans threw the Waggonheim charges out of court, citing the Florida ruling. "I don't see how we can stop it," the judge said.[23]

By the summer of 1976 the Baltimore County Council was ready to try again. Councilman Norman W. Lauenstein introduced a bill to prohibit drive-ins from showing any films on screens visible to the general public outside the theater. Ostensibly the measure was aimed at traffic problems. Linda Orant of the Carrollwood Civic Improvement Association testified that in the area of drive-ins "there was a lot of bumper-type accidents and slamming of brakes."

However, neither she nor a half dozen other speakers in favor of the bill could recall seeing an accident caused by visible movie screens. The objection to ozoners that kept surfacing the most was against "dirty" movies that "corrupt the young and distract the adults." A particular target was the Bengies Drive-In, owned by Hank Vogel. This ozoner used to screen X-rated movies but discontinued them on May 4, 1976, after numerous complaints, before the proposed bill was introduced. Other drive-in owners opposed the bill because it would be too costly for them to erect the necessarily very high fences to comply with the proposal. Lauenstein complained that sex films turned a shopping-center parking lot near the Bengies into a "bedroom" during weekends. "Patrons of the outdoor theatre," he said, "were broadcasting on their citizens' band radios the soundtrack of the movies and their running comments to youngsters gathered in the parking lot." This bill was killed at a council meeting a week after it was introduced. Last-minute lobbying by theater owners helped but more important was a pledge by Vogel not to "play any X-rated films unless it is technically feasible to restrict the viewing to an area within the boundaries of our property."[24]

The city council in Charlotte, North Carolina, considered an even more restrictive bill when an ordinance was introduced that would have made it unlawful for a drive-in screen to be visible from the street. This was ostensibly for purposes of traffic safety, but in reality it was to keep "drivers' eyes from being diverted by overwhelming sex to the screen and away from their driving." Owners throughout the Carolinas joined forces to oppose the bill, calling it an invitation to drive-ins "to close up and get out of town." The cost of necessary fencing was again cited as prohibitive for the owners. As only two of the ozoners in the area ever screened X films, lobbying efforts prevailed. The Charlotte city council voted unanimously to kill the proposal.[25]

At the same time the Charlotte proposal was dying, police were arresting Clyde A. Bolt, Jr., owner of the Fox Drive-In, in Anderson, South Carolina. He was charged under a South Carolina law that erotic scenes were not to be visible beyond the theater. Bolt's screenings had been monitored by the two hundred–member Citizens for Decency. Group organizer Elaine Childers said that at her group's request, local lawmen notified the Fox by letter to "shape up" within thirty days as its film selection did not meet with the approval of the group, which considered them to be obscene. When this deadline passed with unsatisfactory results from the group's point of view Childers said: "I called the police department."[26]

Herb Snow was one of the owners of the Meridian Drive-In located near Greenwood, Indiana. Toward the end of the 1978 drive-in season, police and the White River Township Planning Coalition received complaints from nearby residents that the Meridian was showing lewd films that could be seen from their homes and by people on the highway. Brought before the Planning Coalition Board, Snow said he wouldn't show any X films during the coming season but he would continue to show soft-core R films. According to this owner, he would have preferred to show G- or PG-rated films but economics dictated otherwise. "I don't play those R-rated films because I personally want to watch them," Snow said. "I'm in business for economics. I'm showing them to make a dollar. I've been in the theatre business eight years and I've sat through one X-rated movie, and I don't care to see another one again." When someone suggested that he could erect a fence around his property, Herb stood his ground, refusing to spend his money on a fence when he was operating within the law. After due consideration the Planning Coalition Board decided against becoming involved in the matter.[27] It was a rare example of the authorities backing off from a fight with a drive-in.

A similar situation arose at the same time in Philadelphia, when the 61st Street Drive-In, owned by Claude J. Schlanger, came under fire for screening X films such as *Barbara Broadcast, Climax of Blue Power,* and *Prisoners of Love.* District Attorney Edward G. Rendell reported that complaints came from citizens, the police, and neighborhood businesses and that "traffic has often come to a complete stop when the more provocative and graphically depicted sexual scenes are shown." Rendell was seeking an injunction to prevent the ozoner from showing sexually explicit films on the ground that the operation was a public nuisance. By proceeding that way, he hoped to avoid the difficulty of gaining a conviction under any type of obscenity charge, as this tactic was often viewed by the courts as an attack on First Amendment rights.[28] In this case a compromise seems to have been reached.

The state of Ohio went ahead with action although it had no specific case in hand. Many drive-ins were located just outside cities in unincorporated areas. In those cases city law didn't apply, only state law. Anticipating problems, Ohio passed a law, effective in 1979, which required all drive-ins in Ohio that showed X films to have a shield, "either tangible or intangible," so that the picture was not visible from outside the theater. Initially the law was to require all drive-ins to cover up by erecting a fence around their property. The NATO in Ohio lobbied the state legislature so that the law applied only to ozoners showing porn. NATO also successfully lobbied to have the fence provision changed to a barrier either tangible or intangible.[29] At that time the drive-in industry still awaited the much-hoped-for "miracle" screen that would contain the image within the property (the "intangible barrier").

An example of perseverance by the authorities in their battle against drive-ins can be seen in Minnesota. Prior to 1980 only one X-rated film had ever been shown at a Minnesota ozoner—*Deep Throat*, screened on only one day in 1973 at a drive-in in Verndale. The next year state representative Glen Sherwood introduced a bill to ban X-rated films at drive-ins. Opposing the bill was the North Central NATO group. The bill failed that year, and each succeeding year Sherwood would reintroduce it only to see it fail again. His persistence started to pay off in 1978, when the Minnesota House passed the bill unanimously only to have it killed in the Senate's judiciary committee.

As usual Sherwood was back with his bill in 1979, the sixth year in a row. North Central NATO president Gerald Carisch sighed: "It's the same bill, same author, nothing's changed. The amount of money we've spent fighting this thing is awful, but we're going to do it again." Stengthening the prospects of the bill this time around was a coalition of "pro-decency" and antiabortion advocates who pushed hard for its passage. The prolifers considered the issue a test of their strength. Once again the bill was passed by the House. When the bill reached the Senate judiciary committee, it was stripped of one provision, which would have permitted county attorneys to obtain injunctions against films they considered obscene before the films appeared on drive-in screens. This amended bill was passed by the full Senate becoming law in Minnesota in the spring of 1979.[30]

In Bible-belt areas of the United States, confrontations between townspeople and film exhibitors had become a regular spring occurrence as the drive-in season began. One target, in 1976, was Butler Felts, who owned a drive-in as well as an indoor house in Lamar, Missouri. A group of twenty people organized a letters-to-the-editor campaign against him, complaining about the R films he showed. (No X-rated films were ever shown.) Leading the group was Mrs. Davie Barger, wife of the pastor of Lamar's Christian Church. Mrs. Barger, who grew up in the 1950s, complained that she had been able to see only three films in the previous three years because of the dearth of good films. Her group had been drawn to its current campaign when their Bible study class came across an injunction in Romans to "hate evil." (Barger didn't explain how that specifically led them to drive-in movies.) Felts said he would stick to his policy of mixing up his films, something for everybody. While he would like to oblige his critics it was the R films that did the most business at the box office. Drive-in operators in the area agreed that R pictures outgrossed those rated G and PG by 3 or 4 to 1.

One letter to the editor said: "If you are opposed to the filthy movies, then please don't compromise with Satan—stay away," while another commented, "Please make movies that can be watched by grandmas, grandkids, the family dog, etc., without any embarrassment." Publisher David Palmer of the local paper said the issue surfaced every year. The indignant letters often arrived several in one envelope.[31]

Wilbraham, Massachusetts, enacted an ordinance in 1977 requiring restaurants, theaters, and other places of amusement to be shut between 2:00 and 5:00 A.M. Harry L. Schwab of the Parkway Drive-In claimed it was an economic hardship on him as he couldn't start his summer shows until 9:00 P.M. His three-feature program normally concluded after 2:00 A.M. Schwab argued that no such restrictions were in force in 1950 when the Parkway began operations. Complaints mainly stemmed, he thought, from one complaining couple who built a house next to his ozoner in the mid- to late-1960s. Complaints against the Parkway were registered on account of patron noise, adult films being screened, and those films being visible from outside the property. Due to the complaints Schwab said he had spent $10,000 to erect a solid fence and install new lighting. Mr. and Mrs. Karl Dygon were the complaining couple, who charged Schwab with violating the 2:00 A.M. closing ordinance, that speakers were not turned down, and that the Parkway management invited people in vans who became loud and intoxicated at the Parkway. While the Dygons scored the Parkway for screening "dirty movies," Schwab stated he hadn't screened an X film in more than eighteen months. Charges and countercharges were tossed around at a public hearing on the issue. The owner of a nearby motel cited vandalism to his property, laying blame for this on Parkway patrons. Schwab's lawyer told the hearing that "we are not here to be antagonistic. We will act in a reasonable, rational way to correct problems." Chairman of the Wilbraham selectmen, John Lovejoy, retorted: "Your client has promised to turn down the speakers for five long years. Schwab's record of cooperation is very, very narrow.... If there was a firm, honest commitment, we wouldn't be here tonight."[32]

Prompted by "ministerial constituents," two state legislators in Arkansas pushed a bill through the 1979 General Assembly in that state that would have required drive-in owners to erect tall fences to screen themselves from outside view. The governor vetoed the bill. Chicago's Starview drive-in spent several years fighting a Cook County ordinance that regulated the type of films that drive-ins were allowed to screen. During that time the Starview constructed a fence and planted eleven hundred poplar trees to screen itself off. It continued to show X-rated features.[33]

During the late 1970s and into the 1980s much of the assault on drive-ins over the type of films they played was led by fundamentalist religious types. One such was Gordon DeMeritt who, at twenty-six, moved his family out of New York to get away from bad influences there. A devout Baptist he settled his family in Luray, Virginia, a rural area eighty miles outside of Washington. Around October 1981 DeMeritt was driving his family home from church on a Sunday evening when his seven-year-old son suddenly exclaimed "Boy!" The lad's eye had been caught by a larger-than-life simulated-sex scene from the R-rated film *The Sensuous Nurse* being shown by the Luray Drive-In. Gordon was shocked and offended.

Over the course of the 1981 drive-in year the Luray had a policy of alternating popular films such as *Star Trek II, On Golden Pond,* and *Grease II* with more obscure R fare having titles like *Sex and the Other Woman* and *Cindy and Donna*. According to theater owner Charles E. Bowen, it was always the R films that did best at the box office. "We've had a number of requests for more sexually oriented movies," he said. "We attempt to show movies the people want to see." The Luray never screened X motion pictures.

Charlton Heston as Moses in *The Ten Commandments* before an audience of cars in Utah.

DeMeritt began a campaign to put an end to such goings-on. Soon the meetings of county supervisors rang with the cry of "public decency." Petitions were circulated and signed, warning that the showing of "adult" films at the drive-in "will have a severe effect on the moral health" of the community. Luray mayor Ralph Dean said: "If you go out and talk with the people in the county, they could care less about what's playing at the theater. As I see it, there's no way you can drive past the drive-in at 55 miles per hour and even see the screen anyway. Not if you're keeping your eyes on the road." But Gordon and his friends cared. He said, "Basically, I see it as a community issue. Does this man have the right to display on the highway anything he wants to display? . . . I wouldn't expose my children to it at home so why should I let one man's business decision affect then?" For Bowen it was a First Amendment fight.

The county attorney discovered that there was a state criminal statute that might apply, but the County Board of Supervisors declined to take action to regulate the Luray. Subsequent to that, charges were laid under that statute. A juvenile court judge threw those charges out of court when he learned that no allegedly offensive films were to be introduced as evidence by Commonwealth Attorney John T. Hennessy — the reason being that his office was unable to come up with the $450 needed to set up a private screening of the films. "This was a considerable amount," Hennessy explained.

At one point during the campaign against the ozoner, DeMeritt's lawyer contacted Bowen, asking why he didn't show "Christian" movies so that committed Christian families could attend the drive-in. One suggested film was *Chariots of Fire*. Having already booked it, Bowen was disappointed on screening it to find that "not a single, solitary one of them [DeMeritt and his supporters] showed up." Over the three years he had operated the Luray the film that grossed the least for Bowen was Disney's *Sleeping Beauty*. Despite the fact the squabble lasted a year or more Bowen remained committed to conducting his business as he saw fit. "We're not going to change our method of operation one iota. We are neither going to book less nor more of these movies," he said.[34]

A grassroots campaign against sex on the drive-in screens in West Valley City, Utah, a community of $72,000 people ten miles southwest of Salt Lake City, had concrete results. Citizen annoyance at the R films shown at the two area drive-ins led the city, in 1980, to pass a law creating a commission on public decency. This group consisted of twelve volunteer members who served one-year renewable terms at the discretion of the city manager. Under the law the drive-ins had to notify the city attorney when they planned to show an X or R film. The commission then reviewed these films prior to screening. Many of these films were shipped back to the distributor unshown in West Valley City, while cuts of "objectionable" material were ordered in others.

Wes Webb owned one of the drive-ins, the Valley-Vu. He said: "It's a pain to be faced with this, wondering what you can play. It gives a small element of people the opportunity, whenever they see something on the screen they don't like, to scream it's time to enforce the law. ... We show very few R-rated movies any more. ... I still don't think a soft-R picture with an occasional bare breast is offensive to children." When he played *Private Lessons* Webb darkened the screen during scenes the commission felt were objectionable. Commission on Public Decency chairman Steve Allen commented: "If a lady was to stand outside a drive-in theater and take off her top, she could be arrested for indecent exposure. At the same time we can show that same scene 40 times larger. That bothers me." The commission was primarily concerned with ozoners, but occasionally it checked out indoor theaters, store magazine shelves, and video rental outlets for possible infractions. City attorney Ron Greenhalgh said: "We let the theater owners know we stand behind the commission and we're not afraid to take legal action. ... The big thing we've got going for us is holding a sword over their heads. ... And the cooperation of the theater people has been great."[35]

In Memphis, Ken Robinson claimed that indecent films on the screen of the Frayser Drive-In could be seen from his home. When he found that his seven-year-old son and a friend had been watching sexually explicit films from the boy's bedroom in the house, Robinson "steamed to a boil." Along with about one hundred others Robinson picketed the drive-in. A committee was soon formed that called itself "Memphians Against Degeneracy." Responding to this public pressure, the police raided the drive-in, seized two films, *Women in Love* and *Ecstasy* — neither of which were X rated — and charged owners and employees under a state law that prohibited the showing of sex-oriented films in open-air theaters. Only recently had the Frayser switched to porn. It was a move that quadrupled attendance, complained protesters, whose action shut down the theater. When he learned of this a jubilant Robinson said: "It's great to see it closed and if they open, we will picket again and again."[36]

Clifford Faw and his brother Wade owned the Monroe Drive-In in Monroe, North Carolina, from 1952 onward. While they started showing X films in 1972, it was not until 1983 that a drive, led by religious groups, to have the theater shut was mounted against them. A year later the Faws were forced to submit two films, *Garage Girls* and *Hot Pursuit*, to the courts for review. Unwisely the Faws altered the films before submission, cutting about seventeen minutes out of them (each ran for one hour). When this was discovered the brothers were found guilty of contempt of court. Clifford Faw, then seventy-two, was sentenced to ten days in jail and fined $250, while Wade Faw was sentenced to ten days in jail or a $100 fine. The brothers also signed a consent order promising to screen no more X films. The Faws were then trying to sell the theater.[37]

Other ways existed to get rid of offending ozoners. In northern California the Sonomamarin Drive-In sat in Sonoma County right by the Marin County border. With the screen facing away from the highway it posed no problem to motorists. In fact the only people reportedly disturbed were the Corda family, who owned a farm in Marin County. According to the Cordas the drive-in turned to X films in the mid–1970s, causing the Cordas no end of troubles as they had to shoo trespassers away who were trying to see free movies. "You ought to see some of the people we have to deal with," said Tom Corda. "Our kids can't even play outside at night the way we did." The family kept their curtains closed so their children wouldn't be exposed to any on-screen sexual activity. Complaints to officials in both counties brought no relief, or so the Cordas thought, feeling that jurisdictional problems were at least partly to blame. However, the complaints were noticed by Supervisor Jim Harberson of Sonoma, who came up with a plan to buy the property, raze the theater, and use the land as a flood plain to hold overflowing water during heavy rains. It was much cheaper to do that than to raise the highway. Owner Dan Tocchini was happy to oblige. He got title to the ozoner as one theater in a much larger package he had purchased. Tocchini claimed it was only by showing X-rated films that he could make any money with the drive-in. Aware that county officials wanted him out, Dan said: "And I want out, but every time I get an offer they deny a permit because the area is designated as a scenic corridor." Supervisor Harberson was happy. "It's almost too good to be true," he said. "I'm really interested in flood control, but I wouldn't exactly be sorry to see the drive-in close."[38]

Cities and states continued to draft legislation against drive-ins during the 1980s. Hamond, Louisiana, adopted an ordinance in 1983 prohibiting the showing of films at drive-ins if they could be seen from the street. This was struck down by a federal judge as an unconstitutional violation of First Amendment rights. An ozoner in Berlin, Connecticut, that showed films with a sexual content had installed a fence around its property, at the request of the authorities, to prevent people outside the grounds from being able to see the film. When officials discovered a large hole in the fence town executives ordered the ozoner closed down. Prior to that a number of "nuisance" inspections by town officials had harassed the owner. A federal judge ordered the reopening of the Berlin Drive-In.[39]

The state of Maine enacted a law in 1983 making it an offense to exhibit obscene films where they could be viewed by minors under eighteen from any public thoroughfare or from a residence. This law was put on the books after year-long campaigns in two different communities. Demonstrators picketed the Ellsworth-Trenton drive-in along the major highway to Bar Harbor, charging that it screened films that degraded women as well as featuring all kinds of sexual activity. Owner Fred Freda echoed the sentiments of so many other owners by saying only X-rated films brought in any money. Freda said he would close down his ozoner when the new law took effect. Enfield was the other area with ozoner problems. Rose Hatch managed the targeted drive-in there. She said she took in more money on one weekend with an X film than she did in an entire month of G and PG fare. Before anyone could be prosecuted under the Maine law, a court had to first rule that the film under scrutiny fit the law's definition of obscenity.[40]

A long, heated battle took place in Rockford, Illinois, between the Sunset Drive-In theater and Winnebago County. Sitting just outside Rockford city limits, the Sunset showed its age with the concession stand peeling badly and weeds sprouting up all over the parking area. While the Sunset faced the highway, a thicket of trees plus the fact the screen was positioned on low ground effectively blocked any images from escaping to passing motorists. Some surrounding homes were on high ground. They had a view of the screen. The Sunset had shown only "acceptable" fare at one time, but like so many other ozoners it was suffering a rapid decline in business. Ownership changed in 1983. So did the type of films screened with selection going to R and X films. Neighbors were shocked when they looked out their windows at night. A war was joined.

Area resident Sandra Muraski said: "We kept out kids inside at night and stayed home the whole first summer. We didn't even want to bring a babysitter up here and expose her to it." Husband Stan added: "I had a very difficult talk with the kids. They were about 10 years old. I had to tell them, 'Adults don't really do stuff like that. Or if they do, they don't let anybody film it.'" Neighbors reported they were plagued by trespassers on their property trying to get a good view.

A raid was carried out by Winnebago authorities not long after the first complaints started to come in. The authorities closed down the drive-in and arrested the manager and projectionist. Fighting back, since it regarded the whole issue as a First Amendment case, the Sunset won a restraining order in federal court allowing the show to go on. Winnebago Sheriff Donald Gasparini declared: "Things that occur in a place like Las Vegas should not go on in Rockford." During April 1984 Gasparini's men raided the Sunset four nights in a row. The Sunset got a judge to order him to stop. Trials were held as a result of these raids. One ended in a mistrial after a local minister marched around the courtroom with a placard that read "Don't License Lust." A second trial ended when the jury found the film *Deep Throat* not to be obscene. A third trial resulted in a jail sentence of 140 days for the theater owner.

In an attempt to make the image unviewable to the neighbors, the Sunset installed a number of high-intensity lights shining outward at neighboring houses. Though less than fully effective, they did succeed in enraging the residents to new heights of anger. A real estate developer who had holdings he wished to develop near the theater sued the Sunset, claiming what with trespassers, the X films, and the high-intensity lights, his land had been made unfit for "respectable occupation." He lost.

Later in 1984 Winnebago County adopted an outdoor theater ordinance closely patterned on successful ones that seemed to have held up in court. It required drive-ins to agree not to show films depicting sexual activity if their screens could be seen from public streets or private residences. The Sunset fought this all the way to the U.S. Supreme Court. The high court declined to hear the Sunset's appeal, in effect letting the law stand. Residents in Winnebago breathed a sigh of relief. At last it was over. They had won. Less than two weeks after that decision the Sunset opened for the 1986 drive-in season. The opening attraction was *Beverly Hills Exposed*, which was to be followed a week later by *Naked Scents*. The Sunset was thumbing its nose at the courts. Neighbors were infuriated. But it was an ultimately futile act. For Winnebago County it was only necessary to go through the required procedure to revoke the Sunset's license, shutting it for good.[41]

Chapter 18

Decline and Stagnation, 1960s and 1970s

While the 1950s were a period of wild growth for the drive-ins and accompanying extensive media coverage, the 1960s, and into the 1970s, were periods of relative quiet. The industry stagnated, showing little inclination to expand or contract. Much less attention was paid by the media. Even the oil shock of the early 1970s caused little attention. This was followed by a brief ray of hope that ozoners would undergo a new period of growth. Only in the last years of the 1970s was it mentioned that the drive-in was in a serious decline.

General Drive-In Corporation owned twenty outdoor and sixteen indoor theaters in the eastern part of the country in 1960. That year they reported that 70 percent of their revenue, and a higher percentage of their profits, came from their outdoor houses. These were big units averaging more than eleven hundred cars each. During the summer these ozoners operated at 75 percent capacity on weekends, 25 percent on weekdays. For the rest of the year it was 50 percent capacity on weekends, 20 percent the rest of the week. Thirteen operated year-round. Thirty-three percent of the combined gross came from concession sales, compared to 11 percent from indoor spots. Operating profit margin for the drive-ins, 15.5 percent, was almost double that from indoor venues.[1] This period started well for almost every outdoor operator. It would end badly for almost all of them.

Community relations remained an integral part of hyping a new theater, or of the rehabilitation of an old one. When Pacific Drive-In Theatres opened the 1,612-car, $750,000 Sunnyside Drive-In at Fresno, California, on May 24, 1965, executive Robert Selig was on hand to explain it all. Letters of invitation were sent to the main Parent-Teacher Association officers, the clergy, and to high school journalism teachers and classes. These groups arrived for daylight tours of the Sunnyside at 10:00, 2:00 and 4:00 P.M., respectively. Response rates were said to have been: 60 percent PTA, 40 percent clergy, and 90 percent from journalism classes.

Letters to the first two groups stressed that the company would debunk any ideas these people might hold that ozoners were still passion pits. "Are they sinful fancies or legitimate sources of wholesome relaxation? . . . Please do join us in the shadow of the world's largest screen for an hour of what we think will be unusual enlightenment of an honest, sparkling clean and properly motivated community enterprise," went part of the letter to the clergy. To the journalism classes was stressed the idea that they would be exposed to news in the making. Once these groups were on site Selig and five executive underlings gave them a guided tour of the facilities complete with free refreshments. Pointing out that the aim of the drive-in was to provide wholesome entertainment for all ages, Selig told each group:

> We wish Walt Disney could make a picture a week—or a day—so that we could always give you a clean, amusing Disney picture, but unfortunately that isn't possible, so we do out utmost to give you the best, most wholesome pictures from all sources that can be had. . . . We wanted you to come and see us in the daytime, which is something that few people have occasion to do, so that you can balance the facts that you have seen against the unfounded derogatory rumors you sometimes hear from critics.[2]

Almost a decade later Pete Hudnall and Phil Gibson took over the Suburbia Drive-In in Gainesville, Florida. Previous owners had allowed it to run down and become a place for gangs to hang out in. Business was poor. The new owners turned things around by adding two more screens, modernizing and enlarging the concession stand, and adding attractions such as pinball machines, electronic games, and a jukebox. Food selections offered at the refreshment stand included fish, corn dogs, and barbecued ribs. Shows were programmed to appeal to the area's large university student population. Following graduation ceremonies at Gainesville High School, each graduate was given a T-shirt with the school name on the front, compliments of the drive-in. Business at the Suburbia thrived. Soon a laundromat and bakery were added to the amenities. Explained Hudnall and Gibson: "What we are trying to do here is to create a self-contained unit in which people of all ages can enjoy themselves, while at the same time have the opportunity to fulfill certain necessary household duties."[3]

Playgrounds remained an important part of the drive-ins during the 1960s but slowly started to slip away, especially at outlets which switched to partly or mostly screening R or X films. Most other novelty entertainment forms disappeared entirely in the 1960s. Two outdoor theaters in Minneapolis each set up a small dance floor and provided a five-piece rock and roll band allowing patrons to dance from 7:30 P.M. until 9 P.M. when the show started. While this type of activity was common in the 1950s Minneapolis was the exception rather than the rule when they instituted dancing in June 1967. One of the reasons they did so was because that was the year that saw the permanent nation-wide introduction of daylight saving time.[4]

The Suburbia Theatre at Gainesville, Florida. This building contained concessions and restrooms on the first floor, a 350-seat enclosed auditorium on the second, and the projection room on the third, the tip of which is just visible, about 1953.

More typical of the fate of extras introduced in the 1960s took place at Wineland's Laurel Drive-In in the Washington, D.C. area. Opened in 1965, it also had a walk-in patio that seated 250, advertising itself as a "drive-in and walk-in." Motorized golf carts were available at the box office for people who came without a car, allowing them to drive around the lot. It was very successful for a year, then died completely when the novelty wore off. A dozen years later the carts were rusting away unused in storage.[5]

When drive-ins went searching for extras in the 1960s and 1970s, it was usually a type of extra that would bring in some money, not cost them any. Three drive-ins participated in an experiment in Boston in 1963. With the aid of federal money the three ozoners were turned into park-and-ride lots in the daytime for commuters who parked in the lot, then took Boston buses to work. Those using the service were reminded that they had to remove their cars before the drive-ins opened for business in the evening or they would have to pay the outdoor theater's admission fee to retrieve their vehicles.[6]

Los Angeles tried a similar plan a decade later when the city's transit authority, RTD, used five of Pacific Theatres' drive-ins for park-and-ride lots. Commuters parked on the lots for two dollars a month plus paid ten dollars for a monthly RTD pass. Pacific was guaranteed $2,000 a month from the RTD for each drive-in used, with five hundred spaces set aside for parking in each one. It was a deal that made Pacific's Robert Selig jubilant. "In my 29 years in the theatre business, with many spent in drive-in operations, we always have searched for new ways to combat nonproductive time," he enthused.[7] Nonproductive time was anytime an ozoner was closed, which was most of the day. Unfortunately these park-and-ride experiments were failures.

More typical of extra income ventures were the swap meets that many drive-ins held once in a while in their lots. The Long Beach Drive-In in Long Beach, California, ran a daytime swap meet on Wednesdays, Saturdays, and Sundays. The Timonium Drive-In near Baltimore, Maryland, leased its lot for $150 a day on the weekends for a combined flea market and auto sales operation. Only a few of Pacific's ozoners were used for swap meets. None were held in theaters in or near the city of Los Angeles as there was too much competition from garage sales and church bazaars.[8]

Contests and giveaways took place less frequently. The Northmain Drive-In in Winnipeg, Manitoba, held a draw at its concession stand to give away three $50 silicone-ignition wire sets. Per patron concession income was significantly higher the weekend of the draw. Next the Northmain gave away a $1,500 motorcycle, donated by a local merchant. This contest ran ten weeks with patrons having to deposit their ballots in a box located in the concession building. Over that time Northmain recorded a 10 percent per person increase in concession stand income.[9]

More modest was the contest run at the Palmer Drive-In near Washington, D.C. Between the first and second features six ticket stubs were drawn with the winning numbers being posted in the refreshment stand. Winners got one dollar off on anything, admission or food. Actually this contest has other motives as Palmer official Harry Robinson explained, "This is our way of keeping the people in the box office honest by making customers ask for their stubs, and of keeping the customers honest. There's less temptation to sneak in the trunk or through the woods with the incentive of a dollar's worth of free popcorn."[10]

When the oil shock of the early 1970s struck even it was translated into a potential money making opportunity by the outdoor exhibitors. Toward the end of 1973 the nation's gas stations threatened a shut down to protest retail gas price ceilings. It was a move deplored by NATO executive B. V. Sturdivant, who denounced the threat as "an unacceptable danger to more than 4,500 drive-in theatres of the nation." NATO then undertook a feasibility study to determine ways of putting ozoners into use as filling stations. Paul Roth, president of NATO, wanted to broaden the study to look for a variety of ways of generating extra income. "I think it makes sense for NATO to look into additional uses for theatres . . . that will produce revenue during times when theatres would not ordinarily be open, or on ground or in facilities that don't normally produce anything." Roth explained. "I'm neither particularly carried away with, and certainly not upset with the suggestion that we explore filling stations. I just don't think it will be productive to limit it to that."[11] Nothing came of the gas station idea.

Horn-honking by patrons came to be an annoyance to owners in the 1970s. Prior to that it seemed to have drawn no comment except rather obliquely when owners told Detroit, in a list of requests for a better vehicle, that horns should be made inoperable when the ignition was off. Owner Ed Price was perturbed that some of his patrons repeatedly honked their horns during the intermission. Price reasoned it was either based on genuine objection or downright devilment, opting for the latter as the explanation.[12]

Honking before the show started was apparently more common. This was often caused by impatient patrons who felt it was dark enough to start the show. When this happened at the Scarboro Drive-In near Toronto, Ontario, the manager came on the loudspeaker saying: "Honking your horns is stupid and just annoys the people around you. If we turned the movie on now you'd see a blank screen. You paid to see a movie. If you want to see a blank screen we'll turn it on." The honking stopped. Manager Dick Stemen had the same problem at the Corral Drive-In near Flatwoods, Kentucky. "Horn blowing is like yawning or coughing, it's contagious. If you don't stop it at the beginning, the whole field soon will be going," he commented. "I don't pick the starting time. It must be dark enough for a good presentation. I want to give them the best show I can even if it means starting five minutes later." Another reason for curtailing horn blowing was to avoid a rash of complaints from neighboring residents irate over the noise. Once it got so bad at the Corral that one patron left his car and ran to the front of the lot where he tried to lead the horns, like a musical conductor. Most drive-ins refused to start a film until the tooting stopped. "Why let three antagonists spoil the show for everybody?" said Dick. "The guy next to him will tell him to stop if I say 'no show' till all the horns stop."[13]

Asked about which type of films drew the best at his theater Stemen said that good action pictures outdrew any other types, including sexploitation films. Generally he programmed "good" movies during the June through September period, when kids were out of school. At the end or beginning of the season sex films dominated the bill. At the "bottom of the heap" in terms of drawing customers, Stemen placed the cheap, independently produced horror and science fiction films.[14]

A survey of 14 outdoor theaters around Washington, D.C., in the summer of 1977 indicated that two played X-rated films, three played R material, two mixed R and PG, while one mixed R and horror films. Four screened mostly PG fare with action and horror dominating. One mixed in some G material. Only two of the fourteen screened mostly "bland" G material such as Walt Disney films, when available.[15]

Lou Ratner owned two ozoners in the Akron, Ohio area. Like many other exhibitors, as his family dominated business trailed off in the 1960s, he programmed more sex oriented material. Speaking of these sex films Ratner said that in the early 1970s "that is what almost all the drive-ins were showing: the cheerleaders, the nurses, the student teachers with sexploitation subjects like that. We can't deny it. That must have been about 60 percent of the business." By the end of that decade the tide had turned again; this time action features predominated. Films that did best at Ratner's outlets then were the Burt

Reynolds and Clint Eastwood types of flicks. Sexploitation films fell out of vogue, thought Lou, because the audience found them to be all alike.[16]

In the mid-1960s Bart Pirosh was an executive at the Pacific Drive-In chain, with many years of film booking experience behind him. Pacific resisted any trend to screen sex films doggedly trying to program for a family audience. Pirosh found the best grossing pictures to be big westerns, big outdoor pictures and "real good family pictures." Examples cited included *The Vikings, The Alamo, Ben-Hur, The Carpetbaggers, The Parent Trap,* and Beatles' films. His company refused to book a film like *The Lovers* for fear of objections from patrons who complained strenuously when *Shot in the Dark* and *Tom Jones* were screened. Foreign films were rarely played at the Pacific chain. One problem was that a subtitled print couldn't be used, as the titles couldn't be read at drive-ins. Pacific and the distributor of *La Dolce Vita* did dicker about playing that film; however, they couldn't develop a larger subtitle. As well, the producer couldn't or wouldn't provide a dubbed version, so the film was never screened by Pacific. Pirosh felt that even if it had been it would have grossed poorly.[17]

At one drive-in in the Midwest during the summer of 1976, the bill of fare presented was headed by soft porn and hot-car movies, the two largest categories. Completing the bill were horror and disaster films. Representative titles were *Blazing Stewardesses, Revenge of the Cheerleader, The Creature from Black Lake, Dirty Mary, Crazy Larry,* and *Airport 1975*. Seven of the sixteen titles were sex films. Hot-car movies did the best box office at that location that summer.[18]

While the most popular film genre at the drive-in may have changed from time to time what remained constant was the fact that ozoners almost never got first run major Hollywood product during the 1960s and 1970s. As always they remained stuck with second- and third-run or with B or worse films. When a Chicago chain managed to play two major first-run films at its ozoner during the same season, *The Deep* and *Star Wars*, it marked a first for the industry. The year was 1977.[19] So cut off from mainstream films were the drive-ins that a production industry developed especially to service them. Best known of this group was American International Pictures (AIP), founded in 1954. AIP went on to great success, producing quickly made, low-cost films, usually science fiction and or horror, supplied to drive-in outlets. The most famous AIP alumnus is Roger Corman. Many of the films produced by AIP, and others like it, were never screened at all in indoor theaters.[20]

One South Carolina operator split his films between X-rated soft porn and religious-type material such as *The Robe, The Sign of the Cross* and *The Ten Commandments*. Anything with Elvis Presley was also a guaranteed big draw. Owner Terry Holman said:

> The Pentecostals will line up for Pat Boone's "The Cross and the Switchblade" and anything with an Art Linkletter voice-over. But then there's a lot of folks

> down here who would just as soon see what Linda Lovelace is doing, too. You want to know the best drive-in movie ever made? *Thunder Road*. Don't ask me why. Maybe it's the chases, maybe it's Robert Mitchum. But it's a door-buster. I could bring it in tomorrow and I'd be packed.[21]

The Midwest survey cited above also mentioned *Thunder Road* (1958) as a seminal ancestor of hot-car pictures.

Evidence for the powerful impact of television on film attendance, at least in 1963, came from Pacific's Bart Pirosh, who said the biggest box office weekend he ever had in his three decades in the business was the weekend after the assassination of President John F. Kennedy. "The people came just in droves," he recalled, "because they couldn't see regular television programs." Similarly, a Georgia owner said that the week after the assassination was the biggest he ever had. "They lined up out here for two and three hours. Face it, they were cut off from their crap on the tube. The next big surge was during the moonshots. The moonshots were the best thing that's happened to drive-ins since Elvis."[22]

At Pacific's Southern California ozoners, Pirosh said the company made it a policy to start their films on time, at a specific time, as patrons wanted to see everything from the start as opposed to earlier, more family-oriented times, when a family didn't care so much if they arrived in the middle of the film. Many ads for ozoners listed the start times simply as "dusk." Pacific charged about $2.50 a carload then, in the middle 1960s, while indoor prices in the area were $2.50 to $3.50 for first run. Pirosh described his patrons as an "unsophisticated audience" drawn primarily from two groups: families and those in their teens and young adults—daters. Reviews of movies were entirely ignored by these ozoner patrons, who were the "moderates, the middle class." Pressure was still exerted on Pacific at that time against booking certain films. If the company tried to book a Charlie Chaplin film they got intense pressure from the American Legion. In order not to offend its moderate patrons Pacific wouldn't book anything they felt to be out-and-out propaganda for the Communists, the John Birch Society, the Ku Klux Klan, and so on.

Of his audience Pirosh added:

> Now I doubt very much whether the majority of our people read a book in a year. I just don't believe it . . . of any kind. These are people who possibly went through high school and who were not literate, no literary bent, probably went through on C's and D's. They are working in factories and in jobs that do not require high intelligence. . . . So these are the people that are the backbone of our business, and they're not interested in art forms. They don't know from nothing about art forms and they care less.[23]

Pirosh may have avoided booking sex films into Pacific theaters in favor of family-type offerings, but he didn't mind the low quality. He admitted:

"We get some of the so-called important pictures first run. We get all the junk offered as first run because of the type of service we have. We get our patrons in on all our junk . . . so why stick them with something good."[24]

Toward the middle and end of the 1970s admission prices at drive-ins ranged from $2.00 a head in Los Angeles to $4.00–$6.00 per carload in New England to $2.50 a person in Texas to from $1.00 per head to $4.00–$5.00 per carload in Chicago to $2.00 a ticket in the Midwest.[25]

When an advertising agency looked at movie-going audiences in the mid–1970s, the company found the indoor patrons to be career-minded, confident, financially stable, future-oriented, and socially active while the ozoner patron was described as a financially worried, dissatisfied, lonely blue-collar worker.[26]

Vans became a popular mode of transportation, and they turned up in increasing numbers both on the highways and in the drive-ins. Some parked their vans backwards opening the back doors to watch the film while lounging on pillows or on foam mattresses. Others sat outside on folding lawn chairs. Kids occasionally viewed the film while lying on the roof of the van. Some parked sideways, viewing the picture through open side doors. In Los Angeles patrons were described as middle income. Men came dressed in T-shirts while women could still be seen in hair curlers. Upscale vehicles could be seen among the vans. Mercedes and Jaguars drove in to see *Chinatown* while Cadillacs turned out in numbers for any Barbra Streisand film. Linda Parker came with her six-year-old daughter and her mother. After paying $4.00 admission for the two adults, Linda bought three boxes of popcorn, two double hamburgers, two corn dogs, two Cokes, and three chocolate bars from the refreshment stand at a total cost of $6.25. "I come to drive-ins whenever I get the money," Linda said. "I like them because you don't have kids hollering and running up and down the aisles." Gary Gough was there with his girlfriend, in his van. They brought their own food and booze. "You can do what you want to. Nobody bothers you," said one attendee. Patron Donald Almuete commented, "You create your own environment here. It's very private, and you can be within yourself." Just out of high school Don Riley and his friends went to the drive-in to party. Some of his friends worked a scam wherein each would park his car in a different theater (it was a triple-screen ozoner); then the people, not the cars, would change places during intermissions.[27]

With a low regard for the kind of films he screened, the Georgia operator said: "I been shoveling this crap to them for thirty years now. Sometimes, when I get drunk enough, I get a little sad about it all. I mean it. That crowd out there is the crowd that skinned through high school on C-minuses and D's. They're still wearing their football sweaters. And I mean they don't read one book a year, any year."[28]

Or, as another observer put it, commenting on the 1970s drive-in experience: "There was the feeling that the movie itself meant less than in other circumstances; that what really mattered, whether it was the sexplay of the adolescents or the family togetherness of the others, was what happened down below in the cars. One sensed that the quality of the popcorn, say, was more important than the quality of the film."[29]

Problems of vandalism and theft increased. Leon Back, head of NATO's chapter in Maryland, reported that an ozoner might lose as many as 20 percent of its speakers over the course of a season. It was this loss rate which first made Back think about converting to radio sound for his own operation. Terry Holman in South Carolina noted he lost three air-conditioning units from his ozoner in just one month. "Those things weigh damn near a hundred pounds. Hell, they'll steal anything, steal the speakers and take them over to Georgia and sell them to another drive-in." When asked if he would buy stolen Carolina speakers a Georgia operator laughed and said: "Hell, yeah. They buy ours."[30]

One of the stranger, and more tragic, legal cases involving drive-ins started in 1971 when nineteen-year-old Demetrius Terentiuk and a seventeen-year-old female companion attended an outdoor theater in Geauga County, Ohio. As it was a cool evening Terentiuk kept the motor of his eleven-year-old car running to keep warm. The couple were overcome by carbon monoxide fumes and not discovered by patrolling police until three hours after the drive-in closed for the night. Terentiuk emerged from a four-month-long coma with permanent crippling injuries; his companion died. Five years later a lawsuit against the drive-in went against Terentiuk when it was held that neither the theater operator nor the corporation could be held liable.[31]

The art of concession selling maintained its scientific height through the use of a series of trailers strung together and run throughout the length of the intermission period. Operator Ed Price, after consultation with other owners, had what he considered the optimally efficient trailer film, or as he called it, "clock." It began with an opening title, such as "Visit Our Concession Stand," followed by "Ten Minutes till Showtime." Then came several short food clips touting various food and beverage products available at the refreshment stand. Each ran ten or twenty seconds. After sixty seconds of those came "Nine Minutes till Showtime," followed by sixty more seconds of short food clips. After eight minutes to go was announced, came long food clips such as two of thirty seconds' duration each. For the remaining time between each one minute countdown came one period of public service trailers; the other periods were filled with normal sixty second ads paid for by local or national merchants. Toward the end of the clock warnings that time to visit the refreshment stand was getting low were increased. Food trailers were still supplied free to the theaters by suppliers such as Coca-Cola.

Clips touting concession products were all aired early in the clock where "they'll do the most good." Price felt this type of ordering of the trailers was important for if they were assembled in the clock in a confused or hodgepodge way, without rhyme or reason, they would work much less efficiently. Ideally the clock was to be run just once a night, between the previews and the feature, or between the previews and the second film if a double bill was screening. Price was aware that his patrons often honked their horns throughout the clock but offered the thought that "despite all the surface objections to it, I feel that patrons not only expect the clock, but demand it."[32]

Writer Joyce Maynard endured just such a clock. It was very much as Price suggested except that it ran for only eight minutes and may have included many more food clips than Ed thought prudent. Between the minute-countdown titles Maynard reported she was "subjected to pictures of doughnuts, hot dogs, potato chips, popcorn, chocolate bars, Orange Crush, hamburgers, Cracker Jack, ice cream bars, corn chips, Life Savers, and peanuts." Unhappy as she was about the mind manipulation and brainwashing she felt were at work, Maynard had to admit how "successful that intermission was—how, at every reminder that there were only a few minutes left to stock up on 'tasty treats,' the members of the viewing audience obediently opened their car doors and headed, robotlike, for the refreshment counter."[33]

Some observers refused to believe that drive-ins would fade away. Even in the middle 1970s some accounts spoke of an increase in ozoner attendance, of a revival, or a renaissance. For many of these observers, both inside and outside the industry, what would fuel new growth would be the imminent technological improvements—the containment screen and radio sound. The former never arrived, while the latter was not so major an advance as hoped for.[34]

For General Cinema Corporation the handwriting was on the wall by 1973, when it announced an ambitious expansion program to add new screens—all indoors. They also said they would phase out of the ozoner business as soon as leases expired and they could redevelop land they owned.[35]

By the end of the 1970s the drive-in decline was readily admitted. Texas had 475 drive-ins in 1959. The number was down to 384 by 1965. By 1969 there were 350 drive-ins comprising 311 single screens, 32 twins, 6 triples, and 1 four-screen operation. Ten years later the number was down to 268; 213 single screens, 40 twins, 12 triples and 3 four-screen venues. Al Reynolds, president of NATO's Texas chapter, attributed the decline to much higher film rental rates, the introduction of daylight saving time, which delayed start times by one hour making it too late for much of the family business that was the mainstay of outdoor theaters. As well he thought informality of dress became so standard in the 1960s that people dressed casually for indoor theaters, robbing ozoners of informality as a prime selling point. "Obsolescence and a declining trade area in addition to daylight time, contributed to the demise of most of this type of operation," Reynolds concluded.[36]

Southern New Jersey had around forty drive-ins operating between 1973 and 1975. By 1978 it was down to twenty. Don Warner, manager of one of those outlets, blamed the decline on a lack of suitable product, saying: "The pictures they show today at drive-ins are the whole reason the industry is failing. It will never be the same." There were no longer the popular Western and horror films that used to fill the lot for Warner.[37]

Joe Zazzaro, manager of the Memorial Drive-In near West Springfield, Massachusetts, attributed the decline in business to a lack of quality films and the drop in family attendance. When he screened Walt Disney's *Gus* the year before, he pulled it after two days because nobody came. Zazzaro contended that the people who did turn up had no respect for property. Picnic tables used to grace the grounds but were stolen or trashed by vandals. Three hundred speakers a year had to be replaced because patrons stole them.[38]

Escalating land prices were an incentive to sell outdoor theaters. As cities moved out toward them, they became increasingly valuable. Those that had located on choice sites, such as the intersection of major roads, were even more in demand. As ozoners disappeared they were replaced by shopping malls, condos, apartment buildings, offices, parking lots, supermarkets, K Marts, hotels, and so on. Outdoor theaters faced higher expenses such as increased rental fees but also higher maintenance costs for everything from repainting the screen to repaving the lot.

When the drive-in went into the start of its steep decline, the indoor theater was beginning to arrest its own long decline. The indoor houses did this by multiplexing, converting old large units into two or more screens in the same area, or much more usually, by building new multiscreen theaters in new areas with each screen having considerably smaller seating capacity than the old single units. Extremely infrequent would be the construction of a new indoor theater with just one screen. There was a payroll saving, since a five-screen multiplex could be run by fewer employees than if those five were all separate units. More importantly these theaters were of a smaller size reflecting the changing pattern of the audience and the fact that giant units would never again by viable.

Drive-ins still had what were basically far-too-large-sized units. Some multiplexing was being done by the 1970s, but only about 10 percent of ozoners were then multiplexes, compared to about one-third of indoor locations. There had always been a few multiplex drive-ins around right from 1950, when there was at least one twin and one fourplex in the country. The fourplex ozoner opened in Chicago in 1950. Each section held three hundred automobiles. Unlike modern multiplexes, which usually screen different films in each part, this drive-in showed the same movie on all the screens. Multiplexing here was done as an elaborate method of traffic control. Two areas were filled first, then short subjects were screened. While the shorts ran, the other two areas were filled up. When all four areas were in the feature started. At the end the first two sections emptied while the other two watched the shorts. Sections were color-coded so patrons wouldn't get lost returning to their cars from the common refreshment area.[39]

The Twin Drive-In near Amarillo, Texas, about 1953.

It was much harder to multiplex an ozoner, since an owner wouldn't want a screen facing directly into the setting sun—delaying a late summer start even more. If his one screen was carefully shielded from highway view, an owner might have been a little gun-shy of facing one that way, fearing a wave of complaints from neighbors. Cost of shielding it may have been prohibitive. Even changing a sixteen hundred–car drive-in into a threeplex may have left each section still too large for the contemporary market. Indoor theaters could and did respond to a shifting audience by building six-, eight-, ten-, twelve-, or more-screen complexes. Drive-ins couldn't. A very few of the ozoners went to four screens or more, but it was a desperation measure that didn't work. The only viable conversion an ozoner could make, from the point of view of customer enjoyment, was to a two- or three-screen operation. And that was not enough of a response to save them.

At the end of the 1970s a great number of the ozoners were twenty-five to thirty years old—an age at which capital improvements were needed in many instances. Screen towers were made of wood in many cases; insects and weather were taking a toll. Speaker wiring was likely shot, or going that way, and so on. Faced with large expenditures for replacement or even larger expenditures for upgrading, as from in-car speakers to radio sound, many owners decided to get out. For when they looked down the road it didn't look very promising to invest in something designed to last another quarter century.

General Cinema executive Melvin Wintman said of the ozoner industry in 1979: "Its future is behind it." That same year the last drive-in in Marin County, California, closed. At the wake nineteen-year-old patron Carol Dutra wondered where she and her friends would go, saying: "We're too young to get into discos. We can't smoke or talk at indoor theaters. At drive-ins police don't hassle you. What good is affluence if it means drive-in freaks are going to be culturally deprived?"[40]

From the census data drive-ins held up fairly well into the mid–1970s. The number of outdoor theaters changed little in that time, after an initial drop. In 1963 there were 3,502 drive-ins, 3,375 of them with a payroll. Every one dollar of payroll expense that year generated $5.19 in receipts (including tax) for drive-ins, compared to $3.99 for indoor theaters. This was a low point for the indoor venues, from which they would begin to recover. Drive-ins took 24 percent of the combined gross admissions in 1963. Average indoor admission was 98 cents, 91 cents outdoors. Each dollar of admissions at an indoor venue produced 10.4 cents in concession sales, 21.1 cents outdoors. The average ozoner drew 84,877 patrons, enough to fill the lot to capacity fifty-eight times.[41]

For the 1967 and 1972 census only abbreviated data was published by the government. Every payroll dollar generated $4.37 indoors in 1967, $4.67 in 1972; $5.26 outdoors in 1967, then $5.09 in 1972. Of the combined gross ticket sales drive-ins took 24.4 percent in 1967, their highest mark ever, slipping to 22.75 percent in 1972. There were 3,384 outdoor theaters with a payroll in 1967, 3,342 in 1972.[42]

A recovery by indoor theaters can be seen in 1977 census data when a payroll dollar generated $5.66 compared to $5.16 outdoors. This marked the first time that indoor theaters outperformed their outdoor kin on this measure. Drive-ins took just 16 percent of the combined gross that year. At the concession stand indoor houses took in 16.6 cents per dollar admission compared to 27 cents outdoors. Average admission price was $2.60 indoors, $2.61 at the ozoners. That year the average drive-in drew 58,347 patrons, enough to fill the lot to capacity just thirty-seven times. In number they were down to 2,882.[43]

If the decline of the drive-in was noted fairly frequently at the end of the 1970s, and it was, nobody spoke of its death, nobody wrote an obituary. That would be left for the 1980s.

Chapter 19

Rapid Descent, 1980s and Beyond

Typical of the 1980s were the following stories. When the Copiague opened in Copiague, New York, during the mid–1950s halcyon drive-in days, it was a blockbuster of a place holding two thousand automobiles, a full service restaurant and a Ferris wheel, among other attractions. Twenty-five years later the restaurant was closed, the Ferris wheel dismantled and gone. On a typical summer night in 1982 it played two second-run films to just fifty autos. Projectionist Pierre Jelis, Jr., commented: "Drive-ins are going downhill. It's sad. Now you go to sterile movie houses to watch a screen not much bigger than a television set."[1] Not long after the Copiague was gone.

The Morris Plains Drive-In near Parsippany, New Jersey, was erected on fourteen acres of rural land purchased in 1947 for a total cost of $10,750. In 1981 the site was sold to a developer for $1.25 million. On the West Coast the Frontier Drive-In in San Diego was sold in the middle 1980s to build a shopping center. Its eleven acres were purchased for $11 million. Herb Burton, Frontier manager, said: "My heart says drive-ins will survive, but my mind tells me they're going to be like '56 Corvettes—you're not going to find them." Near the start of the decade Sumner Redstone, president of U.S. Northeast Theatre Corporation, thought: "Drive-ins are rapidly becoming part of our nostalgic past. I foresee their extinction by the end of the decade."[2]

The long-standing problems ozoners had in getting first-run films continued through the 1980s. The owner of the last drive-in on Cape Cod built a four-screen indoor house right beside it. Eleanor Hazen of the South Wellfleet Drive-In insisted that one of the reasons for building it was the fact that "distributors continually refused the drive-in first-run features."[3]

Owners of ozoners near Pittsburgh, Pennsylvania, despaired of the same problem, in 1983. George Pastor of the Twin Hi-Way lamented an ongoing problem of unavailability of major pictures soon enough. Tom and Aglaia Zaimes had operated the Monroeville for thirty-seven years. Mrs. Zaimes said: "I feel drive-ins will become extinct if the distributors don't give independent exhibitors a break and allow us to play first-run pictures." Her husband was more adamant and angrier: "Distributors like to let movies stay put in the indoor theaters they maintain have the largest grossing potential. Screens relegated to late-run status routinely are told no prints are available. There are anti-trust laws but independents don't want to pursue law enforcement for every picture they play. These youngsters are quitters. They don't stand up for their rights." Added Mrs. Zaimes: "We had an anti-trust suit that was never resolved. The booking problem still continues. There's no let-up."[4]

Another veteran owner in the Pittsburgh area was Marty Warren of the South Hills Drive-In. Regarding his experience with the film *E.T.*, Warren remarked: "Them's fightin' initials to most exhibitors." Universal didn't make their all-time money-making film available to drive-ins until almost a full year after its release. And 20th Century–Fox was irritating outdoor theater owners with a similar no-drive-in policy on its then-current blockbuster *Return of the Jedi* by telling exhibitors they would have to wait a year to obtain a print.[5]

Typical, perhaps, of the distributors' attitude was that voiced by Sidney Ganis, vice president in charge of marketing for Lucasfilm Ltd., who said, "We don't have any major regard for drive-ins because they're such a small percentage of our profits."[6] A few drive-ins, such as the Pacific chain in the Southwest, did regularly screen first-run major films but more didn't.

Even the old-faithful, small independent producers who had so long been a staple supplier of cheap product to the outdoor houses began to diminish. Roger Corman moved on from AIP to form New World in 1970. Initially they released films primarily to drive-ins but soon branched out into other areas, such as releasing foreign films by directors like Ingmar Bergman to the art-house market. It was an attempt to move away from an image of New World as simply an exploitation company like AIP. The decline in the number of drive-ins also pushed Corman to target the ozoner less heavily. Crown International Pictures (CIP) was another production company that produced a great deal of its product specifically for outdoor theaters. Well over 50 percent of their market was in drive-ins, decreasing to around 30 by 1981. CIP president Mark Tenser felt there was no chance that the downward curve of drive-ins would level off or be reversed. More and more, CIP was targeting multiplex indoor houses, which offered the promise and fulfillment of extended runs. Speaking in 1981 Tenser said: "Drive-ins are a diminishing market. . . . Five years ago we were making pictures basically for drive-ins."[7] Other competition for the independent film was provided by the advent and flowering of cable TV and home video markets. Independent filmmakers would sometimes bypass drive-ins to sell directly to these outlets. It was often possible to reach a larger audience and make bigger profits going direct to home video or to cable TV release.

Outdoor theaters continued to screen something less than the best quality films. For every outlet that stuck to wholesome family fare there seemed to be another featuring nothing but hard-core porn. Most mixed up the bill of fare with a little of everything, as long as it was light. If it wasn't aimed at children an ozoner looked for films with lots of blood and guts, action, chases, and soft-core porn in their product selection. In Long Island, New York, the Westbury strove for a middle ground avoiding both X- and G-rated product. Manager Bill Mitchell said: "We show comedies, science fiction, karate, scary movies, light stuff mostly. We'd never have, like *Passage to India*."[8] A film distributor in the Washington, D.C., area claimed an ideal night at the drive-in would begin with "a shoot-'em-up Clint Eastwood cop film, followed by a punch-'em-up Sly Stallone epic, a kick-'em-up Chuck Norris karate film, topped off by a slash-'em-up horror movie."[9]

A survey conducted by Dennis Giles in 1982 compared the type of films screened at indoor and outdoor theaters in Cleveland, Ohio. From the point of view of genre Giles found little difference. Each type screened a lot of family fare, a lot of comedy, a lot of science fiction, and so on. There was a major difference in terms of film classifications, however. G-rated films made up 3.9 percent of indoor theater fare, 2 percent of drive-in offerings; PG movies were screened 56.8 percent of the time indoors, 32.3 percent outdoors. R-rated material was shown 39.3 percent of the time indoors, 63.6 percent outdoors. Indoor theaters showed no X-rated films, while outdoor theaters screened X material 2.1 percent of the time. Giles noted that few drive-ins played first-run material, that their films were more explicit, aimed at a younger target audience, and dominated by certain subgenres such as sexploitation and drug comedy (Cheech and Chong). Most of the films aired at the Cleveland drive-ins were second run, including some five- to ten-year-old material, or from small independent distributors. While both types of theaters screened a lot of comedy, indoor houses tended to more adult comedies such as *Author, Author* or *Victor/Victoria*, while ozoners heavily favored teenage-oriented comedies.[10]

The all-time favorite drive-in movie was *Texas Chain Saw Massacre*, according to drive-in movie critic Joe Bob Briggs, whose weekly movie review column "Joe Bob Goes to the Drive-In" started running in the *Dallas Times Herald* and soon spread by way of syndication to other newspapers. Joe Bob's other favorite films include *Basket Case, The Beast Within, I Dismember Mama,* and *Mad Monkey Kung Fu*. Joe Bob is the tongue-in-cheek alter ego of film critic John Bloom. Adopting a redneck persona, Joe Bob claimed to be "representative of the typical drive-in patron"—a beer-swilling, commie-hater who despised foreign films and indoor movie houses, which he said catered to people too poor to drive cars. A typical Joe Bob movie critique went: "Nothing can prepare you for the finish of this movie, which has nudity, bondage, child murder, axes used two different ways on two different people. . . . Joe Bob says check it out."[11] Besides Roger Corman and *Texas Chain Saw Massacre*, drive-ins made famous such films as *Walking Tall, Billy Jack,* and such people as Russ Meyer and George Romero.

Ozoner fare, claimed Joe Bob, can basically be described as "blood, breasts and beasts." Burt Reynolds drew praise from Joe Bob for films such as *W. W. and the Dixie Dancekings*. Reviewing the bomb *Stroker Ace*, which starred Reynolds and Loni Anderson, Joe Bob wrote: "Five motor-vehicle chases. Eight crashes. No beasts. No breasts but Loni comes close. One beer-joint brawl. One guy through a plate-glass window and into the swim pool. No kung fu. No plot. Two and a half stars (one off for a lack of sufficient Loni anatomy). Joe Bob says check it out."[12]

Beverly and Ferd Sebastian made a number of cheap exploitation movies with southern themes for the drive-in trade, such as *Gatorbait*. Asked to describe the type of films the couple made Mrs. Sebastian replied: "We make redneck romper-stompers." One they didn't make, but of that genre, was the low-budget *Bayou*, distributed by United Artists in 1957. *Bayou* starred Peter Graves, in a role he'd probably rather forget, as a man trying to win the love of a young Cajun girl. The film was abysmal, doing little or no business. Four years later the producer, Mike Ripps, bought his film back. Deciding it needed suggestive inserts, Ripps shot them with a new cast, since the originals weren't available. In one scene Graves goes into a clinch with the female lead. Cut to an insert of the clinch it finished off by two people who bear no resemblance to the first pair. With a new ad campaign, *Bayou* was rereleased as *Poor White Trash*. In addition to the initial production cost of $200,000, Ripps spent another $50,000. *Poor White Trash* went on to gross an estimated $10 million, much of it at drive-ins.[13]

Larry Buchanan kept busy in the 1960s churning out thirty or more films, mostly for under $20,000 each. His Azalea Pictures turned out such ozoner hits as *Mars Needs Women, It's Alive,* and *Zontar: The Thing from Venus*. Buchanan related that outdoor owners told him: "If you can keep making them that cheap we'll buy them."[14]

Larry Collins booked films for a number of ozoners in the Pittsburgh area. The outlet that made the most money was the Maple in North Huntingdon, Pennsylvania, which he programmed only with X films. When the Maple opened each year, around April 15, five weeks of mainstream films had to be played as the Maple waited for the trees that lined its perimeter to sprout a full set of leaves. The trees were planted to shield the screen from nearby residents who complained about sex films being visible. Collins said the Maple would gross $8,000 in a week with X films, while second-run major Hollywood product took in around $1,500 per week. The bad news was that concession sales were lower at ozoners that screened X material. Operator Jon Showe said: "Normally you figure $1 per capita at the concession stand, but for a drive-in that runs X's, it's traditionally lower—closer to 35–50 cents. X's seem to inhibit people from getting out of their cars."[15]

Off-beat films were a staple of the drive-ins. The Delray Drive-In, Delray, Florida, ran *Invisible Strangler*, an independent film that started shooting in

1976 but wasn't completed until the 1980s, as well as a 1982 reissue of CIP's 1974 *The Teacher.* Miami's Boulevard Drive-In offered a grab bag of trashy films, often ten to fifteen years old. One such was the 1972 release *Please Don't Eat My Mother*, a soft-core imitation of *Little Shop of Horrors*. When it screened at the Boulevard, in 1982, it was disguised in the ad and on the marquee as *Sexpot Swingers*. It was not uncommon for drive-ins to resell old pictures to hapless customers by giving the films new, random titles (with the new title crudely handwritten, then inserted on the print.[16]

But then what was on the screen didn't seem to matter very much. For many owners there was something more important to consider. As a Chicago owner put it: "I don't try to book the very best movie I can. You see there's a helluva profit in Cokes and popcorn. I want pictures that tread that fine line between being 'a draw' and being boring enough so that people will get restless and go to the refreshment counter."[17]

Admission prices in the early 1980s ranged from $3 to $3.75 per head in Chicago to $4.00 in the Washington, D.C., area to $3.00 around Pittsburgh dropping to $1.50 per head on Mondays and or Tuesdays at many Pittsburgh outlets. In all these cases kids under twelve were admitted free. One exception to that policy was for certain Walt Disney pictures. As early as the 1950s, Disney had insisted that a per-capita charge be levied on these pictures, on children, even in drive-ins. Usually it was a token amount such as 50 cents.[18]

In the latter half of the decade prices had moved up, but not by a great deal. Houston, Texas ozoners charged $4.50 a person, $2.00 on Monday and Tuesday, while Pittsburgh charged $3.00 to $3.50 and also offered $2.00 bargains on Monday and Tuesday. Baltimore, Maryland's, ozoners charged $2.50 to $3.75 per person, the higher end for first-run features. One had a $7.50 carload rate on Tuesdays. The Pratt-Mont in Prattville, Alabama, charged $5.00 a carload, while the tariff in Los Angeles was $4.50 per person. Once again children under twelve got in free in all these locations.[19] A family of four could attend the drive-in for $9.00 in Los Angeles when the indoor tariff would have been $14.00 for the two adults plus the cost of two children's tickets. Nonetheless, though it may have been a bargain, it didn't fill the lot.

Sneaking in remained a popular pastime in the 1980s. One difference between the contemporary form from the 1950s version was that operators were more likely to try to prevent the practice in order to get every admission dollar they could. In the 1950s owners were more likely to look the other way. Those trying to sneak in were no smarter than those of more than 30 years previous. Mary Sheeler sold tickets at Chicago's Cascade Outdoor Theatre all through the 1980s. After eight years she has a very skilled eye. "From being here so long I have a knack for knowing which people are lying to me," explained Sheeler. "There's always that big car with two people in it, yet the back bumper is almost scraping the ground. Then you have ninety-degree weather and people have six blankets in the back." Ann Carol Perry, operator of a Newton, New

Jersey, drive-in commented: "Kids haven't gotten any smarter about sneaking in. A single teen-ager will drive up. Sometimes you hear giggling in the trunk. The drivers are always very chatty and overly polite."[20]

Bill Martin, operator of the Laurel near Washington, D.C., recalled: "One guy came in with four bags of potato chips, two six-packs of beer, two foot-long hot dogs and he's by himself and his car's just about scraping the bottom. We let him see us and then we park next to him and wait for the pounding from the trunk. Eventually those guys want out of there." A ticket seller at another ozoner in that area said she had a lot of people pretending to be younger than they were to get in free as an under-twelve child. "A lot of times you get 16-year-old girls coming in with their fathers, in pigtails, with pillows over their chests and sucking their thumbs. It's pathetic."[21]

Sam Pradun was assistant manager of Chicago's Skyhi, where he and his staff "basically look for the single person driving in alone. If the back end of the car is riding low, we ask them to pull over and open their trunk. Nine times out of 10 they do, and if there's somebody in there, we usually all have a good laugh."[22] Sneaking in by driving your car in through the exit was another time-honored method of getting in for free. Some drive-ins, like the Skyhi, stationed somebody at the exit to guard against that practice. Today it's not uncommon to have armed security guards at drive-ins who systematically check the contents of cars, particularly trunks. Primarily they aren't looking for freeloaders trying to sneak in. They are looking for weapons, guns, rifles, and so on. Unfortunately they find some.

All attempts at turning the nonproductive time of a drive-in into something with a financial return for the owner have failed. Many still used their lots as places to hold swap meets and flea markets. (Much less was written on the subject.) Some who adopted the practice abandoned it; holding such affairs at drive-ins was, at best, only marginally successful for the drive-ins. Indicating the dying status of the outdoor theaters was the fact that no new ideas emerged as to how to generate other income. Nor were any new means suggested as to how to efficiently hype the ozoner, except for a mild burst of nostalgia. This was an even surer sign of impending death.

In 1981 Dave Gibson was a forty-two-year-old Huntington Beach, California, resident who ran an ad in the paper to find people who wanted to do what he wanted to do—go cruising "like we did in the 1950s." From this a group was formed, and on the first Friday of each month Orange County Cruise Night took place, on occasion drawing more than one hundred old cars, which converged on a fifties A&W restaurant and Angelo's Drive-In in Anaheim. The nostalgia was for the entire fifties erea, not just drive-ins. Club member Ron Shaltz said: "The kids really didn't have any place to hang out. The drive-in was a place you could go and kick back and be with your peers. . . . It makes me feel good to be here. I guess the reason for that is it reminds me of happier times." Angelo's owner, Tony Stramiello, was happy too. "We kind of fit the '50s 'Happy Days' concept," he said. "It's great. We like the cars, we like the people. They're real nice. We've never had a rowdy incident since we've been doing this. There's no drug culture, no heavy drinking, it's just good clean fun."[23]

Car-club members arrived early at a drive-in in Westbury, New York, to show off their fifties and sixties vehicles, while near Pittsburgh the Starlite held Cruise Night every Friday and Saturday night. Patrons with older cars brought them early to park in the front rows. Others also arrived at the drive-in early to check out the old cars. Owner George Welsh explained: "We give door prizes. We're planning a '50s night in which we'll invite patrons to come in costumes from the period and bring cars from the '50s, too. We're seeing a lot of enthusiasm."[24]

The nostalgia craze even reached an official level, when the Los Angeles Conservancy held a Nifty Fifties Night complete with fifties music, a Hula-Hoop contest, and *The Girl Can't Help It*, a 1956 rock-and-roll film. This event was held in August 1989 in honor of the Studio Drive-In in Culver City, which was slated for eventual demolition. Among those present was Tom Ewell, who starred with Jayne Mansfield in *The Girl Can't Help It*. Then eighty years old, Ewell admitted he's never been to a drive-in in his life.[25]

The height of the craze was reached in 1988 in New York City. While Manhattan was never home to a drive-in, that year it gained the distinction of becoming the only place to have an *indoor* drive-in, which came complete with automobiles. Michael Dezer was born in Israel in 1941. After arriving in the United States in 1962 he proceeded to make a fortune in real estate. Along the way he indulged in his love for automobiles by amassing a large collection of vintage cars. By 1985 Dezer had so many cars he needed a bigger place to store them, so he purchased a warehouse in Manhattan for $5 million. After spending another $5 million on renovations, he opened Dezerland, a 1950s dreamland. Dezerland contained Hot Rod, an oldies dance floor; Rock 'n' Roll Heaven, which featured live weekly flashback acts; a memorabilia store; a museum; and the American Classics Drive-In. Located inside the Dezerland warehouse, it had thirty-six vintage convertibles neatly parked in rows at the screen. Admission was $5.00 a head on weekdays, $7.50 on weekends. Dezer said: "I'm addicted to the '50s phenomenon. That's why I'm going to build Dezerlands all over the world. . . . I was born into loving cars, especially American cars."[26] The American Classics Drive-In was still operating in 1990 but was only available for private parties.

At least one drive-in, the Frontier in San Diego, California, was able to cash in by hyping the fiftieth anniversary of the institution. Running an extensive media campaign, the Frontier got newspaper, radio, magazine, and television coverage in June 1983. The lot was jammed with prices rolled back to what they were *said* to have been in 1933—$1 per adult. (The actual price had been a quarter.)[27]

Dallas, Texas, played host to the First World Drive-In Movie Festival and Custom Car Rally in 1982, held for three days at the Gemini Drive-In in North Dallas. It was an offshoot of the USA Film Festival. Many of the board members of that group were reluctant to have a drive-in festival, considering it not respectable to sponsor an event that showed "that kind of movie." Twenty-four of the "Greatest Drive-In Movies in the History of the World" were shown back to back. An area woman was crowned Miss Custom Body while featured guest Roger Corman, "King of the Drive-In Movie," received the Joe Bob Briggs Life Achievement Award, an engraved Chevy hubcap.[28]

During one of his seminars there Corman explained that editing a film down to about eighty-two minutes was necessary for drive-in movies "because the audience tends to have a limited attention span." One of his early films was titled *Five Guns West* as his budget allowed for only five actors. Some of his early efforts were completed in five days or less with results Corman acknowledged were "lamentable." At New World he often took as long as three weeks to complete a film. On occasion, Corman admitted, he inserted footage from old movies into new ones to cut costs. "There was the same burning house scene that appeared in at least three of them," he said. Drive-ins were declining, thought Corman, "Not because they're losing popularity, but because of land values. It has become more practical to turn drive-ins into shopping centers."[29]

One year later the Seattle Film Festival programmed one night in its schedule for a Salute to the Golden Age of Drive-Ins. The festival took over the Aurora Drive-In, charging patrons $5 a carload for "those kinds of movies." Featured films were Paul (*Eating Raoul*) Bartel's first Hollywood effort, *Death Race 2000*. Next were Corman's 1960 cult item, *Little Shop of Horrors, The Abominable Dr. Phibes* (with Vincent Price), and last was Corman's *The Trip*. The Seattle Festival staff had no reluctance to program such an event, which started with a car-club cavalcade through the city to the Aurora. Festival co-director Dan Ireland said, "Everyone has been to a drive-in, whether they're sophisticated moviegoers or not. This is intended as an affectionate salute to that period in our lives." Ireland's partner, Darryl Macdonald, added: "Drive-in movies gave birth to the careers of some great directors, including Francis Coppola, Peter Bogdanovich, and Martin Scorsese. There are those who will argue that they made even better movies back then."[30] All these examples of nostalgia had the appearance of a wake—a wake at which the patient is not yet dead, not quite.

Playgrounds for children began to disappear in the late 1960s. By the 1980s it was hard, if not impossible, to find one. The culprit was always the same—the cost of insurance. Robert Ricouard elminated the playgrounds from his New Orleans area outdoor theater in the 1960s when the cost for insurance against injuries became too high. At the Starlite near Pittsburgh owner Jim Nash commented: "We used to have a $60,000 playground here. Maintaining it today is out of the question because of insurance costs. We sold all we had except the roller coaster, which has been inoperable for several years. I didn't charge for rides. Everything was free. Those were the glory days." The Loew's chain in the northeast no longer owned any ozoners by 1986. Vice president of Loew's, Ted Arnow, recalled, "We used to have miniature railroads and some theaters even had miniature golf. But that was years ago."[31]

The multiplexing of drive-ins continued at a faster rate in the 1980s, although not nearly so rapidly as with indoor houses. Some drive-ins went beyond four to six or even eight screens. Ultimately, it didn't help. No matter how many times they carved them up the drive-in remained too large to be viable. Sometimes a larger, old indoor house was multiplexed where it stood. More usually it was closed with a new multiplex built somewhere else, inside a mall, for example. This never happened with ozoners. They were either closed or multiplexed where they stood; no new ones were built. If a drive-in's location was in any way responsible for some of its declining audience, then multiplexing would not help. Less multiplexing was done with outdoor theaters because it involved a large capital expenditure. With falling business, many owners viewed the idea as throwing good money after bad. Two or three screens would be the maximum in any lot, for customer satisfaction; beyond that an owner was taking what were already poor technical aspects in a single-screen venue and making it worse in a lot with four or more screens.

One study of multiplexing at drive-ins indicated that twinning was the most profitable for the outdoor theater since it increased revenues 30 to 50 percent. Adding a third screen created a revenue increase of 10 to 20 percent, while adding screens beyond that number contributed only 5 to 10 percent additional revenues. At the time of that study, 1983, there were only 212 multiplexed ozoners; 162 twins, 30 triplexes, 14 quadriplexes, 2 with five screens and 4 with six. The vast majority remained single-screen operations.[32]

Despite the obvious decline in drive-ins, both in attendance and number of outlets, many insiders refused to acknowledge that fact preferring denial instead. Pacific executive Robert Selig said: "It would appear we're far from dead," although he did grant that "We're not fools. If that land becomes more productive for another use, we're not stubbornly going to continue to run drive-ins." When the Frontier ran its fiftieth anniversary of the drive-in celebration manager Herb Burton insisted that the industry was "alive and we're doing well."[33] Within a few years the Frontier was gone.

Journalist Ed Blank said, in 1987, that the fortunes of drive-ins were up that summer, although admitting the reversal might be temporary. Selig insisted that same year: "Drive-ins are thriving in the Sunbelt states," while fellow Pacific executive Milton Moritz added: "The worst may be over."[34] Brave words they may have been, but in no case did they reflect reality. The decline of drive-ins was steady and relentless during the 1980s. The patient was terminally ill, yet some refused to even admit it was ailing.

In 1982 Selig claimed that the audience at Pacific drive-ins was much the same as in the past. According to a survey they took, 72 percent of their patrons were young married couples with two or more children. "They can't afford a baby-sitter or parking so they come to the drive-in," said Selig.[35]

Yet the atmosphere at most of the 1980s drive-ins was considerably different. Writer Toby Thompson aptly described the scene at a Texas ozoner, but it could have been anywhere in the country: "Hundreds of vehicles are lined up like pigs before a trough, grunting their approval—horns honking, tape decks blaring, an odd rocket arching toward the screen. If you look past the speaker hung from your window, you gaze on the Texas moon riding high above this most remarkable celebration; you note hibachi campfires, smoke rising from barbecued ribs, lawn chairs planted in the beds of pick-up trucks, hammocks strung between speaker poles, patrons splayed out on blankets atop vans, and a Western 'Rocky Horror' punk fest of sixteen-year-olds crowded around the concession stand. You smell pot sweeping through the night, sweet as sagebrush. And all around you Texans are mating."[36]

The practice of parking pickup trucks and vans backwards and sitting in the back or on lawn chairs on the ground around the vehicle started in the South and the West as a way of beating the heat and humidity. It soon spread all over the land. Teenager Thomas Layton said: "I'll swipe a couple of my parents' lawn chairs or sit on the toolbox in back of my pickup and watch a double feature. The main reason I own a pickup is for the drive-in. Out there you can take in your cooler and you can move around some." His girlfriend Laurel Reed added: "People make cracks in a hardtop. In a drive-in you've got privacy if you want it. Some of the best times, though, are when kids are tossing Frisbees or playing touch football around the speaker poles. On a summer night it's like a three-ring circus."[37]

Tillatha Whitlock, in her mid-forties in 1988, couldn't remember the last time she went to the drive-in, but back in the late 1960s she often went with her husband and kids. "It was practical for five small children," she explained. "You didn't have to get a baby-sitter, you could take the children with you. It was also a solution to satisfy a need for a form of recreational entertainment." Janine Jackson attended Baltimore area outdoor theaters with her husband and two children. When she was in high school in the 1960s, Jackson remembered drive-ins as the hot spot for teens, saying: "That's where everybody went, even in the freezing cold. If you didn't go to the drive-in on Friday night, you were nobody. . . . You would think that today's teenagers would want to come to the drive-in. I think its the fact that it's an adventurous thing to do. The whole idea is not to see a particular movie. It's to bring the food you want and move around."[38]

Family groups still turned out at the ozoners for the same reasons as in the past, only in much smaller numbers. At the Winnetka Drive-In in Chatsworth, California, Mike Brown, his wife, and four children came with lawn chairs, blankets, and a cooler of refreshments to "camp out." They preferred the price, convenience, and casual atmosphere of the outdoor theater. "It's a great place to bring the kids. You don't need a baby-sitter, and you don't have to worry about how much noise you make," said Mrs. Brown. At the other end of the country Dorothy Striano said she, her husband, and seven kids attended the Westbury in Long Island, New York, because: "It's a great way to get the kids out of the house. We wouldn't bring them to a movie theater. We wouldn't put other people through that. Besides, it's cheaper here, just a dollar a kid. If they closed this place I don't know what we'd do."[39]

Asked what it was that drew him to drive-ins, as he sat in his car at the Cascade Outdoor Theatre near Chicago, Stan DeGloria replied, "You don't have to worry about anyone that smells terrible sitting next to you."[40]

Clarence Johnson, thirty-nine in 1985, was a self described drive-in vet from the 1960s when: "Me and the old lady used to come out here to, you know, we'd get romantic. We still come out and remember what it was like in the '60s. It's kinda like reliving your youth. But tonight I'm with my neighbor and our sons. I been coming here since '61. I musta lost count of every drive-in I been to." On that 1985 night Johnson attended the Bel-Air in Cicero, Illinois, with a neighborhood buddy. Each man had his teenaged son with him. The two men sat outside the car on lawn chairs while the teens stayed inside blowing the horn every time a young female passed by. Johnson's wife was home playing cards with friends while Clarence kept "the kid out of her hair" for a time. Horn honking was so pervasive at the Bel-Air that night that the projectionist began the film early — one of the few to do so under such provocation. As a result the nudity of the R-rated feature passed unnoticed, in the early stages, as there was still enough light in the sky to render the film next to invisible. Johnson explained his reasons for being at the Bel-Air by saying, "We bring some food from the Home Run Inn, you know, some pizza. Can't afford the food here. We bring a few beers and these chairs here, and we're cool. I think more people come here 'cause of the convenience and the economics. It's cheaper, cost us $12 for me, him and the two kids. I used to sneak in in the trunk sometimes, but now I'm more responsible."[41]

Early in the 1980s Diane and Donald Huff regularly attended ozoners in the Washington, D.C., area, taking their three-year-old and twelve-year-old with them. From the back of their pickup truck Diane watched while reclining on a patio lounger. Donald sat on a folding lawn chair next to a Styrofoam cooler filled with diet soda, beer, and a fifth of Chivas Regal. The family arrived an hour before dark to let the kids run around in the playground for a while. "It gets them aired out and, hopefully, ready to conk out," said Diane. Donald commented: "If it weren't for the drive-in, we'd probably be sitting home fighting tonight." When she was asked about the decline in drive-ins Diane replied: "I just hope they never get rid of drive-ins. It would be like taking a piece of America."[42]

At the same time as Selig was announcing that Pacific's patrons were mostly young families with children, according to their survey, the results of another survey were released by Bruce Austin, professor of communication at the Rochester, New York Institute of Technology. Austin found that only 15 percent of the audience he polled was made up of families. The remainder were young couples. As with patrons in the past, Austin found that the film being screened was almost inconsequential for his respondents.[43]

The number of drive-ins in Kansas City had been twenty-five screens at twenty sites in the mid-1960s. By 1981 it was sixteen screens at twelve sites; nine screens at seven sites in 1986. The number in Chicago and area dropped from twenty at the peak down to seven in 1987. Connecticut had thirty-five drive-ins in 1980. Eight years later five remained. Greater Cincinnati had four drive-ins open for the 1989 season, down from close to two dozen in the late 1950s. One was the Oakley Drive-In, owned by National Amusements. That company's chief executive officer, Ira A. Korff, said, of the twenty-two ozoners they were opening that season: "None of our drive-ins are that profitable. The ones that we're keeping open are either break-even or just somewhat profitable." Any major repair could push a marginal theater into unprofitability. "And that's when we take another hard look at it," he said. Korff added: "If there were demand out there, the other business considerations would pale. It would be profitable for the two or three months that you have them open. But I sense the demand just isn't there anymore. Everyone is lamenting the decline of the drive-in, but nobody's going." Holiday Amusements operated three ozoners in Greater Cincinnati in 1988, none in 1989. Joanne Cohen of Holiday remarked: "The problem is the property taxes. And you can't forget about the maintenance either." Repairs to a screen could amount to as much as $20,000 to $30,000. While some of the Cincinnati drive-ins had operated year-round in the past, the 1989 season was just four months long—Memorial Day to mid-September. Mark Siegel's company had leased Holiday's outdoor theaters for the 1989 season, hoping to turn things around. "Traditionally drive-ins were family entertainment," he said. "But, as families were drawn away by other amusements and by shopping malls, drive-ins turned to different sorts of movies—mostly potboilers—which had the effect of making sure families wouldn't come back."[44]

In 1987 the Pacific chain decided to spend $4.5 million to turn its Thousand Oaks, California, outdoor theater into a ten-screen indoor multiplex. Seating two thousand people, it would use six and a half acres, including parking, of the outdoor site. The remaining nineteen and a half acres would be given over to other development.[45]

To many ozoner owners cable TV and video recorders were major villains responsible for the decline of the outdoor theater. D. G. Bell, one of the longtime owners of the St. Bernard Drive-In in New Orleans said: "Drive-ins are being driven under by television and all its improvements. You can get cable, which heavily emphasizes movies, and you can get a video recorder for your television to record movies for later viewing. You can almost build your life around television. Cable is the main thing, if you want to name one thing. People just don't go to the show anymore when they can stay home and watch movies on television." Bart McLendon, owner of a Houston, Texas, ozoner stated, "Home video, including VCRs and cable TV, also is having an impact. A lot of people won't go to an indoor theater these days, let alone a drive-in. It's hurting both sides of the theater business." David Baker owned the Mountain View Drive-In in Stanton, Kentucky. He said, "VCRs have hurt us more than anything else that has come down the pike."[46]

Another factor in the decline was the automobile itself. With escalating costs to buy and operate a vehicle, people turned more and more to compact cars—cars that were less comfortable and practical to sit in for long periods. In such cars the back seat was next to useless to try and view films from cramped quarters through a smaller windshield and around headrests. The front seat was no longer bench-style, usually divided in the middle by a gear box or storage area. As Malcolm Green said when he was president of NATO, "People now are less devoted to driving around in a car. The idea of just sitting in a car has dwindled."[47] One always went to the drive-in in a Chevrolet or Pontiac, not in a Honda or Toyota.

Jan Peters operated the Gateway Drive-In near Pittsburgh. While he booked no R or X material, he found "the family audience died out with family films." Between the 1982 and 1983 season he twinned the Gateway, a procedure that cost $60,000 to $90,000 at the time. Operator Vince Ranalli of the nearby Greentree said of the industry:

> It's a different business today. I think drive-ins have had their heyday. It's a combination of a lot of things: cable TV, underabundance of product, not as many good pictures, loss of the family audience. It's partly the industry's fault. The proliferation of complexes has hurt us tremendously. It eats up a lot of product. There's nothing left to play. Our second features are on cable before we can even get to them.

At Pittsburgh's Kenmawr, owner Lou Lambro was barely hanging on, saying: "I lose money on movies. Whatever we make at the concession stand, I use to pay off the movies. I did nothing on *E.T.* when they finally let us have it. Lost money on it. I dropped dead on *Tootsie* too. I would never get in this business again. I'd open a hot-dog stand somewhere instead. Honest to God."

Multiplexes had many advantages. As with all indoor houses they operated twelve months a year and as many hours in the day as the owner chose. In addition they responded to changing patterns by locating where people were, such as shopping malls. The malls had become prime hang-out areas for youth. Any multiplexing of ozoners took place on the old site; no new ones were developed. Films that were not viable in huge indoor houses were playable at the smaller multiplexes, sometimes for months on end. They soaked up much more of what product remained for a longer period of time. With some exceptions drive-ins couldn't book first-run films. Even when multiplexed, ozoners were still too large for the business they generated.

And then there was the rocketing land values of these theaters, which took up such a huge amount of land. Mark Manson, an investment house analyst, said: "Drive-ins are cultural dinosaurs. The car is not a part of American culture as it used to be." Fred Wineland owned several drive-ins around Washington, D.C. He commented: "In general, drive-ins aren't operated at their most valuable and productive use. So you sit on them until you can sell them, rent them, or build them up yourself."[48]

At one time Gustave Allmacher owned several drive-ins in New York State. "My father used to say," he recalled, "that a drive-in was a business you went into to make a living while real estate values went up."[49]

According to the 1982 census the number of drive-ins (with payroll) was down to 2,129. Every one dollar of payroll expense produced $5.25 in admission sales at indoor houses, compared to just $3.78 at drive-ins. When all receipts, tickets and concessions, were combined the figures were $6.48 and $5.04 for indoor and outdoor spots, respectively. Of the latter combined total receipts, ozoners took 9.8 percent. For combined gross ticket sales, drive-ins accounted for 9.2 percent. Indoor admissions averaged $2.52, outdoors it was $2.05. Only at the concession stand did the ozoners continue to hold a strong edge. Every dollar spent on tickets produced 22.5 cents indoors compared to 31.3 outdoors. In 1982 the average drive-in drew 60,430 patrons, enough to fill the lot to capacity twenty-five times in the year. About half of the 7,215 indoor theaters were multiplexes. They accounted for 75 percent of the indoor receipts. Fifteen percent of drive-ins were multiplexes. They accounted for almost 40 percent of the outdoor gross receipts.[50]

Only abbreviated data was published for the 1987 census. One dollar of payroll generated $6.91 in indoor revenue; $5.01 at drive-ins. Of the combined gross receipts drive-ins accounted for a meager 4.2 percent. There were more outdoor screens than the number of locations, however, in 1987 the number of drive-ins was down to 999. A second source listed the number of ozoner screens at 1,545 in 1988, down 38 percent from 2,507 in 1987. At the same time the number of indoor screens moved from 21,048 in 1987 to 21,689 in 1988, up 3 percent.

The idea that ozoners did well in the good weather areas such as the South and the West is not borne out by the census data. In Arizona drive-ins captured a little more than 6 percent of the gross spent at theaters in that state, in Florida it was a bit less than 3 percent. In Ohio it was a little over 5 percent while in Michigan it was 5 percent. Just by the fact of being open twice as long as their outdoor counterparts in colder states drive-ins in warm states should do double the percentage just to stay even. They don't. The best state for drive-ins was California; however, even there drive-ins captured only 8 percent of the money spent at motion picture theaters.[51]

Optimists could still be occasionally found. The *New York Times* ran an article in the spring of 1990 claiming that ozoners were gaining back some of their old fans. In June of that year there were two drive-ins left on Long Island, New York. One was a triplex at Westbury, which was screening *Total Recall* at 8:50 and 11:10 P.M., *Another 48 Hours* at 9:00 and 11:15 P.M. and *Back to the Future III* at 8:40 and 11:00 P.M. Admission was $6.00 for adults, $1.00 for children, and $3.50 for those sixty-two and older. When asked about the future of outdoor theaters, Mary Ann Grasso, executive director of the National Association of Theater Owners, said: "I'm sure we're never going to see a new one built. But we are finding that folks with young families are going to drive-ins more than they were, so I'm hoping that more will stay open."[52]

Historian Oscar Handlin, who taught a popular culture course at Harvard, said of the drive-ins: "They're obsolete. Their decline is a sign that a certain stage in American life is over."[53]

Chapter 20
Conclusion

While still alive and kicking today, just barely, the drive-in is very much dated. It belongs to the 1950s, the era of the Hula Hoop, of "Leave It to Beaver," of Ike, of the family, of the pinball machine, of huge cars guzzling cheap gas. They are all gone now. The family still exists, of course, but its dynamics, its psychosociological structure is vastly different, and no longer suited to ozoners. The pinball machine lived on by becoming something entirely different with more complexity, more glitter, and more flash. It survived by becoming almost unrecognizable, by adapting. The drive-in has never been able to adapt to a radically changing environment. Because of this inability to adapt it will become an example of Darwinism at its simplest: It will die. The oft made comparison of drive-ins to dinosaurs is not inappropriate. But it had a wonderful life. The 1950s were truly golden years for the industry—perhaps too good, for it could do no wrong. It grew fat, rich and lazy convinced customers would never stop coming. Drive-ins seemed to be full all the time. All of this made it much more difficult to try and adapt once a decline set in. In the end they couldn't.

The drive-in roared to a huge popularity in the late 1940s and through the 1950s in the face of many reasons why it should have fallen flat. The films screened were old and of low quality; technical aspects of presentation—audio and video—were abysmal; while the indoor theater seat may not be the most comfortable spot, it is markedly better than sitting in a car for hours; exposure to the weather was a negative factor; the drive-in was closed much of the year in much of the country, which is not the best way of building a steady, regular week-in, week-out clientele; because of daylight films couldn't be screened until hours after screenings started at indoor houses, especially in the middle of the summer.

Despite these obstacles the drive-in thrived. A major factor behind its success was the American love of the automobile. The country's affluence coupled with its cheap gas put ownership and operation of an automobile within the reach of almost everyone. And Americans loved to drive. It was the United States that institutionalized that most banal of activities—the Sunday afternoon drive. The outdoor theater quickly became a favorite destination for car lovers. After you arrived you still got to stay in your car.

From the beginning family groups were attracted to ozoners. Parents didn't have to pay for a baby-sitter nor did they have to worry about their offspring being noisy or disruptive. Drive-ins catered to the family unit, and it soon came to be the dominant patron group. With its various amenities the drive-in came to be almost a community recreation center or mini amusement park.

Admission prices were geared to the family, for whom it was a cheap night out. For a single individual or a couple, the drive-in was never cheap, particularly when the age and quality of the films was taken into consideration. One reason for the family turning en masse to the drive-in may have had to do with the fact that it fulfilled a desire on the part of families to spend time together as a unit, a strong 1950s concept, particularly after the disruptions of World War II. The kids got to play around while the parents could watch something on the screen later at a time when the youngsters, after fresh air and exercise, might be less rambunctious or even sleepy. Furthermore, everybody got to eat. It was all fast food at vastly inflated prices but the family got to eat together, play together, be entertained together all in one night, after driving for miles in their beloved automobile and never having to stray very far from it.

Plenty of films were available in those days. If they weren't much good at least parents could have little trouble in finding a "safe" film, one they felt would not warp little Johnny. With that exception, what film was being screened mattered little (if at all) to patrons.

The only other group of note to attend the drive-ins was the teen and young adult segment. Unlike other patrons they didn't go to outdoor theaters for the movies, they went for sex. With the traditional family intact, it was difficult for a teen couple living with their respective parents to find time alone together since, typically, each mother was home all day. A drive-in was the ideal place. Drive-in owners were so concerned with their family image that most vigorously denied anything of that sort took place at their establishments. At the same time they vigorously patrolled their lots in a futile effort to make sure it didn't happen. Nevertheless, everyone knew what was on your mind when you parked in the infamous and legendary back ramp of the drive-in. Teen sex at ozoners got more play in the press than it deserved. It was the family group that dominatted and that produced big profits for operators. Teens were a small minority.

Then it all started to unravel for the industry. A significant decline in the early 1960s was followed by a stagnant decade and a half. This was followed by a steady decline, which commenced in the late 1970s and continues to the present as the drive-in inexorably follows the path of the dinosaur. The shakeout between 1958 and 1963 likely represented the exit of the most inefficient operators, a response to overbuilding as more and more people rushed into the industry in an attempt to make a quick million. The decline from the late 1970s onward is a response to lack of business.

People went to the drive-in for many reasons but, unlike patrons at indoor shows, the film itself was hardly ever a major priority. They went to drive-ins to let their kids play, to have sex, to party, to spend time with their kids, to be outdoors, to enjoy the various amenities available at most ozoners, to be with their cars, and so on. By the time the 1980s rolled around drive-ins had divested themselves of all their amenities, such as playgrounds. Other reasons for attending that didn't involve ozoner amenities either didn't exist anymore or were satisfied in different ways. Nobody went to the drive-in to see the movie in the fifties and sixties, but, ironically, by the 1980s that was all the drive-ins had left to offer patrons. There were fewer and fewer takers.

Many of the reasons for the decline lay within the industry itself. As indoor attendance began to decline in 1948, major Hollywood studios responded by radically cutting back on the number of films they produced. This was much easier to do after the government broke the industry monopoly, ordering it to sell off its theaters. When they owned their own houses studios had to fill them with product. Not owning any theaters, combined with waning attendance, facilitated production cutbacks. Among the first to go were B films and family-type fare. Drive-ins had less to choose from—fewer films patrons considered to be inoffensive to their children.

Drive-in owners never banded together in the 1950s, when they were at their strongest, to try and lobby for better and earlier product for their outlets. Financially they were doing so well it didn't seem necessary. When they went into decline they were too weak to have any impact. Owners of independent cinemas and ozoner operators should have combined into a natural alliance against the majors who dominated and dictated terms to both groups. That never happened. Instead, independent indoor owners displayed open hostility to the outdoor men, blaming them for their declining fortunes even though drive-ins weren't responsible. Ozoners became whipping boys for indoor exhibitors, particularly the independent indoor people. The evidence indicates that, by and large, the audiences were different groups without a lot of overlap. Ozoners did not steal business from indoor houses because as their attendance zoomed from near nil in January to its August peak, indoor attendance also rose to its peak in the summer. Drive-in patrons didn't rush to indoor theaters in the cold weather because as ozoner attendance plunged in the fall and winter so did it decline indoors.

When indoor exhibitors started multiplexing in the late 1970s, the position of the drive-in was further eroded. These new and smaller units were built in areas with a high visibility and concentration of pedestrian traffic. Malls were a favorite location. Being smaller, they could and did hold a film for weeks and months further delaying and drying up product for outdoor markets. Some ozoners tried to emulate the indoor example by multiplexing themselves, but this effort was doomed to failure. Indoor theaters could easily contain ten, twelve, or more screens. Outdoor shows were limited to a few screens at most. Anything more and the patron was being treated with utter contempt. Indoor multiplexes moved to where the people were. Drive-ins multiplexed where they stood. In view of the declining audience for films, drive-ins were vastly oversized. To be comparable in size to the new smaller indoor auditoriums, a drive-in today should hold no more than around 100 to 150 cars. Multiplexing an old 1,000-car ozoner into two, three or even four screens still left it vastly too large. There was no way it could be economically viable.

Worst of all were the technical aspects of the drive-in's presentation. The audio and video were, and remain, of low quality in comparison to indoor houses and to home entertainment systems. At the best of times when the outdoor screen is new and clean it is about one-fifth as bright as its indoor counterpart. It is not very visible. It is distorted. It is fuzzy. Outdoor screens degraded faster than indoor ones from direct exposure to the elements. As grime built up, the brightness level decreased further. With dropping revenues, owners tended to put off cleaning and repainting their screens. Sound over the car radio is an improvement over that from the in-car speaker yet both are poor quality. The effect of a musical film was totally lost at an outdoor house. No real attempt was made by the industry to address these problems. Again, things were so good in the 1950s owners came to believe the public didn't care. They filled the lots under abominable conditions. Why waste money trying to improve technical aspects when the lot was full?

The one area of research into technical improvements the ozoner industry did pursue were pie-in-the-sky ventures to create the daylight containment screen. This was not to make conditions better for patrons but to get moralists off their backs, and more importantly, to increase revenues by allowing extra screenings in dusk and or full daylight hours, which was not possible with a standard screen. Advice to owners was given on how to save on energy costs by cutting back lamp size (with the never-to-be-realized screen) so brightness would remain at one-fifth that of the indoor standard. Patrons of drive-ins have never been foreign film buffs; however, such films couldn't be screened at drive-ins anyway as the technical aspects were so poor that subtitles couldn't be read.

Drive-ins were greedy in other ways, always at the patrons' expense. Over time longer projector throws meant a bigger image and a bigger screen which led to larger lots holding more and more cars. Some owners added more rows than was technically acceptable. If technology dictated a maximum of twelve rows some put in fifteen, and so on. Some parked cars too far to the left or to the right. Regardless of brightness levels, these patrons would view a technically unacceptable image. Those at the front were overwhelmed by the size of the image. Those at the back were underwhelmed by the same image. Indoor exhibitors never treated patrons with anywhere near this kind of disdain. Patrons went to an indoor house for one reason—to see the film. As this wasn't the case at ozoners owners got away with this type of behavior in the early years. They would pay the price when the film itself was all they had left to offer to potential customers.

Families stayed away as the number of available films dropped off. Real community centers mushroomed, as did large and elaborate amusement parks for children. All these recreational facilities provided by drive-ins in small amounts gradually became available on a larger scale at other locations. This further drained patronage. Family structure altered with more single parent families, more families with both parents employed outside the home. There was less time and energy in such households left for drive-ins. Parents spent less time with their offspring as a unit. No longer was that concept as important as it was in the 1950s.

Teens had less reason to go to drive-ins for sex. Less parental presence and supervision made it easier for them to be alone together in one or other of the parental homes. Vans became popular, and private, vehicles. Parental attitude toward sex perhaps became more open. Long before teens were old enough to drive they were hanging out at the new in-place—the malls. It was a habit that continued after they did get a driver's license. Malls were usually handier. They were climate controlled. They were open for long hours. They had plenty of fast food outlets, at much cheaper prices than at an ozoner.

As the family audience deserted the drive-in many turned to screening porn. This alienated any family-type audience that remained, got the community moralists going and further downgraded an already low ozoner image, from bad to worse. Overwhelmingly the family audience was the backbone of the drive-in. Its loss could not be replaced by a much smaller group whose tastes ran to porn. It could not be replaced at all.

Weather may make a trip to an indoor theater unpleasant but once you arrive you are comfortable. At a drive-in it was often too hot, or too cold, or too windy, or too rainy, or too humid, or too buggy for comfort. Daylight saving time dictated some very late starts in summer. None of these climatic problems were ameliorated by the industry.

The industry often worried about daylight saving time with many blaming it for its falling attendance. What little evidence there is suggests that daylight time had no effect on drive-ins. If ozoners are associated strongly with the 1950s they are equally associated with the summer. One went to the drive-in in the summer when it was still light out. This was due to the ozoner offering, from the patron's point, an entertainment event. Its amenities were best enjoyed when it was warm and when it was light. Many owners in the cold weather areas opened year-round. All talked bravely about doing well. In fact (see page 237), they didn't. Hardly anybody attended drive-ins in the winter in any part of the country, even warm-weather areas.

Everywhere, of course, was television, then cable, and then video recorders to compete against, and win audience away from, the drive-in, and film exhibitors in general. At first drive-ins successfully beat off the challenge of television growing enormously through the 1950s right when the tube was taking over the nation. Finally the proliferation of stations, specialized services of cable and the watch-it-anytime potential of video recorders took its toll. The very fact that drive-ins were perceived by patrons as more than places which screened films allowed them to resist the inroads of television for so long.

Over all those years the value of land—of which drive-ins occupied so much—skyrocketed. Offers were made to owners by developers that they didn't resist. Beginning in the late 1970s many ozoners reached 25 to 30 years of age, or were getting there. It was an age that marked the life expectancy of much of the equipment such as a possibly rotting away wooden screen tower or 10,000 feet or more of buried wiring which was about shot. The necessity for major capital expenditures was often an important factor in the decision to sell. The number of drive-ins plummeted downward through the 1980s. From a peak of 4,063 in 1958 to 2,882 in 1977 to 2,129 in 1982 to 999 in the 1987 census.

Drive-ins today sit poised on the edge of extinction. The last handful may be around yet for decades. A few may be kept alive as sort of living museums, perhaps subsidized. But they are finished as a part of the American landscape. New ones will never be built. It is only a matter of time.

Appendices

Patented May 16, 1933 **1,909,537**

UNITED STATES PATENT OFFICE

RICHARD M. HOLLINGSHEAD, JR., OF RIVERTON, NEW JERSEY

DRIVE-IN THEATER

Application filed August 6, 1932. Serial No. 627,704.

My invention relates to a new and useful outdoor theater and it relates more particularly to a novel construction in outdoor theaters whereby the transporation facilities to and from the theater are made to constitute an element of the seating facilities of the theater.

My invention relates more particularly to a novel construction in outdoor theaters wherein the performance, such as a motion picture show or the like, may be seen and heard from a series of automobiles so arranged in relation to the stage or screen, that the successive cars behind each other will not obstruct the view.

My invention further relates to other novel features of construction, all as will appear more fully from the following detailed description.

For the purpose of illustrating my invention, I have shown in the accompanying drawings one form thereof which is at present preferred by me, since the same has been found in practice to give satisfactory and reliable results, although it is to be understood that the various instrumentalities of which my invention consists can be variously arranged and organized and that my invention is not limited to the precise arrangement and organization of the instrumentalities as herein shown and described.

May 16, 1933. R. M. HOLLINGSHEAD, JR 1,909,537

DRIVE-IN THEATER

Filed Aug. 6, 1932 3 Sheets-Sheet 1

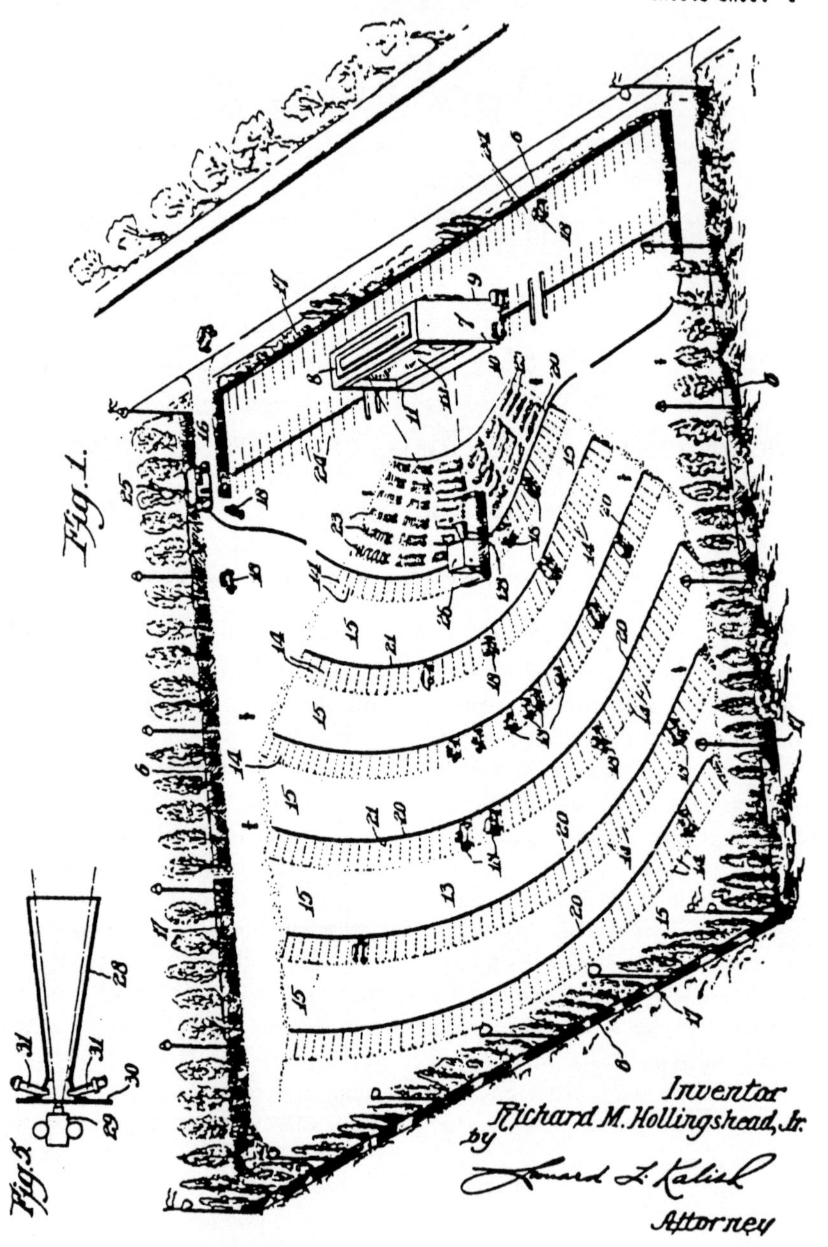

May 16, 1933. **R. M. HOLLINGSHEAD, JR** **1,909,537**

DRIVE-IN THEATER

Filed Aug. 6, 1932 3 Sheets-Sheet 2

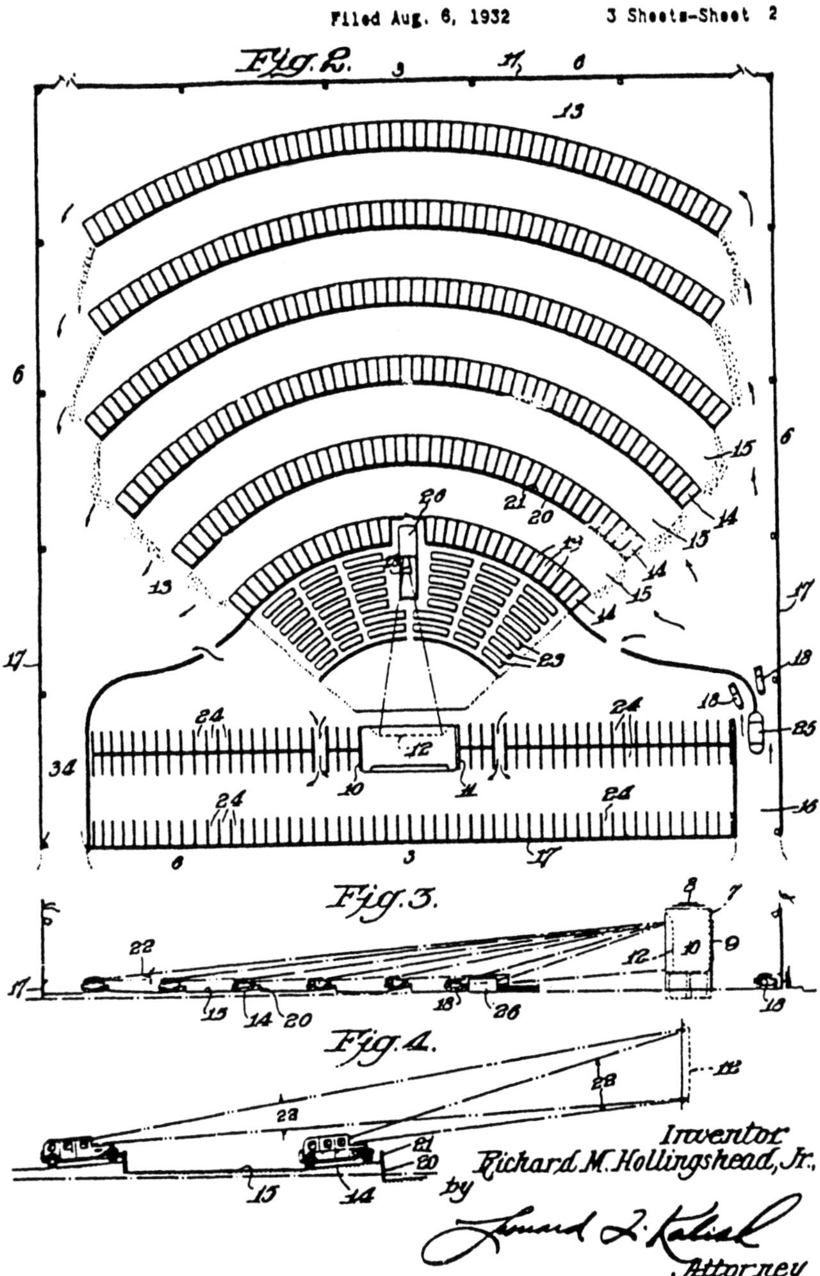

May 16, 1933. R. M. HOLLINGSHEAD, JR 1,909,537

DRIVE-IN THEATER

Filed Aug. 6, 1932 3 Sheets-Sheet 3

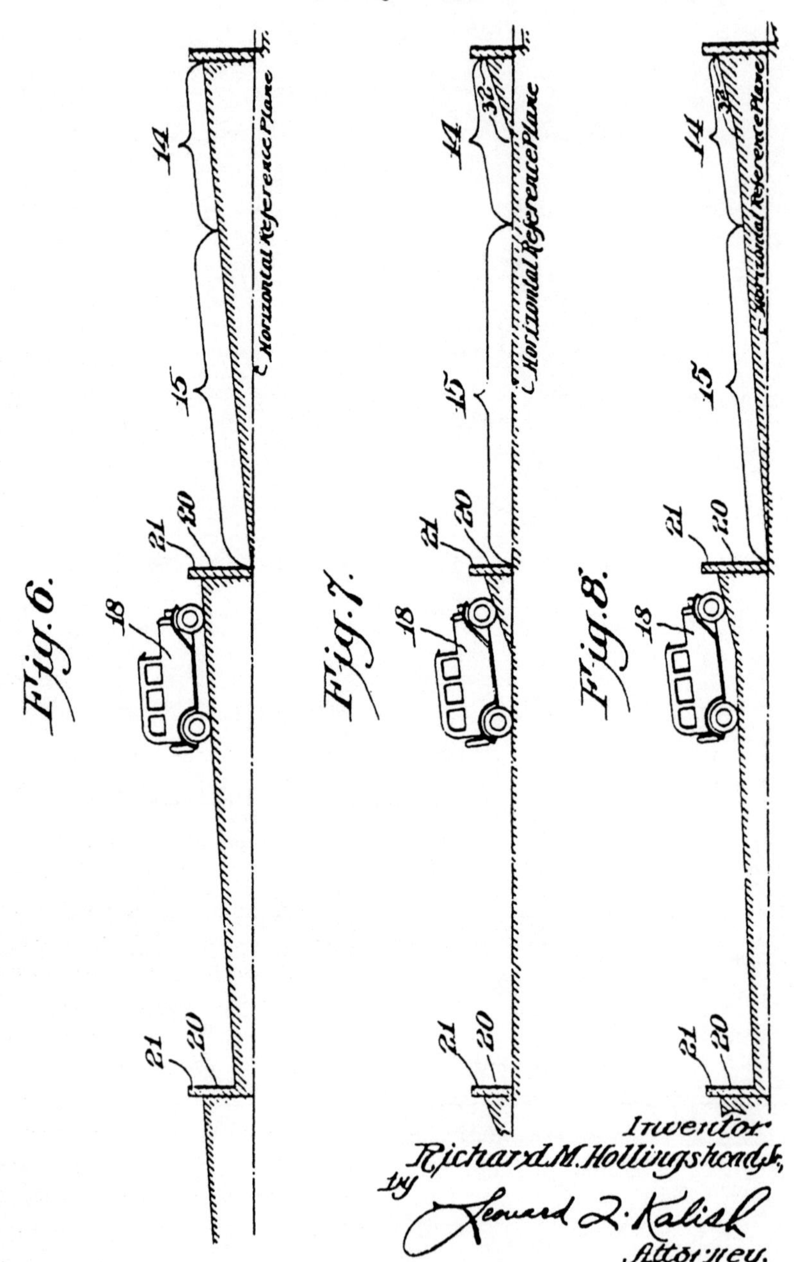

Referring to the drawings in which like reference characters indicate like parts:

Figure 1 represents a perspective view of an outdoor theater embodying our invention.

Figure 2 represents a top plan view of the same.

Figure 3 represents a section on line 3—3 of Figure 2.

Figure 4 represents a view similar to that shown in Figure 3 on a somewhat larger scale and with the angular relationship of elements somewhat exaggerated in order to bring more clearly to view these angular relationships, which otherwise would not be clearly visible on such reduced scale as this drawing, because the angles in actual practice are comparatively small.

Figure 5 represents a somewhat diagrammatic sectional view of the projection guard and guarding means employed.

Figure 6 represents a diagrammatic sectional view of a modified embodiment of my invention.

Figure 7 represents a diagrammatic sectional view of a still further modified embodiment of my invention.

Figure 8 represents a further modified embodiment of my invention.

According to my invention, I provide a suitable plot of ground as shown in Figures 1 and 2, preferably having one boundary, such as the boundary 6 bordering upon the highway or street.

At a point near the boundary 6, I provide a screen house 7, of any suitable frame construction, sufficient to resist wind and other weather conditions, and including top 8, back wall 9, and side walls 10 and 11, and having a screen 12 facing the field 13, and set into the screen house a suitable distance, so that it might be shielded to some extent from foreign sources of light.

The surface of the field 10 in front of the screen 12 is graded with a slight generally down grade towards the screen, as shown particularly in Figures 3 and 4, and alternate arcuate stall-ways and drive-ways 14 and 15 are arranged generally about the screen as the center of the arcs. The stallways 14 are each inclined upwardly at a slight angle as seen particularly in Figures 2 and 3, while the drive-ways 15 may be generally horizontal, and the rear boundaries of the drive-ways 15 are at a level below the front boundaries of the next succeeding stall-way.

The automobiles enter through a gateway 16 which is formed in the fence or other suitable enclosure 17 surrounding the field, and after paying the admission fee, the car 18 is driven by its occupant into any one of the driveways 15, and then into the first stall 19 which may be open or unoccupied in the stall-way 14 directly in front of the driveway into which the car has been driven;—so that the automobile will face the screen.

The individual "stalls" or individual automobile-receiving spaces of the stallways are preferably marked off by any suitable markings or lines of division, either on the ground or surface of the stall-ways, or slightly above the ground or surface of the stall-ways; — though obviously, it is not necessary or essential to the practice of the present invention to "mark off" individual automobile-receiving spaces or individual "stalls." Thus, it is not necessary for the practice of the present invention, to in any way either mark off, or to separate adjacent automobile-receiving spaces or "stalls" from each other, within the respective "stall-ways"; — though some such marking may be desirable to facilitate the convenient spacing of adjacent automobiles within each "stall-way." Hence the term "stall-way" is intended to mean, and should be understood to mean, the areas adapted to receive the automobiles in adjacent relation to each other, facing the stage or screen.

The front boundaries of the stall-ways 14 may be retained by suitable bracings or plankings 20, which bracings or plankings 20 may project slightly above the front of the stall-way 14 so as to form an upwardly projecting abutment 21, for limiting the forward movement or the position of the automobile in its stall.

As will be observed from the drawings, the stall-ways 14 are each inclined upwardly at a slight angle in a forward direction, so that the automobile will be tilted upwardly to an extent sufficient to bring the angle of vision 22 between the car and the screen 12, clear of the top of the car and the screen 12, clear of the top of the car ahead of it; — each stall-way, however, being slightly below the stall-way behind it, so that the angle of vision from each car to the screen will clear not only the car directly ahead of it, but all cars ahead of it. By this means also, each automobile may be backed into its drive-way 15 without starting the engine, and the same may coast backward.

The stall-ways are made approximately 15 or 16 feet wide while the drive-ways are made approximately thirty-five feet wide.

If desired, rows of seats 23 may also be provided in front of the first row of automobiles, and to accommodate the occupants of the seats 23, I may also provide parking spaces 24 for automobiles outside of the zone of visibility of the screen 12.

As the automobiles 18 drive in through the drive-way 16, they pass through any suitable collection booth 25, and are then driven through one of the drive-ways 15 into an empty stall. Due to the arcuate arrangement of the stall-ways 14, each space or stall 19 is of generally tapered form, wider at its entrance end or its end joining the drive-way 15. This facilitates the movement of the automobiles into and from the stall or space.

A projection booth 26 is provided at a suitable distance from the screen 12, below the angle of vision. From this projection booth, the motion pictures are projected onto the screen 12, and the sound of talking motion pictures may be reproduced through any suitable electrical sound reproducers or amplifiers directly in the vicinity of the screen 12, or the sound may be reproduced through electrical sound reproducers or amplifiers distributed at suitable points in the field. The motion picture projection apparatus and the sound reproducing apparatus are not shown in the drawings, as any conventional sound reproducing and motion picture projecting means may be employed.

In order to eliminate all insects from the path of the light from the motion picture projector to the screen, particularly in proximity to the motion picture projector, I provide a funnel-shaped guard member 28 directly ahead of the motion picture projector 29, outside of the wall 30 of the projection house;—said funnel-like member having an angle sufficient to afford suitable passage for the light without any obstruction. The funnel-like member is of any suitable length, as for instance, three to six feet, and from a suitable fan or blower, (not shown), clean or filtered air is blown into the small end of the funnel 28 through suitable nozzles 31, so that a clean stream of air passes through the guard funnel 28 and out through its large end. This stream of air tends to prevent insects from gathering in the funnel, or approaching the lens of the projector. At a distance equal to the length of the guard, or at a greater distance, an insect in the path of the light will not be as conspicuous as would be the same insect in the path of the light in close proximity to the lens of the projector. In this manner, the projection of the motion picture may be rendered more free of undesirable obstructions, through insects passing through the beam of light in proximity to the lens.

It is contemplated through my invention to provide means whereby an audience, particularly in rural sections, may view a motion picture without the necessity of alighting from the automobile, and as a matter of fact, the automobile serves as an element of the seating facilities.

If desired also, the entire field may be inclined to a suitable extent towards one or the other side, or towards both sides from the center, so that the automobiles may not only be backed into the drive-ways, but may be coasted along the drive-ways until they entirely clear the drive-way, so that interference due to sound of the engine may be minimized.

If desired, the inclination of the stall-way portion may continue through the corresponding drive-way portion, as indicated particularly in Figure 6. Thus, the drive-way may be rearwardly inclined to the same extent as the stall-way, so as to lower the car more clearly below the lowest line of vision of the cars in the next succeeding stall-way.

I may also provide, as shown in Figures 7 and 8, front wheel lifts or risers at the front end of each stall-way or space, onto which the front wheels of the automobile are adapted to be driving to a varying extent, in order not only to more sharply incline the front of the car upwardly, but so as also to permit each car to be inclined to a greater or lesser degree, at the will of the driver or occupant. Thus, the riser portion 33, is of a greater inclination than the portion onto which the rear wheels of the car be placed, and by driving the front wheels onto the riser portion 33, to a greater or lesser extent, the front end of the car may be raised to varying degrees, and the car thereby inclined upwardly to varying degrees.

This provision thus enables the occupants of each car to adjust the inclination of their car to the particular relative height of seats to windshield, or to the particular height of the occupant in relation to toe seats and windshield of the car. Thus, while some automobiles have relatively high seats and large windshields, other automobiles have relatively low seats and windshields of relatively small vertical dimension placed at various heights. By this means, the angle of vision may be adjusted individually and selectively for each individual occupant without interference with any other automobile.

I may also raise or elevate the entrance 16 and the side of the field on which said entrance is located, in relation to the exit 34 and the side of the field on which said exit is located, so that automobiles entering through the entrance 16 may coast into any one of the drive-ways 15 without power and also enter any of the stall-ways under the influence of momentum. When it is desired to leave the stall-way and drive-way, the car may be backed into the drive-way from the stall-way ahead of it, by coasting, at the same time by turning the rear end of the car towards the up incline of the drive-way, the car can be permitted to coast forwardly out through the drive-way on the down incline thereof, towards the side of the field on which the exit 34 is located, and may be permitted to coast right out through said exit gate 34. By this means, with a reasonable amount of skill and care, the automobiles may be placed into the stalls and removed from the stalls without the use of the engine, or the use of the engine may be minimized, depending upon the skill of the driver. In this manner, the disturbance due to the engine starting, and due to the racing of the engine, may also be minimized, if not entirely eliminated.

In order to simplify the definition of the present invention the term "stage" is employed to designate a motion picture screen or other zone or field of action, and wherever the word "stage" appears in the claims, it is intended to mean, and is intended to include, both a motion picture screen (that is, the "stage" for motion picture projection) as well as any other "stage" for visual entertainment. So, too, the words "inclination" or "inclined" or "angle" appearing in the claims and referring to the stall-ways is intended to refer to the effective inclination or angularity of the stall-way. Thus, as will be seen particularly from Figures 3, 6, 7 and 8, the entire surface of the stall-way may be uniformly "inclined" or may be at a uniform "angle" as particularly shown in Figures 3, 4 and 6, or only a portion of the stall-way, that is the front portion may be "inclined" or at an "angle" as shown in Figure 7, yet producing for the whole "stall-way" an effective inclination or angle between the front and rear wheel-contract points or automobile-supporting points or zones of the stall-way. So, too, as seen in Figure 8 of the drawings, the angle or inclination of the stall-way may be different at the front than at the rear;—again producing an effective "inclination" or "angle."

I am aware that my invention may be embodied in other specific forms without departing from the spirit or essential attributes thereof, and I therefore desire the present embodiment to be considered in all respects as illustrative and not restrictive, reference being had to the appended claims rather than to the foregoing description to indicate the scope of the invention.

Having thus described my invention, what I hereby claim as new and desire to secure by Letters Patent, is:

1. An outdoor theater comprising a stage, alternate rows of automobile drive-ways and vertically inclined automobile stall-ways arranged in front of the stage, said stall-ways being adapted to receive automobiles disposed adjacent to each other and facing the stage;—said automobile stall-ways being at a vertical angle with respect to the stage such as will produce a clear angle of vision from the seat of the automobile, through the windshield thereof to the stage, free of obstruction from the automobiles ahead of it.

2. An outdoor theater comprising a stage, alternate rows and curvilinear automobile drive-ways and curvilinear and vertically inclined automobile stall-ways arranged in front of the stage, said stall-ways being adapted to receive automobiles disposed adjacent to each other and facing the state;—said automobile stall-ways being at a vertical angle with respect to the stage such as will produce a clear angle of vision from the seat of the automobile, through the windshield thereof to the stage, free of obstruction from the automobiles ahead of it.

3. An outdoor theater comprising a stage, alternate rows of automobile drive-ways and vertically inclined automobile stall-ways arranged in front of the stage, said stall-ways being adapted to receive automobiles disposed adjacent to each other and facing the stage;—said automobile stall-ways being at a vertical angle with respect to the stage such as will produce a clear angle of vision from the seat of the automobiles ahead of it, and an abutment along the front boundary of each of said stall-ways for limiting the forward position of the automobiles therein.

4. An outdoor theater comprising a stage, alternate rows of curvilinear automobile drive-ways and curvilinear and vertically inclined automobile stall-ways arranged in front of the stage, said stall-ways being adapted to receive automobiles disposed adjacent to each other and facing the stage;—said automobile stall-ways being at a vertical angle with respect to the stage such as will produce a clear angle of vision from the seat of the automobile, through the windshield thereof to the stage, free of obstruction from the automobiles ahead of it, and an abutment along the front boundary of each of said stall-ways for limiting the forward position of the automobiles therein.

5. An outdoor theater comprising

a screen, alternate rows of automobile drive-ways and vertically inclined automobile stall-ways arranged in front of the screen, said stall-ways being adapted to receive automobiles disposed adjacent to each other and facing the screen; — said automobile stall-ways being at an angle with respect to the screen as will produce a clear angle of vision from the seat of the automobile, through the windshield thereof to the screen, free of obstruction from the automobiles ahead of it, a motion picture projection booth in operative relation to said screen and electrical sound reproducing means in operative relation to said stallways.

6. An outdoor theater comprising a screen, alternate rows of automobile drive-ways and vertically inclined automobile stall-ways arranged in front of the screen, said stall-ways being adapted to receive automobiles disposed adjacent to each other and facing the screen; — said automobile stall-ways being at an angle with respect to the screen such as will produce a clear angle of vision from the seat of the automobile, through the windshield thereof to the screen, free of obstruction from the automobiles ahead of it, an abutment along the front boundary of each of said stall-ways for limiting the forward position of the automobiles therein, and a motion picture projection booth in operative relation to said screen, and electrical sound reproducing means in operative relation to said stall-ways.

7. An outdoor theater comprising a stage, alternate rows of automobile stall-ways and automobile drive-ways arranged in front of the stage, said stall-ways being adapted to receive automobiles disposed adjacent to each others and facing the stage; — said automobile stall-ways being at an effective angle with respect to the stage, such as will produce a clear angle of vision from the seat of the automobile through the windshield thereof to the stage, free of obstruction from the automobiles ahead of it, and said driveways being inclined towards an outer end thereof, thereby to permit the coasting of automobiles from said drive-ways.

8. An outdoor theater comprising a stage, alternate rows of automobile stall-ways and automobile drive-ways arranged in front of the stage, said stall-ways being adapted to receive automobiles disposed adjacent to each other and facing the stage; — said automobile stall-ways being at an effective angle with respect to the stage, such as will produce a clear angle of vision from the seat of the automobile through the windshield thereof to the stage, free of obstruction from the automobiles ahead of it, and means for permitting the egress of automobiles from the stall-ways and drive-ways without power.

9. An outdoor theater comprising a stage, alternate rows of automobile drive-ways and automobile stall-ways arranged in front of the stage, said stall-ways being adapted to receive automobiles disposed in generally adjacent relation to each other and facing the stage, and means associated with said stall-ways for raising the front end of an automobile disposed therein in order to produce a generally clear angle of vision from

the seat of the automobile through the windshield thereof to the stage, generally free of obstruction from the automobiles ahead of it.

10. An outdoor theater comprising a stage, alternate rows of automobile drive-ways and automobile stall-ways arranged in front of the stage, said automobile stall-ways being adapted to receive automobiles disposed in generally adjacent relation to each other and facing the stage, and means for longitudinally tilting the automobiles in said stall-ways in order to produce a generally clear angle of vision from the seat of the automobile through the windshield thereof to the stage, generally free of obstruction from the automobiles ahead of it.

11. An outdoor theater comprising a stage, alternate rows of automobile drive-ways and automobile stall-ways arranged in front of the stage, said automobile stall-ways being adapted to receive automobiles disposed generally adjacent to each other and facing the stage, said automobile stall-ways being so disposed with respect to the stage that the vertical included angle between the stage and the effective automobile-supporting surface of the stall-ways is more than 90°.

12. An outdoor theater comprising a stage, alternate rows of automobile drive-ways and automobile stall-ways arranged in front of the stage, said automobile stall-ways being adapted to receive automobiles disposed generally adjacent to each other, said automobile stall-ways being vertically inclined with respect to the horizontal.

13. An outdoor theater comprising a stage, alternate rows of automobile drive-ways and automobile stall-ways arranged in front of the stage, said automobile stall-ways being adapted to receive automobiles disposed generally adjacent to each other, said automobile stall-ways being vertically inclined with respect to the horizontal, and successive stall-ways, removed from the stage, being at successively lesser angles with respect to the horizontal.

14. An outdoor theater comprising a stage, alternate rows of automobile drive-ways and automobile stall-ways arranged in front of the stage, said automobile stall-ways being adapted to receive automobiles disposed generally adjacent to each other, said automobile stall-ways being vertically inclined with respect to the horizontal, and successive stall-ways, removed from the stage, being successively higher.

15. An outdoor theater comprising a stage, alternate rows of automobile drive-ways and automobile stall-ways arranged in front of the stage, said autmobile stall-ways being adapted to receive automobiles disposed generally adjacent to each other, said automobile stall-ways being vertically inclined with respect to the horizontal, and successive stall-ways, removed from the stage, being successively higher, and successive stall-ways, removed from the stage, being at successively lesser angles with respect to the horizontal.

16. An outdoor theater comprising exhibiting means and space for

spectators in front thereof, inclined means for supporting automobiles in such space in rows further and further from said exhibiting means, the supporting means in the rows further and further away from the exhibiting means being higher and less inclined successively to an extent as will produce a clear line of vision from the seat of an automobile in a row, through a windshield thereof to the exhibiting means, free of obstruction from the automobile ahead of it, and an automobile drive-way leading to and from said supporting means of a row.

17. An outdoor theater comprising exhibiting means and space for spectators in front thereof, means for supporting automobiles in such space in rows further and further from said exhibiting means, the supporting means in the rows being inclined vertically to an extent as will produce a clear line of vision from the seat of an automobile in a row, though a windshield thereof to the exhibiting means, free of obstruction from the automobile ahead of it,and an automobile driveway leading to and from said supporting means of a row.

18. An outdoor theater comprising exhibiting means and space for spectators in front thereof, vertically inclined means for supporting automobiles in such space in rows further and further from said exhibiting means, the supporting means in the rows further and further away from the exhibiting means being higher successively to an extent as will produce a clear line of vision from the seat of an automobile in a row, through a windshield thereof to the exhibiting means, free of obstruction from the automobile ahead of it, and an automobile driveway leading to and from said supporting means of a row.

19. An outdoor theater comprising exhibiting means and space for spectators in front thereof, inclined means for supporting automobiles in such space in rows further and further from said exhibiting means, the supporting means in the rows further and further away from the exhibiting means being higher and less inclined successively to an extent as will produce a clear line of vision from the seat of an automobile in a row, through a windshield thereof to the exhibiting means, free of obstruction from the automobile ahead of it, and an automobile driveway at the front and an automobile drive-way at the back of the automobile supporting means.

20. An outdoor theater comprising exhibiting means and space for spectators in front thereof, means for supporting automobiles in such space in rows further and further from said exhibiting means, the supporting means in the rows being inclined vertically to an extent as will produce a clear line of vision from the seat of an automobile in a row, through a windshield thereof to the exhibiting means, free of obstruction from the automobile ahead of it, and an automobile drive-way at the front and an automobile drive-way at the back of the automobile supporting means.

In testimony whereof I have hereunto set my hand.

RICHARD M. HOLLINGSHEAD, Jr.

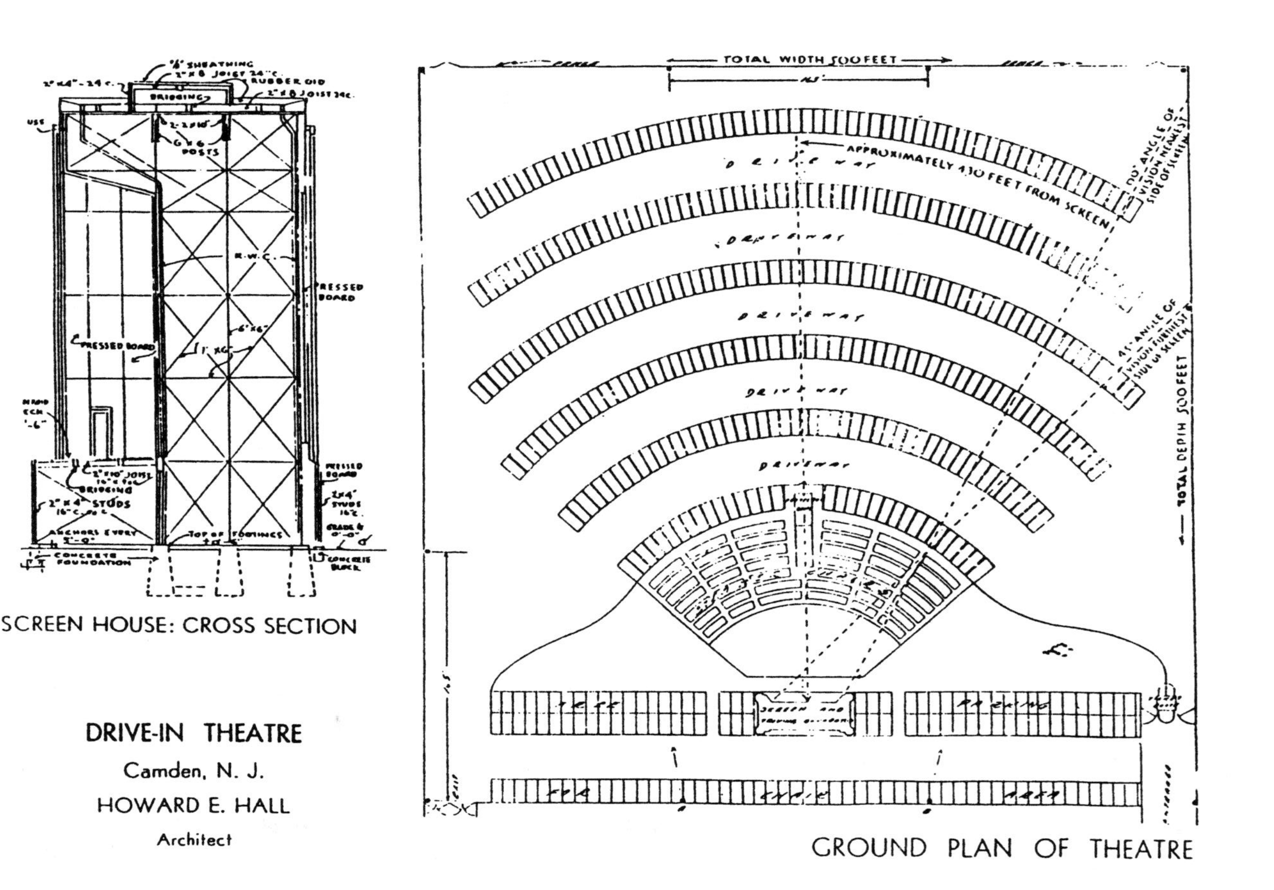

SCREEN HOUSE: CROSS SECTION

GROUND PLAN OF THEATRE

DRIVE-IN THEATRE

Camden, N. J.

HOWARD E. HALL

Architect

Patented Dec. 21, 1937 **2,102,718**

UNITED STATES PATENT OFFICE

2,102,718

THEATER

Louis P. Josserand, Houston, Tex.

Application December 14, 1933, Serial No. 702,294

1 Claim. (Cl. 20–1.12)

The invention relates to an improvement in the arrangement and construction of drive-in theater wherein the theater is so constructed that the patrons may drive their automobiles into the theater and observe the performance while seated in the automobile.

It is one of the objects of the invention to provide an efficient, economical, and convenient construction so that the greatest number of vehicles may be parked within a minimum area in order to provide a maximum of attendance.

Another object of the invention is to provide entry ways for the vehicles in such a manner that two rows of vehicles may be arranged adjacent each driveway.

Another object of the invention is to so concave the surface of the theater that each vehicle will have a clear view of the performance without interference by the rows of vehicles in front thereof.

Another object of the invention is to provide a drive-in theater wherein the entrance and exits are conveniently arranged with respect to the parking areas so that the minimum of disturbance will be created by vehicles entering and leaving the theater.

Other and further objects of the invention will be readily apparent when the following description is considered in connection with the accompanying drawings wherein:

Fig. 1 is a top plan view of the theater showing the arrangement of the entrances and exits as well as the parking areas and driveways.

Fig. 2 is a section taken on the line 2–2 of Fig. 1 looking in the direction of the arrows and illustrating the general concaved arrangement of the parking areas and driveways.

Fig. 3 is an enlarged vertical sectional view of one of the driveways and showing the vehicles parked in position to observe the performance.

In Fig. 1 the location of the theater is illustrated as adjacent two intersecting streets such as 3 and 4, but it may be located otherwise if desired.

With such a location, however, the entrance to the theater may be at the corner 5 so that only one box office 6 is necessary. The entrances are shown at 7 and 8, but only one entrance may be desired.

A suitable enclosure, such as a fence or shrubbery 9 may be arranged on all sides of the theater spaced so that only those entering the enclosure may observe the performance. Two exits 10 and 11 have been illustrated, one on each of the intersecting streets. In this manner the vehicles leaving the theater will not interfere with those entering the theater and a minimum of disturbance will be created by the moving vehicles.

The theater enclosure will be provided with a suitable stage or screen 12 from which the performance will be given. In event it is merely a moving picture theater the picture will be displayed on a screen on this stage. The projection room has not been illustrated but it is to be understood that it can be either in front or in back of the stage as desired.

Arranged in front of the stage 12 are the parking places such as 13, 14, 15, and 16. The number of these parking places will vary with the size of the theater desired. These parking spaces are shown as being curvilinear. The parking areas may be described as double parking areas such as 13 and 14. It is intended, however, that the vehicles in the parking area 13 will move into the parking position by passing in front of the parking area as at 17, and backing into the parking area such as best seen in Fig 3, while the vehicles entering the parking area 14 will pass into the driveway 18, which is between the parking areas 14 and 15. As will be apparent, the vehicles after passing the box office will move along the side drive 20 until they arrive at the desired driveway, such as 18 or 22. The vehicles which intend to park in the area 14 will turn in the driveway 18 and move into the position shown in Fig. 3 by driving forwardly; whereas the vehicles which are to park in the area 15 will pass into the driveway and back into position.

While the entrance or exit of the vehicles through the driveways may interfere momentarily with the view of some of the patrons in the parked cars, such interference will be very slight because the sight lines, such as 25, extending to a position 26, which is slightly below the center of the stage 12, will pass above the top of the vehicles moving along the driveway, such as 18.

In arriving at the spacing of the parking areas 13, 14, 15 and 16, and the driveways therebetween, the height of present day vehicles has been very carfully considered and the inclination of the parking areas has been so calculated that the sight line from the center of the windshield of the vehicle in one row permits a clear line of vision over the top, such as 27, of the vehicles in the preceding parking area.

As clearly observed in Figs. 2 and 3, the surface 30 of the theater has been inclined and divided into parking areas and driveways and so concaved that when sight lines from each

Dec. 21, 1937. L. P. JOSSERAND 2,102,718

THEATER

Filed Dec. 14, 1933 2 Sheets-Sheet 1

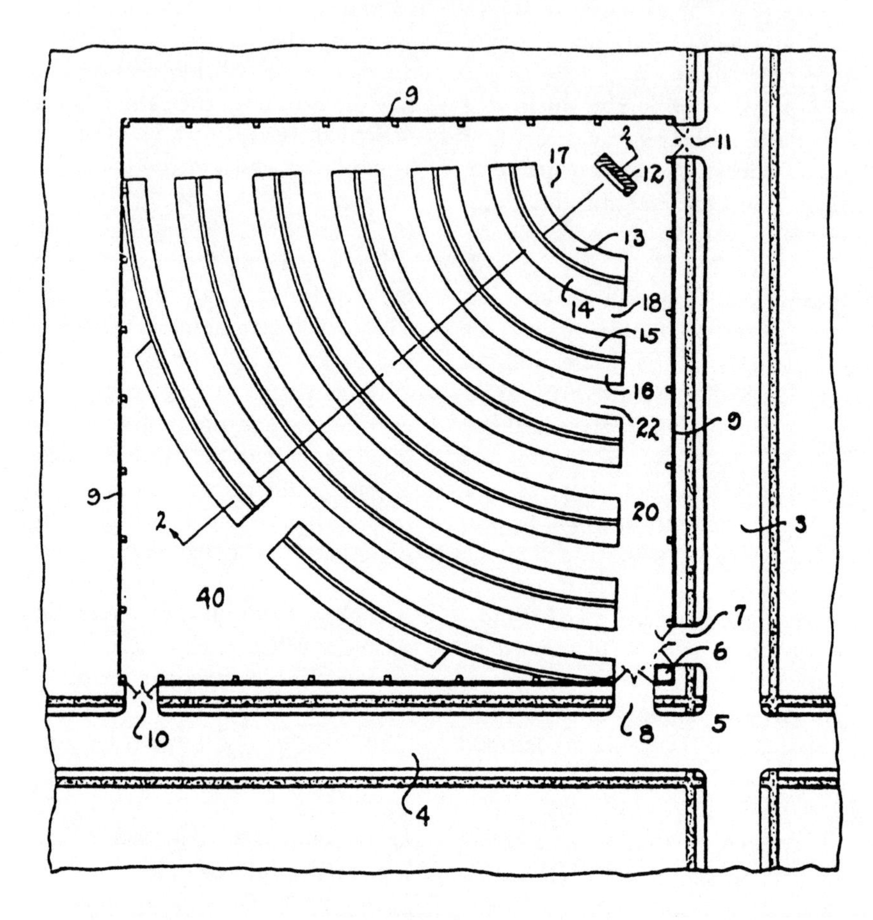

Fig. 1.

Inventor

LOUIS P. JOSSERAND.

By Jesse R. Stone
Lester B. Clark

Attorneys.

Dec. 21, 1937. L. P. JOSSERAND 2,102,718

THEATER

Filed Dec. 14, 1933 2 Sheets-Sheet 2

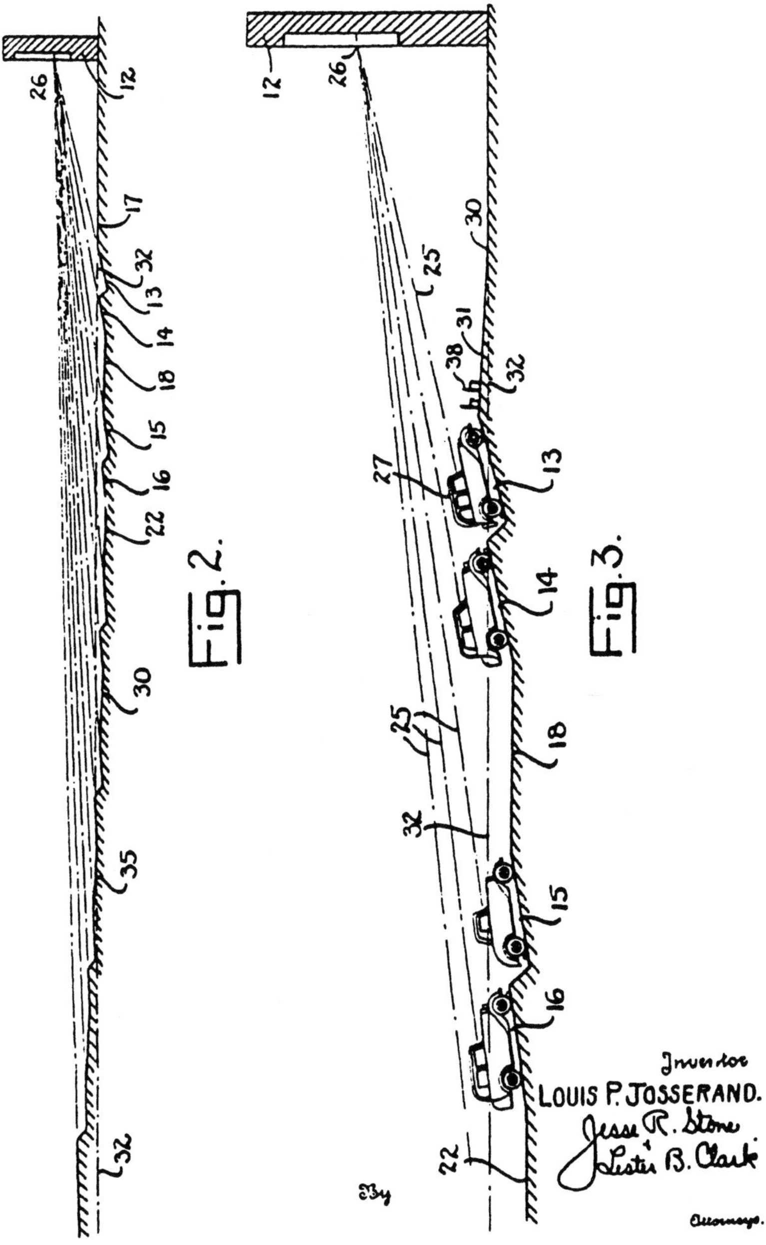

parking area are drawn to converge at the point 26 each slight line will clear the top of the vehicles in the preceding parking areas. As best seen in Fig. 3, the first area 31 is inclined upwardly slightly with respect to the normal ground line 32. This normal ground line is shown as extending across both Figures 2 and 3 to indicate the concaved arrangement of the surface 30. The parking area 13 is shown as tipping quite sharply downward from the normal horizontal plane so that the sight line 25 from the focus point 26 will be parallel to the line of sight of a person seated in the vehicle. This makes a convenient and comfortable parking angle for the vehicle. The area 14 is shown as being inclined upwardly from the driveway 18 at such an angle that the sight line from the focus 26 is also parallel to the line of sight of persons seated in the vehicle. In order to accomplish this, however, the drive 18 is shown as being at an elevation somewhat below the ground line 32, because if the driveway 18 were on the level with the ground line, the cars in the rearward parking areas could not have a clear view of the screen. The parking area 15 is inclined downwardly in somewhat the same manner as the parking area 13 but at a somewhat lesser angle because this parking area is spaced further from the screen and the sight line clears the top of the vehicles in the parking area 14.

From Fig. 2 the general contour of the surface 30 will be observed as concaved and at substantially the point 35 the surface rises above the ground line 32. The inclination of the parking areas gradually decreases from the front of the theater toward the rear so that in all probability no two of the parking areas would be inclined at the same angle with respect to the horizontal.

In building a theater of this type it would be possible to use the earth removed in constructing the front part of the theater to be deposited in the back part of the theater so that the cut and fill would practically balance each other and no supply of earth from an outside source would be required. In this manner the theater could be constructed at a minimum cost and it would only be necessary to landscape the surface in accordance with the showing of these drawings.

While it is possible that the sight lines could be more closely spaced together, the arrangement has been such that the sight lines will be two feet six inches apart when measured at the windshield in any one parking area. In other words, there will be a two feet six inch clearance between the line of sight in one parking area and the line of sight in the next succeeding parking area. It is considered that this is sufficient to clear the top of the average vehicle now in use. With the trend, however, of lower vehicle bodies it is possible that as the higher cars gradually disappear a theater could be constructed with the sight line spaced a lesser distance apart and in this manner the inclination of the parking areas could be arranged at a lesser angle with respect to the horizontal. Any suitable inclination to the parking areas with respect to the horizontal or with respect to the driveways may be arranged so that an unobstructed view of the stage may be had by the occupants of every vehicle.

The particular advantage of the present arrangement is that a maximum number of vehicles can be accommodated in a minimum of space, each driveway serving two parking areas and two parking areas being closely adjacent each other.

It is contemplated, of course, that if desired seats 38 may be placed in front of the parking area for such patrons as desire to leave their vehicles and observe the performance more closely. The area 40 behind the last parking area may be used to park vehicles where the patrons desire to be seated with friends in another vehicle or where the patrons desire to occupy the space in front of the parking area 13. It is contemplated, of course, that the entrances and exits may be arranged in any manner desired other than here shown, but it is believed that the present arrangement is convenient.

What is claimed is:

An outdoor theater for vehicles comprising a stage, a generally concaved surface located in front of the stage, spaced driveways on said surface, a parking area located on each side of each driveway, the area in front of each driveway being inclined upwardly therefrom and the area in the rear of each driveway being inclined downwardly therefrom in such a manner that the occupants of the vehicle parked on said parking areas will have an unobstructed view of the stage.

LOUIS P. JOSSERAND.

Appendix 4: Early Drive-ins

Specific Starting Dates

The first four ozoners listed are the first opened in the United States. The date for Shankweiler's is questionable. See text for details on all four. The list that follows the first four is a selection for which specific dates are available, followed by the source for each. (They are not the next fourteen to be opened in the country.)

1. June 6, 1933, Drive-In Theatre, Camden, New Jersey, owned by Richard Hollingshead
2. April 15, 1934, Shankweiler's Auto Park, Orefield, Pennsylvania, owned by Wilson Shankweiler
3. July 5, 1934, Drive-In Short Reel Theater, Galveston, Texas, owned by Louis Josserand
4. September 9, 1934, Pico (named this some time after opening), Los Angeles, California
5. May 6, 1936, Weymouth Drive-In Theatre, Weymouth, Massachusetts, owned by Thomas DiMaura and James Guarino (*Boxoffice*, April 30, 1938, p. 143)
6. Summer, 1937, Starlight Auto Theatre, Akron, Ohio (*Boxoffice*, August 3, 1940, p. 51)
7. July, 1937, Lynn Open Air Theater, Lynn, Massachusetts, owned by Elias M. Loew (*Boxoffice*, April 30, 1938, p. 143)
8. July 21, 1937, Providence, Rhode Island, owned by Elias M. Loew (*United States Patent Quarterly*, 72:471)
9. February 25, 1938, Miami, Florida, owned by Elias M. Loew and Peter Landatti (*Boxoffice*, March 19, 1938, p. 91)
10. June 2, 1938, Detroit, Michigan, owned by Phil Smith group (*Boxoffice*, June 4, 1938, p. 71)
11. June 1938, Cleveland, Ohio, owned by Phil Smith group (*Boxoffice*, June 4, 1938, p. 71)
12. June 1938, Shrewsbury, Massachusetts, owned by James Guarino and Thomas DiMaura (*Boxoffice*, June 4, 1938, p. 79)
13. June 10, 1938, San-Val, Burbank, California, owned by Seth D. Perkins (*Motion Picture Herald*, December 10, 1938, p. 15)
14. Summer 1938, Merrimack Auto Theatre, Methuen, Massachusetts, owned by Joe Cifre and George Swartz (*Boxoffice*, July 30, 1938, p. 75)
15. August 10, 1938, Valley Stream, Long Island (*New York Times*, August 14, 1938, sec. 9, p. 3)
16. March 1939, Corpus Christi, Texas, owned by Nick Katsaris, Pete

Katsaris, Leon Newman, C. A. Richter, F. D. Smith (*Boxoffice*, March 30, 1940, p. 126)

17. July 15, 1939, Saco Drive-In, Portland, Maine (*Portland Press Herald*, July 15, 1989)

18. December 6, 1939, Atlantic Drive-In, Jacksonville, Florida, owned by George Wilby (*Boxoffice*, April 1, 1974, p. SE1)

Earliest Known List of Existing Drive-ins

The following list is for mid–February 1942 and lists a total of ninety-five ozoners in twenty-seven states. Missing from this list are numbers 2, 8, and 17 from above. (*Film Daily Year Book 1942*, pp. 854–55.)

Alabama

Auto Movies Amusement Co., Birmingham
Auto Movies Amusement Co., Montgomery

Arizona

Phoenix Drive-In Theater, Phoenix
Tucson Drive-In Theater, Tucson

Arkansas

North Little Rock Drive-In, Route 70, North Little Rock
Pine Bluff Drive-In Theater, Route 65, Tampo Pike, Pine Bluff

California

Pico Drive-In Theater, Pico Boulevard, Los Angeles
Orange Drive-In Theater, 101 Highway at Placentia Avenue, Santa Ana
San-Val Drive-In Theater, San Fernando Road at Winona Road, Burbank
Drive-In Theater, San Diego

Connecticut

College Open Air Theater, Middletown
Milford Drive-In Theater, Boston Post Road and Cherry Street, Milford

Florida

Jacksonville Drive-In Theater, Beach Road, Jacksonville
Miami Drive-In Theater, NW 7th Avenue at 19th Street, Miami
Orlando Drive-In Theater, Orlando

Pensacola Drive-In Theater, Pensacola
St. Petersburg Drive-In Theater, St. Petersburg
Tampa Drive-In Theater, Tampa

Georgia

Augusta Drive-In Theater, Augusta
Piedmont Road Drive-In Theater, Piedmont Road, Atlanta
Macon Drive-In Theater, Jeffersonville Road, Macon
Savannah Drive-In Theater, Savannah
Stewart Avenue Drive-In Theater, Stewart Avenue, Atlanta

Illinois

Illinois Drive-In Theater, Waukegan and Golf Roads, Chicago
Drive-In Theater, North Shore, Chicago
Drive-In Theater, U.S. Highway 50, East St. Louis
Morton Grove Drive-In Theater, Morton Grove

Indiana

Drive-In Theater, Pendleton Pike, Indianapolis
Drive-In Theater, Route 67, Indianapolis
Drive-In Theater, Route 20, Michigan City
Park-In Auto Theater, 13th at Poplar Street, Terre Haute

Kentucky

Drive-In Theater, Louisville and Shelbyville Road, Louisville

Louisiana

Drive-In Theater, Canal Boulevard, New Orleans
Shreveport Drive-In Theater, Shreveport

Maryland

Open-Air Theater, Governor Ritchie Highway, Baltimore

Massachusetts

Dartmouth Auto Theater, Fall River and New Bedford, Fall River
Lynn Open Air Theater, Lynn
Riverside Park Drive-In Theater, Springfield
Merrimack Park Drive-In Theater, Route 110, Lawrence-Lowell Boulevard, Methuen

Salisbury Open Air Auto Theater, Route 1A, Salisbury
Saugus Drive-In Theater, Newburyport Turnpike and Route 1, Saugus
Shrewsbury Drive-In Theater, Boston-Worcester Pike at Route 9, Shrewsbury
Sturbridge Drive-In Theater, Sturbridge
Weymouth Drive-In Theater, South Shore Road and Route 3A, Weymouth

Michigan

Drive-In Theater, Eight-Mile at Coolidge Highway, Royal Oak
Westside Drive-In Theater, Eight-Mile at Schaefer Street, Detroit
Eastside Drive-In Theater, Harper Street at Seven-Mile, Detroit

Mississippi

Drive-In Theater, Highway 80, Jackson

Missouri

Drive-In Theater, East Prairie
St. Louis Drive-In Theater, Manchester Road, St. Louis

New Hampshire

Berlin Drive-In Theater, Milan Road, Berlin
Pine Island Park-In Theater, Manchester

New Jersey

S. & G. Theaters, Inc., Route 29 at Chestnut Street, Union

New York

Drive-In Theater, Schenectady-Albany-Amsterdam Road, Albany
Hellman's Auto Drive-In, Latham's Corners, Albany
Drive-In Theater, Niagara Falls Boulevard, Buffalo
Buffalo Drive-In Theater, Harlem Road and Genessee Street, Buffalo
Sunrise Auto Theater, Inc., Valley Stream, Long Island

North Carolina

Charlotte Drive-In Theater, Wilkinson Blvd., Charlotte
Durham Drive-In Theater, Hillsboro Road, Durham
Greensboro Drive-In Theater, Greensboro

Ohio

Auto Theater, Route 2 and 224, Creston

Boyer's Auto Theater, Navarre
Eastside Drive-In Theater, Route 8, Cleveland
Westside Drive-In Theater, Prook Park Road, Cleveland
Drive-In Theater, Montgomery Pike, Montgomery
Bluebird Auto Theater, Greentown
Starlight Auto Theater, Akron
Riverside Auto Drive-In, 5800 Riverside Drive, Columbus
Drive-In Theater, Toledo
Lake Erie Drive-In Theater, Maumee
LaVerne Drive-In Theater, Warren

Pennsylvania

South Parks Drive-In Theater, Pittsburgh
Skyway Theater, West Lake Road, Erie
Seventh Street Drive-In Theater, Seventh Street, Allentown
Kishacoquillas Park, Lewistown
Drive-In Movies, Evergreen Park, Hazelton
Drive-In Theater, North Main Street, Providence

South Carolina

Drive-In Theater, Garner's Ferry Road, Columbia

Tennessee

Drive-In Movies, Lamar Avenue, Memphis
Met-N-Mo V, Jackson

Texas

Drive-In Theater, Austin
Rio Grande Valley Drive-In Theater, Alamo
Drive-In Theater, Highway 9, Corpus Christi
South Main Drive-In Theater, Houston
Northwest Highway Drive-In, Dallas
Fort Worth Highway Drive-In, Dallas
Fort Worth Drive-In, Fort Worth
San Antonio Drive-In, San Antonio

Virginia

Open-Air Theater, Bowling Green
Delmar Drive-In Theater, Delmar
Drive-In Theater, Williamsburg

Mt. Vernon Open Air Theater, Route 1, Alexandria
Norfolk Drive-In, Sedge Road, Norfolk

Wisconsin

Drive-In Theater, Blue Mound Road, Milwaukee

A Few Other Countries

Canada—July 10, 1946, Stoney Creek, Ontario (*Financial Post*, September 8, 1962, p. 23)
Mexico—May 1950, Auto Cinema Lomas, Mexico City, owned by Raul Castellanos (*Variety*, May 10, 1950, p. 12)
Australia—1954 (*Film Daily*, April 4, 1956, p. 7)
Italy—August 29, 1957, Drive-In Cine, Rome (*New York Times*, August 30, 1957, p. 10)
Denmark—July 1961, Copenhagen (*Illustrated London News*, July 22, 1961, p. 126)
Germany—before 1968, Gravenbruch, Frankfurt (*Variety*, August 23, 1978)
France—before June 1968, Toulon (*Variety*, June 19, 1968, p. 31)
Japan—November 1, 1969, Iwata (*New York Times*, October 12, 1969, p. 79)
Israel—February, 1973, Tel Aviv (*Variety*, February 7, 1973)

Appendix 5: Financial Data

San-Val Drive-In, opened June 10, 1938, Burbank, California. 618-car capacity. Itemized cost of construction (excluding land):

Screen building, projection building, concession ticket office and fence, labor and materials	$31,121
Plumbing	1,200
Grading and oiling ramps, complete	4,351
Painting	1,684
Electric wiring and fixtures	4,934
Horns, installed	1,530
Sound equipment, complete	5,609
Projection room equipment	3,236

Other equipment, such as furnishings for manager's office, ushers' room, rest rooms, ticket office, and janitor's supplies	898
Total cost	$54,563

Source: C. A. Balch, *Motion Picture Herald*, December 10, 1938, p. 14.

Drive-in construction cost in 1948, based on several projects with capacity averaging 700 autos (excluding land):

Grading and surfacing (oiled crushed stone) ramps and drives	$17,000
Refreshment-Projection-Restroom building, including toilet fixtures but no refreshment-service equipment	1,500
Fencing (enclosure and ornamental)	2,000
Electrical wiring, not including speakers	3,300
Painting (additional to that of main structure)	500
Projection and sound equipment, installed (including in-car speakers and posts)	25,000
Screen tower (steel construction, with frame housing at base for manager's office, attendants' room, switchboard)	14,900
Landscaping	1,000
Office, ticket booth equipment, lockers, etc.	2,000
Attraction panels and letters and name signs, miscellaneous signs	10,000
Light fixtures and installation, including "moonlight" lighting	2,000
Plans and contingency allowances	2,700
Total cost	$96,000

Source: George Schutz, *Motion Picture Herald*, February 11, 1956, p. 12.

Drive-in construction cost in 1956, based on several projects with capacity averaging 1,000 autos (excluding land):

Grading—including clearing, soil tests, rough grading and drainage (the latter being, however, a highly variable item)	$25,000
Surfacing (crushed stone with two oil treatments; blacktop would add $15,000 to the amount given here)	30,000
Sewage disposal and water supply	15,000
Electrical—including wiring for speakers and road lighting, floodlighting, and all lighting fixtures, building wiring and main power line	40,000
Screen tower (approx. 120 × 52-foot screen), complete	26,000
Refreshment-projection-restroom building (approx. 70 × 60 feet)	45,000
Refreshment service equipment (cafeteria)	25,000
Theater and attraction sign and letters	5,000
Fencing (including playground) and guard rails	3,000
Projection and sound equipment—including speakers	22,000
Playground equipment (medium facilities)	7,500
Landscaping	4,000
Total cost	$254,000

For winter operation:

In-car heaters—including ramp and terminal wiring, and additional electric power service for 300 heaters	12,000
Heating installation for main building	10,000
Total cost for all-season operation	$276,000

Source: George Schutz, *Motion Picture Herald*, February 11, 1956, p. 13.

Drive-in construction cost in 1953, based on 500 car capacity:

Preliminary

Cost of site, approx. 11 acres @ $500 an acre	$ 5,500
Architectural fee	2,000

Legal fees	500
Engineering fees, survey, and topography	350
	$ 8,350
Construction	
Grading and drainage	$ 7,000
Surfacing ramps and drives	8,000
Water supply, drilled well, and equipment	2,000
Sewage disposal, septic tank, and filter bed	1,500
Screen structure, screen size 50 × 37 ft. 6 in.	10,000
Projection room, concession, and restrooms	7,500
Ticket office	800
Attraction board	1,000
Plumbing	2,200
Electric wiring and fixtures	2,000
Speaker posts and underground wiring	3,000
Fencing, various	1,800
Landscaping	1,500
Signs, neon and painted	2,500
	$50,800
Equipment	
Projection and in-car speakers	$16,000
Concession equipment	3,500
	$19,500
Miscellaneous	
Office furniture and equipment	$ 200
Playground equipment	1,000
Moonlight floodlighting	500
Uniforms, ushers and car hops	200
Silhouette sign letters	500
	$ 2,400
Total Cost	$81,050

Source: George M. Petersen, *Drive-In Theatre: Manual of Design and Operation*. Kansas City, Missouri, Associated, 1953, p. 27. (Petersen estimates a range of $40,000 to $150,000.)

Estimated operating cost of a 700-car drive-in, based on several operating ozoners and based on a twenty-six-week season, 1953:

	Season	Week
1. Film	$13,000.00	$ 500.00
2. Advertising	2,600.00	100.00
3. Booth supplies	78.00	3.00
4. Carbons	163.00	6.26
5. Film delivery	260.00	10.00
6. Lamps, floodlights, etc.	260.00	10.00
7. Sound service	260.00	10.00
8. Sound supplies and repairs	26.00	1.00
9. Tickets	52.00	2.00
10. Express	54.00	2.07
11. Records for non-sync	52.00	2.00
12. Janitors' supplies	104.00	4.00
13. Payroll (*see below*)	16,250.00	625.00
14. Office expense	435.00	16.70
15. Insurance premiums	761.00	29.20
16. Light and power	2,080.00	80.00
17. Miscellaneous expense	1,300.00	50.00
18. Taxes, social security, unemployment	1,133.00	43.50
19. Telephone and telegraph	260.00	10.00
20. Trucking and freight	112.00	4.30
21. Legal and accounting	260.00	10.00
22. Laundry and cleaning	260.00	10.00
23. Licenses	41.60	1.60
24. Park and yard maintenance	390.00	15.00
25. Subscriptions and dues	26.00	1.00
26. Uniforms, new and repairs	260.00	10.00
27. Building maintenance	260.00	10.00
28. Depreciation of equipment	1,466.00	56.50
29. Donations	130.00	5.00
Total Estimated Operating Cost	$42,333.00	$ 1,628.00

Estimated Payroll Expense

Manager	$ 1,950.00	$ 75.00
Projectionists (two)	5,200.00	200.00
Deputy sheriff	780.00	30.00
Watchman	650.00	25.00

Estimated Payroll Expense, *continued*

Cashier	650.00	25.00
Yard man	780.00	30.00
Ushers (fifteen)	5,200.00	200.00
Carhops	780.00	30.00
Miscellaneous	260.00	10.00
Total	$16,250.00	$ 625.00

Average Gross Income Based on Six-Month Operation:

180,000 adult admissions at 60 cents each	$108,000.00
30,700 child admissions at 25 cents each	7,675.00
	$115,675.00

Average Net Earnings:

Gross admissions	$115,675.00
Taxes, Amusement, inc. local	28,381.00
Net Admissions	$ 87,294.00
Operating costs from above	42,333.00
Net Earnings from Admissions	$ 44,961.00
Net Earnings from Concession	15,000.00
Total Net Earnings	$ 59,961.00

Source: George M. Petersen, *Drive-In Theatre: Manual of Design and Operation* (Kansas City, Missouri: Associated, 1953), pp. 25–26.

Appendix 6: Number of Drive-ins, by State

	1948	1954	1958	1963	1967	1972	1977	1982	1987
Alabama	13	93/87	96/86	75/71	69	72	55	26	6
Alaska	N	N	N	1/1	2	1	1	0	0
Arizona	4	29/29	49/49	37/37	38	40	47	20	7
Arkansas	5	56/52	57/55	42/42	45	46	40	32	10
California	44	159/153	180/176	202/196	223	219	192	147	113
Colorado	9	48/48	61/55	37/37	50	44	59	38	20
Connecticut	6	27/27	34/34	38/38	42	31	29	16	9
Delaware	0	9/7	6/6	8/8	7	5	9	7	1
Florida	22	158/144	155/141	126/124	123	133	117	93	42
Georgia	13	128/120	119/113	89/87	96	84	74	44	10
Hawaii	N	N	N	5/5	5	2	4	3	2
Idaho	8	32/30	35/31	29/29	30	27	20	19	11
Illinois	25	106/100	123/113	107/103	106	125	96	68	25
Indiana	28	111/111	125/121	109/103	108	110	89	74	40
Iowa	7	68/62	58/56	48/48	67	59	48	41	22
Kansas	11	107/107	125/113	84/84	80	68	55	37	16
Kentucky	16	105/99	117/109	103/99	97	86	77	54	28
Louisiana	9	67/63	54/46	40/38	44	30	30	12	3
Maine	2	36/36	35/35	30/30	36	32	33	26	7
Maryland	5	33/33	47/41	43/43	42	42	34	24	2
Massachusetts	21	58/58	86/84	78/78	80	83	60	52	20
Michigan	28	87/81	110/106	108/102	94	106	103	96	48

Appendix 6: Number of Drive-ins, by State, *continued*

	1948	1954	1958	1963	1967	1972	1977	1982	1987
Minnesota	7	46/38	77/61	65/61	69	80	59	42	15
Mississippi	5	65/61	69/67	48/46	45	33	36	19	9
Missouri	16	124/118	121/111	108/106	93	99	85	62	23
Montana	2	27/27	39/35	34/30	29	31	20	14	8
Nebraska	3	41/37	43/41	31/29	34	38	35	32	14
Nevada	2	7/7	9/9	9/9	11	8	10	9	5
New Hampshire	2	20/18	21/21	23/21	19	20	18	16	6
New Jersey	7	31/31	44/44	39/39	46	38	32	22	8
New Mexico	3	45/45	49/45	42/42	47	43	31	21	6
New York	33	126/122	147/141	154/148	128	114	107	95	48
North Carolina	66	206/194	209/179	153/133	116	120	104	73	23
North Dakota	0	16/12	16/14	22/20	15	17	10	11	4
Ohio	88	164/162	196/186	188/178	189	181	165	144	83
Oklahoma	29	95/95	93/91	93/91	83	80	63	47	14
Oregon	3	67/67	69/65	51/51	48	59	47	29	17
Pennsylvania	59	165/161	181/177	166/161	170	126	141	115	75
Rhode Island	1	9/9	12/12	10/10	14	8	6	5	2
South Carolina	36	99/89	72/70	56/50	46	42	40	25	12
South Dakota	5	23/23	31/29	24/24	24	23	19	19	7
Tennessee	15	107/103	112/102	90/84	86	98	86	43	19
Texas	88	388/374	382/358	315/311	263	280	192	137	56
Utah	10	34/34	32/30	30/28	30	30	19	20	10
Vermont	1	22/22	23/21	21/21	19	19	17	11	8

Virginia	26	118/114	143/135	115/105	90	102	87	56	16
Washington	16	56/54	58/54	47/47	56	71	66	49	24
West Virginia	18	76/72	73/69	58/58	60	55	46	35	19
Wisconsin	3	60/54	43/43	49/49	50	59	50	35	18
Wyoming	0	21/21	27/25	22/20	20	23	19	14	8

Notes: N - Data for Alaska and Hawaii not reported until after they attained statehood.
No drive-ins reported in any of these census years for the District of Columbia.
For census years 1954, 1958, and 1963 two figures are reported. The first is the total number of establishments; the second is the total number with a payroll. The single number for other census years is the number with a payroll, the only one given.

Number of Drive-ins and Gross Receipts, United States

	Number of Indoor theaters	Number of Drive-ins	Receipts, indoor theaters $1,000s estabs. with payroll	Receipts, drive-ins $1,000s estabs. with payroll
1948	17,689	820	1,312,013	40,385
1954	14,716/13,760	3,775/3,611	1,170,401	225,910
1958	12,291/11,271	4,063/3,805	928,128	230,417
1963	9,150/ 8,665	3,502/3,375	803,458	253,766
1967	8,094	3,384	969,991	313,012
1972	8,328	3,342	1,402,758	413,158
1977	7,814	2,882	2,130,142	440,167

Number of Drive-ins and Gross Receipts, United States, *continued*

	Number of Indoor theaters	Number of Drive-ins	Receipts, indoor theaters $1,000s estabs. with payroll	Receipts, drive-ins $1,000s estabs. with payroll
1982	7,215	2,129	3,224,241	351,496
1987	6,777	999	3,809,209	167,869

Note: Double figures for 1954, 1958, and 1963 represent total number of establishments and total number with a payroll, respectively. Gross receipts for those years include admission taxes, excluded for 1948, not specified for other years.

Sources: *United States Census of Business 1948*, vol. 7, *Service Trade—Area Statistics* (Washington, D.C.: United States Bureau of the Census, 1951).
54 Census of Business, vol. 5, *Selected Service Trades—Summary Statistics* (Washington, D.C.: United States Bureau of the Census, 1957).
1958 Census of Business, vol. 5, *Selected Services—Summary Statistics* (Washington, D.C.: United States Bureau of the Census, 1961).
1963 Census of Business, vol. 6, *Selected Services—Summary Statistics* (Washington, D.C.: United States Bureau of the Census, 1966).
1967 Census of Business, vol. 5, *Selected Services—Area Statistics, Part 1* (Washington, D.C.: United States Bureau of the Census, 1970).
1972 Census of Selected Service Industries (Washington, D.C.: United States Bureau of the Census, 1975).
1977 Census of Service Industries, vol. 1, *Subject Statistics* (Washington, D.C.: United States Bureau of the Census, 1980).
Census of Service Industries (1982) (Washington, D.C.: United States Bureau of the Census, n.d.).
1987 Census of Service Industries, Geographic Area Series—United States (Washington, D.C.: United States Bureau of the Census, 1989).

Appendix 7: Monthly Film Attendance by Type of Theater, 1952–1954

In millions of admissions

	1952		1953		1954	
Month	Indoor	Drive-in	Indoor	Drive-in	Indoor	Drive-in
January	37.2	.3	36.0	.3	31.7	.4
February	42.1	.4	37.4	.4	35.4	.4
March	40.7	.9	32.2	.9	37.5	1.0
April	39.6	3.9	32.6	3.8	32.1	6.5
May	37.5	6.9	31.7	7.9	34.1	9.1
June	33.7	18.5	34.6	21.2	38.1	21.8
July	36.3	38.5	37.9	29.9	40.8	31.7
August	39.6	40.9	40.7	33.8	40.9	39.2
September	35.6	30.1	40.6	24.5	41.1	24.7
October	38.2	9.1	32.6	9.5	35.1	9.9
November	41.8	4.7	31.2	4.5	39.0	4.6
December	34.4	.4	24.0	.2	32.0	.3

Source: *Film Daily Year Book 1955* (New York: Film Daily, 1955), p. 143).

Notes

Chapter 1: A Backyard Invention

1. Richard M. Hollingshead, Jr., United States Patent number 1,909,537.
2. Floyd E. Stone, "Father of Drive-Ins Says 'Never Again,'" *Motion Picture Herald*, January 28, 1950, p. 38.
3. "The Drive-In Theatre: A Motor-Age Experiment," *Motion Picture Herald*, July 1, 1933, p. 15.
4. Stone, "Father of Drive-Ins."
5. Ibid.
6. Harry M. Potter, "The World's First Drive-In Theatre," *South Jersey Magazine*, October-December 1974, p. 3.
7. "Drive-In Theatre to Be Opened Here, *Courier-Post* (Camden, N.J.), May 17, 1933.
8. Potter, "The World's First Drive-In," p. 3.
9. "Open Air 'Drive-In' Theatre for Cars," *Variety*, June 13, 1933, p. 5.
10. Ibid.; "Drive-in Theater," *Business Week*, August 5, 1933, p. 19; "Camden's Drive-In Theater," *Literary Digest* 116:19, July 22, 1933; "Movie Theater Lets Cars Drive Right In," *Popular Science Monthly*, 123:19, August 1933; "Drive-In Movie Holds Four Hundred Cars," *Popular Mechanics*, 60:326, September 1933.
11. See note 10; "First Drive-In Theatre in the World," one-page sheet from Camden County Historical Society and Camden Public Library, n.d.
12. "The Drive-In Theatre: A Motor-Age Experiment," pp. 15–17.
13. "R. M. Hollingshead, Jr. Dies: Originator of Drive-Ins, *Boxoffice* 107:7, May 26, 1975.
14. Lewis Beale, "Drive-ins: The Thrill Is Gone," *Washington Post*, June 5, 1983, p. F4.
15. Tony Muldoon, "Film Credits May Roll for Local Man Who Pioneered Drive-In Theaters," *Courier-Post* (Camden, N.J.), June 9, 1985, p. 6A.
16. Beale, "Drive-Ins: The Thrill Is Gone," p. F4.

Chapter 2: Patent Battles

1. Brad Angier, "New England Open-Air Theatre Situation Forsakes Ozone for Courtroom Battles," *Boxoffice*, April 30, 1938, p. 143.
2. Ibid., pp. 143, 148–49.

3. Ibid.; Drive-In Theatres Corporation v. Park-In Theatres et al., *United States Patent Quarterly* 38:41–42.

4. Park In Theatres, Inc., v. Rogers et al., *United States Patent Quarterly* 55:103–6.

5. Park-In Theatres, Inc., v. Loew's Drive-In Theatres, Inc., *United States Patent Quarterly* 72:470–77.

6. Park-In Theatres, Inc., v. Ochs et al., *United States Patent Quarterly* 75:4–5; Park In Theatres, Inc., v. Ochs et al., *United States Patent Quarterly* 77:43–49

7. Park-In Theatres, Inc., v. Paramount-Richards Theatres, Inc., et al., *United States Patent Quarterly* 76:353–55; Park-In Theatres, Inc., v. Paramount-Richards Theatres, Inc., et al., *United States Patent Quarterly* 80:6–14.

8. Park-In Theatres, Inc., v. Paramount-Richards Theatres, Inc., et al., *United States Patent Quarterly* 82:90–92; Park-In Theatres, Inc., v. Paramount-Richards Theatres, Inc., et al., *United States Patent Quarterly* 85:346–48; Park-In Theatres, Inc., v. Paramount-Richards Theatres, Inc., et al., *United States Patent Quarterly* 85:353–58; Park-In Theatres, Inc., v. Paramount-Richards Theatres, Inc., et al., *United States Patent Quarterly* 88:165.

9. Park-In Theatres, Inc., v. Paramount-Richards Theatres, Inc., et al., *United States Patent Quarterly* 85:347.

10. Loew's Drive-In Theatres, Inc., v. Park-In Theatres, Inc., *United States Patent Quarterly* 81:149–55.

11. Park-In Theatres Inc., v. Loew's Drive-In Theatres, Inc., *United States Patent Quarterly* 83:543.

12. Park-In Theatres, Inc., v. Waters et al., *United States Patent Quarterly* 87:291–93; Park-In Theatres, Inc., v. Perkins, et al., *United States Patent Quarterly* 90:163–68.

13. North Park Theatre Corporation v. Park-In Theatres, Inc., et al., *United States Patent Quarterly* 114:474–79.

14. Floyd E. Stone, "Father of Drive-Ins, Says 'Never Again,'" *Motion Picture Herald*, January 28, 1950, p. 38.

Chapter 3: A Very Slow Start, 1933–1944

1. Louis Josserand, United States Patent Number 2,102,718; Josserand v. Taylor Jr., *United States Patent Quarterly* 59:140–49; Josserand v. Taylor Jr., *United States Patent Quarterly* 72:357–64; In Re Josserand. *United States Patent Quarterly* 89:371–81.

2. "Drive-In Theater Opening Tomorrow," *Los Angeles Examiner*, September 8, 1934, p. 9.

3. "Merrimack Auto Theater," *Boxoffice*, July 30, 1938, p. 75; "Detroit Drive-In," *Boxoffice*, February 25, 1938, p. 121; "Hyannis Ozone Theatre," *Boxoffice*, March 19, 1938, p. 55.

4. "Drive-Ins Hit by Hurricane Include Odd Dual Theatre," *Motion Picture Herald*, October 15, 1938, p. 8.

5. "Loew Drive-In Theatre, *Boxoffice*, March 19, 1938, p. 91; "Miami Drive-In Cuts Admission Price," *Boxoffice*, April 30, 1938, p. 152.

6. "Drive-Ins for Hub Showmen," *Boxoffice*, June 4, 1938, p. 79, "Detroit Drive-In Opened in Rain," *Boxoffice*, June 4, 1938, p. 71; "Detroit Drive-In Draws City-Wide Patronage; Rain Does Not Retard," *Boxoffice*, June 25, 1938, p. 106.

7. "Detroit Drive-In Draws."

8. Scott Fosdick, "Ritchie Drive-In," *News American* (Baltimore), April 1, 1984.

9. Ted Cohen, "Saco Drive-In's 50th Birthday Stirs Memories," *Portland* (Maine) *Press Herald*, July 15, 1989.

10. "Outdoor Auto Movie House, First in State," *New York Times*, July 3, 1938, p. 4; Thomas M. Pryor, "Evolution of the Drive-In, *New York Times*, August 14, 1938, sec. 9, p. 3.

11. "First Florida Drive-In Built in 1939 in Jacksonville," by Horace Denning, *Boxoffice*, April 1, 1974, pp. SE1, SE7.

12. "N. S. Barger Opening Chicago Drive-In," *Boxoffice*, May 24, 1941, p. 96.

13. Jerry Dean, "Drive-In Heyday Passes; 'Chevrolet Nights,' Family Films Yield to a Different Kind of Fare," (Little Rock) *Arkansas Gazette*, February 8, 1983.

14. C. A. Balch, "The Plan and Construction of One of the Newest Drive-In Theatres," *Motion Picture Herald*, December 10, 1938, pp. 14–15, 40–41; S. D. Perkins, "Policy and Technical Factors in Drive-In Theatre Operation," *Motion Picture Herald*, December 10, 1938, pp. 15, 41.

15. Ordinance number 74733, Los Angeles City Council, passed February 7, 1935; "Drive-In Noises Go for Test Tomorrow," *Daily Variety*, April 3, 1935, p. 8; "Legality of Murmur Law Is Hit in Drive-In House Closing Suit," *Daily Variety*, April 5, 1935, p.25; "Drive-In Theatre Operator Found Guilty by Jury," *Los Angeles Times*, June 5, 1935, sec. 1, p. 5; "Drive-In Theater Head Given Fine Under Noise Law," *Los Angeles Times*, June 7, 1935, sec. 2, p. 12; "Drive-In Theater Originator Dies," *Los Angeles Times*, December 28, 1936, sec. 2, p. 2.

16. "Restrainer Demand Threatens Drive-In," *Boxoffice*, July 9, 1938, p. 50.

17. "Hearings Slated on Writ Bid Against Drive-In," *Boxoffice*, September 14, 1940, p,. 95.

18. "Are Drive-In Pixers a Public Nuisance?" *Variety*, May 9, 1945, p. 6.

19. "Decision on Sound Volume at Riverside Due Soon," *Boxoffice*, August 10, 1940, p. 43.

20. "Claims Only Woman Drive-In Manager," *Boxoffice*, March 3, 1940, p. 89; *Boxoffice*, July 13, 1940, p. 27.

21. "Drive-Ins," *Boxoffice*, September 13, 1941, p. 42, Western edition.

22. "389 New Theatres Entered Field in 1939," *Boxoffice*, February 10, 1940, p. 17.

23. William Price Fox, "The Drive-In," *Esquire* 84:156, December 1975.

24. Dale Schneck, "America's Oldest Drive-In Theatre," *Boxoffice*, September 1983, p. 122.

25. Brad Angier, "DiMaura Emerges Victor in First Legal Skirmish over the Drive-In Theatres, Inc.," *Boxoffice*, November 26, 1938, p. 71.

26. "Drive-Ins," *Time* 38:66, July 14, 1941.

27. *Film Daily Year Book 1957* (New York: Film Daily, 1957), p. 111.

28. "Theatre Attendance Down Five Million," *Boxoffice*, February 22, 1941, p. 6.

29. "Spread of Drive-In Cinemas May Become a Worry to Regular Ops; Dixie Belt Can Stay Open All Year," *Variety*, July 6, 1938, p. 21.

30. "Cincinnati Drive-In Building Protested," *Boxoffice*, January 20, 1940, p. 55; Angier, "DiMaura Emerges."

31. George M. Petersen, *Drive-In Theatre* (Kansas City, Mo.: Associated Publications, 1953), p. 16.

32. *Film Daily Year Book 1942* (New York: Film Daily, 1942), pp. 67, 854–55; *Film Daily Year Book 1943* (New York: Film Daily, 1943), p. 51; *Film Daily Year Book 1944* (New York: Film Daily, 1944), p. 51; *Film Daily Year Book 1945* (New York: Film Daily, 1945), p. 49; *Film Daily Year Book 1946* (New York Film Daily, 1946), p. 51;

Film Daily Year Book 1947 (New York: Film Daily, 1947), p. 57; *United States Census of Business 1948*, vol. 7, *Service Trade—Area Statistics* (Washington, D.C.: Bureau of the Census, 1951), p. 0.04; *1954 Census of Business*, vol. 5, *Selected Service Trades—Summary Statistics* (Washington, D.C.: Bureau of the Census, 1957), p. 8-2.

33. Park-In Theatres, Inc. v. Loew's Drive-In Theatres, Inc., *United States Patent Quarterly* 72:471; Fosdick, "Ritchie Drive-In."

Chapter 4: Postwar Surge, 1945–1949

1. Material for this brief overview of the industry's monopoly hold comes from Michael Conant, *Antitrust in the Motion Picture Industry* (Berkeley, Calif: University of California Press, 1960); "Court Orders Divorce of Loew's, 20th–Fox and Warner Theatres," *Motion Picture Herald*, July 30, 1949, pp. 13–14ff.

2. Lloyd Wendt, *The Wall Street Journal* (Chicago: Rand McNally, 1982), p. 300.

3. Ansel M. Moore, "The Drive-In Theory: Basically Sound But Badly Interpreted," *Boxoffice*, December 8, 1945, p. 10, Western edition.

4. Ibid., pp. 10, 21.

5. Rodney Luther, "Drive-In Theaters: Rags to Riches in Five Years," *Hollywood Quarterly* 5:405, Summer 1951; Bruce A. Austin, "The Development and Decline of the Drive-In Movie Theater," in *Current Research in Film*, vol. 1 (Norwood, N.J.: Ablex, 1985), p. 68.

6. Elsie Loeb, "The Drive-In Story," *Boxoffice*, October 4, 1947, p. 22.

7. Charles Irwin, "Drive-Ins Boom in Ohio, Six in Dayton Alone," *Boxoffice*, July 13, 1946, p. 16.

8. John Harti, "Drive-Ins Survive, But Land Values Threaten," *Seattle Times*, August 22, 1982.

9. Irwin, "Drive-Ins Boom"; Loeb, pp. 22–23.

10. Irwin, Drive-Ins Boom."

11. Loeb, "The Drive-In Story," p. 22.

12. Dave Wielenga, "Moviegoers by the Carful," *Press-Telegram* (Long Beach, Calif.), August 25, 1988, p. D1.

13. George Spires, "Service—by Bar or Cart—Brings Drive-In Sales," *Motion Picture Herald*, August 13, 1949, p. 43.

14. "AP Columnist Tells of Flexer Drive-In," *Boxoffice*, November 29, 1947, p. 89.

15. "Drive-Ins Appeal to Family Groups," *Boxoffice*, August 9, 1947, p. 52.

16. David Barrett, "Exhibitors Favor Year-Round Operation," *Boxoffice*, October 3, 1953, p. 42.

17. "A Drive-In Pioneer Looks at the Record," *Motion Picture Herald*, December 2, 1950, p. 22; "Indianapolis," *Boxoffice*, July 26, 1947, p. 121; George M. Petersen, *Drive-In Theatre: Manual of Design and Operation* (Kansas City, Mo.: Associated, 1953), p. 186.

18. "Ozoners Reverse Current B.O. Dip, Drive-Ins Up 10% Over '48 Revenue," *Variety*, June 8, 1949, p. 14; "The Roof's the Sky and Sky Is Drive-In Limit," *Motion Picture Herald* 172:16, July 17, 1948.

19. "The Roof's the Sky."

20. National Theatre Supply ad, *Boxoffice*, September 15, 1945, p. 29; RCA ad, *Boxoffice*, February 2, 1946, pp., 24–25.

21. "Drive-Ins Offered as Package Deal," *Boxoffice*, February 28, 1948, p. 22; "Drive-In Growth," *Boxoffice*, September 24, 1949, p. 7.

22. "Twice as Many Drive-in Theaters?" *Business Week*, January 1, 1949, p. 44.
23. "AP Columnist"; "The Roof's the Sky"; Fred Hift, "Drive-Ins A'Bloom in Spring—By Hundreds," *Motion Picture Herald* 174:22, March 26, 1949.
24. "Magnolia Drive-In," *Boxoffice*, July 1, 1950, p. 40; "Denver Drive-In," *Boxoffice*, July 12, 1949, p. 59.
25. "Drive-In Growth"; "A Theatre Architect Looks Ahead," *Boxoffice*, April 1, 1950, pp. 10–11.
26. George Schutz, "The New Drive-In Economics and How They Got That Way," *Motion Picture Herald*, February 11, 1956, p. 12.
27. Sumner Smith, "Drive-Ins Up from 100 to 761 in 20-Month Building Boom," *Boxoffice*, November 13, 1948, p. 25; "743 Drive-Ins Operating; 137 All Year, MPAA Says," *Motion Picture Herald*, November 6, 1948, p. 15.
28. *United States Census of Business 1948*, vol. 7, *Service Trade—Area Statistics—Amusements* (Washington, D.C.: United States Bureau of the Census, 1951).
29. *Film Daily Year Book 1957* (New York: Film Daily, 1957), p. 111. These figures are cited in all *Film Daily Yearbooks* as well as in, for example, Cobbett Steinberg, *Film Facts* (New York: Facts on File, 1980), p. 46.
30. Edward de Grazia, *Banned Films* (New York: Bowker, 1982), p. 69; Rodney Luther, "Marketing Aspects of Drive-In Theaters," *Journal of Marketing* 15:44, July 1950.
31. "Hellman Fears Drive-Ins Are Being Overbuilt," *Boxoffice*, October 18, 1947, p. 56.

Chapter 5: Drive-ins Battle the Industry

1. "Pre-Hearing Accord in Drive-In Case," *Boxoffice*, April 19, 1941, p. 83; "Austin Drive-In Asks 30-Day Availability," *Boxoffice*, November 29, 1947, p. 81.
2. "Two Theatres Seek Reduced Clearances Through Decree," *Daily Variety*, March 5, 1942, p. 4.
3. "Twin City Indies Fear Invasion of Drive-In Theatres," *Variety*, September 17, 1947, p. 20; "Drive-In Exhib Charges Twin City Theatres Stifling Competition," *Variety*, September 17, 1947, p., 20; "Secret Meetings Held to Battle Threatened Drive-In Invasion," *Boxoffice*, September 13, 1947, p. 28.
4. "Minn. Distribs Profit from Ozoners Operated by Non-Theatre Owners," *Variety*, September 13, 1950, p. 22.
5. "First Run Bid Rights Granted to Drive-In," *Boxoffice*, April 16, 1949, p. 11.
6. Fred Hift, "Drive-Ins A'Bloom in Spring—By Hundreds," *Motion Picture Herald* 174:19, March 26, 1949.
7. "Drive-Ins Are Now Fighting for Clearance Improvement," *Boxoffice*, May 21, 1949, p. 8.
8. "Product Day at the Convention," *Boxoffice*, November 4, 1950, p. 19.
9. "Anti-Drive-In Bill Dies," *Boxoffice*, May 6, 1950, p. 68.
10. "Drive-Ins Press for First Runs," *Variety*, August 31, 1949, p. 20.
11. *Film Daily Yearbook 1957* (New York: Film Daily, 1957), p. 111.
12. "Drive-Ins Are Now Fighting for Clearance Improvement," *Boxoffice*, May 21, 1949, p. 8.
13. "Ozoner Loses Suit to Force Paper to Take Ads," *Variety*, April 30, 1952, p. 4.
14. "20th–Fox Established Policy on Selling Drive-In Accounts," *Boxoffice*, March 12, 1949, p.14.

15. "Drive-Ins Get Eighth of Total Patronage," *Boxoffice*, September 2, 1950, p. 9.

16. "First-Run Licenses to Drive-Ins Denied," *Hollywood Reporter*, October 20, 1949; "Drive-Ins," *Boxoffice*, August 31, 1949; "Drive-Ins Press for First Runs," *Variety*, August 31, 1949, p. 20.

17. Ibid.; "Chicago Drive-Ins Sue on Clearances," *Boxoffice*, June 4, 1949, p. 11; "Chi Ozoner Talks Suing for 1st Runs," *Variety*, August 24, 1949, p. 25; "Drive-Ins Talk Suing for Better Film Clearances," *Variety*, August 17, 1949, pp. 4, 9.

18. "Penna. Court Rules Ozoners Entitled to 1st-Run Treatment," *Daily Variety*, November 29, 1950; "Allentown Ozoner Asks Equal 1st-Run Clearance," *Variety*, February 15, 1950, p. 18; "Majors Expect Verdict in 2 Weeks on Pennsy Drive-In Bid Appeal," *Variety*, July 25, 1951, pp. 7, 16; "Drive-In Clearance Case Taken to Supreme Court," *Hollywood Reporter*, March 18, 1952; "U.S. Supreme Court Rules Distribs Cannot Favor Theatres Over Drive-Ins," *Variety*, April 22, 1952.

19. "Ozoners Can't Gross Enough for Top Bids, Sales Chiefs Believe," *Variety*, April 4, 1951, pp. 5, 13.

20. "Coast Drive-Ins Sue Majors for First Run Recognition," *Hollywood Reporter*, December 13, 1950; "N.J. Drive-In Files Anti-Trust Suit," *Variety*, June 7, 1950, p. 18; "Ill Drive-In Asks Million in Trust Suit," *Variety*, January 25, 1951, p. 5.

21. "Drive-In Owners Want Per Person Admission, Earlier Product Runs," *Motion Picture Herald*, June 30, 1951, p. 13.

22. "Fair Trade Practices Code for Drive-Ins Is Demanded," *Boxoffice*, November 11, 1950, p. 9.

23. "By-the-Busload, Boxtop Operators Not to Get Top MGM Availability," *Boxoffice*, November 11, 1950, p. 9.

24. "Ozoners the Best Answer to TV," *Variety*, July 23, 1952, pp. 3, 23.

25. "Drive-Ins' Eagerness for Parity with Hardtops on First Runs (Via Court Orders) Worrisome," *Variety*, August 3, 1955, p. 23.

26. "Drive-In Theatre Sues Movie Trust," *New York Times*, October 10, 1954, p. 82; "Pa. Drive-In Theatres File Clearance Action," *Film Daily*, May 9, 1956, p. 15.

27. Steven Ginsberg, "Indoor Sites Forced to 8 Weeks; Protest Drive-In 'Half Runs,'" *Variety* 291:27, July 5, 1978.

Chapter 6: Communities Battle Drive-ins

1. "Traffic Hazard Stymies Toronto Drive-In, But Many Others Planned," *Variety*, May 7, 1947, p. 33.

2. "Drive-In Theatres a Factor," *New York Times*, September 28, 1949, p. 29; "Drive-Ins as 'Highway Hazards' Probed by Pennsy Commission," *Variety*, July 6, 1949, p. 25.

3. "Drive-Ins Seen Highway Menace by State Groups," *Variety*, July 12, 1950, p. 7; "Urge Tighter State Drive-In Regulation," *Motion Picture Herald*, June 10, 1950.

4. Joseph C. Ingraham, "Drive-In Movies Held Car Hazard," *New York Times*, December 2, 1956, p. 142.

5. "It's a New, Brighter Year for Drive-Ins," *Motion Picture Herald*, May 20, 1950, p. 23; "City Planning Body Scored by Murdock," *New York Times*, March 16, 1950, p. 35.

6. "Would Bar Drive-In Shows," *New York Times*, August 20, 1950, p. 42; "Drive-In Theatre Plan Fails," *New York Times*, January 29, 1950, p. 53; "Drive-Ins Bitten as Mayors Snarl," *Motion Picture Herald*, January 21, 1950, p. 16.

7. "Chi Council Cracks Down on Ozoners; New Ordinance Bans 'Em Inside City," *Variety*, May 10, 1950, p. 19; "Chicago Court Rules City Cannot Bar Drive-Ins," *Motion Picture Herald*, January 28, 1950, p. 22.

8. "Ozoner Operator Sues Chi Suburban Village for $1,000,000 Over Permit," *Variety*, April 12, 1950, p. 20; "Cold Weather Hits Midwest Ozoners; Many Folding; Other Drive-In News," *Variety*, October 18, 1950, p. 16; "Drive-In a Menace to Health, Village Sez," *Variety*, August 30, 1950, p. 16.

9. "Drive-In Curfew Upset," *New York Times*, December 6, 1958, p. 25; "Chicago Mayor Would Halt Construction of Drive-In," *Film Daily*, May 11, 1956, pp., 1, 3.

10. Wilfred P. Smith, "Management of a Drive-In," *Motion Picture Herald*, February 4, 1950, pp. 13–14.

Chapter 7: The Golden Years, 1950s

1. Al Hine, "The Drive-Ins," *Holiday* 12:6, July 5, 1952; John Durant, "The Movies Take to the Pastures," *Saturday Evening Post* 223:24, October 14, 1950.

2. Durant, "The Movies," pp. 25, 85.

3. Ibid, p. 90; "Drive-Ins," *Architectural Record* 108:140, August 1950.

4. "A Ban on New Construction," *Boxoffice*, December 27, 1952, p. 24.

5. Petersen, *Drive-In Theatre*, pp. 25–27.

6. "Drive-Ins Steal the Show," *Business Week*, August 15, 1953, p. 114.

7. Frank J. Taylor, "Big Boom in Outdoor Movies," *Saturday Evening Post*, September 15, 1956, pp. 100–101.

8. Petersen, *Drive-In Theatre*, p. 30.

9. "Million-Dollar Drive-In Offers Films, Fun and Food," *Popular Science Monthly* 171:118–121, September 1957; "The Colossal Drive-In," *Newsweek* 50:85, July 22, 1957.

10. *International Motion Picture Almanac 1951–1952* (New York: Quigley, 1952), p. 511; *International Motion Picture Almanac 1957* (New York: Quigley, 1958), pp. 549ff.; *International Motion Picture Almanac 1959* (New York: Quigley, 1960), pp. 560ff.; Taylor, "Big Boom," p. 102; "Pulman, R. E. Drive-In Theatre Operation," *British Kinematography* 32:105, April 1958.

11. "Drive-In on the Subway," *Motion Picture Herald*, November 5, 1949, p. 18.

12. Taylor, "Big Boom," pp. 100, 102.

13. "Adapting a Drive-In to Its Countryside," *Motion Picture Herald*, October 1, 1949, pp. 25–26.

14. "Tinted Windshields," *Boxoffice*, March 21, 1953, p. 19.

15. Rita Reif, "Drive-In Theatre Extends Horizon," *New York Times*, June 9, 1957, p. 14; "Drive-In Theatres: Happy But Griping," *Business Week*, May 9, 1953, p. 131.

16. Durant, "The Movies," p. 90.

17. Leonard Spinrad, "Burgeoning Drive-Ins," *New York Times*, March 1, 1953, p. 5.

18. "Drive-In Owners Want Per Person Admission, Earlier Product Runs," *Motion Picture Herald*, June 30, 1951, p. 13.

19. Marguerite W. Cullman, "Double Feature—Movies and Moonlight," *New York Times Magazine*, October 1, 1951, p. 72.

20. "Drive-In Owners Want," pp. 13–14.

21. Cullman, "Double Feature," p. 68.

22. "Drive-In Owners Want," pp. 14, 19; Pulman, p. 106.

23. "Drive-In Theaters: Happy," p. 129.

24. "Kids-for-Free, Filled Cars at $1 Snarl Distribs," *Variety*, June 28, 1950, pp. 5, 16; "The Colossal Drive-In," p. 86.

25. "Drive-Ins Cut Charlotte First-Runs Down to Two," *Variety*, July 16, 1952, p. 4; "Swarm of Expected Closings Seen Correcting; Drive-In Impact Strong," *Variety*, July 5, 1950, pp. 3, 22; "Price Dispute Clouds Bright Drive-In Year," *Motion Picture Herald*, June 2, 1951, p. 13.

26. "Drive-Ins Like Daisies, Popping Out All Over," *Motion Picture Herald*, April 14, 1951, p. 13.

27. "Price Dispute."

28. "It's a New, Brighter Year for Drive-Ins," *Motion Picture Herald*, May 20, 1950, p. 23.

29. "Drive-In Owners Want," pp. 13, 19.

30. *Film Daily Year Book 1966* (New York: Film Daily, 1967), p. 103.

31. Dana L. Thomas, "Flicker of Hope?" *Barron's* 38:3, June 23, 1958.

32. "Drive-Ins Zoom Nationally," *Variety*, June 4, 1952, pp. 7, 22; "Drive-Ins: Their Relation to Car Registration," *Boxoffice*, June 7, 1952, p. 19.

33. *Film Daily Year Book 1955* (New York: Film Daily, 1956), p. 143.

34. George Schutz, "The New Drive-In Economics and How They Got That Way," *Motion Picture Herald*, February 11, 1956, p. 13.

35. "See $35,000,000 in 1950 Rentals from Drive-Ins," *Variety*, June 14, 1950, pp. 1, 6.

36. Nevin I. Gage, "Average Drive-In's Concession Gross Is Nearly Fifty Per Cent of the Ticket Dollar," *Boxoffice*, February 2, 1952, p. 31.

37. *Film Daily Year Book 1955* (New York: Film Daily, 1956), p. 143.

38. *1954 Census of Business*, vol. 5, *Selected Service Trades—Summary Statistics* (Washington, D.C.: United States Bureau of the Census, 1957), tables 8A–8F.

39. *1958 Census of Business*, vol. 5, *Selected Service Trades—Summary Statistics* (Washington, D.C.: United States Bureau of the Census, 1961), tables 8A–8E.

Chapter 8: The Golden Years, Showmanship

1. "Some Drive-Ins May Play Acts," *Variety*, March 22, 1950, p. 1; "Reade Ozoners Use Circus Acts to Up B.O.," *Variety*, July 23, 1952, p. 23.

2. "Drive-Ins Are Showbusiness—But That Ain't All, *Motion Picture Herald*, February 4, 1950, pp. 28–29.

3. Paul Petersen, "Cultivating Carriage Trade—Drive-In Style," *Motion Picture Herald*, February 7, 1953, pp. 9, 37.

4. "The Derby-Port Drive-In," *Boxoffice*, May 4, 1951, p. 37.

5. "Lakeland Plan and Policy," *Motion Picture Herald*, July 7, 1956, p. 36.

6. Wilfred P. Smith, "Management of a Drive-In," *Motion Picture Herald*, February 4, 1950, p. 36.

7. "It's a New, Brighter Year for Drive-Ins," *Motion Picture Herald*, May 20, 1950, p. 23.

8. "Fish and Films," *American Magazine* 156:57, July 1953.

9. "Breweries Eye Drive-In Outlets," *Variety*, March 7, 1951, p. 20.

10. "Drive-Ins Doubling as Churches on Sunday," *Daily Variety*, May 27, 1953.

11. "Church Services at Three Drive-Ins Builds Goodwill in Jacksonville," *Boxoffice*, July 18, 1953, p. 23.

12. "Lakeland Plan"; "Drive-In Theatre Serves as Church on Sunday," *New York Times*, August 13, 1951, p. 12.
13. "3-D Drive-Ins," *Business Week*, February 13, 1954, p. 59; "Marketing Briefs," *Business Week*, October 10, 1953, p. 56.
14. Allen Widem, "Conn. Theatres Aim for Kiddie Trade," *Film Daily*, July 14, 1956, pp. 1–2.
15. "Playgrounds for Extra Lure," *Motion Picture Herald*, June 9, 1956, pp. 10–11.
16. "150,000 Playland Rides a Year for Free," *Boxoffice*, February 6, 1954, pp. 24–25.
17. Petersen, *Drive-In Theatre*, pp. 185–87.
18. "Golf, Paying Rides Are Sidelines at Drive-In," *Film Daily*, June 8, 1956, p. 20.
19. "Special Service for Drive-In Theatres," *Motion Picture Herald*, July 14, 1956, p. 41, Managers' Round Table Section.
20. Wilfred P. Smith, "They're Lots of Ways for the Drive-In to Use Showmanship," *Motion Picture Herald*, May 5, 1951, pp. 40–41.
21. "Record Drive-In Load—58 in One Car," *Boxoffice*, September 13, 1952, p. 26.
22. Petersen, *Drive-In Theatre*, p. 150.
23. "Business-Building Methods Keyed to Drive-In Operations," *Motion Picture Herald*, February 20, 1960, pp. 32–35.
24. "He'd Have Drive-Ins Offer More Than Movies," *Motion Picture Herald*, November 5, 1949, p. 22.

Chapter 9: The Golden Years, Selling Food

1. Nevin I. Gage, "Average Drive-In's Concession Gross Is Nearly Fifty Per Cent of the Ticket Dollar," *Boxoffice*, February 2, 1952, p. 30.
2. "New Concession Talk-Back System Speeds Patron Service at Park," *Boxoffice*, October 7, 1950, p. 50.
3. Frances Harding, "Cafeteria Service Spells CASH at the Drive-In," *Boxoffice*, July 7, 1951, pp. 33–34.
4. Ibid.
5. "Munching at the Motor Movies, *Motion Picture Herald*, April 15, 1950, pp. 50–51.
6. "Drive-In Owners Want Per Person Admission, Earlier Product Runs," *Motion Picture Herald*, June 30, 1951, p. 13.
7. "Drive-In Theatres," *Motion Picture Herald*, March 26, 1955, p. 52; "Drive-In Theatres," *Motion Picture Herald*, March 24, 1956, p. 46.
8. "Controlling Quality and Servings at the Drive-In Snack Stand," *Motion Picture Herald*, April 11, 1953, p. 26.
9. "Hot Dog! Detroit Drive-Ins' Trailers Boost Biz (Concession, That Is) 20%," *Daily Variety*, June 23, 1953.
10. "Intermission Trailers Boost Drive-In Refreshment Sales," *Motion Picture Herald*, January 10, 1953, pp. 22, 27.
11. Gage, "Average Drive-In's," p. 32.
12. "Drive-In Theatres," *Motion Picture Herald*, March 26, 1955, p. 52.
13. "Controlling Quality," p. 34.
14. Philip L. Lowe, "In Refreshment Sales What Is Your Potential?" *Motion Picture Herald*, July 4, 1953, p. 10.

15. Gage, "Average Drive-In's," p. 31.

16. "Roll It to 'Em for Greater Drive-In Profit," *Motion Picture Herald*, May 20, 1950, p. 53.

17. Spires, George, "Service—By Car or Cart—Brings Drive-In Sales," *Motion Picture Herald*, August 13, 1949, p. 41.

18. Lowe, "In Refreshment Sales," pp. 10, 43.

19. "Controlling Quality," p. 34.

20. Wilfred P. Smith, "Is Your Refresheteria Ready for 1951?" *Motion Picture Herald*, January 6, 1951, p. 26.

21. "Trends in Vending," *Motion Picture Herald*, April 7, 1952, p. 38.

22. "Controlling Quality," p. 34.

23. Gage, "Average Drive-In's," p. 30.

24. "Chinese Egg Rolls, Pizza Pie Show Up at Drive-In Counters," *Boxoffice*, February 6, 1954, p. 56; John Harti, "Drive-Ins Survive, But Land Values Threaten," *Seattle* (Wash.) *Times*, August 22, 1982.

25. Edward Cope, "Drive-In Promotes 'Family Dinner' Theme," *Boxoffice*, November 21, 1953, pp. 52ff.

26. "Chinese Egg Rolls," "Concession Business Vaults as Patrons Whet Appetites at Drive-In Square Dance," *Boxoffice*, November 7, 1953, p. 27.

27. "Efficiency: Key to Profit in Drive-In Refreshment Selling," *Motion Picture Herald*, February 3, 1951, p. 32.

Chapter 10: Strange Drive-ins

1. "Fly-In, Drive-In Theatre Is Opened in New Jersey," *New York Times*, June 4, 1948, p. 13; "The Roof's the Sky."

2. "Iowa's First Fly-In Theatre to Open at St. Ansgar," *Boxoffice*, July 11, 1953, p. 22.

3. "Develops New-Type Drive-In Theatre," *Boxoffice*, August 18, 1953, p. 16.

4. "The Drive-In Lie-In," *Newsweek* 62:78, July 8, 1963.

5. "Circular Drive-In Is a West Coast First," *Boxoffice* 103:W8, June 4, 1973.

6. "The Drive-In Lie-In."

7. Rodney Luther, "Marketing Aspets of Drive-In Theaters," *Journal of Marketing* 15:47, July 1950; Anthony Downs, "Drive-Ins Have Arrived," *Journal of Property Management* 18:161–62, March 1953.

8. John Cocchi, "Drive-In Operator Praises Sound System," *Boxoffice* 106:MT19, February 16, 1975.

9. "Super Drive-Ins to Key Ten Breakthroughs," *Boxoffice* 97:3, August 10, 1970.

Chapter 11: Foreign Drive-ins

1. "See Mohammedanism Big B.O. Booster for Drive-In Pic Theatres," *Variety*, April 25, 1951, pp. 3, 15.

2. "Drive-In Theatre Spreads to Italy," *New York Times*, August 30, 1957, p. 10; "Drive-In Cine," *New York Times Magazine*, September 29, 1957, p. 32.

3. "2d Cine-Auto to Bow in France Near Swiss Line," *Variety* 251:31, June 19, 1968.

4. "A Window on the World," *Illustrated London News*, July 23, 1961, p. 126.
5. "First Mex Drive-In in Big Brass Sendoff," *Variety*, May 10, 1950, p. 12; "Israel's 1st Drive-In," *Variety*, February 7, 1973.
6. "Drive-In Movie for Japan," *New York Times*, October 12, 1969, p.79; "Japanese Utilize Parking Lots for Suburban Drive-In Havens," *Variety* 314:2, 150, March 21, 1984.
7. "German Drive-Ins Boom," *Variety* 287:39, July 27, 1977; "W. German Cinemas Dip to 3,072; Drive-Ins Big, with 20 Now Operating," *Variety* 292:51, August 23, 1978.
8. Billy Kocian, "Costs, Red Tape, Public Opposition Keep German Drive-Ins Few," *Variety* 284:150, October 20, 1976; "Cars (For Sale) Filling German Drive-In Lots," *Variety* 330:7, April 6, 1988.
9. "Alford's Drive-In," *Film* 119:6, October 1983; "Drive-In Madness," *Film* 142:4, January 1986.
10. "Ozoner Biz to Get New Try in Britain," *Variety* 315:47, June 27, 1984; "London's Passion Pit a 1-Night Stand," *Variety*, June 21, 1989.
11. "New Zealand Stalls All Drive-In Plans," *Variety* 282:140, May 5, 1976.
12. "Kiwis Get Drive-In Okay, But Demand Is Dubious," *Variety* 326:32, December 24, 1986; "First N.Z. Ozoner," *Variety* 327:91, April 29, 1987.
13. R. E. Pulman, "Drive-In Theatre Operation," *British Kinematography* 32:93–94, April 1958.
14. Peter Morrison, "Hoyt's (Fox)-GUT Group Wins Drive-In Appeal," *Film Daily*, February 28, 1956, pp. 1, 8; Peter Morrison, "M-G-M in Drive-In Race Down Under," *Film Daily*, April 4, 1956, p. 7; "John Pye's American Idea Lift Develops 12 Australian Ozoners," *Variety* 303:99, May 6, 1981.
15. "John Pye's American Idea."
16. "Greater Union to Ax 12 Oz Convertibles," *Variety* 314:43, March 28, 1984; Don Groves, "Aussie Ozoners Out in the Cold; Videocassettes, Breath Tests Cited," *Variety* 316:45, September 19, 1984.
17. "Third Ontario Drive-In Opens Near London," *Boxoffice*, July 12, 1947, p. 112; David Thompson, "Lure of Great Outdoors Proves Big Cinema Boon," *Financial Post* (Toronto), September 8, 1962, p. 23.
18. Thompson, "Lure of Great Outdoors," pp. 23, 26.
19. "Quebec's Belated Drive-In OK," *Variety* 247:15, June 21, 1967; "Quebec Drive-Ins," *Variety*, July 26, 1989.
20. "Canada's Drive-Ins Thrive on Families," *Financial Post*, February 12, 1949, p. 9.
21. Peter Newman, "Horse Operas Move to the Country," *Financial Post*, May 30, 1953, p. 15.
22. Ibid.
23. Thompson, "Lure of Great Outdoors," p. 23; Ted Ferguson, "Drive-In Capital," *Canadian Magazine*, November 4, 1978, pp. 22–23.
24. Ferguson, "Drive-In Capital," p. 22.
25. Richard Cairney, "The Pits for Passion Pits," *Alberta Report* 12:10, September 9, 1985; F. H. Leacy, ed., *Historical Statistics of Canada*, 2nd ed. (Ottawa: Statistics Canada, 1985), Series V420–423; Statistics Canada Reference Phone Service; Kathryn Young, "Theatre Attendance Down," *Times-Colonist* (Victoria), July 27, 1990, p. B12.

Chapter 12: Drive-ins Battle the Elements

1. "Drive-Ins Steal the Show," *Business Week*, August 15, 1953, p. 114; "Fan Units to 'Control' Weather at Drive-Ins," *Motion Picture Herald*, June 18, 1956, p. 37.

2. "How We Operate Our Drive-In," *Boxoffice*, August 6, 1949, p. 29.

3. Carl F. Boester, "Air Conditioned Drive-In Theaters," *Heating and Ventilating* 46:57–58, July 1949.

4. "Drive-In Owner Offers Yardstick for In-Car Heater Selection," *Boxoffice*, November 3, 1951, pp. 44–45.

5. "Sound and Heat Supplied Drive-In Car by a Tube," *Motion Picture Herald*, December 3, 1949, p. 23.

6. Wilfred P. Smith, "Taking the Tour at Tesma," *Motion Picture Herald*, December 2, 1950, p. 44.

7. David Barrett, "Exhibitors Favor Year-Round Operation," *Boxoffice*, October 3, 1953, pp. 42–44.

8. "Auto Heater for Drive-Ins," *New York Times*, February 6, 1951, p. 20.

9. "Bob Hope and Oilheating Too!" *Fueloil and Oil Heat* 17:68, May 1958.

10. Ibid, pp. 67–68; "Central Heating Due for Drive-Ins," *New York Times*, December 10, 1958, p. 61; "Drive-In Theater Goes First Class, Warm Air for Patrons, Heated by Gas," *American Gas Journal* 188:33, February 1961.

11. "Cloth Net for Cars to Keep Out Insects," *Motion Picture Herald*, May 12, 1956, p. 27.

12. "Effective Methods of Mosquito Control," *Boxoffice*, November 21, 1953, pp. 68ff.

13. "Fogging Out Drive-In Theatre Mosquitos," *Motion Picture Herald*, December 3, 1949, p. 24.

14. "Fogging Method for Killing Drive-In Insects," *Motion Picture Herald*, April 9, 1949, p. 13.

15. Sandy Warren, "Life at the Movies," *Houston Post*, November 4, 1984, p. 22 (magazine).

16. "Insect-Free Theatre Packs 'Em In," *Boxoffice*, October 3, 1953, p. 47.

17. Jerry Dean, "Drive-In Heyday Passes," (Little Rock) *Arkansas Gazette*, February 8, 1983.

Chapter 13: Drive-ins Pray for a Miracle

1. "Sero Joins Fights on Daylight Time," *Variety*, August 31, 1949; "Drive-In Chain Head Tosses Firecracker on TOA Floor," *Hollywood Reporter*, September 16, 1949; "Drive-Ins Rejoice, Daylight Savings Makes the Appetites Grow Stronger," *Variety*, June 21, 1951.

2. Warren, "Life at the Movies."

3. Dean, "Drive-In Heyday Passes;" "Drive-Ins in Danger of Disappearing," *Hollywood Reporter*, July 5, 1988, p. 102.

4. Thomas M.Pryor, "Metal Brightens Drive-In Screens," *New York Times*, January 10, 1955, p. 27; "Porcelain Screen Made for Drive-Ins," *Film Daily* 124:7, January 13, 1964.

5. Glenn Berggren, "Puzzle Asks Readers to Solve Problem of Twinning Ozoner," *Boxoffice* 107:MT4ff., July 21, 1975; Tony Francis, "Improving Drive-In Picture and Sound," *Boxoffice* 118:56, March 1982.

6. Robert E. Tuffing, "Peeling Screen Calls for Prompt Attention," *Boxoffice*, 110:MT32–33, February 14, 1977.

7. "Daylight Drive-Ins Are Next," *Hollywood Reporter*, February 17, 1953, p. 1.

8. "Pre-Sunset Shows for Drive-Ins as Technical Goal," *Variety* 240:20, November 10, 1965; "Ozoners Quest: 'Light' Screen," *Variety* 240:7, 27, February 23, 1966; "Grope for Sharp Daylight Screen; Also Urge Distrib Service Prints Better Suited to Outdoor Need," *Variety* 243:17, June 29, 1966; "Study Daytime Use of Drive-In Theatres," *Motion Picture Herald* 236:1, 4, July 13, 1966; "'Dusk' Projection Test Encouraging," *Variety* 246:4, February 22, 1967.

9. "New Process for Daylight Use of Drive-In Theatres," *Hollywood Reporter* 221:1, 13, May 18, 1972; "Daylight Ozoners Screen Demonstrated," *Daily Variety* 155:2, May 19, 1972; Will Tusher, "New Technology Big Boost to Drive-Ins," *Hollywood Reporter* 221:1, 3, May 19, 1972.

10. "Ozone Operators Raise 100G Kitty Find New Screen," *Daily Variety* 157:1, 6, November 20, 1972; "NATO to Present 'Containment' Plan for Drive-Ins," *Daily Variety* 157:1, 6, November 13, 1972; Peter Vlahos, "Containment Screen for Drive-In Theaters," *Journal of the Society of Motion Picture and Television Engineers* 82:95, February 1973; "Containment Screen Model Expected Next Year," *Boxoffice* 104:10, October 15, 1973; "Scientist Maps Progress on New Screen During Annual NATO Convention," *Boxoffice* 104:10ff., October 15, 1973.

11. Steve Toy, "New Containment Drive-In Screen Debuting in June," *Daily Variety* 162:1, 8, January 31, 1974; A. D. Murphy, "NATO-AMPTP's 'Containment' Screen for Ozoners Within Six Months of a Prototype," *Daily Variety* 163:1, 6, May 24, 1974.

12. Cynthia Kirk, "Unveil Drive-In Screen Details," *Hollywood Reporter* 233:1, 13, October 10, 1974.

13. "Drive-In Prototype-Screen Costs Exceeding Projections," *Daily Variety* 166:11, February 26, 1975; Ralph Kaminsky, "Experimental Drive-In Containment Screen Slated for Late Spring, Early Summer Trial," *Boxoffice* 106:MT26–27, March 17, 1975.

14. Will Tusher, "Shutin Screen for Drive-Ins Finally Ready," *Hollywood Reporter* 238:1, 10, September 23, 1975; "Final Drive-In Containment Screen Design Under Way," *Boxoffice* 108:4, March 1, 1976.

15. Harris M. Plotkin, "Protolite Screen: Drive-In Breakthrough," *Boxoffice* 119:64–65, March 1983.

16. R. E. Pulman, "Drive-In Theatre Operation," *British Kinematography* 32:94–95, April 1958.

17. Toy, "New Containment," p. 8; Murphy, "NATO-AMPTP's 'Containment,'" p. 6; "Containment Screen Model Expected Next Year," *Boxoffice* 104:10, October 15, 1973; Glenn Berggren, "Myths Tend to Cloud Facts About Drive-In Screen Light," *Boxoffice* 106:MT6, February 17, 1975.

18. R. Mathews, "A Sunbelt Favorite: Movies in the Great Outdoors," *San Francisco Chronicle*, September 3, 1987, p. 66.

Chapter 14: Drive-in Sound

1. "New 'In-Car' Speaker for Drive-In Theatres," *Boxoffice*, July 20, 1946, p. 33.

2. Burton L. Clark, "Protect Your Drive-In," *Boxoffice*, October 23, 1954, p. 72; George M. Petersen, *Drive-In Theatre: Manual of Design and Operation* (Kansas City, MO: Associated, 1953), p. 145.

3. "A Leash for Straying Speakers," *Boxoffice*, October 3, 1953, p. 48.

4. W. Flaherty, "Drive-In Theatre," *British Kinematography* 23:69, September 1953.

5. "Controlling Speaker Theft," *Motion Picture Herald*, December 5, 1953, p. 47.

6. Anthony Downs, "Drive-Ins Have Arrived," *Journal of Property Management* 18:161, March 1953.

7. "Theatreman Invents Unit to Carry Drive-In Sound Through Car Radios," *Boxoffice*, September 1, 1951, p. 14.

8. "How It All Came About," *Boxoffice* 104:6, January 14, 1974.

9. "Schwartz to Show New Cinema Radio," *Variety* 269:1, 78, November 15, 1972.

10. John Cocchi, "Drive-In Operator Praises Sound System," *Boxoffice* 106:MT19, February 17, 1975; "Cinema Radio Allows Patrons to Hear Sound over Car Radio," *Boxoffice* 104:6, 11, January 14, 1974.

11. "New 'Cine-Fi' Drive-In Sound System Introduced at Industry Tradeshow," *Boxoffice* 112:MT18–19, November 21, 1977.

12. Ralph Kaminsky, "Cine-Fi Maps Marketing Expansion," *Boxoffice* 112:10, October 10, 1977.

13. Barbara Slavin, "It's Technology to the Rescue of Drive-In Movie Theaters," *New York Times*, August 8, 1978, p. A12.

14. Wesley Trout, "Cinema Radio's Innovative Sound System Like Small Radio Station," *Boxoffice* 111:MT12ff., June 13, 1977.

15. Gary Burch, "Drive-In Trends Continue to Focus on Sound System and Conversion," *Boxoffice* 112:MT8–11, February 13, 1978; "Drive-In Radio Sound Systems," *Boxoffice* 116:35–36, December 1980; Daniel Braverman, "Drive-In Radio Sound — An Historical Overview," *Boxoffice* 121:43–45, June 1985.

16. "Drive-In Broadcast Sound System," *Boxoffice* 118:54, March 1982; Braverman, "Drive-In Radio Sound," p. 43.

17. Peter Stack, "A Drive-In Movie Gizmo," *San Francisco Chronicle*, November 8, 1984.

18. Will Tusher, "Low-Power AM Ban Protested by Drive-Ins," *Daily Variety*, 224:1, 19, July 24, 1989.

Chapter 15: The Audience

1. Richard M. Hollingshead, United States patent number 1,909,537, p. 2.

2. Bruce A. Austin, "The Development and Decline of the Drive-In Movie Theater," in *Current Research in Film*, vol. 1 (Norwood, N.J.: Albex, 1985), p. 60; "Drive-Ins — Are Getting the Play Now," *Motion Picture Herald*, August 4, 1956, p. 35.

3. "Drive-Ins Creaking New Audiences, Says Rodgers," *Hollywood Reporter*, July 20, 1949, "Drive-Ins Creating New Audiences for Pictures, Says Rodgers," *Variety*, July 20, 1949, p. 18.

4. W. R. Wilkerson, "Trade Views," *Hollywood Reporter*, September 12, 1949.

5. Rodney Luther, "Marketing Aspects of Drive-In Theaters," *Journal of Marketing* 15:45–46, July 1950; Rodney Luther, "Drive-In Theaters: Rags to Riches in Five Years," *Hollywood Quarterly* 5:409–411, Summer 1951; "Drive-Ins Luring Patrons over 30-Year Mark," *Variety*, October 26, 1949; "Survey Shows Who Attends Drive-Ins," *Boxoffice*, January 7, 1950, p. 45.

6. "52% of Drive-In Patrons Own TV Sets But They Still Prefer Movies," *Boxoffice*, July 1, 1950, p. 21.

7. "Drive-Ins Get One Eighth of Total Patronage," *Boxoffice*, September 2, 1950, p. 9; "1 in 8 Pic-Goers Went to Drive-Ins in July," *Variety*, September 6, 1950, p. 4.

8. Austin, "The Development and Decline," p. 68.

9. Ibid., p. 69.

10. Ibid., pp. 73–75.

11. Ibid., p. 75.

12. "Drive-In Movie Fan Is Solid Consumer TsAB Report Says," *Advertising Age* 31:86, March 14, 1960; Austin,"The Development and Decline," p. 75.

13. Austin, "The Development and Decline," p. 75.

14. Ibid., pp. 76–87.

15. Ibid., pp. 69–70, 83.

Chapter 16: Sex in the Drive-in

1. "The Drive-In Theatre: A Motor Age Experiment," *Motion Picture Herald* 112:15, July 1, 1933.

2. Lewis Beale, "Drive-Ins: The Thrill Is Gone," *Washington Post*, June 5, 1983, p. F4.

3. "A Drive-In Pioneer Looks at the Record," *Motion Picture Herald*, December 2, 1950, p.22; "Spread of Drive-In Cinemas May Become a Worry to Regular Ops; Dixie Belt Can Stay Open All Year," *Variety*, July 6, 1938, p. 21; "Drive-Ins," *Time* 38:66, July 14, 1941.

4. "Detroit Drive-In Singles 4 Days," *Boxoffice*, May 24, 1941, p. 115.

5. "Could It Be Necking Has Something to Do with It?" *Variety*, May 23, 1945, p. 7.

6. "Traffic Hazard Stymies Toronto Drive-In, But Many Others Planned," *Variety*, May 7, 1947, p. 33; Charles Irwin, "Drive-Ins Boom in Ohio, Six in Dayton Alone," *Boxoffice*, July 13, 1946, p. 16.

7. "Moon-Washed," *New Yorker* 25:20, October 1, 1949.

8. John Durant, "The Movies Take to the Pastures," *Saturday Evening Post* 223:24, October 14, 1950.

9. Marguerite W. Cullman, "Double Feature—Movies and Moonlight," *New York Times Magazine*, October 1, 1950, p.69; Petersen, *Drive-In Theatre*, p. 147.

10. "Chicago Court Rules City Cannot Bar Drive-Ins," *Motion Picture Herald*, January 28, 1950; Thomas M. Pryor, "Impact of Movies on Youth Argued," *New York Times*, June 17, 1955, p. 24.

11. "Drive-Ins Labeled Only 'Licensed Petting Places,' So $1,000 Fee, Curfew Set," *Variety*, December 17, 1947, p. 1.

12. "Yamins Rep. Rips Into Drive-Ins as 'Not Clean,'" *Film Daily*, April 11, 1956, pp. 1, 3.

13. "Dusk-to-Dawn Ozoners ('Passion Pits with Pix') K.O.d by San Antone Clergy," *Variety*, April 1, 1953; "Cook Those Passion-Pits TOA Advises Drive-Ins," *Variety*, November 2, 1953.

14. Stan Goldstein, "A Night at the Drive-In," *Cue* 39:11, July 4, 1970; Betty Liddick, "Charge of the Night Brigade," *Los Angeles Times*, September 8, 1974, sec. 10, p. 12; Roger Rapoport, "The Last Drive-In in Marin," *San Francisco Chronicle*, July 28, 1979, p. 4.

16. Tony Rutherford, "Management of a Drive-In Requires Creativity, Ingenuity—and Patience," *Boxoffice* 114:ME5, October 23, 1978; William Price Fox, "The Drive-In," *Esquire* 84:157, 221, December 1975.

17. Gerald Clarke, "Dark Clouds over the Drive-Ins, *Time* 122:64, August 8, 1983; Rachel Altman, "The Last Studio Drive-In Picture Show," *Los Angeles Times*, August 22, 1989, pt. 6, p. 3; Gene Siskel, "1981's Drive-Ins: Fast Fadeout for Passion Pit Image," *Chicago Tribune*, August 16, 1981; Dale Schneck, "America's Oldest Drive-In Theatre," *Boxoffice* 119:122, September 1983.

18. Siskel, "1981's Drive-Ins"; Richard Harrington, "Drive-Ins Now: Making Do in a Shrinking Market," *Washington Post*, June 5, 1983, p. F11; Toby Thompson, "the Twilight of the Drive-In, *American Film* 8:47, July/August 1983.

19. Thompson, "The Twilight of the Drive-Ins," p. 48.

Chapter 17: Sex on the Drive-in

1. "Trouble for Drive-Ins on Last Season Bills," *Boxoffice*, October 27, 1951, p. 14.

2. Richard S. Randall, *Censorship of the Movies* (Madison, Wis.: University of Wisconsin Press, 1968), p. 155.

3. Edward de Grazia, *Banned Films* (New York: Bowker, 1982), pp. 306–7.

4. "Supreme Court Declines to Review Pontiac School Busing Order," *New York Times*, October 27, 1971, p. 32.

5. Larry Michie, "High Court Overturns Drive-In Rap," *Daily Variety*, March 21, 1972, p. 6.

6. Randall, *Censorship of the Movies*, p. 154.

7. de Grazia, *Banned Films*, pp. 296–97.

8. Randall, *Censorship of the Movies*, p. 154.

9. Ibid., pp. 152, 154.

10. Ibid., p. 151.

11. "Alabama Seizes Six Films as Obscene," *New York Times*, July 11, 1969, p. 16.

12. Randall, *Censorship of the Movies*, p. 155.

13. "Rockefeller Vetoes Film Bill," *New York Times*, May 22, 1970, p. 40; "NY Passes Strict Law Affecting Drive-Ins," *Boxoffice*, June 19, 1972, p. E1.

14. Randall, "Censorship of the Movies," pp. 362–63, 343–45.

15. "Ban On X Movies Backed," *New York Times*, July 21, 1971, p. 70; Allen M. Widem, "Masschusetts Is Urged to Control Drive-In X Films," *Hollywood Reporter*, February 4, 1972, p. 13.

16. B. Drummond Ayres, "Rival Charges Hruska Peddles Smut," *New York Times*, November 1, 1970, p. 64.

17. Jack Boettner, "A Tale of 2 Screens: No X Films in Anaheim," *Los Angeles Times*, January 21, 1970, pt. 2, p. 8.

18. "Drive-In Film Nudity Ban Upset by High Court, 6–3," *New York Times*, June 24, 1975, p. 18; "High Court Ozoner Ruling Confuses Local Censors," *Boxoffice*, July 14, 1975, p. 6.

19. "High Court Ozoner."

20. Ibid.

21. "First Blush of Fall," *New York Times*, October 26, 1975, p. 58; "Drive-In Cited for 'Free' X-Rated Film," *San Francisco Chronicle*, May 12, 1976, p. 3; Kim Lem, "Drive-In Theater Once Showing X-Rated Films Now Raising Funds for Church," *New York Times*, July 27, 1975, p. 65.

22. "Must Shield Ozoners Showing X Pictures," *Boxoffice* 104:E1, February 11, 1974.
23. "Roadside Glom Case Lost, But State Will Appeal," *Variety* 281:6, November 12, 1975.
24. "Drive-Ins Threatened by County Screen Bill," *Boxoffice* 109:E1 July 19, 1976; "Baltimore County's Airer Bill Killed at Hearing," *Boxoffice* 109:E7, July 26, 1976.
25. "Drive-Ins Beef at Visibility Ordinance," *Variety* 285:6, December 29, 1976; "Vote Down Ord to Bar Drive-Ins' Giant-Size Sex," *Variety* 286:28, February 23, 1977.
26. "Larger-Than-Life Sex Brings Cops," *Variety* 286:28, February 23, 1977.
27. "Drive-In to Continue to Run R-Rated Films," *Boxoffice* 114:C4, February 12, 1979.
28. "District Attorney Aims for Drive-In Closing," *Boxoffice* 114:E1, February 19, 1979.
29. "Ohio Ordinance Limits Drive-In Screen Sex," *Boxoffice* 114:ME2–3, February 5, 1979.
30. "No. Cent. NATO Fights Minn. Bill to Ban X-Rated Pix at Drive-Ins," *Variety* 294:27, February 14, 1979; "Single 'Deep Throat' Date (in 1973) Brings Curb on Ozoners' Porn," *Variety* 294:44, March 21, 1971; Bob Rees, "Minnesota Lowers the Boom on Hardcore Drive-In Exhib'n," May 30, 1979, library clipping not further identified.
31. "Warm Nights and Drive-Ins Open, Small Burgs Protest 'R' Pics," *Variety* 283:24, June 23, 1976.
32. Allen M. Widem, "Ozoner Owner Fights Town's Curfew Law," *Boxoffice* 113:NE1, August 7, 1978; "Showman Harry L. Schwab Mulls Suit Against Town Board of Selectmen," *Boxoffice* 113:NE1, September 11, 1978.
33. Dean, "Drive-In Heyday Passes"; Siskel, "1981's Drive-Ins."
34. Don Nunes, "Flesh Tones on the Silver Screen Make Some See Red," *Washington Post*, September 18, 1982, pp. B1, B5.
35. Bob Mims, "Drive-Ins Bow to Law, Forgo R-Rated Films," *Salt Lake Tribune*, November 14, 1982.
36. "Memphis Ozoner, Seen by Nabes, Shuttered over Steamy, Non-X Pix," *Variety* 309:6, 32, December 15, 1982; Mark Howard, "Drive-Ins Not Reeling," (Memphis, Tenn.) *Commercial Appeal*, December 26, 1982.
37. "N.C. Porn Drive-In Must Close in Sept.," *Variety* 315:7, 32, July 25, 1984.
38. Jim Brewer, "Hot to Get Rid of an X-Rated Landmark," *San Francisco Chronicle*, March 2, 1987, p. 2.
39. "Drive-In Theater Gets Temporary OK to Show Films," *Times-Picayune* (New Orleans), June 29, 1982, sec. 5, p. 15; "Drive-In Battles Berlin, Conn. Closure to Suppress Sexplicity," *Variety* 306:31, February 3, 1982.
40. "Maine Anti-Porn Law Hits Ozoners; Op Says 'X' Pix Are Sole Earners," *Variety* 312:6, September 21, 1983.
41. Eric Zorn, "Unstoppable Drive-In X-Asperates," *Chicago Tribune*, April 11, 1986, sec. 2, pp. 1, 7; "Ban on Sex Scenes at Drive-Ins Upheld," *Daily Variety*, March 26, 1986, p. 6.

Chapter 18: Decline and Stagnation, 1960s and 1970s

1. "General Drive-In Views Profits Rise When New Bowling Units Get Rolling," *Barron's* 40:24–25, September 26, 1960.
2. William R. Weaver, "An Exercise in Community Relations," *Motion Picture Herald* 233:6–8, June 9, 1965.

3. Ruben Betancourt, "Suburbia D-1: An Experiment in Entertainment," *Boxoffice* 105:6, 8, July 8, 1974.

4. "Mpls. Drive-Ins Serve Up Dance Music Till It's Dark Enough to Screen Pix," *Daily Variety* 136:5, June 20, 1967.

5. Adrienne Cook, "Rating the Big Fourteen," *Washington Post*, July 24, 1977, Potomac Section, p. 22.

6. "Unique Boston Experiment Uses Drive-Ins for Daytime Car Parks," *Variety*, August 28, 1963, p. 16.

7. Syd Cassyd, "Pacific Has Key Role in LA Transit Plan," *Boxoffice* 105:6, June 3, 1974.

8. "Drive-In Movies Keep in Step," *Los Angeles Times*, January 1, 1978, sec. 5, p. 14; "Maryland Underskyers Facing Period of Decline in Attendance, Income," *Boxoffice* 114:E1, October 16, 1978.

9. Robert Hucal, "Creative Showmanship, Hard Work Boost Off-Season Ozoner Business," *Boxoffice* 111:MT4, June 13, 1977.

10. Cook, "Rating the Big Fourteen," pp. 12, 18.

11. Will Tusher, "Gas Pumps at Drive-Ins Would Keep B.O. Open," *Hollywood Reporter* 228:1, 19, October 3, 1973.

12. Ed Price, "Secret to Drive-In Clock's Success Lies in the Way It Is Constructed," *Boxoffice* 108:MT29, February 16, 1976.

13. Marshall Delaney, "The Popcorn's Taste Is What Matters Most," *Saturday Night* 86:36, August 1971; Tony Rutherford, "Management of a Drive-In Requires Creativity, Ingenuity—and Patience," *Boxoffice* 114:ME5, October 23, 1978.

14. Rutherford, "Management of a Drive-In."

15. Cook, "Rating the Big Fourteen," pp. 12ff.

16. "Exhibitors Say Drive-Ins Must Adapt to the Changing Times," *Boxoffice* 113:NC1, June 12, 1978.

17. David Paletz, "The Exhibitors," *Film Quarterly* 19:17, Winter 1965–66.

18. Andrew Horton, "Turning on and Tuning Out at the Drive-In," *Journal of Popular Film* 5:240 n., 3/4 1976.

19. Steven Ginsberg, "Drive-Ins Rate Firstrun; Hardtop Sites Re-Valued," *Variety* 290:23, April 26, 1978.

20. Robert H. Stanley, *The Celluloid Empire* (New York: Hastings House, 1977), p. 243.

21. William Price Fox, "The Drive-In," *Esquire* 84:157, December 1975.

22. Paletz, "The Exhibitors," p. 22; Fox, "The Drive-In," p. 223.

23. Paletz, "The Exhibitors," pp. 15ff.

24. Bruce Austin, "The Development and Decline of the Drive-In Movie Theater," in *Current Research in Film*, vol. 1 (Norwood, N.J.: Ablex, 1985), p. 70.

25. Betty Liddick, "Charge of the Night Brigade," *Los Angeles Times*, September 8, 1974, sec. 10, p. 1; "New England Ozoners Adhere to Status Quo," *Boxoffice* 113:ME5, June 26, 1978; "Ozoners Still Popular Across State of Texas," *Boxoffice* 113:E6, August 21, 1978; "Relaxed Atmosphere of Drive-Ins Appeals to Chicagoland Patrons," *Boxoffice* 108:C6, December 8, 1975; Horton, "Turning On," p. 236.

26. Ginsberg, "Drive-Ins Rate Firstrun."

27. Liddick, "Charge of the Night Brigade," p. 12.

28. Fox, "The Drive-In," p. 224.

29. Delaney, "The Popcorn's Taste," p. 37.

30. "Maryland Underskyers"; Fox, "The Drive-In," p. 157.

31. "Drive-In Owner Not Liable," *Variety* 282:26, March 31, 1976.

32. Price, "Secret to Drive-In," pp. 30ff.

33. Joyce Maynard, "Peanuts, Popcorn and Pictures," *Producers Guild of America Journal* 16:25 n. 4, 1974.

34. Liddick, "Charge of the Night Brigade," p. 1; Horton, "Turning On," p. 236; "Drive-Ins Are Experiencing a Renaissance Across U.S.," *Boxoffice* 113:NC1, September 4, 1978; "Drive-In Survey Discussed by Reynolds," *Boxoffice* 113:SW6, July 31, 1978; "Maryland Underskyers."

35. "Smith's Ozoner Slant: No Family Pix," *Variety*, May 9, 1973, p. 5.

36. "Drive-In Survey."

37. "Number of South Jersey Underskyers Down Nearly 50 Percent in 5 Years," *Boxoffice* 114:4, December 18, 1978.

38. Neal Weinberg, "Now Playing: Last Tango in U.S. for Drive-Ins?" *Springfield* (Mass.) *Republican*, August 21, 1977.

39. "Four Screen Drive-In Is Opened," *Motion Picture Herald*, June 24, 1950.

40. Jay Newquist, "The Slow Fade-Out of Drive-In Theaters," *New Haven* (Conn.) *Register*, September 16, 1979; Roger Rapoport, "The Last Drive-In in Marin," *San Francisco Chronicle*, July 28, 1979, p. 4.

41. *1963 Census of Business*, vol. 6, *Selected Services—Summary Statistics* (Washington, D.C.: United States Bureau of the Census, 1966), pp. 8-1/8-29.

42. *1967 Census of Business* vol. 5, *Selected Services—Area Statistics* Part 1 (Washington, D.C.: United States Bureau of the Census, 1970), pp. 1-1; *1972 Census of Selected Service Industries* (Washington, D.C.: United States Bureau of the Census, 1975), p. 9.

43. *1977 Census of Service Industries*, vol. 1, *Subject Statistics* (Washington, D.C.: United States Bureau of the Census, 1980), pp. 4-1/4-29.

Chapter 19: Rapid Descent, 1980s and Beyond

1. Lynn Langway, "The Disappearing Drive-In," *Newsweek* 100:65, August 9, 1982.

2. Ibid.; Patrick O'Driscoll, "A Tradition Refuses to Flicker Out," *USA Today*, June 22, 1987, p. D1.

3. Alice Hoffman, "The Drive-In, at Twilight," *New York Times*, September 4, 1988, p. 18.

4. Ed Blank, "Is Drive-In Movie Era Flickering to an End?" *Pittsburgh Press*, June 26, 1983.

5. Ibid.

6. Gerald Clarke, "Dark Clouds over the Drive-Ins," *Time* 122:64, August 8, 1983.

7. Squire, Jason E., *The Movie Business Book* (New York: Simon & Schuster, 1986), p. 286; Will Tusher, "Crown: Drive-Ins Losing Impact," *Daily Variety*, November 30, 1981, p. 1.

8. Clifford D. May, "Drive-In: Tradition Beneath the L.I. Stars," *New York Times*, September 1, 1986, p. 27.

9. Adrian Havill, "The Home of the Picnic with Visual Effects," *Washington Post*, September 2, 1983, Weekend Sec., p. WE17.

10. Dennis Giles, "The Outdoor Economy: A Study of the Contemporary Drive-In," *Journal of the University Film and Video Association* 35:72–73 n. 2, 1983.

11. Toby Thompson, "The Twilight of the Drive-In," *American Film* 8:46, July/August 1983.

12. Joan Liftin, "Films Alfresco," *American Film* 10:42, July/August 1986; Clarke, "Dark Clouds."

13. Jimmy McDonough, "Hillbilly Heaven," *Film Comment* 21:55–56, November/December 1985.

14. Douglas St. Clair Smith, "How Bad Were They," *Texas Monthly* 14:209, May 1986.

15. Blank, "Is Drive-In Movie Era Flickering?"

16. Lawrence Cohn, "Whole 'Nother Way to Go Provided in South Florida by Adventurous Ozoners," *Variety* 318:44, March 13, 1985.

17. Siskel, "1981's Drive-Ins."

18. Ibid.; Havill, "The Home of the Picnic"; Blank, "Is Drive-In Movie Era Flickering?"

19. Jay Frank, "The Last Picture Show," *Houston Post*, August 3, 1986, p. 3J; Ed Blank, "The Drive-In," *Pittsburgh Press*, June 28, 1987; Leslie Williams, "Some Survivors Scratch by with Flea Markets," (Baltimore) *The Evening Sun*, July 21, 1988; O'Driscoll, "A Tradition Refuses"; Rachel Altman, "The Last Studio Drive-In Picture Show," *Los Angeles Times*, August 22, 1989, part 6, p. 3.

20. Robert Blau, "Drive-Ins Going Way of Silent Movies," *Chicago Tribune*, August 21, 1987, sec. 1, pp. 1, 2; William E. Geist, "Drive-In Movies: An Innovation Hits 50 and Passes Its Prime," *New York Times*, June 7, 1983, pp. B1, B5.

21. Harrington, Richard, "Drive-Ins Now: Making Do in a Shrinking Market," *Washington Post*, June 5, 1983, pp. F1, F11.

22. Siskel, "1981's Drive-Ins."

23. Dennis McLellan, "Drive-In Cruising," *San Francisco Chronicle*, December 20, 1981, p. 5, Sunday Punch section.

24. "Drive-In Theaters Become Dinosaurs on the Movie Landscape," *Wall Street Journal*, July 21, 1988, p. 1; Blank, "The Drive-In."

25. Altman, "The Last Studio Drive-In."

26. Kelli Pryor, "A Night at the Drive-In," *New York* 21:35, May 9, 1988; Patricia Freeman, "Michael Dezer Just Hated to See the '50s Disappear So He Brought Them Back," *People* 30:97–98, August 29, 1988.

27. "Drive-Ins Forever," *Boxoffice* 120:39–40, May 1984.

28. John Hartl, "A Salute to Drive-Ins," *Seattle Times*, June 5, 1983; Thompson, "The Twilight of the Drive-In," pp. 46–47.

29. Mike Shropshire, "Drive-In Movie Freaks Celebrate a Bygone Era," *Dallas Morning News*, November 1, 1982.

30. Hartl, "A Salute to Drive-Ins."

31. Steve Cannizaro, "Victim of TV," *Times-Picayune* (New Orleans), April 4, 1982, sec. 7, p. 1; Blank, "Is Drive-In"; May, "Drive-In Tradition."

32. Bruce A. Austin, "The Development and Decline of the Drive-In Movie Theater," in *Current Research in Film*, vol. 1 (Norwood, N.J.: Ablex, 1985), pp. 70–71.

33. Blank, "The Drive-In"; "Drive-Ins Forever," p. 39.

34. Mark Howard, "Drive-Ins Not Reeling, Owners Say," (Memphis) *Commercial Appeal*, December 26, 1982; Jack Mathews, "A Sunbelt Favorite," *San Francisco Chronicle*, September 3, 1987, p. 66; "Scene Change," *Los Angeles Times*, August 7, 1989, part 4, p. 5.

35. Howard, "Drive-Ins Not Reeling."

36. Thompson, "The Twilight of the Drive-In," pp. 45–46.

37. Ibid., p. 47.

38. Williams.

39. Elizabeth L. Levitan, "The Drive-In Is Still Thrivin'," *Christian Science Monitor*, September 8, 1988, pp. 1, 6; May.
40. Blau, "Drive-Ins Going," p. 2.
41. Paul Sullivan, "A Love Affair with the Stars," *Chicago Tribune*, July 26, 1985, sec. 7, p. 3.
42. Leon Wynter, "Over a Six-Pack, Under the Stars," *Washington Post*, July 30, 1981, pp. MD1, MD3.
43. Barbara Vobejda, "Where Have All the Drive-Ins Gone?" *Washington Post*, November 5, 1984, pp. B1, B7.
44. "Drive-In Season Opening in K.C. Marked by Closings," *Daily Variety*, March 12, 1986, p. 27; "Drive-In Theaters Become Dinosaurs"; Blau, "Drive-Ins Going"; David Lyman, "Twilight of the Drive-In," *Cincinnati Post*, May 25, 1989.
45. "Pacific Theaters to Cap Another of Its Drive-Ins," *Variety* 328:7, 41, October 7, 1987.
46. Cannizaro, "Victim of TV"; Frank, "The Last Picture Show"; "Drive-Ins in Danger of Disappearing," *Hollywood Reporter*, July 5, 1988, p. 102.
47. "Drive-Ins in Danger of Disappearing."
48. Blank, "Is Drive-In"; Barbara Bradley, "Drive-Ins Sit on Real Estate Gold Mines," *Houston Post*, December 13, 1982, p., D3.
49. Betsy Brown, "Whatever Happened to the Drive-In Movies?" *New York Times*, February 1, 1987, sec. 8, p. R10.
50. *Census of Service Industries (1982)* (Washington, D.C.: United States Bureau of the Census, n.d.), pp. 1–28, 1–72, 4–3/4–28.
51. *1987 Census of Service Industries, Geographic Area Series: United States* (Washington, D.C.: United States Bureau of the Census, 1989), pp. US–11, US–16, US–20, US–48; *International Motion Picture Almanac 1990* (New York: Quigley, 1990), p. 31A.
52. "Drive-Ins Endure, and Woo Back Some Old Fans," *New York Times*, June 17, 1990, p. 42.
53. Clarke, "Dark Clouds."

Bibliography

"Adapting a Drive-In to Its Countryside." *Motion Picture Herald*, Oct. 1, 1949, pp. 25–26.
"Alabama Seizes Six Films as Obscene." *New York Times*, July 11, 1969, p. 16.
"Alford's Drive-In." *Film* 119:6 Oct. 1983.
"Allentown Ozoner Asks Equal 1st-Run Clearance." *Variety*, Feb. 15, 1950, p. 18.
Altman, Rachel. "The Last Studio Drive-In Picture Show." *Los Angeles Times*, Aug. 22, 1989, part 6, p. 3.
Angier, Brad. "DiMaura Emerges Victor in First Legal Skirmish over the Drive-In Theatres, Inc." *Boxoffice*, Nov. 26, 1938, p. 71.
________. "New England Open-Air Theatre Situation Forsakes Ozone for Courtroom Battles." *Boxoffice*, April 30, 1938, p. 143.
"Anti–Drive-In Bill Dies." *Boxoffice*, May 6, 1950, p. 68.
"AP Columnist Tells of Flexner Drive-In." *Boxoffice*, Nov. 29, 1947, p. 89.
"Are Drive-In Pixers a Public Nuisance?" *Variety*, May 9, 1945, p. 6.
Austin, Bruce A. "The Development and Decline of the Drive-In Movie Theater," in *Current Research in Film*, vol. 1. Norwood, N.J.: Ablex, 1985.
"Austin Drive-In Asks 30-Day Availability." *Boxoffice*, Nov. 29, 1947, p. 81.
"Auto Heater for Drive-Ins." *New York Times*, Feb. 6, 1951, p. 20.
Ayres, B. Drummond. "Rival Charges Hruska Peddles Smut." *New York Times*, Nov. 1, 1970, p. 64.
Balch, C.A. "The Plan and Construction of One of the Newest Drive-In Theatres." *Motion Picture Herald*, Dec. 10, 1938, pp. 14–15ff.
"Baltimore County's Airer Bill Killed at Hearing." *Boxoffice*, July 26, 1976, p. E7.
"Ban on Sex Scenes at Drive-Ins Upheld." *Daily Variety*, March 26, 1986, p. 6.
"Ban on X Movies Backed." *New York Times*, July 21, 1971, p. 70.
Barrett, David. "Exhibitors Favor Year-Round Operation." *Boxoffice*, Oct. 3, 1953, pp. 42–44.
Beale, Lewis. "Drive-Ins: The Thrill Is Gone." *Washington Post*, June 5, 1983, p. F4.
Berggren, Glenn. "Myths Tend to Cloud Facts About Drive-In Screen Light." *Boxoffice*, Feb. 17, 1975, p. MT6.
________. "Puzzle Asks Readers to Solve Problem of Twinning Ozoner." *Boxoffice*, July 21, 1975, p. MT4ff.
Betancourt, Ruben. "Suburbia D-I: An Experiment in Entertainment." *Boxoffice*, July 8, 1974, pp. 6, 8.
Blank, Ed. "Is Drive-In Movie Era Flickering to an End?" *Pittsburgh Press*, June 26, 1983.
________. "The Drive-In." *Pittsburgh Press*, June 28, 1987.

Blau, Robert. "Drive-Ins Going Way of Silent Movies." *Chicago Tribune*, Aug. 21, 1987, sec. 1, pp. 1, 2.
"Bob Hope and Oilheating Too!" *Fueloil and Oil Heat* 17:68, May 1958.
Boester, Carl F. "Air Conditioned Drive-In Theaters." *Heating and Ventilating* 46:57–58, July 1949.
Boettner, Jack. "A Tale of 2 Screens: No X Films in Anaheim." *Los Angeles Times*, Jan. 21, 1970, part 2, p. 8.
Bradley, Barbara. "Drive-Ins Sit on Real Estate Gold Mines." *Houston Post*, Dec. 13, 1982, p. D3.
Braverman, Daniel. "Drive-In Radio Sound — An Historical Overview." *Boxoffice*, June 1985, pp. 43–45.
Brewer, Jim. "How to Get Rid of an X-Rated Landmark." *San Francisco Chronicle*, March 2, 1987, p. 2.
"Breweries Eye Drive-In Outlets." *Variety*, March 7, 1951, p. 20.
Brown, Betsy. "Whatever Happened to Drive-In Movies?" *New York Times*, Feb. 1, 1987, sec. 8, p. R10.
Burch, Gary. "Drive-In Trends Continue to Focus on Sound System and Conversion." *Boxoffice*, Feb. 13, 1978, pp. MT8–MT11.
"Business-Building Methods Keyed to Drive-In Operations." *Motion Picture Herald*, Feb. 20, 1960, pp. 32–35.
"By-the-Busload, Boxtop Operators Not to Get Top MGM Availability." *Boxoffice*, Nov. 11, 1950, p. 9.
Cairney, Richard. "The Pits for Passion Pits." *Alberta Report* 12:10, Sept. 9, 1985.
"Camden's Drive-In Theater." *Literary Digest* 116:19, July 22, 1933.
"Canada's Drive-Ins Thrive on Families." *Financial Post* (Toronto), Feb. 12, 1949, p. 9.
Cannizaro, Steve. "Victim of TV." *Times-Picayune* (New Orleans), April 4, 1982, sec. 7, p. 1.
"Cars (For Sale) Filling German Drive-In Lots." *Variety*, April 6, 1988, p. 7.
Cassyd, Syd. "Pacific Has Key Role in LA Transit Plan." *Boxoffice*, June 3, 1974, p. 6.
Census of Service Industries (1982). Washington: United States Bureau of the Census, n.d.
"Central Heating Due for Drive-Ins." *New York Times*, Dec. 10, 1958, p. 61.
"Chi Council Cracks Down on Ozoners; New Ordinance Bans 'Em Inside City." *Variety*, May 10, 1950, p. 19.
"Chi Ozoner Talks Swing for 1st Runs." *Variety*, Aug. 24, 1949, p. 25.
"Chicago Court Rules City Cannot Bar Drive-Ins." *Motion Picture Herald*, Jan. 28, 1950, p. 22.
"Chicago Drive-Ins Sue on Clearances." *Boxoffice*, June 4, 1949, p. 11.
"Chicago Mayor Would Halt Construction of Drive-In." *Film Daily*, May 11, 1956, pp. 1, 3.
"Chinese Egg Rolls, Pizza Pie Show Up at Drive-In Counters." *Boxoffice*, Feb. 6, 1954, p. 56.
"Church Services at Three Drive-Ins Builds Goodwill in Jacksonville." *Boxoffice*, July 18, 1953, p. 23.
"Cincinnati Drive-In Building Protested." *Boxoffice*, Jan. 20, 1940, p. 55.
"Cinema Radio Allows Patrons to Hear Sound Over Car Radio." *Boxoffice*, Jan. 14 1974, pp. 6, 11.
"Circular Drive-In Is a West Coast First." *Boxoffice*, June 4, 1947, p. W8.
"City Planning Body Scored by Murdock." *New York Times*, March 16, 1950, p. [illegible].
"Claims Only Woman Drive-In Manager." *Boxoffice*, March 3, 1940, p. 89.
Clark, Burton L. "Protect Your Drive-In." *Boxoffice*, Oct. 23, 1954, p. 72.

Clarke, Gerald, "Dark Clouds over the Drive-Ins." *Time* 122:64, Aug. 8, 1983.
"Cloth Net for Cars to Keep Out Insects." *Motion Picture Herald*, May 12, 1956, p. 27.
"Coast Drive-Ins Sue Majors for First-Run Recognition." *Hollywood Reporter*, Dec. 13, 1950.
Cocchi, John. "Drive-In Operator Praises Sound System." *Boxoffice*, Feb. 17, 1975, p. MT19.
Cohen, Ted. "Saco Drive-In's 50th Birthday Stirs Memories." *Portland Press Herald* (Maine), July 15, 1989.
Cohn, Lawrence. "Whole 'Nother Way to Go Provided in South Florida by Adventurous Ozoners." *Variety*, March 13, 1985, p. 44.
"Cold Weather Hits Midwest Ozoners; Many Folding." *Variety*, Oct. 18, 1950, p. 16.
"The Colossal Drive-In." *Newsweek* 50:85, July 22, 1957.
Conant, Michael. *Antitrust in the Motion Picture Industry*. Berkeley: University of California Press, 1960.
"Concession Business Vaults as Patrons Whet Appetites at Drive-In Square Dance." *Boxoffice*, Nov. 7, 1953, p. 27.
"Containment Screen Model Expected Next Year." *Boxoffice*, Oct. 15, 1973, p. 10.
"Controlling Quality and Servings at the Drive-In Snack Stand." *Motion Picture Herald*, April 11, 1953, p. 26.
"Controlling Speaker Theft." *Motion Picture Herald*, Dec. 5, 1953, p. 47.
Cook, Adrienne. "Rating the Big Fourteen." *Washington Post*, July 24, 1977, Potomac sec., p. 22.
"Cool Those Passion-Pits TOA Advises Drive-Ins." *Variety*, Nov. 2, 1953.
Cope, Edward. "Drive-In Promotes 'Family Dinner' Theme." *Boxoffice*, Nov. 21, 1953, pp. 52ff.
"Could It Be Necking Has Something to Do with It?" *Variety*, May 23, 1945, p. 7.
"Court Orders Divorce of Loew's, 20th–Fox and Warner Theatres." *Motion Picture Herald*, July 30, 1949, pp. 13–14.
Cullman, Marguerite W. "Double Feature—Movies and Moonlight." *New York Times Magazine*, Oct. 1, 1950, pp. 72ff.
"Daylight Drive-Ins Are Next." *Hollywood Reporter*, Feb. 17, 1953, p. 1.
"Daylight Ozoners Screen Demonstrated." *Daily Variety*, May 19, 1972, p. 2.
Dean, Jerry. "Drive-In Heyday Passes." (Little Rock) *Arkansas Gazette*, Feb. 8, 1983.
"Decision on Sound Volume at Riverside Due Soon." *Boxoffice*, Aug. 10, 1940, p. 43.
de Grazia, Edward. *Banned Films*. New York: Bowker, 1982.
Delaney, Marshall. "The Popcorn's Taste Is What Matters Most." *Saturday Night* 86:36, Aug. 1971.
"Denver Drive-In." *Boxoffice*, July 12, 1949, p. 59.
"The Derby-Post Drive-In." *Boxoffice*, May 5, 1951, p. 37.
"Detroit Drive-In." *Boxoffice*, Feb. 25, 1938, p. 121.
"Detroit Drive-In Draws City-Wide Patronage; Rain Does Not Retard." *Boxoffice*, June 25, 1938, p. 106.
"Detroit Drive-In Opened in Rain." *Boxoffice*, June 4, 1938, p. 71.
"Detroit Drive-In Singles 4 Days." *Boxoffice*, May 24, 1941, p. 115.
"Develops New-Type Drive-In Theatre." *Boxoffice*, Aug. 18, 1953, p. 16.
"District Attorney Aims for Drive-In Closing." *Boxoffice*, Feb. 19, 1979, p. E1.
Downs, Anthony. "Drive-Ins Have Arrived." *Journal of Property Management* 18:161ff, March 1953.
"Drive-In Battles Berlin, Conn. Closure to Suppress Sexplicity." *Variety*, Feb. 3, 1982, p. 31.

"Drive-In Broadcast Sound System." *Boxoffice*, March 1982, p. 54.
"Drive-In Chain Head Tosses Firecracker on TOA Floor." *Hollywood Reporter*, Sept. 16, 1949.
"Drive-In Cine." *New York Times Magazine*, Sept. 20, 1957, p. 32.
"Drive-In Cited for 'Free' X-Rated Film." *San Francisco Chronicle*, May 12, 1976, p. 3.
"Drive-In Clearance Case Taken to Supreme Court." *Hollywood Reporter*, March 18, 1952.
"Drive-In Curfew Upset." *New York Times*, Dec. 6, 1958, p. 25.
"Drive-In Exhib Charges Twin City Theatres Stifling Competition." *Variety*, Sept. 17, 1947, p. 20.
"Drive-In Film Nudity Ban Upset by High Court, 6–3." *New York Times*, June 24, 1975, p. 18.
"Drive-In Growth." *Boxoffice*, Sept. 24, 1949, p. 7.
"The Drive-In Lie-In." *Newsweek* 62:78, July 8, 1963.
"Drive-In Madness." *Film* 142:4, Jan. 1986.
"Drive-In Movie Fan Is Solid Consumer TsAB Report Says." *Advertising Age* 31:86, March 14, 1960.
"Drive-In Movie for Japan." *New York Times*, Oct. 12, 1969, p. 79.
"Drive-In Movie Holds Four Hundred Cars." *Popular Mechanics* 60:326, Sept. 1933.
"Drive-In Movies Keep in Step." *Los Angeles Times*, Jan. 1, 1978, sec. 5, p. 14.
"Drive-In Noises Go for Test Tomorrow." *Daily Variety*, April 3, 1935, p. 8.
"Drive-In on the Subway." *Motion Picture Herald*, Nov. 5, 1949, p. 18.
"Drive-In Owner Not Liable." *Variety*, March 31, 1976, p. 26.
"Drive-In Owner Offers Yardstick for In-Car Heater Selection." *Boxoffice*, Nov. 3, 1951, pp. 44–45.
"Drive-In Owners Want Per Person Admission, Earlier Product Runs." *Motion Picture Herald*, June 30, 1951, p. 13.
"A Drive-In Pioneer Looks at the Record." *Motion Picture Herald*, Dec. 2, 1950, p. 22.
"Drive-In Prototype-Screen Costs Exceeding Projections." *Daily Variety*, Feb. 26, 1975, p. 11.
"Drive-In Radio Sound Systems." *Boxoffice*, Dec. 1980, pp. 35–36.
"Drive-In Season Opening in K.C. Marked by Closings." *Daily Variety*, March 12, 1986, p. 27.
"Drive-In Survey Discussed by Reynolds." *Boxoffice*, July 31, 1978, p. SW6.
"Drive-In Theater." *Business Week*, Aug. 5, 1933, p. 19.
"Drive-In Theater Gets Temporary OK to Show Films." *Times-Picayune* (New Orleans), June 29, 1982, sec. 5, p. 15.
"Drive-In Theater Goes First Class, Warm Air for Patrons, Heated by Gas." *American Gas Journal* 188:33ff, Feb. 1961.
"Drive-In Theater Head Given Fine Under Noise Law." *Los Angeles Times*, June 7, 1935, sec. 2, p. 12.
"Drive-In Theater Opening Tomorrow." *Los Angeles Examiner*, Sept. 8, 1934, p. 9.
"Drive-In Theater Originator Dies." *Los Angeles Times*, Dec. 28, 1936, sec. 2, p. 2.
"Drive-In Theaters: Happy But Griping." *Business Week*, May 9, 1953, p. 131.
"Drive-In Theaters Become Dinosaurs on the Movie Landscape." *Wall Street Journal*, July 21, 1988, p. 1.
"The Drive-In Theatre: A Motor Age Experiment." *Motion Picture Herald*, July 1, 1933, p. 15.
"Drive-In Theatre Operator Found Guilty by Jury." *Los Angeles Times*, June 5, 1935, sec. 1, p. 5.
"Drive-In Theatre Plan Fails." *New York Times*, Jan. 29, 1950, p. 53.

"Drive-In Theatre Serves as Church on Sunday." *New York Times*, Aug. 13, 1951, p. 12.
"Drive-In Theatre Spreads to Italy." *New York Times*, Aug. 30, 1957, p. 10.
"Drive-In Theatre Sues Movie Trust." *New York Times*, Oct. 10, 1954, p. 82.
"Drive-In Theatre to Be Opened Here." *Courier Post* (Camden, N.J.), May 17, 1933.
"Drive-In Theatres." *Motion Picture Herald*, March 26, 1955, p. 52.
"Drive-In Theatres." *Motion Picture Herald*, March 20, 1956, p. 46.
"Drive-In Theatres a Factor." *New York Times*, Sept. 28, 1949, p. 29.
"Drive-In Theatres Corporation v. Park-In Theatres, et al." *United States Patent Quarterly* 38:41–42.
"Drive-In to Continue to Run R-Rated Films." *Boxoffice*, Feb. 12, 1979, p. C4.
"Drive-Ins." *Architectural Record* 108:140ff, Aug. 1950.
"Drive-Ins." *Boxoffice*, Sept. 13, 1941, p. 42, Western edition.
"Drive-Ins." *Boxoffice*, Aug. 31, 1949.
"Drive-Ins." *Time* 38:66, July 14, 1941.
"Drive-Ins: Their Relation to Car Registration." *Boxoffice*, June 7, 1952, p. 19.
"Drive-Ins a Menace to Health, Village Sez." *Variety*, Aug. 30, 1950, p. 16.
"Drive-Ins Appeal to Family Groups." *Boxoffice*, Aug. 9, 1947, p. 52.
"Drive-Ins Are Experiencing a Renaissance Across U.S." *Boxoffice*, Sept. 4, 1978, p. NC1.
"Drive-Ins Are Fighting for Clearance Improvement." *Boxoffice*, May 21, 1949, p. 8.
"Drive-Ins Are Getting the Play Now." *Motion Picture Herald*, Aug. 4, 1956, p. 35.
"Drive-Ins Are Showbusiness—But That Ain't All." *Motion Picture Herald*, Feb. 4, 1950, pp. 28–29.
"Drive-Ins as 'Highway Hazards' Probed by Pennsy Commission." *Variety*, July 6, 1949, p. 25.
"Drive-Ins Beef at Visibility Ordinance." *Variety*, Dec. 29, 1976, p.6.
"Drive-Ins Bitten as Mayors Snarl." *Motion Picture Herald*, Jan. 21, 1950, p. 16.
"Drive-Ins Creating New Audience for Pictures, Says Rodgers." *Variety*, July 20, 1949, p. 18.
"Drive-Ins Creating New Audiences, Says Rodgers." *Hollywood Reporter*, July 20, 1949.
"Drive-Ins Cut Charlotte First-Runs Down to Two." *Variety*, July 16, 1952, p. 4.
"Drive-Ins Doubling as Churches on Sunday." *Daily Variety*, May 27, 1953.
"Drive-Ins' Eagerness for Parity with Hardtops on First Runs." *Variety*, Aug. 3, 1955, p. 23.
"Drive-Ins Endure, and Woo Back Some Old Fans." *New York Times*, June 17, 1990, p. 42.
"Drive-Ins for Hub Showmen." *Boxoffice*, June 4, 1938, p. 79.
"Drive-Ins Forever." *Boxoffice*, May 1984, pp. 39–40.
"Drive-Ins Get One Eighty of Total Patronage." *Boxoffice*, Sept. 2, 1950, p. 9.
"Drive-Ins Hit by Hurricane Include Odd Dual Theatre." *Motion Picture Herald*, Oct. 15, 1938, p. 8.
"Drive-Ins in Danger of Disappearing." *Hollywood Reporter*, July 5, 1988, p. 102.
"Drive-Ins Labeled Only 'Licensed Petting Places,' So $1,000 Fee, Curfew Set." *Variety*, Dec. 17, 1947, p. 1.
"Drive-Ins Like Daisies, Popping Out All Over." *Motion Picture Herald*, April 14, 1951, p. 13.
"Drive-Ins Luring Patrons Over 30-Year Mark." *Variety*, Oct. 26, 1949.
"Drive-Ins Offered as Package Deal." *Boxoffice*, Feb. 28, 1948, p. 22.
"Drive-Ins Press for First Runs." *Variety*, Aug. 31, 1949, p. 20.
"Drive-Ins Rejoice, Daylight Savings Makes the Appetites Grow Stronger." *Variety*, June 21, 1951.

"Drive-Ins Seen Highway Menace by State Groups." *Variety*, July 12, 1950, p. 7.
"Drive-Ins Steal the Show." *Business Week*, Aug. 15, 1953, p. 114.
"Drive-Ins Threatened by County Screen Bill." *Boxoffice*, July 19, 1976, p. E1.
"Drive-Ins Zoom Nationally." *Variety*, June 4, 1952, pp. 7, 22.
Durant, John. "The Movies Take to the Pastures." *Saturday Evening Post* 223:24ff, Oct. 14, 1950.
"'Dusk' Projection Test." *Variety*, Feb. 22, 1967, p. 4.
"Dusk-to-Dawn Ozoners ('Passion Pits with Pix') K.O.d by San Antone Clergy." *Variety*, April 1, 1953.
"Effective Methods of Mosquito Control." *Boxoffice*, Nov. 21, 1953, pp. 68ff.
"Efficiency: Key to Profit in Drive-In Refreshment Selling." *Motion Picture Herald*, Feb. 3, 1951, p. 32.
"Exhibitors Say Drive-Ins Must Adapt to the Changing Times." *Boxoffice*, June 12, 1978, p. NC1.
"Fair Trade Practices Code for Drive-Ins Is Demanded." *Boxoffice*, Nov. 11, 1950, p. 9.
"Fan Units to 'Control' Weather at Drive-Ins." *Motion Picture Herald*, June 18, 1956, p. 37.
"Father of Drive-In Says 'Never Again.'" *Motion Picture Herald*, Jan. 28, 1950, p. 38.
Ferguson, Ted. "Drive-In Capital." *Canadian Magazine*, Nov. 4, 1978, pp. 22–23.
"52% of Drive-In Patrons Own TV Sets But They Still Prefer Movies." *Boxoffice*, July 1, 1950, p. 21.
Film Daily Year Book, 1942, 1943, 1944, 1945, 1946, 1947, 1955, 1957, 1966. New York: Film Daily, 1942–1947, 1955, 1957, 1966.
"Final Drive-In Containment Screen Design Under Way." *Boxoffice*, March 1, 1976, p. 4.
"First Blush of Fall." *New York Times*, Oct. 26, 1975, p. 58.
"First Florida Drive-In Built in 1939 in Jacksonville by Horace Denning." *Boxoffice*, April 1, 1974, pp. SE1, SE7.
"First Mex Drive-In in Big Brass Sendoff." *Variety*, May 10, 1950, p. 12.
"First N.Z. Ozoner." *Variety*, April 29, 1987, p. 91.
"First Run Bid Rights Granted to Drive-In." *Boxoffice*, April 16, 1949, p. 11.
"First-Run Licenses to Drive-In Denies." *Hollywood Reporter*, Oct. 20, 1949.
"Fish and Films." *American Magazine* 156:57, July 1953.
Flaherty, W. "Drive-In Theatre." *British Kinematography* 23:69ff, Sept. 1953.
"Fly-in, Drive-In Theatre Is Opened in New Jersey." *New York Times*, June 4, 1948, p. 13.
"Fogging Method for Killing Drive-In Insects." *Motion Picture Herald*, April 9, 1949, p. 13.
"Fogging Out Drive-In Theatre Mosquitos." *Motion Picture Herald*, Dec. 3, 1949, p. 24.
Fosdick, Scott. "Ritchie Drive-In." *News American* (Baltimore), April 1, 1984.
"Four Screen Drive-In Is Opened." *Motion Picture Herald*, June 24, 1950.
Fox, William Price. "The Drive-In." *Esquire* 84:156ff, Dec. 1975.
Francis, Tony. "Improving Drive-In Picture and Sound." *Boxoffice*, March 1982, p. 56.
Frank, Jay. "The Last Picture Show." *Houston Post*, Aug. 3, 1986, p. 3J.
Freeman, Patricia. "Michael Dezer Just Hated to See the '50s Disappear So He Brought Them Back." *People* 30:97–98, Aug. 29, 1988.
Gage, Nevin I. "Average Drive-In's Concession Gross Is Nearly Fifty Per Cent of the Ticket Dollar." *Boxoffice*, Feb. 2, 1952, pp. 30–31.
Geist, William E. "Drive-In Movies: An Innovation Hits 50 and Passes Its Prime." *New York Times*, June 7, 1983, pp. B1, B5.

"General Drive-In Views Profits Rise When New Bowling Units Get Rolling." *Barrons* 40:24–25, Sept. 26, 1960.
"German Drive-Ins Boom." *Variety*, July 27, 1977, p. 39.
Giles, Dennis. "The Outdoor Economy—A Study of the Contemporary Drive-In." *Journal of the University of Film and Video Association* 35:72ff, n2, 1983.
Ginsberg, Steven. "Drive-Ins Rate Firstrun; Hardtop Sites Re-Valued." *Variety*, April 26, 1978, p. 23.
________. "Indoor Sites Forced to 8 Weeks; Protest Drive-In Half Runs." *Variety*, July 5, 1978, p. 27.
Goldstein, Stan. "Automobile Movie Born Here." *Courier-Post* (Camden, N.J.), Oct. 7, 1975.
"Golf, Paying Rides Are Sidelines at Drive-In." *Film Daily*, June 8, 1956, p. 20.
"Greater Union to Ax 12 Oz Convertibles." *Variety*, March 28, 1984, p. 43.
"Grope for Sharp Daylight Screen, Also Urge Distrib Service Prints Better Suited to Outdoor Need." *Variety*, June 29, 1966, p. 17.
Groves, Don. "Aussie Ozoners Out in the Cold; Videocassettes, Breath Tests Cited." *Variety*, Sept. 19, 1984, p. 45.
Harding, Frances. "Cafeteria Service Spells CASH at the Drive-In." *Boxoffice*, July 7, 1951, pp. 33–34.
Harrington, Richard. "Drive-Ins Now: Making Do in a Shrinking Market." *Washington Post*, June 5, 1983, p. F11.
Harti, John. "Drive-Ins Survive, But Land Values Threaten." *Seattle Times*, Aug. 22, 1982.
Havill, Adrian. "The Home of the Picnic with Visual Effects." *Washington Post*, Sept. 2, 1983, Weekend section, p. WE17.
"Hearings Slated on Writ Bid Against Drive-In." *Boxoffice*, Sept. 14, 1940, p. 95.
"He'd Have Drive-Ins Offer More Than Movies." *Motion Picture Herald*, Nov. 5, 1949, p, 22.
"Hellman Fears Drive-Ins Are Being Overbuilt." *Boxoffice*, Oct. 18, 1947, p. 56.
Hift, Fred. "Drive-Ins a'Bloom in Spring—By Hundreds." *Motion Picture Herald*, March 26, 1949, p. 22.
"High Court Ozoner Ruling Confuses Local Censors." *Boxoffice*, July 14, 1975, p. 6.
Hine, Al. "The Drive-Ins." *Holiday* 12:6, July 5, 1952.
Hoffman, Alice. "The Drive-In at Twilight." *New York Times*, Sept. 4, 1988, p. 18.
Hollingshead, Richard M. Jr. *United States Patent number 1,909,537*.
Horton, Andrew. "Turning On and Tuning Out at the Drive-In." *Journal of Popular Film* 5:240ff, n 3/4, 1976.
"Hot Dog! Detroit Drive-Ins' Trailers Boost Biz (Concession, That Is) 20%." *Daily Variety*, June 23, 1953.
"How It All Came About." *Boxoffice*, Jan. 14, 1974, p. 6.
"How We Operate Our Drive-In." Boxoffice, Aug. 6, 1949, p.29.
Howard, Mark. "Drive-Ins Not Reeling, Owners Say." (Memphis) *Commercial Appeal*, Dec. 26, 1982.
Hucal, Robert. "Creative Showmanship, Hard Work Boost Off-Season Ozoner Business." *Boxoffice*, June 13, 1977, p. MT4.
"Hyannis Ozoner Theatre." *Boxoffice*, March 19, 1938, p. 55.
"Ill Drive-In Asks Million in Trust Suit." *Variety*, Jan. 25, 1951, p. 5.
In Re Josserand. *United States Patent Quarterly* 89:371–381.
"Indianapolis." *Boxoffice*, July 26, 1947, p. 121.
Ingraham, Joseph C. "Drive-In Movies Held Car Hazard." *New York Times*, Dec. 2, 1956, p. 142.

"Insect-Free Theatre Packs 'Em In." *Boxoffice*, Oct. 3, 1953, p. 47.
"Intermission Trailers Boost Drive-In Refreshment Sales." *Motion Picture Herald*, Jan. 10, 1953, pp. 22, 27.
International Motion Picture Almanac 1951–52, 1957, 1959, 1990. New York: Quigley, 1952, 1958, 1960, 1991.
"Iowa's First Fly-In Theatre to Open at St. Ansgar." *Boxoffice*, July 11, 1953, p. 22.
Irwin, Charles. "Drive-Ins Boom in Ohio, Six in Dayton Alone." *Boxoffice*, July 13, 1946, p. 16.
"Israel's 1st Drive-In." *Variety*, Feb. 7, 1973.
"It's a New, Brighter Year for Drive-Ins." *Motion Picture Herald*, May 20, 1950, p. 23.
"Japanese Utilize Parking Lots for Suburban Drive-In Havens." *Variety*, March 21, 1984, pp. 2, 150.
"John Pye's American Idea Lift Develops 12 Australian Ozoners." *Variety*, May 6, 1981, p. 99.
Josserand, Louis. *United States Patent number 2,102,718.*
"Josserand v. Taylor Jr." *United States Patent Quarterly* 59:140–149 and 72:357–364.
Kaminsky, Ralph. "Cine-Fi Maps Marketing Expansion." *Boxoffice*, Oct. 10, 1977, p. 10.
________. "Experimental Drive-In Containment Screen Slated for Late Spring, Early Summer Trial." *Boxoffice*, March 17, 1975, pp. MT26–MT27.
"Kids-for-Free, Filled Cars at $1 Snarl Distribs." *Variety*, June 28, 1950, pp. 5, 16.
Kirk, Cynthia. "Unveil Drive-In Screen Detail." *Hollywood Reporter*, Oct. 10, 1974, pp. 1, 13.
"Kiwis Get Drive-In Okay, But Demand Is Dubious." *Variety*, Dec. 24, 1986, p. 32.
Kocian, Billy. "Costs, Redtape, Public Opposition Keep German Drive-Ins Few." *Variety*, Oct. 20, 1976, p. 150.
"Lakeland Plan and Policy." *Motion Picture Herald*, July 7, 1956, p. 36.
Langway, Lynn. "The Disappearing Drive-In." *Newsweek* 100:65, Aug. 9, 1982.
"Larger-Than-Life Sex Brings Cops." *Variety*, Feb. 23, 1977, p. 28.
Leacy, F. H. ed. *Historical Statistics of Canada*, 2d ed. Ottawa: Statistics Canada, 1985.
"A Leash for Straying Speakers." *Boxoffice*, Oct. 3, 1953, p.48.
"Legality of Murmur Law Is Hit in Drive-In House Closing Suit." *Daily Variety*, April 5, 1935, p. 25.
Lem, Kim. "Drive-In Theater Once Showing X-Rated Films Now Raising Funds for Church." *New York Times*, July 27, 1975, p. 65.
Levitan, Elizabeth L. "The Drive-In Is Still Thriving." *Christian Science Monitor*, Sept. 8, 1988, pp. 1, 6.
Liddick, Betty. "Charge of the Night Brigade." *Los Angeles Times*, Sept. 8, 1974, sec. 10, pp. 1, 12.
Liftin, Joan. "Films Alfresco." *American Film* 10:42ff, July/Aug. 1986.
Loeb, Elsie. "The Drive-In Story." *Boxoffice*, Oct. 4, 1947, p. 22.
"Loew Drive-In Theatre." *Boxoffice*, March 19, 1938, p. 91.
"Loew's Drive-In Theatres, Inc. v. Park-In Theatres, Inc." *United States Patent Quarterly* 81:149–155.
"London's Passion Pit a 1-Night Stand." *Variety*, June 21, 1989.
Lowe, Philip L. "In Refreshment Sales What Is Your Potential." *Motion Picture Herald*, July 4, 1953, p. 10.
Luther, Rodney. "Drive-In Theaters: Rags to Riches in Five Years." *Hollywood Quarterly* 5:405ff, Summer 1951.

———. "Marketing Aspects of Drive-In Theaters." *Journal of Marketing* 15:44ff, July 1950.
Lyman, David. "Twilight of the Drive-In." *Cincinnati Post*, May 25, 1989.
McDonough, Jimmy. "Hillbilly Heaven." *Film Comment* 21:55ff, Nov./Dec. 1985.
McLellan, Dennis. "Drive-In Cruising." *San Francisco Chronicle*, Dec. 20, 1981, p.5, Sunday Punch section.
"Magnolia Drive-In." *Boxoffice*, July 1, 1950, p. 40.
"Maine Anti-Porn Law Hits Ozoners; Op Says 'X' Pix Are Sole Earners." *Variety*, Sept. 21, 1983, p. 6.
"Majors Expect Verdict in 2 Weeks on Pennsy Drive-In Bid Appeal." *Variety*, July 25, 1951, pp. 7, 16.
"Marketing Briefs." *Business Week*, Oct. 10, 1951, p. 56.
"Maryland Underskyers Facing Period of Decline in Attendance, Income." *Boxoffice*, Oct. 16, 1978, p. E1.
Mathews, Jack. "A Sunbelt Favorite." *San Francisco Chronicle*, Sept. 3, 1987, p. 66.
May, Clifford D. "Drive-In: Tradition Beneath the L.I. Stars." *New York Times*, Sept. 1, 1986, p. 27.
Mayerson, Donald. "A Night at the Drive-In." *Cue* 39:11, July 4, 1970.
Maynard, Joyce. "Peanuts, Popcorn and Pictures." *Producers Guild of America Journal* 16:25ff n4, 1974.
"Memphis Ozoner, Seen by Nabes, Shuttered over Steamy, Non-X Pix." *Variety*, Dec. 15, 1982, pp. 6, 32.
"Merrimack Auto Theater." *Boxoffice*, July 30, 1938, p. 75.
"Miami Drive-In Cuts Admission Price." *Boxoffice*, April 30, 1938, p. 152.
Michie, Larry. "High Court Overturns Drive-In Rap." *Daily Variety*, March 21, 1972, p. 6.
"Million-Dollar Drive-In Offers Films, Fun and Food." *Popular Science Monthly* 171:118–121, Sept. 1957.
Mims, Bob. "Drive-Ins Bow to Law, Forgo R-Rated Films." *Salt Lake Tribune*, Nov. 14, 1982.
"Minn Distribs Profit from Ozoners Operated by Non-Theatre Owners." *Variety*, Sept. 13, 1950, p. 22.
"Moon-Washed." *New Yorker* 25:20, Oct. 1, 1949.
Moore, Ansel M. "The Drive-In Theory: Basically Sound But Badly Interpreted." *Boxoffice*, Dec. 8, 1945, p. 10, Western edition.
Morrison, Peter. "Hoyt's (Fox)-Gut Group Wins Drive-In Appeal." *Film Daily*, Feb. 28, 1956, pp. 1, 8.
———. "M-G-M in Drive-In Race Down Under." *Film Daily*, April 4, 1956, p. 7.
"Movie Theater Lets Cars Drive Right In." *Popular Science Monthly* 123:19, Aug. 1933.
"Mpls Drive-Ins Serve Up Dance Music Till It's Dark Enough to Screen Pix." *Daily Variety*, June 20, 1967, p. 5.
Muldoon, Tony. "Film Credits May Roll for Local Man Who Pioneered Drive-In Theaters." *Courier-Post* (Camden, N.J.), June 9, 1985, p. 6A.
"Munching at the Motor Movies." *Motion Picture Herald*, April 15, 1950, pp. 50–51.
Murphy, A. D. "NATO-AMPTP's 'Containment' Screen for Ozoners Within Six Months of a Prototype." *Daily Variety*, May 24, 1974, pp. 1, 6.
"Must Shield Ozoners Showing X Pictures." *Boxoffice*, Feb. 11, 1974, p. E1.
National Theatre Supply ad. *Boxoffice*, Sept. 15, 1945, p. 29.
"NATO to Present 'Containment' Plan for Drive-Ins." *Daily Variety*, Nov. 13, 1972, pp. 1, 6.
"N.C. Porn Drive-In Must Close in Sept." *Variety*, July 25, 1984, pp. 7, 32.

"New 'Cine-Fi' Drive-In Sound System Introduced at Industry Tradeshow." *Boxoffice*, Nov. 21, 1977, pp. MT18–MT19.
"New Concession Talk-Back System Speeds Patron Service at Park." *Boxoffice*, Oct. 7, 1950, p. 50.
"New England Ozoners Adhere to Status Quo." *Boxoffice*, June 26, 1978, p. ME5.
"New 'In-Car' Speaker for Drive-In Theatres." *Boxoffice*, July 20, 1946, p. 33.
"New Process for Daylight Use of Drive-In Theatres." *Hollywood Reporter*, May 18, 1972, pp. 1, 13.
"New Zealand Stalls All Drive-In Plans." *Variety*, May 5, 1976, p. 140.
Newman, Peter. "Horse Operas Move to the Country." *Financial Post* (Toronto), May 30, 1953, p. 15.
Newquist, Jay. "The Slow Fade-Out of Drive-In Theaters." *New Haven Register*, Sept. 16, 1979.
1987 Census of Service Industries. Geographic Area Series: United States. Washington: United States Bureau of the Census, 1989.
1954 Census of Business. vol. 5. *Selected Service Trades—Summary Statistics.* Washington: United States Bureau of the Census, 1957.
1958 Census of Business. vol. 5. *Selected Service Trades—Summary Statistics.* Washington: United States Bureau of the Census, 1961.
1977 Census of Service Industries. vol. 1. *Subject Statistics.* Washington: United States Bureau of the Census, 1980.
1972 Census of Selected Service Industries. Washington: United States Bureau of the Census, 1975.
1967 Census of Business. vol. 5. *Selected Services—Area Statistics. part 1.* Washington: United States Bureau of the Census, 1970.
1963 Census of Business. vol. 6. *Selected Services—Summary Statistics.* Washington: United States Bureau of the Census, 1966.
"N.J. Drive-In Files Anti-Trust Suit." *Variety*, June 7, 1950, p. 18.
"No. Cent. NATO Fights Minn. Bill to Ban X-Rated Pix at Drive-Ins." *Variety*, Feb. 14, 1979, p. 27.
North Park Theatre Corporation v. Park-In Theatres Inc., et al. *United States Patent Quarterly* 114:474–479.
"N. S. Barger Opening Chicago Drive-In." *Boxoffice*, May 24, 1941, p. 96.
"Number of South Jersey Underskyers Down Nearly 50 Percent in 5 Years." *Boxoffice*, Dec. 18, 1978, p. 4.
Nunes, Don. "Flesh Tones on the Silver Screen Make Some See Red." *Washington Post*, Sept. 18, 1982, pp. B1, B5.
"NY Passes Strict Law Affecting Drive-Ins." *Boxoffice*, June 19, 1972, p. E1.
O'Driscoll, Patrick. "A Tradition Refuses to Flicker Out." *USA Today*, June 22, 1987, p. D1.
"Ohio Ordinance Limits Drive-In Screen Sex." *Boxoffice*, Feb. 5, 1979, pp. ME2–ME3.
"150,000 Playland Rides a Year for Free." *Boxoffice*, Feb. 6, 1954, pp. 24–25.
"1 in 8 Pic-Goers Went to Drive-Ins in July." *Variety*, Sept. 6, 1950, p. 4.
"Open Air 'Drive-In' Theatre for Cars." *Variety*, June 13, 1933, p.5.
Ordinance number 74733, Los Angeles City Council, passed Feb. 7, 1935.
"Outdoor Auto Movie House, First in State." *New York Times*, July 3, 1938, p. 4.
"Ozone Operators Raise 100G Kitty Find New Screen." *Daily Variety*, Nov. 29, 1972, pp. 1, 6.
"Ozoner Biz to Get New Try in Britain." *Variety*, June 27, 1984, p. 47.
"Ozoner Loses Suit to Force Paper to Take Ads." Variety, April 30, 1952, p. 4.

"Ozoner Operator Sues Chi Suburban Village for $1,000,000 Over Permit." *Variety*, April 12, 1950, p. 20.
"Ozoners Can't Gross Enough for Top Bids, Chiefs Believe." *Variety*, April 4, 1951, p. 5, 13.
"Ozoners Quest: 'Light' Screen." *Variety*, Feb. 23, 1966, pp. 7, 27.
"Ozoners Reverse Current B.O. Dip, Drive-Ins Up 10% Over '48 Revenue." *Variety*, June 8, 1949, p. 14.
"Ozoners Still Popular Across State of Texas." *Boxoffice*, Aug. 21, 1978, p. E6.
"Ozoners the Best Answer to TV." *Variety*, July 23, 1952, pp. 3, 23.
"Pa. Drive-In Theatres File Clearance Action." *Film Daily*, May 9, 1956, p. 15.
"Pacific Theaters to Cap Another of Its Drive-Ins." *Variety*, Oct. 7, 1987, pp. 7, 41.
Paletz, David. "The Exhibitors." *Film Quarterly* 19:17ff, Winter 1965–1966.
Park-In Theatres, Inc. v. Loew's Drive-In Theatres, Inc. *United States Patent Quarterly* 72:470–477 and 83:543.
Park-In Theatres, Inc. v. Ochs et al. *United States Patent Quarterly* 75:4–5 and 77: 43–49.
Park-In Theatres, Inc. v. Paramount-Richards Theatres, Inc., et al. *United States Patent Quarterly* 76:353–355; 80:6–14; 82:90–92; 85:346–348ff; and 88:165.
Park-In Theatres, Inc. v. Perkins et al. *United States Patent Quarterly* 90:163–168.
Park-In Theatres, Inc. v. Rogers et al. *United States Patent Quarterly* 55:103–106.
Park-In Theatres, Inc. v. Waters et al. *United States Patent Quarterly* 87:291–293.
"Penna. Court Rules Ozoners Entitled to 1st-Run Treatment." *Daily Variety*, Nov. 29, 1950.
Perkins, S. D. "Policy and Technical Factors in Drive-In Theatre Operation." *Motion Picture Herald*, Dec. 10, 1938, pp. 15, 41.
Petersen, George M. *Drive-In Theatre: Manual of Design and Operation*. Kansas City: Associated, 1953.
Petersen, Paul. "Cultivating Carriage Trade—Drive-In Style." *Motion Picture Herald*, Feb. 7, 1953, pp. 9, 37.
"Playgrounds for Extra Lure." *Motion Picture Herald*, June 9, 1956, pp. 10–11.
Plotkin, Harris M. "Protolite Screen: Drive-In Breakthrough." *Boxoffice*, March 1983, pp. 64–65.
"Porcelain Screen Made for Drive-Ins." *Film Daily*, Jan. 13, 1964, p. 7.
Potter, Harry M. "The World's First Drive-In Theatre." *South Jersey Magazine*, Oct.-Dec. 1974, p.3.
"Pre-Hearing Accord in Drive-In Case." *Boxoffice*, April 19, 1941, p. 83.
"Pre-Sunset Shows for Drive-Ins as Technical Goal." *Variety*, Nov. 10, 1965, p. 20.
Price, Ed. "Secret to Drive-In Clock's Success Lies in the Way It Is Constructed." *Boxoffice*, Feb. 16, 1976, p. MT29.
"Price Dispute Clouds Bright Drive-In Year." *Motion Picture Herald*, June 2, 1951, p. 13.
"Product Day at the Convention." *Boxoffice*, Nov. 4, 1950, p. 19.
Pryor, Kelli. "A Night at the Drive-In." *New York* 21:35, May 9, 1988.
Pryor, Thomas M. "Evolution of the Drive-In." *New York Times*, Aug. 14, 1938, sec. 9, p. 3.
________. "Impact of Movies on Youth Argued." *New York Times*, June 17, 1955, p. 24.
________. "Metal Brightens Drive-In Screens." *New York Times*, Jan. 10, 1955, p. 27.
Pulman, R. E. "Drive-In Theatre Operation." *British Kinematography* 32:93ff, April 1958.
"Quebec Drive-Ins." *Variety*, July 26, 1989.

"Quebec's Belated Drive-In OK." *Variety*, June 21, 1967, p. 15.
"R. M. Hollingshead, Jr. Dies: Originator of Drive-Ins." *Boxoffice*, May 26, 1975, p. 7.
Randall, Richard S. *Censorship of the Movies*. Madison: University of Wisconsin Press, 1968.
Rapoport, Roger. "The Last Drive-In in Marin." *San Francisco Chronicle*, July 28, 1979, p. 4.
RCA ad. *Boxoffice*, Feb. 2, 1946, pp. 24–25.
"Reade Ozoners Use Circus Acts to Up B.O." *Variety*, July 23, 1952, p. 23.
"Record Drive-In Load—58 in One Car." *Boxoffice*, Sept. 13, 1952, p. 26.
Reif, Rita. "Drive-In Theatre Extends Horizon." *New York Times*, June 9, 1957, p. 14.
"Relaxed Atmosphere of Drive-Ins Appeals to Chicagoland Patrons." *Boxoffice*, Dec. 8, 1975, p. C6.
"Restrainer Demand Threatens Drive-In." *Boxoffice*, July 9, 1938, p. 50.
"Roadside Glom Case Lost, But State Will Appeal." *Variety*, Nov. 12, 1975, p. 6.
"Rockefeller Vetoes Film Bill." *New York Times*, May 22, 1970, p. 40.
"Roll It to 'Em for Greater Drive-In Profit." *Motion Picture Herald*, May 20, 1950, p. 53.
"The Roof's the Sky and Sky Is Drive-In Limit." *Motion Picture Herald*, July 17, 1948, p. 16.
Rutherford, Tony. "Management of a Drive-In Requires Creativity, Ingenuity—and Patience." *Boxoffice*, Oct. 23, 1978, p. ME5.
"Scene Change." *Los Angeles Times*, Aug. 7, 1989, part 4, p. 5.
Schneck, Dale. "America's Oldest Drive-In Theatre." *Boxoffice*, Sept. 1983, p. 122.
Schutz, George. "The New Drive-In Economies and How They Got That Way." *Motion Picture Herald*, Feb. 11, 1956, p. 12.
"Schwartz to Show New Cinema Radio." *Variety*, Nov. 15, 1972, pp. 1, 78.
"Scientist Maps Progress on New Screen During Annual NATO Convention." *Boxoffice*, Oct. 15, 1973, pp. 10ff.
"2d Cine-Auto to Bow in France Near Swiss Line." *Variety*, June 19, 1968, p. 31.
"Secret Meetings Held to Battle Threatened Drive-In Invasion." *Boxoffice*, Sept. 13, 1947, p. 28.
"See Mohammedanism Big B.O. Booster for Drive-In Pic Theatres." *Variety*, April 25, 1951, pp. 3, 15.
"See $35,000,000 in 1950 Rentals from Drive-Ins." *Variety*, June 14, 1950, pp. 1, 6.
"Sero Joins Fights on Daylight Time." *Variety*, Aug. 31, 1949.
"743 Drive-Ins Operating; 137 All Year, MPAA Says." *Motion Picture Herald*, Nov. 6, 1948, p. 15.
"Showman Harry L. Schwab Mulls Suit Against Town Board of Selectmen." *Boxoffice*, Sept. 11, 1978, p. NE1.
Shropshire, Mike. "Drive-In Movie Freaks Celebrate a Bygone Era." *Dallas Morning News*, Nov. 1, 1982.
"Single 'Deep Throat' Date (in 1973) Brings Curb on Ozoners' Porn." *Variety*, March 21, 1971, p. 44.
Siskel, Gene. "1981's Drive-Ins: Fast Fadeout for Passion Pit Image." *Chicago Tribune*, Aug. 16, 1981.
Slavin, Barbara. "It's Technology to the Rescue of Drive-In Movie Theaters." *New York Times*, Aug. 8, 1978, p. A12.
Smith, Douglas St. Clair. "How Bad Were They." *Texas Monthly* 14:209ff, May 1986.
Smith, Sumner. "Drive-Ins Up from 100 to 761 in 20-Month Building Boom." *Boxoffice*, Nov. 13, 1948, p. 25.

Smith, Wilfred P. "Is Your Refresheteria Ready for 1951?" *Motion Picture Herald*, Jan. 6, 1951, p. 26.
________. "Management of a Drive-In." *Motion Picture Herald*, Feb. 4, 1950, pp. 13–14.
________. "Taking the Tour at Tesma." *Motion Picture Herald*, Dec. 2, 1950, p. 44.
________. "There're Lots of Ways for the Drive-In to Use Showmanship." *Motion Picture Herald*, May 5, 1951, pp, 40–41.
"Smith's Ozoner Slant: No Family Pix." *Variety*, May 9, 1973, p. 5.
"Some Drive-Ins May Play Acts." *Variety*, March 22, 1950, p. 1.
"Sound and Heat Supplied Drive-In Car by a Tube." *Motion Picture Herald*, Dec. 3, 1949, p. 23.
"Special Service for Drive-In Theatres." *Motion Picture Herald*, July 14, 1956, p. 41.
Spinrad, Leonard. "Burgeoning Drive-Ins." *New York Times*, March 1, 1953, p. 5.
Spires, George. "Service—By Bar or Cart—Brings Drive-In Sales." *Motion Picture Herald*, Aug. 13, 1949, p. 41ff.
"Spread of Drive-In Cinemas May Become a Worry to Regular Ops; Dixie Belt Can Stay Open All Year." *Variety*, July 6, 1938, p. 21.
Squire, Jason E. *The Movie Business Book*. New York: Simon & Schuster, 1986.
Stack, Peter. "A Drive-In Movie Gizmo." *San Francisco Chronicle*, Nov. 8, 1984.
Stanley, Robert H. *The Celluloid Empire*. New York: Hastings House, 1977.
Steinberg, Cobbett. *Film Facts*. New York: Facts on File, 1980.
"Study Daytime Use of Drive-In Theatres." *Motion Picture Herald*, July 13, 1966, pp. 1, 4.
Sullivan, Paul. "A Love Affair with the Stars." *Chicago Tribune*, July 26, 1985, sec. 7, p. 3.
"Super Drive-Ins to Key Ten Breakthroughs." *Boxoffice*, Aug. 10, 1970, p. 3.
"Supreme Court Declines to Review Pontiac School Busing Order." *New York Times*, Oct. 27, 1971, p. 32.
"Survey Shows Who Attends Drive-Ins." *Boxoffice*, Jan. 7, 1950, p. 45.
"Swarm of Expected Closings Seen Corrective; Drive-In Impact Strong." *Variety*, July 2, 1950, pp. 3, 22.
Taylor, Frank J. "Big Boom in Outdoor Movies." *Saturday Evening Post*, Sept. 15, 1956, pp. 100–101.
"A Theatre Architect Looks Ahead." *Boxoffice*, April 1, 1950, pp. 10–11.
"Theatre Attendance Down Five Million." *Boxoffice*, Feb. 22, 1941, p. 6.
"Theatreman Invents Unit to Carry Drive-In Sound Through Car Radios." *Boxoffice*, Sept. 1, 1951, p. 14.
"Third Ontario Drive-In Opens Near London." *Boxoffice*, July 12, 1947, p. 112.
Thomas, Dana. "Flicker of Hope?" *Barron's* 38:3ff, June 23, 1958.
Thompson, David. "Lure of Great Outdoors Proves Big Cinema Boom." *Financial Post* (Toronto), Sept. 8, 1962, p. 23.
Thompson, Toby. "The Twilight of the Drive-In." *American Film* 8:46ff, July/Aug. 1983.
"3-D Drive-Ins." *Business Week*, Feb. 13, 1954, p. 59.
"389 New Theatres Entered Field in 1939." *Boxoffice*, Feb. 10, 1940, p. 17.
"Tinted Windshields." *Boxoffice*, March 21, 1953, p. 19.
Toy, Steve. "New Containment Drive-In Screen Debuting in June." *Daily Variety*, Jan. 31, 1974, p. 1, 8.
"Traffic Hazard Stymies Toronto Drive-In, But Many Others Planned." *Variety*, May 7, 1947, p. 33.
"Trends in Vending." *Motion Picture Herald*, April 7, 1952, p. 38.

"Trouble for Drive-Ins on Late Season Bills." *Boxoffice*, Oct. 27, 1951, p. 14.
Trout, Wesley. "Cinema Radio's Innovative Sound System Like Small Radio Station." *Boxoffice*, June 13, 1977, pp. MT12ff.
Tuffing, Robert E. "Peeling Screen Calls for Prompt Attention." *Boxoffice*, Feb. 14, 1977, pp. MT32–MT33.
Tusher, Will. "Crown: Drive-Ins Losing Impact." *Daily Variety*, Nov. 30, 1981, p. 1.
________. "Gas Pumps at Drive-Ins Would Keep B.O. Open." *Hollywood Reporter*, Oct. 3, 1973, pp. 1, 19.
________. "New Technology Big Boost to Drive-Ins." *Hollywood Reporter*, May 19, 1972, pp. 1, 3.
________. "Shutin Screen for Drive-Ins Finally Ready." *Hollywood Reporter*, Sept. 23, 1975, pp. 1, 10.
"20th–Fox Established Policy on Selling Drive-In Accounts." *Boxoffice*, March 12, 1949, p. 14.
"Twice as Many Drive-In Theaters." *Business Week*, Jan. 1, 1949, p. 44.
"Twin City Indies Fear Invasion of Drive-In Theatres." *Variety*, Sept. 17, 1947, p. 20.
"Two Theatres Seek Reduced Clearances Through Decree." *Daily Variety*, March 5, 1942, p. 4.
"Unique Boston Experiment Uses Drive-Ins for Daytime Car Parks." *Variety*, Aug. 28, 1963, p. 16.
United States Census of Business 1948. vol. 7. *Service Trade — Area Statistics*. Washington: Bureau of the Census, 1951.
"Urge Tighter State Drive-In Regulation." *Motion Picture Herald*, June 10, 1950.
"U.S. Supreme Court Rules Distribs Cannot Favor Theatres over Drive-Ins." *Variety*, April 22, 1952.
Vlahos, Peter. "Containment Screen for Drive-In Theatres." *Journal of the Society of Motion Picture and Television Engineers* 82:95ff, Feb. 1973.
Vobejda, Barbara. "Where Have All the Drive-Ins Gone?" *Washington Post*, Nov. 5, 1984, pp. B1, B7.
"Vote Down Ord to Bar Drive-Ins' Giant-Size Sex." *Variety*, Feb. 23, 1977, p. 28.
"W. German Cinemas Dip to 3,072; Drive-Ins Big, with 20 Now Operating." *Variety*, Aug. 23, 1978, p. 51.
"Warm Nights and Drive-Ins Open, Small Burgs Protest 'R' Pics." *Variety*, June 23, 1976, p. 24.
Warren, Sandy. "Life at the Movies." *Houston Post Magazine*, Nov. 4, 1984, p. 22.
Weaver, William R. "An Exercise in Community Relations." *Motion Picture Herald*, June 9, 1965, pp. 6–8.
Weinberg, Neal. "Now Playing: Last Tango in U.S. for Drive-Ins?" *Springfield* (Mass.) *Republican*, Aug. 21, 1977.
Wendt, Lloyd. *The Wall Street Journal*. Chicago: Rand McNally, 1982.
Widem, Allen M. "Conn. Theatres Aim for Kiddie Trade." *Film Daily*, July 14, 1956, pp. 1–2.
________. "Massachusetts Is Urged to Control Drive-In X Films." *Hollywood Reporter*, Feb. 4, 1972, p. 13.
________. "Ozoner Owner Fights Town's Curfew Law." *Boxoffice*, Aug. 7, 1978, p. NE1.
Wielenga, Dave. "Moviegoers by the Carful." *Press-Telegram* (Long Beach, Calif.), Aug. 25, 1988, p. D1.
Wilkerson, W. R. "Trade Views." *Hollywood Reporter*, Sept. 13, 1949.
Williams, Leslie. "Some Survivors Scratch by with Flea Markets." (Baltimore) *Evening Sun*, July 21, 1988.

"A Window on the World." *Illustrated London News*, July 23, 1961, p. 126.
"Woman Manager." *Boxoffice*, July 13, 1940, p. 27.
"Would Bar Drive-In Shows." *New York Times*, Aug. 20, 1950, p. 42.
Wynter, Leon. "Over a Six-Pack, under the Stars." *Washington Post*, July 30, 1981, pp. MD1, MD3.
"Yamins Rep. Rips into Drive-Ins as 'Not Clean.'" *Film Daily*, April 11, 1956, pp. 1, 3.
Zorn, Eric. "Unstoppable Drive-In X-Asperates." *Chicago Tribune*, April 11, 1986, sec. 2, pp. 1, 7.

Index